Barcode in Back

D0561581

Asia on Tour

With the vast majority of academic theory on tourism based on 'Western' tourists, *Asia on Tour* illustrates why the rapid growth of travel for leisure and recreation in Asia demands a reappraisal of how tourism is analyzed and understood. Examining domestic and intra-regional tourism, the book reveals how improvements in infrastructures, ever increasing disposable incomes, liberalized economies, the inter-connectivities of globalization and the lowering of borders, both physical and political, are now enabling millions of Asians to travel as tourists. Drawing upon multidisciplinary theoretical perspectives and up-to-date empirical research, the twenty-three accessible essays in this volume indicate why a rigorous and critical study of Asian tourism must become integral to both our analysis of this rapidly transforming region and our interpretation of global tourism in the twenty first century.

As a rich collection of essays focusing specifically on Asian tourists, *Asia on Tour* will be of particular interest to students and scholars working in the fields of tourism, Asian studies, geography, heritage, anthropology, development, sociology, and cultural and postcolonial studies.

Tim Winter researches heritage and tourism at the University of Sydney. He is author of *Post-Conflict Heritage, Postcolonial Tourism* and editor of *Expressions of Cambodia.*
Peggy Teo is an independent scholar based in Singapore. Her research interests are in tourism and social gerontological issues.
T.C. Chang is Associate Professor at the Department of Geography, National University of Singapore. His research interests are in urban tourism and arts/culture.

Contributors: Audrey Bochaton, Charles Carroll, Chan Yuk Wah, TC Chang, Sidney C.H. Cheung, Jenny Chio, Youngmin Choe, Maribeth Erb, Olivier Evrard, Jamie Gillen, Nelson Graburn, C. Michael Hall, Prasit Leepreecha, Bertrand Lefebvre, Francis Lim, Pál Nyíri, Shalini Panjabi, Robert Shepherd, Denise Spitzer, Peggy Teo, Tim Winter, Joyce Hsiu-yen Yeh

Asia on Tour

Exploring the rise of Asian tourism

**Edited by Tim Winter, Peggy Teo
and T.C. Chang**

Routledge
Taylor & Francis Group

LONDON AND NEW YORK

First published 2009 by Routledge
2 Park Square, Milton Park, Abingdon, Oxon OX14 5RN

Simultaneously published in the USA and Canada
by Routledge
270 Madison Ave, New York, NY 10016

*Routledge is an imprint of the Taylor & Francis Group,
an informa business*

© 2009 Editorial Selection and matter, Tim Winter, Peggy Teo and
T C Chang. Individual chapters, the contributors

Typeset in Times New Roman by Graphicraft Limited, Hong Kong
Printed and bound in Great Britain by CPI Antony Rowe,
Chippenham, Wiltshire

British Library Cataloguing in Publication Data
A catalogue record for this book is available from the British Library

Library of Congress Cataloging in Publication Data
Asia on tour : exploring the rise of Asian tourism / edited by Tim
Winter, Peggy Teo, and T C Chang.
p. cm.
Includes bibliographical references.
1. Tourism—Asia. I. Winter, Tim, 1971– II. Teo, Peggy.
III. Chang, T. C.

G155.A74A828 2008
338.4′7915—dc22
2008008937

ISBN10: 0-415-46085-9 (hbk)
ISBN10: 0-415-46086-7 (pbk)
ISBN10: 0-203-89180-5 (ebk)

ISBN13: 978-0-415-46085-9 (hbk)
ISBN13: 978-0-415-46086-6 (pbk)
ISBN13: 978-0-203-89180-3 (ebk)

Contents

Figures

Tables

Contributors

Audrey Bochaton is a PhD candidate in Health Geography at the University of Paris X Nanterre. Her research focuses on the movements of Laotian patients seeking health care in Thailand. For the past three years, she has been based in the French Institute of Research for Development (IRD) in Vientiane.

Charles Carroll is a PhD candidate in Cultural Transformation, Political Economy, and Social Practice at University of California, Berkeley, and co-founder of the university's Tourism Studies Working Group. He currently works as an educational media advisor in the Lao Ministry of Information and Culture, while conducting research on changing social practices of the political economy in the Lao People's Democratic Republic. His past research has focused on learning, mathematics, craft practice and tourism in Northern Thailand.

T.C. Chang has a PhD from McGill University and is Associate Professor at the Department of Geography, National University of Singapore. His research interests are in urban and heritage tourism, arts and culture, and geographic pedagogy. His research has included Asian regional tourism, urban waterfronts, heritage sites, and boutique hotels in Malaysia and Singapore. He is the co-editor, with Peggy Teo and K.C. Ho, of *Interconnected Worlds: Tourism in Southeast Asia* (Pergamon, 2001).

Sidney C.H. Cheung is a Professor in the Department of Anthropology, The Chinese University of Hong Kong. His research interests include visual anthropology, anthropology of tourism, heritage studies, indigenous cultures, food and identity. His edited books include *On the South China Track: Perspectives on Anthropological Research and Teaching* (HKIAPS-CUHK, 1998), *Tourism, Anthropology, and China* (White Lotus, 2001), *The Globalization of Chinese Food* (RoutledgeCurzon and Hawaii University Press, 2002) and *Food and Foodways in Asia: Resource, Tradition and Cooking* (Routledge, 2007).

Jenny Chio is a PhD candidate at the University of California, Berkeley. She researches tourism, ethnicity, rural communities, and travel media in

China. Her work was funded by a Fulbright-Hays Doctoral Dissertation Research Award and the Wenner-Gren Foundation for Anthropological Research.

Youngmin Choe has a PhD in Asian Studies from the University of California, Berkeley, and is currently working on a book entitled *Trans-Asian Cinema and the Ideology of Tourism*, which examines the cultural collaborations between Korea, Japan and China in the film and tourism industries, and the formation of a regional cultural network after the Asian financial crisis.

Maribeth Erb is an Associate Professor in the Department of Sociology, National University of Singapore. She is the author of *The Manggaraians* (Times Editions, 1999) and the co-editor of *Regionalism in Post-Suharto Indonesia* (RoutledgeCurzon, 2005), and *Biodiversity and Human Livelihoods in Protected Areas* (Cambridge, 2007). She has also written many articles on tourism, political change, Manggaraian ritual and history, in various journals and edited collections.

Olivier Evrard is an anthropologist at the Institut de Recherche pour le Développement (IRD), France, and is also currently an Associate Researcher at the Social Research Institute, Chiang Mai University. His current work on Thai tourism is part of long-term research on mobility, identities and interethnic relationships in mountainous areas of Thailand and Laos.

Jamie Gillen is a Visiting Assistant Professor at Miami University of Ohio. His current research centers on the competing claims on culture between actors in Ho Chi Minh City, the tourism industry and leaders of the Communist Party of Vietnam. He is also interested in entrepreneurship and the entrepreneurial activities of urban governments.

Nelson Graburn is a social cultural anthropologist at the University of California, Berkeley. He was trained at the universities of Cambridge, McGill and the University of Chicago. His research interests include contemporary tourism issues in Asia (particularly Japan and China), as well as cultural preservation of Inuit arts and autonomy in Nunavut, Canada. His most recent book is *Multiculturalism in the New Japan*, co-edited with John Ertl and Kenji Tierney (Berghahn, 2008).

C. Michael Hall is a Professor in the Department of Management at the University of Canterbury and docent in the Department of Geography at the University of Oulu. Co-editor of *Current Issues in Tourism*, he has published widely in tourism, gastronomy, geography, environmental history and related fields.

Prasit Leepreecha has a PhD in Anthropology from the University of Washington, Seattle. Presently, he is a Researcher at the Social Research Institute, Chiang Mai University. He is the co-editor of *Living in a Globalized World: Ethnic Minorities in the Greater Mekong Subregion* (Mekong Press 2008), and *Challenging the Limits: Indidgenous Peoples of* *the Mekong Region* (Mekong Press, 2008). His main interests include ethnic minorities in Northern Thailand and mainland Southeast Asia, identity, culture change, tourism, nationalism and globalization.

Bertrand Lefebvre is a PhD student from the Department of Geography at the University of Rouen (UMR IDEES), France. Since 2004, he has been affiliated with the Centre de Sciences Humaines in New Delhi, India. He is currently working on his thesis concerning the emergence of corporate hospitals in India.

Francis Khek Gee Lim is an Assistant Professor at the Division of Sociology, Nanyang Technological University. His research interests include religion, globalization, development, and tourism, spanning Nepal, Singapore, China, and Taiwan. He is the author of *Imagining the Good Life: Negotiating Culture and Development in Nepal Himalaya* (Brill, 2008).

Pál Nyíri is the Director of the Applied Anthropology programme at Macquarie University. Most of his research has been on Chinese tourism and international migration. His most recent books are *Chinese in Russia and Eastern Europe: A Middleman Minority in a Transnational Era* (Routledge, 2007) and *Maxikulti* (with Joana Breidenbach, Campus, 2008), the latter being a critical investigation of how the idea of cultural difference has taken governments and corporations hostage.

Shalini Panjabi is an independent researcher based in Bangalore, India. With a PhD in Sociology, her research interests include private education in India, as well as orality, literacy and development. Her field sites have been in Kashmir and Rajasthan. In Kashmir, her research focus has been on the complex interface between development, tourism and heritage conservation in a post-conflict era.

Robert Shepherd is an Assistant Professor of Anthropology and International Affairs at George Washington University in Washington, DC. His work on tourism and cultural heritage issues in Indonesia and China has appeared in the *Journal of Contemporary Asia*, the *International Journal of Cultural Studies*, and *Southeast Asia Research*, among other publications.

Denise Spitzer holds the Canada Research Chair in Gender, Migration and Health at the University of Ottawa where she is affiliated with the Institutes of Women's Studies and Population Health. Trained as a medical anthropologist, she is interested in the impact of marginalization on health and well-being and in the myriad ways in which people and communities resist marginalization. She also researches the transnational migration of people, ideas, and materials. In addition to graduate degrees in Anthropology, she also holds undergraduate diplomas in Biology and Chinese.

Peggy Teo is an independent scholar based in Singapore. Her research interests are in tourism and social gerontological issues. She has looked at tourism and the intersection of the global and local in heritage landscapes and theme parks. She has also used a postcolonial framework to analyze backpacking and boutique hotels in Asia.

K. Thirumaran has a PhD from the National University of Singapore. His research interests focus on the cultural relationships between tourists and hosts, intra-regional tourism and policy dimensions of tourism branding. His doctoral thesis focused on affinity tourism as a way to understand the experiences of Chinese and Indian tourists in Southeast Asia.

Chan Yuk Wah is an Assistant Professor in the Department of Asian and International Studies at the City University of Hong Kong. Her research interests include tourism, gender, identity, historical memories and the China–Vietnam relationship.

Tim Winter is based at the University of Sydney, Australia. He is the author of *Post-conflict Heritage, Postcolonial Tourism: Culture, Politics and Development at Angkor* (Routledge, 2007) and co-editor of *Expressions of Cambodia: The Politics of Tradition, Identity and change* (Routledge, 2006). He is also editor of the ICOMOS journal *Historic Environment*. In addition to working on tourism in Asia, Tim researches the role cultural heritage plays in the re-development and reconstruction of post-conflict societies (for more information, visit www.postconflictheritage.com).

Joyce Hsiu-yen Yeh has a PhD in Sociology from Lancaster University and teaches in the Department of Indigenous Cultures at National Dong Hwa University, Taiwan. She researches material cultures and cultural performances of indigenous peoples. Her current research interests include the sociology of identity and cultural Otherness, cross-cultural consumption, travel as acquisition of cultural capital and performance of personal taste, and indigenous festival and food consumption.

Acknowledgments

The editors of this volume would like to acknowledge the support of the Asia Research Institute, Singapore for hosting the conference *'Of Asian Origin': rethinking tourism in contemporary Asia* in September 2006. Thanks go to Anthony Reid and Chua Beng Huat for supporting the conference theme within ARI's cultural studies cluster. And special thanks are offered to the administrative team at ARI, in particular to Alison Rozells for her tireless efforts and enthusiasm. We would also like to thank the team at Routledge, London, most notably Stephanie Rogers and Leanne Hinves for supporting this volume. Some sections of the Conclusion were previously published in a paper entitled, 'Asian Tourism and the Retreat of Anglo-Western Centrism in Tourism Theory' in *Current Issues in Tourism*, Vol. 11, 2008 (Taylor and Francis, London). Finally we would like to thank our contributors. Producing a publication such as this is a long and circular process, and we thank them for their patience and enthusiasm.

Abbreviations

ADS	Approved Destination Status
APEC	Asia-Pacific Economic Cooperation
ASEAN	Association of Southeast Asian Nations
BAMS	Bachelor of Ayurvedic Medicine and Surgery
BIH	Bangkok International Hospital
CABG	coronary artery bypass graft
CII	Confederation of Indian Industry
CNTO	China National Tourist Office
EFEO	Ecole Française d'Extrême-Orient
HCMC	Ho Chi Minh City
HKSARG	Hong Kong Special Administrative Region Government
ICOMOS	International Council on Monuments and Sites
IT	information technology
ITS	Individual Travel Scheme
JCI	Joint Commission International
JNR	Japanese National Railway
JTB	Japan Travel Bureau
KTO	Korean Tourism Organization
Laos PDR	Laos People's Democratic Republic
MRI	magnetic resonance imaging
NGO	non-governmental organization
NRI	non-resident Indian
NTA	National Tourism Administration
NTO	National Tourism Organization
OCA	Olympic Council of Asia
PATA	Pacific Asia Travel Association
SOE	state-owned enterprise
STB	Singapore Tourism Board
TAT	Thai Authority for Tourism
UEFA	Union of European Football Associations
UNESCO	United Nations Educational, Scientific and Cultural Organization
UNWTO	United Nations World Tourism Organization
URA	Urban Redevelopment Authority
WTO	World Tourism Organization
WTTC	World Travel and Tourism Council

1 Introduction

Rethinking tourism in Asia

Tim Winter, Peggy Teo
and T.C. Chang

Introduction

It is not often that an academic book is inspired by a pair of Speedos. Here is one. As countless postcards, travel shows and holiday brochures tell us, our ideal beach is tropical, sandy and washed over by clear, warm, turquoise-colored waters. Indeed, the scene of 'paradise on earth' is deserted, apart from the romantic couple walking arm in arm towards the sunset or the beautiful bikini-clad woman lying on the water's edge soaking up the sun. Reclining alone, she seduces the viewer through passivity and possibility. She tells us the beach is a space of youthfulness, sexuality, independence, and time spent away from the chaos of everyday life. Crucial to this message is the all-over, carefully cultivated suntan. It is here we need to look closer, as it is in the suntan that we see the beach is not the space of brown skin, but the *browning* of skin, or, to be more exact, the browning of white skin. As a marker of sexuality, health and youthful vigor, the suntan is the desired coloring of pale, white skin. And so as the swimwear exposes this skin to the sun, it also reveals a series of broader, underlying values. Today's post-cards, brochures, websites and television programs not only carefully define where in the world the ideal beach is to be found, but also who are its actors, or imagined consumers. Tracing the genealogy of these images, and the ideals they convey, quickly reveals their European and North American roots. At the beginning of the twentieth century, social commentators on both con-tinents would express shock and contempt for an emerging trend of exposed, tanned bodies. In the wake of World War I, however, much had changed as seaside resorts in California and Southern Europe established themselves as extremely popular places dedicated to the pursuit of leisure and fun. Recent years have seen a number of books trace this evolution of the beach as a space of leisure and recreation (Lenček and Bosker 1998; Urbain 2003; Gray 2006). While their titles and introductions promise the definitive story, their accounts focus on beaches in California, the Mediterranean or the north of England. No mention is given to the cultural histories of beaches in Africa, the Middle East or Asia.

If we turn to Figure 1.1, we see an image of a sunbather that lies outside such historical accounts. Taken in Phuket in 2005, the photograph presents

Figure 1.1 Japanese sunbather in Phuket (Photo by Tim Winter)

the far more unusual image of a Japanese male lying by the sea; one that challenges the commonly held perception that the tourist is white and most likely living in a postindustrial, 'Western' country. By moving the point of focus away from the obligatory white Western female, our reclining Asian male asks us to shift our analytic attention accordingly. To date, the vast majority of studies conducted on tourism in Asia have considered encounters between local hosts and their white, Western guests. The above image demands we ask unfamiliar and important questions concerning the ongoing growth of tourism around the world today and the rapid socio-cultural changes now occurring within Asia. It also illustrates why students and scholars of tourism need to address the analytical imbalances that characterize tourism studies today by focusing on domestic and intra-regional tourists in non-Western contexts. In an Asian region that has placed far less value on the suntan historically, is the beach now being inscribed with new cultural values? Do we need to rethink who the subjects and objects of tourism are? Or how places will be constructed and represented for new forms of consumption in the future? Or indeed, the commonly held assumption that Japanese tourists prefer to travel in groups? In raising such questions and many others, our male sunbather asks us to look more closely, scrutinize assumptions, create new modes of analysis and, where necessary, replace clichés with more rigorous, empirically sensitive accounts.

To this end we adopted the photograph as the poster for a conference on Asian tourism at the National University of Singapore in late 2006. The response was interesting. It became a popular topic among student blogs, many of whom expressed their amazement that such 'a daring image' would be used for an academic conference. A number of posters were torn down. Some were taken as prizes to decorate the walls of student rooms. Others, we later learnt, were removed because the image was deemed too offensive. In one department, a smaller poster was carefully taped over the top, ensuring just the sunbather's mid-rift was masked. Given that the posting of notices and adverts with sexual overtones are commonplace on the university campus, we were surprised by such responses. While a woman in a bikini would have raised few eyebrows, the image of a muscular Asian man posing in white swimming trunks clearly created a tangible and emotive response. For some, perhaps, the image was too homoerotic? Whereas, for others, maybe it merely delivered something unfamiliar in a familiar place, and offered messages that transgressed the conventional?

Away from the campus, Singapore's department stores provide another unlikely source of inspiration for thinking about matters of 'skin tone' and 'good looks.' The range of creams, rubs and lotions on sale in their cosmetics sections indicate the presence of opposing attitudes toward skin color in Singapore today. Along one aisle, body lotions, face creams and masks all promise a 'whiter porcelain, clear complexion.' These products form part of a long-standing cosmetics industry that tailors to entrenched ideas of Asian beauty oriented around paler and lighter skin tones. More recently, however, creams and oils designed to enhance a suntan have become increasingly popular. The side-by-side display of products that promise to both lighten and darken skin offers us a glimpse into the shifting values and symbolic meanings ascribed to skin color in this Southeast Asian nation. In marked contrast to the preferences of their parents for staying out of the sun, many young Singaporeans purchase products that will help them attain the 'uniform glow of a perfectly suntanned body.' 'Working on the tan' is now integral to a day relaxing and partying at the beach. But this has not always been the case. The growing popularity of these new cultural practices can, in large part, be attributed to a convergence between increasingly influential Western conceptions of bronzed beauty and the development of certain beaches in Singapore as venues for water sports and night-time entertainment since the mid-1990s.

The growing popularity of sunbathing in Hong Kong and the fact that our subject in Figure 1.1 is a Japanese tourist on holiday in Thailand suggest such changes are not merely confined to the city state of Singapore. Read together, they indicate that in certain contexts in Asia, long-held ideas about darker skin are being superseded by new values and symbolic associations. But to what degree do these practices extend beyond the urban youth of certain countries? Across much of India today, for example, darker skin continues to be associated with unattractiveness, lower caste/class and lower prospects for marriage. It seems highly unlikely that the suntan will emerge as a marker of social and physical attractiveness across India in the foreseeable future.

Reflecting upon the seemingly simple issue of the suntan, its meanings and its histories provided the impetus for bringing together the diverse set of voices found in this book. As the project evolved, it quickly became apparent that a volume examining tourism in Asia by Asian tourists is framed by three key concerns. First, as we move into the twenty-first century, Asia is witnessing a rapid growth in domestic and intra-regional leisure travel. In some countries, the scale of tourism development can be best described as staggering or unprecedented, and with 40 percent of the world's population living in the region, there is little doubt that this growth in travel will be a long-term trend. The impact it will have on Asia's societies needs to be understood. Second, while much has been written about the rise of Asia, so far, very little attention has been given to the role played by intra-regional and domestic tourism; and how such mobilities create new forms of citizenship, transform local environments and foster unforeseen political tensions. Accordingly, this book sets out to foreground Asian tourism in the bigger picture of a rapidly changing region. Third, reviewing studies of the beach and sunbathing tells us much about the geographic and cultural biases that define tourism studies as a field of scholarship. To date, the vast majority of studies published in English have focused on East/West, North/South encounters between Western guests and their host destinations. Far less attention has been paid to the socio-cultural impacts of intra-regional and domestic movements in non-Western contexts like Asia, Africa or the Middle East. The ongoing growth in leisure-related travel across Asia demands a reappraisal of how tourism is analyzed and conceptualized. In response, our aim here is to offer some modest, but hopefully valuable, insights into the social, cultural and political implications stemming from Asia's transformation from mere host destination into a region of mobile consumers.

Challenging conventions: universalism, cultural relativism and historical voids

The geographic and cultural biases that characterize the field of tourism studies extend far beyond accounts of the beach. Obviously detailing the evolution of modern global tourism or reviewing the literature that has studied it is beyond the scope of this chapter. It is, however, helpful to highlight some of the key factors that have contributed to shaping scholarship, and that are pertinent to the themes of this book. In the first instance, various concepts cultivated in the fields of sociology, geography, management or marketing have often been uncritically applied to a host of tourism contexts. Even in less positivist social science and humanities-based approaches, ideas like authenticity, development, heritage and 'the tourist gaze' emerged in ways that suggested they are universally applicable. Perhaps most crucially here, with the universalisms promised by structuralism and a Foucauldian post-structuralism underpinning MacCannell's (1976) alienated authentic-seeking subject and Urry's (1990) tourist gaze respectively, the idea of *the tourist* solidified as an all-encompassing, analytical monolith. More recently this notion of a singular *subject* has somewhat shifted to a more plural language of *subjectivities* via analytical frameworks oriented around ideas of performance (Edensor 1998), embodiment (Yalouri 2001; Sheller 2003) or consumption as practice (Crouch 1999). Nonetheless, these debates invariably continue to rely upon European and North American citizens as their empirical starting point. Indeed, as already noted, the vast majority of studies have looked at 'Western' forms of tourism and their impact on communities, places and environments. This does not, however, mean that 'non-Western' forms of tourism have been ignored entirely. As we shall see over the course of this volume, contributions from Graburn (1995a), Oakes (1998), Tan *et al.* (2001), Winter (2004), Nyíri (2006) and Notar (2007) are among the various studies conducted on domestic and intra-regional tourism in Asia. But despite these works, scholarship on tourism generally continues to be dominated by certain analytical and conceptual ideas that have been conceived in the historical, cultural and social changes of Europe and North America. In the case of the social sciences and humanities, examples here might include modernity, post-modernity, performed identity, or the cultural economies of leisure consumption. And in the context of management and business studies, countless studies have been driven by destination life cycle theories, consumer profiling models or 'case studies.' Hanging their theoretical import on the hooks of replication and predictability, such approaches have commonly provided the basis for misguided claims of universality.

Moreover, and as Winter (2007a) has documented elsewhere, within a field that has prioritized ideas of a *global* tourism industry impacting upon a *local* environment, less attention has been given to regional, cultural and geographic differences and parallels. Given that the paradigm of tourism has in large part been constructed around an analysis of West-to-East, North-to-South encounters, rooted in ideas of globalization as a process of Westernization, our tourist has been silently conceived as white (and male). Like most fields of scholarship, the global lingua franca is English. The key journals in the field like *Annals of Tourism Research*, *Tourism Management*, *Tourism Geographies*, *Tourist Studies* and *Tourism Economics* are run from institutes in Europe or the USA. The Hong Kong-based *Asia Pacific Journal of Tourism Research* and India-based *Tourism Recreation Research* represent notable exceptions here. But while a number of major universities across Asia increasingly are turning their attention to tourism, we have yet to see a consolidation of scholarship that speaks back to, or transcends, the dominant discourses cultivated in academic departments located in post-industrial, 'Western' societies of the global north.

This book sets out with the ambitious task of countering these historical biases, and it does so by examining the ongoing rise of Asian tourism. It certainly does not proclaim a revolution by naïvely dispensing with the corpus of work built up over the past three to four decades. Indeed, many of the authors that follow draw upon this knowledge to frame their accounts, continually adopting and refuting, endorsing and challenging. In selecting the contributors for this volume we have endeavored to create a plurality of complementary voices. The analytical boundaries of the book have been established in part, by us as editors, and in part by factors beyond our control. Given the enormity of the topic and the multitude of issues arising from the rapid growth in Asian tourism at the beginning of the twenty-first century, we have upheld certain boundaries for the sake of analytical rigor and coherence.

First, the book focuses on Asian tourists in Asia. It does not examine how Asian tourists are transforming other parts of the world. And with the exception of one chapter that offers a comparative study, the book does also not examine tourism in Asia by diasporas living outside the region. Second, the book pursues an interpretative approach. Largely working within the social sciences and humanities, our contributors go beyond growth statistics to offer valuable analytical depth and insight. In order to provide a comprehensive overview of the region, we have endeavored to include pieces on as many countries as possible. With such aims, less attention is given to discussions of topics like marketing, facility management or future trend analysis. Rather, the chapters that follow set out to situate tourism within its wider social, political and cultural contexts, addressing an array of topics, including aesthetics, postcolonialism, heritage, healthcare, and nation-building. In bringing them together in one volume, our intention is to open up new directions of analysis, challenge a variety of underlying assumptions and stimulate further research.

To talk of Asia begs the question of scale. Michael Hall helps set the scene for such ideas in Part I by questioning what is meant by 'Asia' in geographical terms. First, by tracing the historical origins of the term, he demonstrates the different ways in which the region is constructed and represented by organizations such as APEC, ASEAN, UNWTO and PATA. Where do Australia and New Zealand fit in? What regulatory boundaries do airlines use? And why Western Asia is only institutionally weakly linked to the rest of the region are among the questions he addresses. While many of the chapters that follow focus on the nation–state, city or rural village to sustain their arguments, the notion of an 'Asian region' is a theme that re-occurs throughout the book. Given that authors are working across very different scales, the question of extrapolation, and the role of qualitative research for understanding broader trends or patterns, is an important, if not elusive, issue. Throughout the 1970s and 1980s, accounts of tourist typologies were common. As the field evolved, however, such approaches were increasingly regarded as static and empirically untenable. To pursue the 'Asian tourist' as a conceptual category today would be a return to an analytical stasis and intransigence. On the flip side, however, to merely continue using the term 'the tourist' in a universalist, non-critical way would be equally reductive and simplistic, and would present an artificial barrier to important and interesting lines of enquiry. The question remains, then, what is a reliable framework for making assertions about motivations, desires or discernible characteristics? Should it be ethno-cultural, geographic or national? Can we speak of Chinese or Thai tourists, for example? Clearly, the boundaries between recognizing 'traits' or 'charac-teristics,' and reductive typologies are thin and often unclear. A number of the chapters that follow accept such risks in order to ask difficult, but important questions, and cast light on issues that have yet to receive the attention they deserve.

Accordingly, in an attempt to address some of the Western-centric biases that have shaped tourism to date, a number of contributors grapple with the tensions between universalism and cultural relativism. Tim Winter considers such issues in the context of the Cambodian souvenir industry in Chapter 4. To date, the study of souvenirs, as forms of material culture, has been oriented towards the traditional, locally made, and the hand crafted. Debates over the loss of authenticity and cultural commodification rest upon the idea that the tourist dollar is the incoming force of globalization, which both trans-forms and distorts. Within such critiques little attention has been given to the tastes and buying preferences of visitors from different parts of the world: the tourist is once again implicitly seen as Western. Winter suggests that the sale of souvenirs at Angkor to tourists from Northeast Asia requires us to move beyond analyses of the local/global, domestic/imported, authentic/inauthentic. To understand why glass replicas of Angkor Wat lit up by red and green neon diodes or metal ashtrays in the shape of temple carvings are so popular, he claims we need to shift the lens to mass manufacturing or the culturally relative nature of what is deemed 'kitsch.' That many of the replicas and other items such as scarves and key chains are manufactured in China and look suspiciously similar to products sold in souvenir shops in other parts of Asia suggests that we must revisit how we construct knowledge about the circulation of material culture in tourism. As Winter points out, citing Gell, it is not a 'study of the aesthetic principles of this or that culture, but of the mobilization of aesthetics principles . . . in the course of social interaction' (1998: 4). With rapid economic growth in the region and the global expan-sion of consumerism encouraging more spending, discourses on consumption may need to take into account conceptual differences, and similarities, in the concerns about the phenomenon.

Chan Yuk Wah's account in Chapter 5 of Chinese tourists in Southeast Asia follows a similar line of argument. For Chan, the well-trodden path of the alienated post-industrial subject seeking 'authenticity' in the pre-modern other offers little insight for understanding the motivations of Chinese over-seas tourists today. Employing the concept of 'disorganized tourism space,' she documents the touristic quest for modernity as an 'aspiring' journey. Amidst the backdrop of restricted movement in the 1970s, the newly gained mobility through international tourism represents a shake-off of tradition, poverty and political control. To travel is to possess an 'upward-looking mentality,' and the more one visits modern sites, the greater is one's cultural capital as a world citizen. However, Chan argues that the emerging tourism geography of the Chinese is a disorganized one in which negative stereotypes and tense host–guest relations dominate. Unlike mass Western tourists who are often regarded as culturally and economically superior, the Chinese are stereotyped as country bumpkins lacking international exposure and awareness. In Hong Kong, Singapore and Vietnam, Chan shows that Chinese tourists leave in their wake unpleasant memories, images and impacts. However, these impacts vary widely, reflecting the differentiated power relations between tourists and locals in different locales and the ever-morphing identity of the Chinese as they acquire travel experience.

For Peggy Teo in Chapter 3, such discussions need to be situated within the broader context of tourism 'truths.' Using Tribe's (2006) dissection of the 'truth about tourism' as her point of departure, Teo argues that Asia has yet to find its place in the knowledge order of the field. Various data charts detailing the scale of tourism growth across the region are cited to illustrate why this needs to be urgently addressed. She suggests that a middle path needs to be followed, one that reinterprets current Western-centric theoretical constructs for different Asian contexts. Accordingly, neoliberalism and postcolonialism are among the analytical 'force-fields' offered for interpreting today's Asian tourism. But as she points out, one knowledge order should not be prioritized over another. Although mapping trends in infrastructure development or the economic growth coming from the travel industry are important, these knowledge orders need to be balanced by accounts that critically address the societal changes that inevitably follow. For Teo, the pursuit of such goals will help us better reflect upon how knowledge in tourism is formulated.

It thus becomes apparent then, that when read alongside each other, the chapters in Part I suggest that some of field's defining analytical foundations and their claims of universality, need to be critically challenged. In harmony, they call for Asia to become the context from which theory emerges. Equally, however, a number of subsequent chapters illustrate how theories and conceptual frameworks conceived in non-Asian contexts offer illumination, clarity and rigor. By coming to different conclusions regarding the validity and applicability of existing debates within the literature, the volume avoids falling in to the trap of essentializing Asia as somewhere or something that is fundamentally 'different.'

For researchers of Asian tourism, the challenge of scale and its representation are compounded by large voids in the historical record. It was noted earlier that in the case of Europe and North America, extensive studies have shown how the beach evolved as a space of leisure and recreation. Through the work of Walton (1983), Lenček and Bosker (1998) and Gray (2006), we now have a detailed picture of 'seaside' architecture, gender and fashion, and how working-class mass-tourism holidays, the European grand tour and holiday camps all emerged. And yet in the case of Asia, very little has been published concerning the cultural history of the sea and its frontiers as a site of leisure. The same can also be said for many other aspects of tourism in

Asia. There are far fewer historical studies available within which scholars examining today's developments can situate their work. More specifically, the picture across the region is very uneven. In their chapters here, Graburn and Nyíri benefit from a number of earlier studies on domestic tourism in Japan and China respectively. However, for those working on Myanmar, Cambodia or Sri Lanka, to cite a few examples, finding studies that trace a history of domestic tourism poses significantly more challenges. Equally, at the conceptual level, while the social, cultural, geographic and economic histories of traveling concepts ranging from the package tour through to the grand tour have received much attention elsewhere, there are few parallels that can be cited for theoretically framing the historical growth of tourism in Asia.

Clearly, then, this lack of historical context presents scholars and students of Asian tourism with a number of analytical challenges. As a further example, although the scale of tourism in Asia today is clearly unprecedented, the degree to which increasing numbers are delivering social and cultural changes deemed to be qualitatively different or new remains unclear. Do today's patterns of consumption represent a break with tradition? Or is today's travel merely a continuation of previous forms of mobility? The difficulties of historically situating recent events also present a major challenge for those attempting to identify underlying trends. History cannot be offered as a guide to the future. Finally, the jury also remains out as to whether tourism across Asia is creating a series of distinct, even unique, cultural forms as it grows, or whether the region is merely following the same growth curves, or cycles, as those experienced in other parts of the world. Teo, in Chapter 3, for example, suggests the evolution of mass tourism to specialist tourism and from tour groups to independent travelers in Asia is qualitatively different to the pathways followed in Europe or the USA (see also Nyíri 2006). Equally, however, she recognizes that the geographical expansion of Asia's markets – from domestic to regional to long-haul – reflects a globally familiar pattern.

Emerging markets, (re)scripting places

Across Asia, entrepreneurs, governments, real estate developers, hoteliers, tour operators and airlines are all (re)orienting their products towards the Asian leisure consumer. As the statistics presented throughout the volume vividly illustrate, increasing levels of disposable income across the region mean that new markets for both domestic and intra-regional travel are being created all the time. Like their Western counterparts, the upper and upper-middle classes are willing to venture both near and far to garner their own cultural capital. In Part II of the book, the ongoing rise of medical tourism is a case in point that illustrates the considerable media attention given to new markets. Two chapters in this volume examine this phenomenon. In Chapter 10, Denise Spitzer addresses alternative medicine. This form of medical travel seems to encompass people going back to their roots and not merely a matter of cheaper costs. Banking on the popularity of Ayurvedic

Medicine in the recent past, Kerala deploys this method of developing wellness as an identity marker of the Indian nation–state to lure diasporic Indians within Asia (and outside of Asia) as well as North Indians to its many resorts and clinics. Whether it is for rejuvenation or the treatment of serious ailments, Spitzer shows that Ayurvedic Medicine is iconic for Kerala and indicative of a new trend of holistic wellness that has wide appeal.

In the other chapter examining medical tourism, Chapter 7, Audrey Bochaton and Bertrand Lefebvre illustrate how a recent expansion in the Asian market is significantly transforming the medical profession in Thailand and India. They posit that medical tourism has blossomed in Asia because the hospitals were able to provide a haven for ill British, American and other European subjects whose own societies face a crisis of rising healthcare costs. The market has, however, been increasingly replaced by Asian medical tourists who desire the same 'unique experience,' the exclusivity, the individualized attention and the quality care that Indian and Thai hospitals can provide. More like five-star hotels and resorts than hospitals, medical tourism in these countries is indicative of the changing consumption patterns of tourism within Asia.

As part of their account, Bochaton and Lefebvre ask whether the exotic Bumrungrad Hospital in Bangkok can be duplicated in Dubai. After all, the interior designs of hospitals look more like resorts than the antiseptic and functional surroundings expected in any normal hospital. The question of how Asian tourism is altering the aesthetics of design, taste and style is a theme that a number of our authors reflect upon in Part II of this book. The recent emergence of boutique hotels in Singapore provides a rich case in point. Peggy Teo and T.C. Chang demonstrate in Chapter 6 how a number of buildings dating back to the colonial period have been reinscribed with new meanings in a market place driven by hybridity, eclecticism and nostalgia. Far from arbitrary, this stylistic interweaving successfully connects with the aesthetic sensibilities of both local and overseas Singaporeans wanting to combine the comforts of a modern inn with the textualities of a rapidly fading past. For Teo and Chang, an analysis of these historic boutique hotels through a postcolonial lens that prioritizes domestic consumption offers an important counter to the current epistemological biases of existing tourism theory.

The appeal of similar values or cultural traits, derived from a shared 'Asianness,' is also fostering a great deal of intra-regional travel and regional co-operation. The government of India, for example, is now using such ideas to help foster heritage tourism industries that extend far beyond its national boundaries. The idea that the Indic civilization is a cultural legacy that endures across large parts of Southeast Asia is also proving a valuable marketing tool for tour operators and travel agents catering to a rapidly growing Indian middle class. K. Thirumaran examines this phenomenon in the context of Bali in Chapter 9. Frequently held up as the iconic island paradise, Bali has been the subject of much academic attention. In his book, *Bali: A Paradise*

Created, Vickers (1996) argues that a history of Dutch colonialism and modern tourism development have foregrounded representations of the island as the quintessential exotic 'other,' a place imbued with female sexuality, color and primitive culture. Crucially, however, such arguments are made from the perspective of a Western gaze. Thirumaran shifts the analysis to Indian tourists. To interpret both their motivations and encounters with local residents, he develops the concept of cultural affinity tourism. Traditional dance performances of Indian influence provide the context. Innovative in its approach, the account offered by Thirumaran reveals interesting host–guest cultural dynamics that have hitherto been unseen in studies of Balinese tourism.

As a parallel, Chapter 8 by Youngmin Choe examines the phenomenon of *hallyu*-induced tourism in Korea as a contributor to regional political cooperation and friendships (*hallyu* refers to the Korean wave of popular culture). She uses the idea of 'a-ffect' to understand the subtle intersections between what happens on screen and at tourist sites. Unlike feeling and emotion, Choe shows how the unformed and unstructured 'a-ffect' that film sites are able to evoke among tourists helps to overcome political hostilities which once riddled Korean–Japan and Korean–Chinese relations. At these film-induced sites, nuanced body movements and expressions embodied by the actors are understood by Asians because they share the same values and are thus able to 'interpret,' 'experience' and appreciate the melodramatic film-induced sites as well as their Korean counterparts. Hence, the film locations in Korea are being reinscribed as depoliticized affective spaces for domestic Korean tourists, Japanese, Singaporean and Hong Kong tourists alike.

The re-scripting of places will depend a great deal on the driving forces behind the demand. Since the state and private enterprise are among the key innovators here as they attempt to capture more of the tourist dollar, there is little doubt many of Asia's touristic landscapes will witness major change over the coming decades.

National imaginings and tourism development

When attempting to understand the societal implications of rapid tourism growth, we soon come to the inevitable question of its relationship to nation-building and the role the industry plays in a country's socioeconomic development. Since the 1970s, the role of 'international' tourism in such processes in the developing world has received considerable attention (De Kadt 1979; Harrison 1992; Wood 1993; Dahles 2001). In contrast, far fewer scholars have examined how domestic tourism in countries outside Europe and North America impacts upon wider economic and political events and processes. A number of authors here take up this imbalance and they are featured in Part III of the book.

In the case of China, it is evident in the studies by Pál Nyíri in Chapter 11 and Jenny Chio in Chapter 15 that the speed and sheer scale of domestic tourism have enabled it to become a potent force for both unification and alienation, development and inequality. At the political level, the development of tourist sites for domestic consumption is following a formulaic recipe that renders greater legitimacy to the state and its ideological goals. Nyíri refers to it as the 'socialist spiritual civilization' wherein the state's support of tourism development aims to improve the 'quality (*suzhi*) of the people.' Whether the attractions are eco-attractions, heritage sites or theme parks, both the tourists and the 'tourees' (people who live and work in the attraction site) are indoctrinated with the message that modernization is progress and this is done in the name of all Chinese who will benefit equally from the project of development. Even for the tourists, they come 'expecting' signs of modernization – tall buildings, clean environments and paved streets rather than any sense of past authenticity. For Nyíri, then, tourism, as modernization, is an important tool in the state's attempts to create a new national citizenry. The question remains, however, whether this vision can be sustained as more and more Chinese travel abroad and incorporate the Internet into their travel practices.

To complement Nyíri's panoramic analysis, Chio pulls us into the village to tell us about the contradictions and tensions inherent to the development process. She examines the village of Ping'an which is undergoing rapid change but also currently experiencing emotional and psychological distancing as villagers compete with each other for a slice of the tourism pie. Her household surveys indicate that unequal wealth distribution has fomented tensions between families who have benefited unequally through tourism. Intra-village rivalry is compounded by inter-village rivalry as different rural sites compete to attract visitors and development funds. A sense of community has thus been replaced by a feeling of self-centeredness. As one villager told her: 'Some have gotten rich [because of tourism] . . . and there's a bit of selfishness; it's very difficult to manage this – everyone thinks about themselves, and no one thinks about everyone.' While such inequalities are a familiar story, Chio interestingly situates them within a wider national context characterized by a series of cultural, economic and geographic convergences. She argues that as rural development takes place, the concepts of 'distance' and 'mobility' take on new significance. With improved roads and the opening of domestic airports, people in China are moving closer to one another as travel time between places are shortened. However, as her village interviews reveal, uneven development caused by different rates of change has also produced new forms of distancing in terms of socioeconomic and cultural disparities.

Seen together, these chapters, along with the pieces by Shepherd and Lim to be outlined shortly, vividly illustrate how domestic tourists in China have quickly become a powerful force for transformation. But as Jamie Gillen and Maribeth Erb show us, it is not only China that is experiencing such changes. In studying Indonesia, in Chapter 12, Erb demonstrates how a growth in domestic tourism has created an opportunity for planners to manage communities according to certain cultural and political ideals. The staging of cultural festivals in Manggarai province are cited as events that delineate ethnic differences and encourage ways of thinking and 'doing' culture. Distinctive aspects of life – from farming, marriage to other rites and rituals – are laid out as tourist sights and activities, allowing visitors and locals to actively participate in cultural practices. By so doing, tourists and locals internalize what it means to be Indonesian. Parks and beaches, musical concerts and picnic sites are also developed not just as attractions but as means to upgrade local quality of life. If travel and enjoying leisure are marks of civility, promoting domestic tourism and local sites of pleasure are seen as important stepping stones to the socio-cultural advancement of rural inhabitants. Domestic tourism thus constitutes an important process in the 'ordering' and 'civilizing' of the masses. Erb's account is not only of cultural and political value, but economic too. She argues that by focusing primarily on international tourism, the state has failed to fully appreciate the significance of its domestic tourist market. Erb thus rightfully calls for a 're-ordering' of how tourism is understood and prioritized in Indonesia, where domestic (and not just international) tourism has become large and important enough to generate positive economic benefits to local communities.

The marginalization of domestic tourists in Vietnam offers an interesting parallel. Accordingly, Chapter 14 by Gillen takes an unusual look at the travel agency industry of Ho Chi Minh City. He explores how such businesses segment their markets, not in the familiar language of cultural, eco- or special interest tourists, but via a reading of their clients' everyday spending and behavioral habits. Gillen demonstrates how this form of differentiation has emerged largely because Vietnamese domestic tourists disturb and unsettle the assumptions held by travel agents as to what a tourist should be, and how he or she should behave. They drink too much alcohol, behave in an unruly manner and do not partake in the practice of tipping guides and drivers. As Gillen puts it: 'They are not replaying the culturally specific performances that their non-Vietnamese tourist counterparts do.' He thus suggests that such clients run contrary to tourism industry stereotypes of who are its 'insiders' and 'outsiders.' Firm ideas of foreign tourists, as outsiders, have underpinned the growth of the tourism industry since the advent of *doi moi*. The stability of these categories, however, is now under threat; a change, Gillen argues, holds important consequences for the social fabric of Vietnamese identity.

Implicit in all these accounts is an understanding that tourism is an artful practice, one that needs to be learnt (Crouch 1999). Whether it's the everyday conventions of tipping in Vietnam or broader ideas of socio-cultural advancement in Indonesia, it is apparent that the knowledge and skills needed to be a tourist do not merely apply to those crossing borders and entering 'foreign' environments. Even for those traveling within their own country, leisure consumption involves the transmission and acquisition of 'cultural capital,' to use Bourdieu's term.

In Nelson Graburn's account in Chapter 13 of domestic tourists in Japan, we see the acquisition of cultural capital divided into stages. What emerges is a fascinating evolutionary picture, whereby domestic tourism becomes a context within which citizens are prepared for traveling beyond the boundaries of the nation–state. In what he describes as the 'internationalization of domestic tourism,' Graburn observes the steady and more recent emergence of 'sites of foreignness' as attractions for Japanese tourists. These include the *furusato* (rural villages and small towns, considered alien in an age of urbanization), foreign community enclaves (such as Chinatowns and other immigrant neighborhoods), and *gaikoku mura* (themed foreign villages such as German Town or Holland Village). The consumption of foreign landscapes, he argues, allows locals to experiment, play and learn about foreignness from the safety of a home environment. The appreciation of foreign goods, products and lifestyles also serves as a status marker, denoting the tourist as a cosmopolitan being. Graburn documents how sites of foreignness are consumed in different ways by different visitors: as social spaces by families, an opportunity to 'go overseas' by others, and a chance to learn about foreign cultures by yet others. This interest is interpreted as a way of becoming the ideal Japanese – open-minded, cosmopolitan, and appreciative of diverse cultures. Ideologically, it is also a form of cultural consumption that prepares the Japanese for their roles as world citizens, ever ready to embrace difference and diversity. In a globalizing age, being cosmopolitan is considered an essential in economic competition and survival.

The politics of revis(it)ing heritage

The ties between tourism and the politics of nation-building are mobilized nowhere more so than in the context of cultural heritage. As the examples of Angkor, Sukothai, and Borobodur all illustrate, architectural and archaeological remnants of the past not only provide the historical legitimacy for emboldening the actions of today's governments, but also frequently occupy the center-stage in the theater of performed nations. Invariably, this seemingly benign use of culture and tradition conceals more disturbing, pernicious processes. As previously, while the broader implications arising from the use and abuse of culture for the international tourist dollar has garnered a considerable amount of critical attention in recent years, significantly less has been written about how domestic tourists contribute to such processes. We examine these issues in Part IV.

Accordingly, in Chapter 17, Olivier Evrard and Prasit Leepreecha consider the ways in which domestic tourism in Thailand has formed part of a longstanding political process aimed at incorporating the country's northern regions into a political and cultural mainstream. Since the 1960s, northern tribes such as the Hmong have constituted a source of political unease for the government, for fears of their co-option by communist and insurgent forces. Rather than leave them on the political margins, tribal groups have been subsumed within nationalist programs as a way of lessening their strangeness and securing their faithfulness to the state. The Royal Project in 1969 to promote commercial agriculture and crop substitution in the north, as well as the establishment of a souvenir store in Doi Pui village (a Hmong stronghold) in 1971 by no less than the Thai King, marked the government's direct hand in developing the north. Tourism initiatives have included the development of villages as tourist sites and incorporation of tribe members into leisure activities. Sympathetic media and non-government organizations have also worked hard to mitigate the image of a 'wild and frightening other,' promoting the north instead as an exotic yet familiar site of pleasure. However, as Evrard and Prasit argue, the zeal to touristify rural sites has also led to cultural commodification and simplification. Traditional Hmong rituals are transformed to impart a less threatening image to visitors, draining them of their meaning and significance. The practice of *ntoo xeeb*, for example, is marketed as the equivalent of an urban Thai ritual involving the ordination of trees called *buat pha*. The two rituals are completely different. Such a process of cultural conflation underlines a broader ideology of subverting difference and domesticating the 'alien,' of which tourism is an abettor. By making the other 'identifiable' and 'enjoyable,' tourists are beguiled and troublesome marginal groups are co-opted and aligned with national agendas.

In Chapter 18, Robert Shepherd pursues similar themes in Tibet. His account opens with an explanation of how, in the eyes of the West, the region and its people became the quintessential culture of mysticism and spirituality. Decades of films, novels and images have seduced Western tourists to this 'exotic, remote and untouched' part of the world. Turning to representations of Tibet within Chinese domestic tourism, Shepherd suggests these same narrative framings prevail. The exoticization of Tibetan culture within China serves to aestheticize and thus, by implication, depoliticize. Shepherd situates such processes within a cultural-political framework to argue that discourses of heritage protection and tourism promotion are part of a broader effort by Beijing to undercut Tibetan claims of cultural and historical importance. Complicit here is UNESCO, whose policies to protect Potala Palace talk of the artistic, engineering and architectural achievements of 'Tibetan, Han, Mongol, Man, and other nationalities.' Valued as a site of significance to the *peoples* of China, their account erases the site's value as a marker of Tibetan national identity. Moreover, UNESCO's desire to protect Tibetan culture from the destructive forces of modernization, including tourism development, reinforces the image of the region as primitive, pre-modern and mysterious. Drawing on interviews with Chinese tourists and backpackers, Shepherd suggests this retention of 'Shangri-la narratives' frames the historical differences and divides between Tibet and the rest of China as cultural, rather than political.

In tracing such processes, Shepherd and Evrard and Prasit Leepreecha together show how domestic tourism has been used to rein in errant states/communities and enforce a sense of national solidarity. In both Tibet and Northern Thailand, where ethnic groups such as the Tibetans, Hmong and Kayans pose a threat to the nation–state of the PRC or Thailand, they are brought into the fold by depoliticizing difference and reconstituting their territories as spaces of culture and tradition that have tourist appeal. What really catches the eye is the suggestion that the depoliticization process is made possible less so by international tourism and more by domestic tourism. Nyíri's chapter argues the same. Wealth and affluence are driving forces of change and it might thus be argued that tourism is a contributor to integration and peace. On the other hand, however, deeply rooted differences are now glossed over in the name of capitalist gains, the outcome of which may be museumification and commodification of cultures. Worse still, deep social divisions emerge as tourism gains are reaped by some and escape others, as pointed out in Chio's chapter on Chinese village tourism.

Understanding the implications which arise when remote, border territories are imagined in overly romantic and aesthetic terms from other parts of the country is also of concern to Shalini Panjabi. Her account in Chapter 16 of Indian-administered Kashmir highlights a series of tensions between imaginings of paradise and the realities of conflict. Rather than orienting her analysis around the now familiar themes of dark or danger zone tourism, Panjabi looks at the ways in which Indian domestic tourism fits into the everyday lives of Kashmiris who continue to endure a low-level conflict. A mountainous, scenic area, famed for its handicrafts, Mughal gardens, rivers and the historic wooden city of Srinagar, the 'vale of Kashmir' emerged as a popular destination for both tourists and pilgrims alike in the decades after partition. The filming of countless Hindi movies in the valley would visually reinforce its image as 'paradise on earth' for Indians. Such notions of tranquility and beauty would be shattered in the early 1990s, however, as the valley succumbed to militancy and inter-communal violence. Not surprisingly, the local tourist industry has suffered heavily ever since. Tired of the violence, people want to move on. Tourism offers valuable opportunities for fulfilling such desires. But as Panjabi indicates, returning to the erstwhile themes of tranquility and an unspoilt, mountainous paradise is likely to once again remove from view the Kashmiri people, and thus exclude their voices in the redevelopment of the region.

Finally, in this Part, we switch to Sidney Cheung's account of cuisine as a locus of shared patrimony. Tracing the origins of *puhn choi* in Hong Kong, in Chapter 19, Cheung argues that Hong Kongers' desire to return to more pristine and peaceful rural settings engendered the popularity of *puhn choi* which is a single communal dish shared by everyone at a table. Usually eaten during tours to the New Territories, *puhn choi* reinforces the idea that there is a traditional Hong Kong heritage which remains part of their identity in the modern cosmopolitan age. While heritage has always been a hotly debated issue in tourism research, especially representations of heritage and the politics of representation, less appreciated is the fact that domestic tourism plays a critical role in evincing such politics and causing heritage to be re-examined and rethought. The intrusion of globalization on architectural and archaeological heritage sites is a well-rehearsed research theme.

Cheung reminds us why we also need to look at domestic tourism's role in affecting other, less tangible forms of heritage.

Tourism and new social networks

Until now, we have emphasized how the transformations brought about by domestic and intra-regional tourism are bound up in reconfigurations of physical space. In Part V, the chapters by Charles Carroll, Francis Lim and Joyce Hsiu-yen Yeh shift the focus towards the ways in which tourism both constitutes and is constituent of new forms of social space. Carroll, for example, presents in Chapter 20 an ethnographically rich account of family travels in Laos from a participant's perspective. His account of travels between Laos and Thailand reveals how family networks are indeed fluid and can be redefined to suit the needs of domestic travel. Close friends become family members. Relatives of close friends can also become part of a loosely defined social unit called 'family members.' Add-ons are common so long as they help bolster the sharing of costs, emotional support or security of the traveling party. Mutual respect seems to be the order of the day and Carroll suggests that the networks are not temporary convenient arrangements but can have lasting social implications.

Equally, Francis Lim's Chapter 21 on Chinese backpackers reveals unique characteristics that distinguish them from their Western counterparts. He notes that the proliferation of Internet and virtual communities in the 1990s allowed for information exchange, laying the foundation for self-organized backpacking trips. Chinese backpackers are highly educated, urban-based and upwardly mobile professionals. In contrast to other forms of backpacking, travel does not represent an escape from the dictates of society, but rather a transplantation of rules and regulations from a socialist state to the realm of the Internet. Indeed, Chinese backpacking is a highly organized affair from initial notifications posted on travel websites, to planning, division of responsibilities, and post-trip review. Every stage of the process is documented in a virtual environment where backpackers post information, exchange tips and discuss travel 'dos and don'ts.' A traveler's reputation is often reinforced or destroyed on the net, due to his/her conduct and behavior on tour. Real and virtual spaces are thus constantly bridged as travelers move continuously between physical and virtual worlds, both of which constitute the totality of the backpacker experience.

In Chapter 22, Yeh also takes up the intersections between young people's identity, technology and travel, this time from the perspective of photography. Yeh shows how travel, and travel photography in particular, mobilize a reflexivity about what it is to be a young, modern Taiwanese citizen. Her framework for interpreting modernity centers on encounters with the 'other,' as narrated and represented by tourists traveling abroad. As she points out, the adoption of this analytical framework to date has overwhelmingly privileged the othering that occurs through Western tourism. In response, sustained attention is given to the role photographs play in defining self and other within a youthful cosmopolitan Taiwanese identity. This account destabilizes the common perception that Asian tourists travel in groups and place collective values over the individual. The practice of selecting, photographing and displaying what is encountered abroad, enables these young travelers to secure the cultural and social capital which defines self. It thus emerges that the other of a modern individualized identity is not just the foreign abroad, but also the family and friends back home who, together, make up the audience of travel photographs.

The volume concludes with a look at the current state of tourism theory and how Asian tourism challenges many of its assumptions and norms. In the Conclusion, Winter argues that scholarship on tourism continues to suffer from an Anglo-Western centrism. Accordingly, he advocates a position of pluralism as a counter to these core–periphery dynamics. Given that the effects of Asian tourism are still very much evolving, he outlines some of the challenges and opportunities for the long-term development of grounded, critical research and teaching on Asian tourism. Winter argues embarking on such roads is vital if we are to adequately understand the profound social changes Asian tourism is now delivering, and at the same time move beyond the cultural, geographical and racial biases that underpin the bulk of tourism research today.

Part I
Challenging conventions

2 'A long and still-unfinished story?'

Constructing and defining
Asian regionalisms

C. Michael Hall

> Over time, when there's more Asians going to Australia and the population is over 50 per cent nonwhite and the rest white, then maybe you'll [Australians] be regarded as Asians.
>
> > (Singapore Prime Minister Goh Chok Tong at the APEC conference in Bangkok, 20 October 2003)

> Australia will never define its place in any part of the world other than to behave as we are.
>
> > (Australian Prime Minister John Howard at the APEC conference in Bangkok, 20 October 2003, both quoted in Jain 2004: 1)

Introduction

On the surface, the task of defining Asia would appear to be a simple one. For many academic and armchair geographers, and readers of Wikipedia, Asia is traditionally defined as the landmass to the east of the Suez Canal and the Ural Mountains, and south of the Caucasus Mountains and the Black and Caspian Seas. To the east it is bound by the Pacific Ocean and the Bering Strait, to the south by the Indian Ocean, and to the north by the Arctic Oceans. Although the physiographic dimensions of such a definition are somewhat problematic given that Europe and Asia share the same continental landmass, the historical convention has been that they are treated separately, although this may also be as much for political and cultural reasons as spatial concerns. However, such an approach tells us little of the way the concept of Asia has come to be socially constructed and the implications that it has for governance as well as identity.

The concept of Asia is usually regarded as a Western construct. It appears that the word 'Asia' has its origins in Ancient Greece where the term was used to describe the region of Anatolia in present-day Turkey. In *The Iliad*, Homer refers to an ally of the Trojans named Asios that may be associated with a confederation of states in Western Anatolia. However, the term was clearly in common use by about 2,450BP when Herodotus used the word to refer to Anatolia or, with respect to the description of the Persian Wars, to differentiate the Persian Empire from Egypt and Greece. Herodotus was also curious as to why different women's names (Asia, Europa and Libya [with respect to Africa]) were used to describe the land mass surrounding the Mediterranean. Nevertheless, in the history of European thought, the concept of Asia has clearly long been significant within a process of geographic, cultural and political othering (Yapp 1992), although the continental affiliations of countries that cross geographic and cultural boundaries may be quite problematic as in the case of Russia, and more recently countries such as Turkey, Georgia, and Armenia, which have either applied or expressed interest in applying for membership of the European Union, and which are seen as having both European and Asian identities or at least being clearly 'different.'

The application of Turkey, for example, for accession to the European Union has raised substantial questions as to the boundaries between geographical and economic regions as well as the extent to which political and cultural values are shared between regions. In the case of Turkey, there are a number of European states with substantial misgivings about the extent to which Turkey shares European cultural mores (no matter how problematic they may also be to define). Interestingly, such concerns over collective values has also been expressed in Asia, especially with respect to the political and economic relationship of Australia and New Zealand to Asia (Broinowski 2003) and the broader 'Asian values' debate (Jain 2004).

Located at the southern end of Asia, the geographical position of Australia and New Zealand belies a socio-cultural, economic and political problematic about the relationship of these countries to contemporary Asia. Although for many years both countries sought to preserve their European identity, population, economic and political trends have drawn them closer to Asia, with tourism being an integral part of this process. The title of this chapter comes from former Australian Prime Minister Paul Keating's book *Engagement: Australia Faces the Asia-Pacific* in which the unfinished story is 'how the people of Australia, this vast continent on the edge of the Asian landmass, are slowly coming to terms with their implications of their place in the world' (2000). The title is significant not only for the subject matter of Australia's foreign policy in relation to Asia but also the extent to which it reveals a fluidity in Asian–Australasian/Pacific relations that has substantial implications for both parties and in which tourism is playing a very significant role (Broinowski 2003). Keating was a great advocate of bringing Australia closer to Asia and in convincing neighboring countries that Australia was a legitimate part of the region. However, he was not necessarily claiming that Australia could be an Asian nation in a cultural sense, as he stated in a December 1993 speech:

> Claims that the Government is trying to turn Australia into an 'Asian country' are based on a misunderstanding of both my own approach and the direction of government policy. This is something I want to be

understood very clearly because it is at the core of my view of Australia and of the Government's approach to relations with our neighborhood. Put simply, Australia is not, and can never be, an 'Asian nation,' any more than we can – or want to be – European and North American or African. We can only be Australian and can only relate to our friends and neighbors as Australia.

(Keating 2000: 20–1)

Yet Keating's stance was of enormous practical import for diplomatic and trade relations as well as domestic policies with respect to education and cultural policy. Underlying Keating's enthusiasm for Asia was the growing trade and tourism significance of Asia for Australia. Similarly, New Zealand had also experienced an increasing Asianization of trade and tourism. Simultaneously, Australia and New Zealand have experienced significant increases in Asian migration and proportion of population with an Asian heritage. All this has led to substantial consideration of where Australia and New Zealand lie in the world and how relations should be built and encouraged. Rethinking Asian tourism arguably therefore also requires a rethink of Australian and New Zealand tourism as well as the tourisms of the other countries that engage with Asia. Such issues of engagement and identity are clearly not isolated to Australia and New Zealand alone and the social, economic and political changes in these countries also raise substantial questions about the social and political construction of Asian identity and Asian tourism and the countries that engage with Asia. This has been taking place,

Although there has been little consensus about what constitutes Asia, many in the international community perceived . . . that the Asia economies were growing at such a vast scale that the 21st century would be marked by the ascendance of Asia – possibly a Pax Asiana.

(Jain 2004: 1)

Nevertheless, even though there may be little consensus over exactly what constitutes Asia, it is nevertheless apparent, that the role of regionalism matters whether it be in terms of personal, place or political identity.

The notion of a regional or a political space is as much a social construct as it is a representation of physical geography. In the same way that the Orient was constructed as an 'other' by various European imperial powers, so also has the notion of Asia been influenced by European and Northern American constructs. However, 'Asia is a contested notion with different meanings and associations for different people in different places, even within Asian societies' (ibid.: 3). The construction and perception of Asia are different within India (Deshingkar 1999) and Japan (Suehiro 1999) as well as being influenced by historical and political events. The concept of an Asian identity is therefore as much being constructed from within as it is from without.

For example, in the 1990s, considerable political attention was given to the notion of Asian values, particularly by Prime Ministers Mahathir bin Mohamad of Malaysia and Lee Kuan Yew of Singapore (Barr 2000). Asian values have been defined as emphasizing a consensual approach, communitarianism rather than individualism, social order and harmony, respect for elders, discipline, a paternalistic state and the primary role of government in economic development, linked to the premise that 'there are values and patterns of behavior that are common to Asian countries and peoples' (Han 1999: 4). In contrast, Han (ibid.: 7) associates 'Western values' with transparency, accountability, global competitiveness, a universalistic outlook and universal practices, and an emphasis on private initiatives and the independence of the private sector. As Milner (1999) noted, the Asian values concept, although at times confused and contradictory, is part of a much larger and longer process of cultural refiguration that, however problematic it might be in cultural and political terms, is attracting substantial and growing emotional investment. Some of the elements of 'Asian' and 'anti-Asian' values are indicated in Table 2.1.

Such debates are not just part of an intellectual argument, they also have an extremely practical effect on how policy is made, particularly with respect to international trade, investment and the mobility of capital, and the mobility of people. Moreover, despite claims as to the diminished role of state given the rate of contemporary economic globalization, it is nevertheless essential to recognize that the state is the foundation of regulatory regionalism via the bilateral and multilateral series of political and economic relations established by states under international law. The Asian values debate of course is not engaged in just by those from the geographical region of East Asia (Tiek 1999) but also from other places that engage with Asia both intellectually and economically (Beeson and Yoshimatsu 2007). The question of what constitutes Asia is therefore particularly problematic in seeking to rethink contemporary Asian tourism given that values and geographies underlie not only decisions to travel but also the regulatory and cultural framework within which varieties of tourism can exist.

There is insufficient space here to fully explore the creation of Asian regulatory spaces, suffice to briefly note the role of bilateral and multilateral regulation of such factors as visa, aviation and transport networks, and the development of regional tourism policy. Asian regulatory spaces are the product of the large number of political agreements covering economic, cultural, governance and environmental activities between countries that specifically use Asia as an identifying term. For example, agreements under APEC (Asia-Pacific Economic Cooperation) give support for the creation of a specific set of transnational relations and flows within the regulatory spaces of APEC members. Such spaces are not anonymous or blank but are identified with a geographical space which, in turn, has its own implications for the social, economic and political construction of particular identities, as noted at the start of this chapter.

Table 2.1 Asian and anti-Asian values

Elements of Asian Values	Anti-Asian Values Elements
• A set of values as shared by people of many different nationalities and ethnicities living in East Asia. These values include a stress on the community rather than the individual, the privileging of order and harmony over personal freedom, refusal to compartmentalize religion away from other spheres of life, a particular emphasis on saving and thriftiness, an insistence on hard work, a respect for political leadership, a belief that government and business need not necessarily be natural adversaries, and an emphasis on family loyalty. • In seeking to understand the economic success of certain Asian societies credit must be given to the role of 'Asian values.' It is not sufficient to analyze such economic success in culture-free economic terms, or as a result of the adoption of specifically Western values. • In the process of developing modern political systems in Asian societies due recognition must be given to the need to ground these systems in the specific Asian cultures in which they are to be situated. It is not acceptable to reform or criticize such societies solely on the basis of Western liberal-democratic practice. • A belief that a major political and economic international shift is underway, involving the rise of 'the East' and the fall of 'the West.' • An expression of disquiet and misgivings regarding certain 'Western values,' especially related to a perceived excessive stress on the individual rather than the community, a lack of social discipline and too great an intolerance for eccentricity and abnormality in social behaviour. The suggestion is sometimes present that Western countries would do well to learn from 'Asian values.' • A style of policy delivery marked by strong central leadership and close relations between government and business.	• The suggestion that a set of 'Asian values' operated throughout the Asian region, or even just in East Asia, contradicts what we know about the presence of long-standing religious (Islamic, Buddhist, Hindu, Confucian) and other divisions in the region, and of the major social and cultural transformation that has been underway. • Many so-called 'Asian values' are equally Western values, and, in some cases, they have been deliberately inculcated in Asian societies as a consequence of the influence on Asian élites of Western models. • The role in social and economic analysis of 'Asian values,' 'Western values' or 'culture' in general can be questioned: economic change may in fact be seen to be the result of other, deeper processes. Cultures are reconstructed, constructed or invented to serve the specific purposes of their inventors. • The specific purpose iof promoting 'Asian values' in the case of a number of Asian régimes is that of defending illiberal forms of government by cloaking autocratic strategies and methods in arguments of cultural exceptionalism. • 'Asian values' are the ideological constructs of Asian leaderships rather than the genuinely-held beliefs of their subjects. • The ideology of 'Asian values' is a radical conservatism that serves the needs of capitalism at a particular stage of its development in specific Asian societies; it is an ideology that 'combines organic statism with market economies.' • There is disagreement within the Asian region about 'Asian values.' NGO's and even some political leaders, are powerful advocates of 'universal,' liberal values. • As a unifying ideological system in the Asian region, the doctrine of 'Asian values,' like the idea of 'Asia' itself, has proved of little use. • 'Asian values' are based on double standards. For example, those claiming to believe in filial piety are in fact accused of being worried by young people not supporting their parents; those claiming the West is materialistic are accused of being engaged in enriching themselves.

Source: Compiled from Milner 1999; Jain 2004

The shift from national to supranational identities of regulation and control is arguably part of a broader process of the development of post-sovereign governance (MacCormick 1996; Morales-Moreno 2004) in which the creation of supranational governance structures arguably goes hand-in-hand with the formation of new sets of political identities and, potentially in the longer term, social identities. The formation of an Asian identity, albeit highly contested, therefore runs parallel to the development of a series of transnational political spaces. For example, it can be argued that the development of new sets of visa and border agreements between countries as a result of the development of new regulatory spaces also encourages the development of new understandings of citizenship, not only with respect to belonging and identity, but also with mobility. For Isin and Wood, modern citizenship is no longer exclusively tied to membership of a nation–state; that is, restricted to 'legal obligations and entitlements which individuals possess by virtue of their membership in a state' (1999: 4). Instead, citizenship is a more complex form of identity which is distinctive because it is based on reciprocal social relations and common interests among a particular group that new Asian supranational regulatory spaces serve to enhance and reinforce. Although notions of 'expanded citizenship' (van Steenbergen 1994) or cosmopolitan citizenship have tended to be applied more to the European sphere (Coles 2008), there is no reason not to consider the development of an Asian cosmopolitan citizenship given the extent to which accessibility and mobility of certain groups in society are being afforded by structures such as APEC or ASEAN (Association of Southeast Asian Nations).

The new regulatory spaces of Asia not only serve to encourage new Asian mobile identities for some groups by virtue of new forms and rights of citizenship but also provide the political means for influencing the direction of flows and connections between places. For example, the ability to fly between international destinations or to cross borders via particular modes of transport is enabled by the political agreements that exist between countries with respect to air rights, transport connections and networks and border crossings. All of these factors therefore influence the capacity of destination development and international mobility within Asia as well as in terms of long-distance travel. Indeed, intra-regional travel has become proportionately more important over time with respect to tourism growth.

Membership of Asian political institutions is therefore an important element in the development of Asian identities as well as a signifier of Asian space. Table 2.2 records a number of these institutions and their memberships. One of the notable observations is that there has been a far longer tradition of international cooperation in supranational bodies among European nations as compared to Asia, but to a great extent this may be a reflection of the relative short history of nationhood and the influence of colonial powers on international relations in Asia. Nevertheless, the development of 'Asian' institutions has historically tended to be more focused on East Asia than on western Asia. Indeed, it is noticeable that the United Nations

Table 2.2 Membership of select Asian political and economic institutions

Institution		Member countries
Association of South East Asian Nations (ASEAN)	Originally a 1967 defence agreement between the original members of ASEAN: Indonesia, Malaysia, Philippines, Singapore, and Thailand. The association was transformed into a trade relationship in 1992.	Brunei, Cambodia, Indonesia, Laos, Malaysia, Myanmar, Philippines, Singapore, Thailand, Vietnam Observers at ASEAN meetings include Australia, China, India, Japan, New Zealand, Pakistan and South Korea Timor-Leste is a candidate ASEAN member
ASEAN Plus Three	Forum that functions to assist cooperation between ASEAN and three East Asian nations	ASEAN nations and China, Japan and South Korea
Asia-Europe Meeting	Interregional forum established in 1996 between the European Union and the members of the ASEAN Plus Three grouping	India, Pakistan and Mongolia were invited to participate in the 2006 and future meetings
Asia-Europe Foundation	Cultural and education compliment to the Asia-Europe Meeting	Brunei, Cambodia, China, Indonesia, Japan, South Korea, Laos, Malaysia, Myanmar, Philippines, Singapore, Thailand, Vietnam
East Asia Summit	Pan-Asian forum first held in 2005	The ASEAN Plus Three plus Australia, India and New Zealand with Russia as an observer and potential future member Proposed members include Bangladesh, Mongolia, Pakistan, Papua New Guinea, Timor-Leste
Asia-Pacific Trade Agreement (APTA)	Commenced 1975, China joined 2001	Bangladesh, China, India, Lao People's Democratic Republic, Republic of Korea, Sri Lanka
Asia Pacific Economic Cooperation (APEC)	Economic forum established in 1989	Australia, Brunei, Canada, Chile, Chinese Taipei (Taiwan), Hong Kong, Indonesia, Japan, Malaysia, Mexico, New Zealand, Papua New Guinea, People's Republic of China, Peru, Philippines, Russia, Singapore, South Korea, Thailand, United States, Vietnam

Table 2.2 (*cont'd*)

Institution		Member countries
Asia Development Bank	Regional development bank established 1966	Afghanistan, Australia, Armenia, Azerbaijan, Bangladesh, Bhutan, Brunei Darussalam, Cambodia, Cook Islands, Federated States of Micronesia, Fiji, Georgia, Hong Kong, India, Indonesia, Japan, Kazakhstan, Republic of Korea, Kyrgyz Republic, Lao People's Democratic Republic, Kiribati, Malaysia, Maldives, Marshall Islands, Mongolia, Myanmar, Nauru, Nepal, New Zealand, Pakistan, Palau, Papua New Guinea, People's Republic of China, Philippines, Samoa, Singapore, Solomon Islands, Sri Lanka, Republic of China (Taiwan), Tajikstan, Thailand, Timor-Leste, Tonga, Turkmenistan, Tuvalu, Uzbekistan, Socialist Republic of Vietnam, Vanuatu
		Other regions: Austria, Belguim, Canada, Denmark, Finland, France, Germany, Ireland, Italy, Luxembourg, Netherlands, Norway, Portugal, Spain, Sweden, Switzerland, Turkey, United Kingdom, United States
UN Economic and Social Commission for Asia and the Pacific		Afghanistan, Australia, Armenia, Azerbaijan, Bangladesh, Bhutan, Brunei Darussalam, Cambodia, People's Republic of China, Federated States of Micronesia, Fiji, France, Georgia, India, Indonesia, Islamic Republic of Iran, Japan, Kazakhstan, Kiribati, Republic of Korea, Kyrgyz Republic, Lao People's Democratic Republic, Malaysia, Maldives, Marshall Islands, Mongolia, Myanmar, Nauru, Nepal, Netherlands, New Zealand, Pakistan, Palau, Papua New Guinea, Philippines, Russian Federation, Samoa, Singapore, Solomon Islands, Sri Lanka, Republic of China (Taiwan), Tajikstan, Thailand, Timor-Leste, Tonga, Turkey, Turkmenistan, Tuvalu, United Kingdom, United States of America, Uzbekistan, Socialist Republic of Vietnam, Vanuatu

Table 2.2 (*cont'd*)

Institution		Member countries
		Associate members: American Samoa, Commonwealth of the Northern Mariana Islands, Cook Islands, French Polynesia, Guam, Hong Kong, Macau, New Caledonia, Nuie
Economic Cooperation Organization	Founded by Iran, Pakistan and Turkey in 1995	Afghanistan, Azerbaijan, Islamic Republic of Iran, Kazakhstan, Kyrgyzstan, Pakistan, Tajikistan, Turkey, Turkmenistan, Uzbekistan
Black Sea Economic Cooperation	Founded 1992	Albania, Armenia, Azerbaijan, Bulgaria, Georgia, Greece, Republic of Moldova, Romania, Russian Federation, Turkey, Ukraine
Gulf Cooperation Council	Founded 1981	Bahrain, Kuwait, Oman, Qatar, Saudi Arabia, United Arab Emirates
UN Economic and Social Commission for Western Asia		Bahrain, Egypt, Iraq, Jordan, Kuwait, Lebanon, Oman, Palestine, Qatar, Saudi Arabia, Syrian Arab Republic, United Arab Emirates, Yemen
South Asian Association for Regional Cooperation (SAARC)	Founded 1985	Peoples Republic of Bangladesh, Kingdom of Bhutan, Republic of India, Republic of Maldives, Kingdom of Nepal, Islamic Republic of Pakistan, Democratic Socialist Republic of Sri Lanka

Source: Compiled by author

has a separate economic and social commission for West Asia which, with the exception of the Islamic Republic of Iran and, to an extent, Turkey, comprises those countries that in European parlance would be described as the 'Middle East.'

The break-up of the former Soviet Union has led to the emergence of a number of new states that have now become members of the Asian Development ment Bank and the UN Economic and Social Commission for the Asia Pacific. Several of these states have also joined the central and western Asian economic grouping known as the Economic Cooperation Organization and the interregional Black Sea Economic Cooperation group, while the Gulf States, excluding Iran and Iraq, have their own economic grouping. But the confused nature of cultural and geographical identity is illustrated by the fact that several of the countries of western Asia that were formerly part of the Soviet Union: Armenia, Azerbaijan, Georgia, and Kazakhstan, are playing in the UEFA (Union of European Football Associations) nations championship, while Georgia and Armenia have expressed interest in becoming members of the European Union. It is also worth noting that with respect to the Olympic sports movement only Kazakhstan of the above mentioned nations participates in the Asian Games run under the auspices of the Olympic Council of Asia (OCA).

To the east, there is also confusion as to the extent to which the Pacific Islands (sometimes referred to, together with Australia and New Zealand, as Oceania) and the Pacific Rim are also a part of the Asian experience. The Asia-Pacific Economic Cooperation (APEC) forum is perhaps the clearest example of these institutional linkages although the extent to which observer status of ASEAN and the East Asia Summit has been extended also illustrates the expansion of the concept of Asia. Here again sport indicates some interesting changes, as in 2007 Australia competed in the Asian Nations Cup after shifting in 2006 from the Oceania Football Federation. Although Australia is unlikely to compete in the Asian Games in the foreseeable future, the shift to playing football in an Asian context for both club and country raises interesting issues of identity for such a sports-focused country. In one sense a shifting in sporting focus follows changes in political focus. As Jain (2004) observed, the 2002 Bali bombings forced the conservative Australian government under Prime Minister John Howard to engage with Asia in a much more involved way than it had previously espoused under its foreign policy settings. Nevertheless, Howard's clear alignment with the United States and, to a lesser extent, the United Kingdom means that, as with Australia playing football in Asia, involvement in Asia is presently based on highly pragmatic as opposed to ideological grounds. As Jain noted, Howard's 'government seeks little convergence between Australian values and Asian values and appears to be blind to the strategic value of goodwill that Australia had finally managed to begin building under the previous administration, which has now been squandered' (2004: 13).

There are also significant changes in terms of the growing interrelationships between Asian countries. Although the countries of South Asia have been especially slow in achieving economic integration as compared to those of ASEAN, it is noticeable that India and Pakistan have been given a stronger role in ASEAN affairs as well as being invited to participate in Asia-Europe meetings. Therefore, potentially providing something of a complementary role to that played by China, Japan and South Korea in East Asian affairs.

Tourism-specific bodies for the region tend to have a marked East Asia-Pacific Rim orientation. The United Nations World Tourism Organization (UNWTO) organizes member states by six regions: Africa, Americas, East Asia and the Pacific, Europe, Middle East and South Asia (Table 2.3). As of November 2007, there were sixteen full members and two associate members of the UNWTO East Asia and the Pacific region, nine full members of South Asia, and twelve full members of the Middle East and one observer. Unlike the UN categories for the social and economic commissions, Libya is included

Table 2.3 Membership of tourism bodies

Organization	Members
UNWTO	
East Asia and the Pacific	Australia, Cambodia, China, Democratic People's Republic of Korea (North Korea), Fiji, Indonesia, Japan, Lao People's Democratic Republic, Malaysia, Mongolia, Papua New Guinea, Philippines, Republic of Korea, Thailand, Timor-Leste, Vietnam; Associate Members: Hong Kong, Macau
South Asia	Afghanistan, Bangladesh, Bhutan, India, Islamic Republic of Iran, Maldives, Nepal, Pakistan, Sri Lanka
Middle East	Bahrain, Egypt, Iraq, Jordan, Kuwait, Lebanon, Libyan Arab Jamahiriya, Oman, Qatar, Saudi Arabia, Syrian Arab Republic, Yemen; Observer: Palestine
PATA (Pacific Asia Travel Association)	Brunei Tourism Board, Canadian Tourism Commission, China National Tourism Administration, Cook Islands Tourism Corporation, Directorate of Hotels and Tourism (Myanmar), Fiji Visitors Bureau, Federated States of Micronesia Visitors Board – Department of Economic Affairs, Government of Timor-Leste, Kiribati National Tourism Office, Korea Tourism Organization (Republic of Korea), Marianas Visitors Authority, Marshall Islands Visitors Authority, Ministry of Tourism (Cambodia), Ministry of Tourism (Government of India), Ministry of Tourism (Government of Pakistan), Ministry of Tourism (Maldives), National Tourism Administration Democratic Peoples Republic of Korea, National Tourism Authority of Lao Peoples' Democratic Republic, Palau Visitors Authority, Papua New Guinea Tourism Promotion Authority, Philippine Convention & Visitors Corporation, Philippine Department of Tourism, Singapore Tourism Board, Solomon Islands Visitors Bureau, Sri Lanka Tourist Board, State Ministry of Culture and Tourism (Indonesia), Tahiti Tourisme, Tonga Visitors Bureau, Tourism Australia, Tourism Authority of Thailand, Tourism Bureau Chinese Taipei, Tourism Malaysia, Vanuatu Tourism Office, Vietnam National Administration of Tourism
	Sub-national members: China Guangxi Tourism Administration (China PRC), Dalian Travel & Tourism Bureau (China PRC), Guam Visitors Bureau, Hawaii Tourism Authority (USA), Hong Kong Tourism Board, Jeollabuk-Do Provincial Government (Republic of Korea), Kunming Municipal Tourism Bureau, Macau Government Tourist Office, Tourism Commission (Government of the Hong Kong SAR)

Source: Compiled from PATA 2007b, *About Asia Pacific*. http://www.pata.org/patasite/index.php?id=36)

in the Middle East region by the UNWTO. Western Asian countries such as Armenia, Azerbaijan, Georgia, Kazakhstan, Kyrgyzstan, Turkmenistan and Uzbekistan are members of the UNWTO's Europe region along with countries such as the Russian Federation and Turkey that occupy both European and Asian geographical, economic and political space. The self-declared leader of the tourism industry in the Asia-Pacific region is PATA, the Pacific Asia Travel Association. Established in 1952 at the First Pacific Area Travel Conference, the association is an organization that represents a range of industry sector, government and other interests, e.g., education, financial services and media, in tourism. According to PATA (2007a) its goal 'is to help members develop and increase business opportunities through a wide array of products, such as events, market intelligence, communications, networking and industry-wide recognition and exposure through the prestigious PATA brand.' However, in governmental terms PATA primarily consists of East Asian, Australasian and Pacific Island members (Table 2.3) although the Asia Pacific map on its website (PATA 2007b) records a sphere of interest ranging from the Americas (although Hawaii is the only government which has an organization representing it) through to Pakistan in the west (a member), and Russia and the central Asian republics of Kyrgyzstan, Kazakhstan and Turkistan, none of which have government agencies as members of PATA.

The 'Asian' political and economic community is therefore increasingly centered on East Asia with growing interlinkages with South Asia and Australia, and to a lesser extent New Zealand and other members of the Pacific community. The growing economic interdependence between these countries and regions, including tourism, has been mooted as heralding the potential development of an Asian economic community to rival that of the European Union. Although the Asian process lies many years behind the European experience of economic integration, the identification of an 'Asia' community and its associated new regulatory space remains an important component of the reorganization of economic space in Asia and the Pacific Rim (Park 2003). Moreover, such economic and political relations have considerable potential to influence the cultural sphere and the development of new citizenships of mobility within Asia.

Conclusion

This chapter has provided a brief review of some of the implications that arise from how Asia is conceived and defined. It has emphasized that the idea of Asia is socially constructed and continues to be so. Within the region, the Asian values debate, and increasingly perhaps notions of what constitutes Asian tourism, are primarily conceptualized within the complex interplay of Western and East Asian geographies and economic, political, and cultural frameworks. However, (East) Asian geographies and regulatory spaces, along with associated travel flows, are being increasingly extended to South Asia and to Australia and New Zealand. Institutionally, western

Asia is only weakly linked to south and eastern Asia and is not a part of discourses on Asian identity instead tending to participate more in discourses with respect to Islamic and Arabic identity.

The concept of an Asian identity is primarily being constructed by the countries and institutions of East and South Asia, particularly through the Asia-Europe meeting, ASEAN and, to a lesser extent, APEC. However, the new institutions of Asia are also representative of a rapidly growing dense set of new regulatory spaces that espouse Asian identity which not only serve to reinforce the social construction of Asia but have a very practical effect on mobilities and citizenship. Such institutions are significant in terms of media representation and notions of otherness but, more particularly, may have a long-term influence of flows of tourists to and from Asia given that the political-economic frameworks that facilitate international trade also facilitate flows of tourists, thereby further leading to changes in understanding of identity and region. The social construction of Asia and the associated debates with respect to Asian values are therefore a significant part of the capacity to engage in and rethink contemporary Asian tourism both within Asia and outside.

3   Knowledge order in Asia

Peggy Teo

Introduction

In his intriguing piece, 'The truth about tourism,' Tribe (2006) offers an overview of how knowledge about tourism is established. He posits that tourism as a phenomenon is subject to 'force-fields' that resist or promote knowledge creation. Five overarching factors at work in the knowledge force-fields are: person, rules, position, ends and ideology. These five factors are not discrete forces; their overlaps and inter-relationships mediate in the process whereby the phenomenal world of tourism is translated into its known world:

Tourism phenomenon<->knowledge force-field<->tourism knowledge

Tribe says that 'different cultural ensembles sustain different recipes for truth and knowledge . . . [and that] reflecting on cultural situatedness helps to understand the consequences of this fact' (ibid.: 361). The reference to 'who,' 'how,' 'for whom' and 'where' (ibid.: 361) as important questions for research raises the significance of the implications of these thoughts for Asian tourism research which is the remit of this chapter. I provide a perspective on the directions taken by Asian tourism knowledge as tourism becomes more prominent in Asia. In doing so, the idea is not to propound essentialism and to distinguish the emergent Asian tourism as indeed different from Western tourism. A call for an analysis of tourism knowledge formation in Asia does not amount to an intention to discard existing knowledge. Rather, it is to emphasize the need for a reassessment of what we think may be, at the end of the day, reflections on inclusivity of 'truths.' Two bodies of work have contributed to this introspection. First, postcolonialism studies. Hall and Tucker (2004) argue that tourism reinforces and is embedded in postcolonial relationships. In spite of this, postcolonialism remains on the fringes of academic tourism discourses, unlike other disciplines such as geography, anthropology and cultural studies where discussions on the political, economic and socio-cultural impacts and implications of direct and indirect colonial rule are rich and nuanced and include renderings about the bi-directional influences between the colonized and the colonizer. Given the deep inequalities between the North and the South, deconstructing and exposing the underlying discursive and material manifestations of the dominance of Western knowledges and practices in tourism studies helps to reorientate knowledge accumulation processes away from what were once considered innate universalisms. Indeed, as pointed out in Chapter 1, there would be more fruitful intellectual discussion if tourism researchers working on Asia do not uncritically accept notions about authenticity, the tourist gaze, and so on. Hence, the need to include an overview of the manner in which Asian tourism knowledge is constructed.

Second, Chua Beng Huat, whose collection of edited essays on consumption in Asia (2000) suggests that although rapid economic growth in the region and the global expansion of consumerism have encouraged more spending, discourses on consumption are arguably different from the West which emphasizes the symbolic and the personal as conceptual concerns. Instead, consumption is still very much tied to the political economies of the various countries in the region. For example, in spite of higher consumption, the moral rift between 'traditional' thrift and 'excesses' remain a core issue in consumption research in Asia. In evaluating personal attitudes towards consumption by the locals, the debates are not about 'spirituality of high art' (i.e., asceticism in the face of material plenty) versus 'degenerate low art' (immorality of unquenchable materialism) (ibid.: 6). To many Asians, degeneracy lies not in the aesthetics of the consumer goods but in 'Westernization/Americanization' which is to be avoided. The distinction is informative and draws readers once again to how Asia needs to be better understood and researched.

This chapter has two objectives. It outlines the importance of Asian tourism as a major contributor to tourism growth, hence warranting it a place in discourses on tourism 'truths.' Second, the chapter sketches out important arguments that help to get at the truth of Asian tourism, not with the intent of reinventing the wheel with regard to tourism knowledge, but simply to throw light on the need for a more inclusive analysis of this expansive and for many, life-changing phenomenon.

Force-fields in tourism

According to Tribe (2006), force-fields are the lens that will both systematically privilege as well as deny tourism knowledge. Since they carry such weight in research, what precisely do they refer to?

Person. Tribe defines as both the individual in pursuance of knowledge in an objective disembodied manner, searching for truths that can be tested and verified; and the subjective researcher whom Swain (2004, cited in Tribe 2006: 362) describes as seeking to understand tourism and to find the truth about it through the 'corporal self.' The latter is exemplified by Botterill (2003, cited in Tribe 2006: 363) who used an 'autoethnographic' approach whereby his epistemological journey from positivism through social constructivism to critical realism helps him discover the importance of his own 'Welshness' when he does tourism research. Gender studies of tourism represent another branch of work that also employs the subjective in critical ways. Aitchison's work (for example, 1996) shows how patriarchal power and control can construct, communicate, legitimate and reproduce knowledge about leisure and tourism that feeds male, heterosexual dominance.

Rules are defined as conventions that researchers subscribe to. Here Tribe offers a platter:

- *Disciplinary* approaches such as sociological, anthropological or economic that emphasize topical preferences and analytical styles that have been tried and tested over time. Because it has reliability, disciplines act to select what type of research is to be included in order to bolster its own strength as a sub-field of knowledge truths.
- Rules can build into *paradigms*. Paradigms are powerful force-fields that offer very tight control over knowledge truths because of their monopolistic tendency to subscribe to the idea that only *a* particular paradigm is coherent and acceptable e.g., Tribe cites the journal *Tourist Studies* as an attempt to subvert the positivist paradigm pervasive in tourism management and economic literature in order to develop critical perspectives on the nature of tourism as a *social* phenomenon as much as it is an economic one.
- *Traditions* build on precedents and preference whereby researchers prefer to follow a method of knowledge analysis e.g., economic aspects of tourism used to dominate research only to be replaced by sociocultural aspects as tourism became an important leisure phenomenon, especially in the arena of the sociocultural impacts of tourism, finally to be replaced by a new kid in the block, alternative sustainable tourism (Jafari 2003).
- *Discourse*, according to Tribe, is akin to paradigms in terms of admissibility of information except that discourse is more grounded in social relations. Hall (1997: 44, cited in Tribe 2006: 367–8) explains discourse as a 'group of statements which provide a language for talking about . . . a particular topic at a particular historical moment,' regulating what can be discussed and what cannot. As such, discourse can sustain a certain régime of truth irrespective of what is the absolute truth. Managerialism is a discourse in which talk about tourism centers on consumer satisfaction, efficiency and markets, proscribing other issues such as gender politics and authenticity as if they were not truths themselves.
- *Methodology* which Tribe divides into scientific positivist and subjective interpretivist approaches. While the former is selective in what can be studied (only measurable things), the latter permits the 'complex world . . . [to be] understood . . . from the point of view of those who operate within it' (Goodson and Phillimore 2004: 36, cited in Tribe 2006: 369). In other words, 'let the data do the talking' (Jordan and Gibson 2004: 215, cited in Tribe 2006: 369).

Position and *ends* describe a person's or organization's ability to influence research as part of stakeholding. For instance, ethnocentrism involves the promotion of one's own ethnic or cultural group; universities will privilege research by time, funding and number of individuals supported so long as the work promotes its own name and carves it a reputation in the competitive world of knowledge ownership. Representations also fall into the realm of position and ends because they have the desired effect of framing knowledge in the interest of those who are making the representations. Since knowledge is never interest-free, there are three motivations in human enquiry: (1) the technical interest seeks control and management in order to improve technique; (2) the practical interest seeks understanding for better insights of what is happening; and (3) the emancipatory interest seeks freedom from falsehoods and emancipation from oppression. Habermas (1978, cited in Tribe 2006: 373) explains that each of these three interests in knowledge is served by different paradigms. Scientific positivism serves the technical, interpretive methods seek understanding and critical theory seeks emancipation. Research driven by technical interest tends to concentrate only on a small part of tourism phenomenon, e.g., management of tourism resources and planning and concentrates on performativity to justify the ploughing back of more research funding for itself. In contrast, the other two interests tend to take a larger view of tourism and better fit the genre of work done by social scientists.

Finally, Tribe talks about *ideology* as guiding thought and action. For contemporary times, Western capitalism is the ideology most researched and the pressing issue facing researchers is whether Western capitalism and consumerism (read Americanization?) may indeed be hegemonic in tourism. Individual researchers also work within particular ideologies when they seek truths. Whether working from religious standpoints or from class standpoints, it would be instructive to keep this in mind when evaluating knowledge truths because they guide the way the researcher looks at and desires to shape the world.[1]

Asian tourism

The growth of Asian tourism is one of the fastest. According to the World Tourism Organization (WTO) (2006), the global pattern of tourist flows is being redrawn with one out of every five international tourists now choosing a destination in Asia and increasing numbers of Asians themselves traveling overseas. An estimated 156 million tourists visited the region in 2005, up more than 7 percent over the previous year despite the devastating Indian Ocean tsunami. A Ministerial Roundtable on Asia-Pacific Tourism Policies held in Macau in June 2006 identified some megatrends within the region, among which are:

- Asian tourism is becoming more activity-based rather than destination-based.
- Asia is becoming a convention hub.

- Low cost carriers are driving tourism growth in the region.
- India is Asia's leader in real tourism growth.[2]

(WTO 2006)

The World Travel and Tourism Council (WTTC) (2006) reported similar data: Asia captured 20.3 percent of the world market of tourist arrivals in 2006. Of this, Northeast Asia (China, South Korea, Japan, Hong Kong, Macau and Taiwan) held the lion's share at 16.6 percent. Southeast Asia (Singapore, Malaysia, Thailand, Vietnam, Burma, Philippines, Indonesia, Papua New Guinea, Brunei, Cambodia and Laos) captured 3.6 percent and South Asia (India, Sri Lanka, Nepal, Maldives, Pakistan and Bangladesh) 1.1 percent. The contribution of travel and tourism to their GDPs in 2006 was in the region of 3.1 percent, with 1 in every 9.9 jobs coming from the industry. Visitor spending was the highest in Northeast Asia at US$227 billion, US$70.9 billion in Southeast Asia and US$13.5 billion in South Asia (WTTC 2006).

As levels of affluence rise in the region, especially in China and India with over 2 billion people between them, the momentum for outbound tourism is also increasing. Although the USA still tops the list of countries where personal expenditure on travel and tourism by its population was the highest at US$883,324 million in 2005, Japan was second at US$286,836 million and the Chinese spent US$89,889 (WTTC 2006). Table 3.1 shows that the proportion spent on personal travel and tourism[3] as a percentage of total consumption was very high in Northeast Asia, which includes Japan and China. Asia is therefore not only a receiving region but also an outbound region for international and domestic tourism.

Table 3.2 shows that the volume of outbound traffic between 1999 and 2003 has indeed grown in Asia with a very strong showing from China and India. Generally, the amount of tourism expenditure in overseas locations had also increased in keeping with the increased volumes.

According to Pacific Asia Travel Association (PATA), in 2002, 61.4 percent of Northeast Asia travel was intra-regional travel from within its own sub-region. For Southeast Asia, the proportion was 41.9 percent and for South

Table 3.1 Proportion spent on personal travel and tourism as a percentage of total consumption (2006)

	2006
World	9.5
European Union	11.3
Northeast Asia	10.0
North America	9.8
Southeast Asia	5.2
South Asia	3.9

Source: Compiled from WTTC 2006: n.p.

Table 3.2 Departures (in '000) and tourism expenditure overseas (US$ million), 1999–2003 from Asia

	Departures		Expenditure	
	1999	*2003*	*1999*	*2003*
Northeast Asia				
China	9,232	20,222	11,621	16,716
Hong Kong SAR	4,175	4,428	–	–
Japan	16,358	13,296	41,213	36,506
Macau	117	156	–	–
S. Korea	4,342	7,086	5,555	10,901
Taiwan	6,559	5,923	8,722	7,402
South Asia				
Bangladesh	1,103	1,414	375	404
India	4,115	5,351	–	–
Maldives	42	44	58	60
Nepal	125	258	116	119
Pakistan	–	–	447	1,162
Sri Lanka	497	561	341	462
Southeast Asia				
Brunei	–	–	–	–
Burma	–	–	26	36
Cambodia	49	–	41	60
Indonesia	–	–	–	4,427
Laos	–	–	–	17
Malaysia	26,067	32,201	2,382	3,401
Papua New Guinea	58	92[a]	–	–
Philippines	1,755	1,803	1,440	985
Singapore	3,971	4,221	–	–
Thailand	1,655	2,152	2,870	4,046
Vietnam	–	–	–	–

Source: Compiled from WTO 2005

[a] 2002 data

Asia, 16.5 percent (PATA 2003: 6). Table 3.3 shows that the absolute numbers in intra-regional travel are by no means small while Table 3.4 shows the high proportion of intra-regional travel for each country within its own sub-region compared to the other Asian sub-regions. Table 3.5 indicates the top three destinations for Asian countries.

The rise of affluence in China is reported to have contributed to a large increase in domestic tourism in China. The number of domestic tourists was reported to be 1,220 million in 2006 (China National Tourist Office (CNTO 2006a) compared to 870 million in 2004 (National Tourism Administration (NTA) 2004). In both years, almost two-thirds of the domestic tourists were rural residents. The income generated from domestic tourism in China

Table 3.3 Intra-regional travel: from origin countries to destination regions (2002)

Origin Country	Destination Region Northeast Asia	Destination Region Southeast Asia	Destination Region South Asia
Northeast Asia			
Hong Kong SAR	67,886,107		
Macau SAR	19,463,359		
China PRC	12,150,192		
Taiwan	8,637,382		
Japan	7,782,346		
S. Korea	3,996,516		
Southeast Asia			
Singapore		9,636,557	
Malaysia		2,457,544	
Indonesia		2,360,977	
Thailand		2,038,469	
Philippines		553,921	
Brunei		344,540	
Vietnam		253,213	
Cambodia		143,399	
Lao PDR		133,320	
Burma		70,807	
Papua New Guinea		–	
South Asia			
India			149,585
Bangladesh			10,979
Maldives			10,109
Sri Lanka			9,867
Pakistan			9,333
Nepal			2,035

Source: Compiled from PATA 2003

was by no means small. It was RMB344.3 billion in 2004 (NTA 2004) and RMB528.5 billion in 2006 (CNTO 2006a). The average expenditure per capita also rose from RMB395.7 in 2004 to RMB436.1 in 2006.

In India, domestic tourism comprised some 320 million trips in 2000. This total was 67 times the size of foreign arrivals in absolute numbers but only 3.65 times in inbound receipts (Government of India Ministry of Tourism and Culture 2002). The volume is high but the income generated is not as rapid although the potential for growth is good.

The commitment to tourism in Asia is also reflected by travel and tourism capital expenditures by both the public and private sectors in the three Asian sub-regions of the Northeast, South and Southeast. Amounting to between US$20 billion and US$230 billion, they represented between 7.7 percent and 9.6 percent of total investments for the year of 2006 (WTTC 2006).

Table 3.4 Intra-regional visitor arrivals (2002, in percent)[a]

Destination Country	Origin Region South Asia	Origin Region Northeast Asia	Origin Region Southeast Asia
Northeast Asia			
Hong Kong SAR	3.3	46.6	17.3
Macau SAR	0.8	79.0	7.8
China PRC	2.5	41.5	16.8
Taiwan	0.5	55.1	16.1
Japan	1.3	55.2	8.0
S. Korea	1.0	59.6	10.1
Southeast Asia			
Singapore	6.4	29.7	33.5
Malaysia	1.8	9.9	74.4
Indonesia	1.0	25.6	40.8
Thailand	3.8	34.5	22.8
Philippines	1.0	47.5	6.9
Brunei	–	–	–
Vietnam	0	50.2	10.3
Cambodia	0.6	28.3	17.0
Lao PDR	0.3	6.8	69.2
Burma	3.3	32.5	18.8
Papua New Guinea	1.4	8.7	7.4
South Asia			
India	–	–	–
Bangladesh	–	–	–
Maldives	4.1	13.2	1.6
Sri Lanka	22.9	7.1	6.2
Pakistan	22.1	4.9	2.5
Nepal	33.1	11.4	0

Source: Compiled from PATA 2003: 7

[a] Since the emphasis is on Asia, only the regions of interest are listed in the table. Hence, the percentages do not add up to 100%. The remaining proportions of arrivals are divided between the Americas, Europe, Other Asia, Pacific, Middle East and Other Countries.

As much as Western tourism started off with an exploration of Westerners in the Western world before the hordes started to venture further afield to more 'exotic' places, Asian tourism is evolving in a similar way. Starting in domestic destinations, the Asian tourist is exploring 'home' territory first before venturing into regional destinations. For example, the burgeoning Chinese market is still confined to familiar places with some historical links such as Hong Kong, Macau, Japan, Russia, South Korea, Thailand, Vietnam, Singapore and Malaysia. The furthest is the USA which has strong diplomatic ties with China and also receives a large number of Chinese students (NTA 2004). However, it should be noted that the tourism industry's development in Asia is far more rapid than in the West. Travel agencies, national tourist organizations, airlines and all supporting services for tourism have

Table 3.5 Top three destinations of Asian countries (2002)

Origin Country	First Top Destination	Second Top Destination	Third Top Destination
Northeast Asia			
Hong Kong SAR	China PRC (61,879,427)[a]	Macau SAR (5,101,437)	Taiwan (435,080)
Macau SAR	China PRC (18,928,763)	Hong Kong SAR (534,590)	Singapore (5,604)[b]
China PRC	Hong Kong SAR (6,825,199)	Macau SAR (4,240,446)	Thailand (797,976)
Taiwan	China PRC (3,660,565)	Hong Kong SAR (2,428,776)	Macau SAR (1,532,929)
Japan	USA (3,627,264)	China PRC (2,925,553)	S. Korea (2,320,820)
S. Korea	China PRC (2,124,310)	Japan (1,271,835)	Thailand (704,649)
Southeast Asia			
Singapore	Malaysia (7,547,761)	Indonesia (1,422,613)	Thailand (546,796)
Malaysia	Thailand (1,332,355)	China PRC (592,447)	Singapore (548,510)
Indonesia	Singapore (1,392,860)	Malaysia (769,128)	China PRC (274,717)
Thailand	Malaysia (1,166,937)	Lao PDR (422,766)	China PRC (386,328)
Philippines	China PRC (508,572)	Hong Kong SAR (329,604)	S. Korea (215,848)
Brunei	Malaysia (256,952)	Singapore (60,042)	Indonesia (14,089)
Vietnam	Thailand (84,219)	Lao PDR (71,001)	Taiwan (43,810)[b]
Cambodia	Thailand (70,187)	Vietnam (69,658)	Singapore (9,030)[b]
Lao PDR	Thailand (90,717)	Vietnam (37,237)	Cambodia (3,083)
Burma	Thailand (36,111)	S. Korea (30,955)[c]	Singapore (22,339)
Papua New Guinea	–	–	–
South Asia			
India	Singapore (375,634)	Thailand (280,641)	USA (257,271)
Bangladesh	India (431,312)[c]	Thailand (35,928)	Hong Kong SAR (33,032)
Maldives	–	–	–
Sri Lanka	India (112,813)[c]	Singapore (54,686)	Thailand (31,649)
Pakistan	China PRC (83,059)	Hong Kong SAR (55,415)	USA (39,442)
Nepal	India (41,135)[c]	China PRC (25,146)	Thailand (19,933)

Source: Compiled from PATA 2003

[a] Numbers are total visitor arrivals to the destination from the origin countries; [b] 2000 figure; [c] 2001 figure

the benefit of systems that are already well developed. Overnight, the tourism industry in Asia has flourished and become an important part of the social landscape of many Asian countries. Travel agents concurrently promote tourism within and outside of Asia in order to feed the interest of the Asian consumer whose curiosity extends to home as well as faraway places.

Besides transportation routes (rail, roads and airports) bringing together places in Asia, social networks are also being transformed by tourism. As attested by Carroll (2006), in Laos, traveling companions comprise extended family members who help to defray the cost of travel while sharing companionable company. For the more adventurous, the Internet can provide instant friends for travel. Cyberspace is breaking down the barriers to travel both in physical and social distance terms for the Chinese (Lim 2006).

This section has indeed shown the strength of numbers in Asian tourism and that the manner in which the phenomenon has taken shape warrants further attention.

Unearthing 'truths' in Asian tourism

Given the rapid rate of growth of Asian tourism from without as well as within, researchers have played and need to continue to play a key role in knowledge formation for the region. The epistemological problem of what constitutes knowledge of tourism has (in the past and probably will continue in the future) drawn heavily from the theoretical order emanating from the West. It may be argued that the rush by researchers of Asia to embrace this order in tourism literature runs the risk of creating theoretical edifices which have a questionable place in Asian tourism. A middle path can be taken on this point which is that tourism theoretical constructs such as 'authenticity,' 'postmodernism,' and so forth need to be reassessed for how they may be reinterpreted for different situational contexts than the West. Hence, in this section, I examine the force-fields identified by Tribe that, in my view, will direct the shape of 'truths' to come for Asian tourism. What are the ideology, method, discourse/ends and position and rules that matter to Asian tourism?[4] As propounded by Tribe, they intersect one another and will be discussed as an amalgamation rather than fragmented forces.

Ideology

Neoliberalism as ideology will be the cornerstone for tourism order for a period of time. Neoliberalism has been the dominant élite ideology in the industrialized world since the Reagan and Thatcher régimes in the 1980s. It is characterized by faith in market forces to provide an efficient allocation of resources in a society and it embraces free global markets that do not have barriers to trade or investment. Deregulation and privatization will shift decision-making to the private sector (Martinez and Garcia 1996) to maximally benefit everyone. Epitomized by the World Trade Organization, the

International Monetary Fund and the World Bank, neoliberalism is a force to reckon with not only in the Western world, it has also permeated Asia and has been behind the growth of market forces throughout the region, including for tourism.

Ioannides and Debbage (1997), Milne and Ateljevic (2001) and Poon (1993) have written about flexibility in tourism and how local economies engage with global forces in the neoliberal environment. As businesses grow, taking advantage of cross-border opportunities opened up by globalization, neo-liberalism is now embraced by many emergent economies desiring a piece of the economic pie (Hall 2001). This has become the pathway to success and hence an important ingredient to how tourism will develop and therefore, by implication, how tourism knowledge will become constructed. The impact of neoliberalism in Asian tourism development is documented in books such as *Tourism and Economic Development in Asia and Australasia* by Go and Jenkins (1997) and *Tourism and Economic Development: Case Studies from the Indian Ocean Region* by Ghosh, Siddique and Gabbay (2003). The volume by Teo, Chang and Ho (2001) also has two sections devoted to open markets and regional cooperation for air travel and resort and hotel development. Writing from their respective disciplinary interests, geographers, sociologists and architects have in the collection of essays in Askew and Logan (1994) highlighted urban transformation in Asia as a result of 'the profanity of globalism' (McGee 1994: ix).

Cartier (1998) has also documented similar mega-developments in Melaka as the Malaysian government's response to the economic potential of tourism. Nankervis (2000), in contrast, outlines the vulnerabilities of collaboration between unequal partners which Chang (1998; 2001) reinterprets as healthy 'co-opetition' (competition and collaboration) that has contributed to the continued growth of Singapore's tourism sector. The force-field of ideology is without doubt influential in directing the shape of tourism truths in con-temporary Asia. Whether the researchers themselves embrace neoliberal ideology, they cannot help but be captivated by its pervasiveness in the region, bolstering government action for tourism development. Since communism gave little credence to tourism as a research field, neoliberalism has unleashed a democratization of economic planning and social life in Vietnam under *doi moi* reforms (Burns 2001; Lloyd 2003). Xiao's (2006) insightful explica-tion of the 'truth' of Chinese tourism was based on a discourse analysis of Deng Xiaoping's talks on tourism to show how tourism was both a signifier for and showcase of China's successful reform policies in the neoliberal world (see also Oakes 1999; Su 2007).

Methods

The methods that researchers use to analyze information have been broadly divided into quantitative and qualitative/interpretive methods. To under-stand the implications of neoliberalism on tourism, both the objective method that is associated with the management genre of research and the subjective methodologies have been used. For quantitative research methods, research done to achieve planning aims has benefited the most. For instance, PATA reports trends and provides projections for the region. Country reports are also available. National Tourism Organizations are important 'persons' seeking specific ends. As ready sources of information, the data they generate constitute the primary information used to devise tourism development plans and hence to materialize visions and ideals. In Singapore, for instance, a consultancy firm, Pannell, Kerr and Forster provided supporting evidence to help justify the newly constructed Tourism Product Development Plan by the Ministry of Trade and Industry in 1986 (Wong 1988). The involvement of the state and of enterprises is crucial for coping with tourism growth; hence mapping trends, distributions and rates are important in agenda setting. The construction of tourism knowledge in Asia is very much contingent on political and economic realities. The desire to earn more foreign exchange and reach developed country status remains the singular goal for most NTOs within Asia.

To uncover the truth of the material landscapes of planning, subjective methodologies can also be important force-fields. In Penang, Teo (2003) has analyzed the role of Penang Development Corporation in systematically building up a comprehensive collage of attractions that would appeal to tourists as well as investors that will help make the island the Silicon Valley of the East. The data collected in this instance were both quantitative and qualitative in nature. Kahn (1997) likewise documented through a qualitative discourse analysis of government speeches and reports, the state's attempts to 'culturalize' Georgetown in Penang. These subjective methods have been useful in illuminating pertinent issues in Asian tourism. The rapidity with which landscapes are being changed to allow for tourism development has meant that the stakeholders in tourism development are numerous. Through qualitative research, useful discourses that illuminate the realities of the Asian contexts can be shared.

Discourses

Some of the discourses that are particularly relevant to Asia are those on power as discussed by Foucault and LeFebvre which have been more accurately documented because of in-depth qualitative interviews and on-site observations. In countries where those with few resources outnumber the rich, tensions are inevitable where tourism development quickens its pace of growth. Smith (1991) talks about stakeholders in beach front development over Asia and attempts to tease out the tussles in power which are made evident when the subjective is discussed. Lai and Nepal (2006) examined local responses to potential ecotourism development in the Tawushan Nature Reserve located in southeastern Taiwan. Community attitude and intention toward ecotourism, including conservation of natural resources and cultural tradition and sustainable community development were investigated. Analysis was based on data collected using face-to-face questionnaire interviews held with two indigenous communities in the reserve. Dahles and Bras (1999), both cultural anthropologists, were able to elucidate how small entrepreneurs are able to survive in beach and cultural tourism sites in Indonesia by using qualitative interviews.

Grundy-Warr and Perry (2001) also used qualitative data to understand the violence that ensued in Bintan when the private sector took advantage of local villagers and displaced them to build an international resort on the island. In the same way, Muzaini and Yeoh (2005) picked up the strands of argument about inequality in ethnic representation in war commemoration sites in Singapore that are visited by both locals and tourists. Discourses about power are also at the center of works on China (Oakes 1998; Doorne *et al.* 2003) especially where cultural politics reveals Han-minority differences and government/private sector joint ventures that exclude local people. As tourism destroys local features and replaces these by pseudo-landscapes that have a very weak link with the history, life and culture of the people who live or work at the tourism sites, the conflation *and* contestation of history and memory that arise from the 'selling' of heritage have become an important truth, meriting discussion in Asia. The commonness of this problem in Asia is a revelation. Michaud and Turner (2006) talk about the 'left-behind' ethnic minorities in Sapa, North Vietnam, after it opened up to tourism. With many countries vying for World Heritage Status, power has become an important discursive truth for many societies affected by tourism. Black and Wall (2001) have elucidated this for the Borobudur and Prambanan; Su and Teo (2005) have done this for Lijiang; and Winter (2007b) for Angkor.

A related discourse that is a pertinent force-field for Asian tourism is postcolonialism. As many of the countries in Southeast Asia were former European colonies, uncovering Western ethnocentrism and self-orientalizing tendencies in tourism practices constitute important agendas. Sorting out representation and positionality will reveal what Foucault (1979) calls favored régimes of truths in tourism practices that repress alternate versions of reality. Following the tradition of Said's (1978) work, tourism scholars have used content analysis to examine representations of Asian peoples and cultures in guidebooks, brochures, advertisements and websites. These are critiques of Western imaginations of Asia e.g., Bandyopadhyay and Morais (2005) and Bhattacharyya (1997), or are about 'exotic' India while the 'myth of the unchanged' is applied to India, China and Thailand in Echtner and Prasad (2003). Lisa Law's (2000) analysis of Southeast Asian sex workers shows that AIDS prevention activities in the region have placed a strategic emphasis on paid sexual relations between Western men and Asian women even though in reality, there are many forms of paid sex work besides catering to the Western tourists. Using the same postcolonialism discourse, she argues that the sex worker's body becomes conflated with nation to such an extent that it gets invaded by foreign powers who infect it with a fatal virus. Dichotomous models of power seem to permeate AIDS prevention dissertations – the colonized/colonizer binary of nationalist discourse gets conflated with feminist discourses of masculine (read white) oppression and female (read colonized) subordination. This binary reinserts stereotypical images of Asian women as passive and exploited, which is similarly expounded by Leheny (1995) whose work focused on Japanese male tourists and Southeast Asian, especially Thai, sex workers.

Postcolonialism and feminism also frame the work of Teo and Leong (2006) who acknowledge their positionality as Asian women researchers trying to unpack how Asian backpackers negotiate for inclusion in the space allocation of Khao San's predominantly Western backpacking space. In the reverse, focusing on the colonizer, Siegenthaler's (2002) work on representations of Hiroshima and Nagasaki in Japanese guidebooks unravels the consequences of Japanese attempts to occupy Asia during the Second World War. The price the Japanese have to pay for misguided aspirations during this period continues to hound the nation, making their occupation efforts the Achilles' heel of the Japanese post-postwar national identity. Finally postcolonialism discourse has helped to decipher new nationalisms. Teo and Chang (2007) argue that postcolonial landscapes are also emblems of alterity and innovative ways have been used in which past architectural distinctions become entwined with the consumer needs of the present to fashion new landscapes that are counterfoils to the colonial past. In this paper, the tropes of 'hybridization,' 'transculturation' and 'simultaneity' are used to demonstrate that postcolonial possibilities in landscapes are indeed open and discursive. Du Cros (2004) shares a similar outlook for Hong Kong.

Globalization is a discourse with wide currency in Asia. Lanfant (1995) explains that landscapes can be corporate mandates (re)configured by global capitalism for touristic consumption. In Asia, the weight of this has been brought to bear by many tourism researchers. Bunnell (2004) discusses the global image of Kuala Lumpur, Chang (1997) of Singapore, Teo (2003) of Penang, and Cartier (2001) and Wang, N. (2005) of Guangzhou and/or Southern China. In tandem with neoliberalism, the political will to forward these places as global cities has meant that transformation is to be expected, with tourism accounting for a large component of its success.

Besides global cities, theme parks provide further discussion about global influences in tourism truths in Asia. In theme parks, elements of the real world are scissored away from their local contexts and playfully bonded together in a pleasing pastiche for the global tourist. Because these established signifiers have subtended collective understandings of the real world, tourism researchers have a genuine concern for the negative impacts of commodification and Disneyfication. Nonetheless, this universality of superficial postmodern landscapes in theme parks does not completely erase local identity. In spite of the strong influence of global forces, the *raison d'être* for tourism movement is still local identity. Hence, in many of research pieces, the discussions center on refining globalization discourse as a meshing of the global with the local, especially in Asia. For example, Raz (1999) showed how, in Tokyo Disneyland, the Japanese have successfully domesticated the hegemonic model of American leisure by producing their own cultural readings of onstage shows and by the manner it treats and welcomes its guests. Ultimately, Tokyo Disneyland is a simulated America showcased by and for the Japanese rather than an agent of Americanization (read homogenization as a result of globalization). Teo and Yeoh (2001) similarly argue that local identity gets worked into international theme parks in the manner of food types, mascots, type of rides and so forth so as to reassert the Asian way of consuming a highly globalized tourism practice. While globalization discussions reveal the implications for landscape changes across the world, reinterpreting globalization for Asian-context theme parks depends on researchers' positionality as Asian academics working to forward the end of their own institutions as premier research universities in Asia.

Rich in history and in some instances, a strong desire to hang on to cultural roots, Asia's playground provides rich fodder for examining how global influences are balanced against each society's ability to maintain continuity with their cultural pasts. Researchers, for example, have analyzed the complex power relations inherent in such global-local interactions of cultures in the Indonesian Flores (Erb 2000a), in China (du Cros and Lee 2007), in Nepal (Hepburn 2002), and of festivals in South Korea (Jeong and Santos 2004). Local identity will always bring to bear its own imprint and impulses in spite of the pre-eminence of postmodernism marking a rise in the aestheticism of experience. As Ooi (2002) avers, using Singapore and Copenhagen as contrasts, there is a need for a dialogic understanding of tourism in which the world is understood in *inter-related* terms.

Embodiment as a discourse in tourism is fairly new and even more so in Asia. As a natural outgrowth of literature exploring representation, existentialist conceptions of the tourism experience is a way to 'reframe authenticity in terms of the tourists rather than the cultures he or she encounters while touring' (Kelner 2001: 1). Following this line of thought, Choe (2006) explores the embodied affective experience of corporal intensity which she claims is similar to that gained while viewing *hallyu* (this refers to what is known as the 'Korean Wave' in which music, television dramas and movies, fashion and food originating from Korea became highly popular across Asia) melodramas. In spatially traversing these filmic sites, emotions associated with the films are evinced. The popularity of *hallyu* melodramas across Asia has led to the creation of drama tours in search of the same existential authenticity. Muzaini's (2006) discussion of backpacking in Southeast Asia also picks up on his embodied Asianness as crucial for facilitating deeper cultural immersions with native peoples in the region. Edensor (1998) in his analysis of tourists at the Taj Mahal in India divided tourist spaces into a continuum from enclavic on one end to heterogeneous on the other. Contrary to what has been discussed in much of the literature on themed/enclavic environments with their trained 'cast' members, he argues that these spaces do not necessarily create dystopian views wherein stereotypical signifiers guide interpretation and practice along preferred lines. Tourist performances can articulate many praxes and dispositions, depending on whether the tourist actors want to conform to group behavior and peer-group pressure; depending on their willingness to transgress routine enactions; and whether they feel a desire to mock performative codes (ibid.: 202–3). Improvisation in performative conventions of walking, gazing, photographing, listening, relaxing and socializing is conditional on a combination of the qualities of the space (heterogeneous or enclavic) and reflexivity on the part of the tourist actor. Lew and Wong (2005) expand on similar reflexivities in the homecoming experiences of overseas Chinese visiting their 'homeland' in China. In contradistinction, Malam's (2004) work is not on the 'receivers' of tourism but is refocused on the 'givers' of tourism. In analyzing how male bar and bungalow workers in Koh Phangon, Thailand, use their bodies to attract Western female tourists, she asserts that these workers are able to reimagine their gendered and classed subject positions on the island. By becoming intimate with Western female tourists, they actually gain access to international capital.

Rules

Finally, discipline-based research will always have a place in tourism research. For Asia, names like Graburn (1983), Picard (1996a), Cohen (1996), Richter (1989), Hall and Page (2000), Wall (2001), Go and Jenkins (1997), and Lea (1988) have blazed early and current truths about Asian (and Western) tourism using the disciplinary approaches of anthropology, sociology, political science, geography and economics. Rules and methods of research associated with discipline-based boundaries are helpful because they decide what is worthy of study, hence postcolonialism studies is a discourse that derives from anthropology's interminable concern for smaller social groups. By monitoring social interactions and behavior, sociologists' elucidation on consumerism have pushed tourism studies forward theoretically, especially for Asia where the 'new rich' (Robison and Goodman 1996) is an immensely large group. In the same manner, the geographer's concern with globalization has helped to break ground on the impact of global forces in the economies and societies of Asia. Economics and business studies have been unwavering in their support for tourism development in the region, taking into account foreign exchange generated, employment created and numerous multiplier effects. Multidisciplinary collaborations have also yielded fruitful collaborations. Picard and Wood (1997), Hitchcock, King and Parnwell (1993), and Mowforth and Munt (1998) are just some examples illuminating the socio-cultural and environmental impacts of Asian tourism developments and practices.

Conclusion

In each of the discussions above, the truths revealed about Asian tourism are significant. The intents of the academics are complex. Depending on the predominant ideology in their environs, their disciplinary training combined with their personage, positionality and preferences with regard to paradigms, traditions, discourses and methods, knowledge outcomes have been variously influenced. The ends they seek can include forwarding technical knowledge, as these are crucial for tourism development plans that are both responsive as well as prescriptive of the way Asian tourism has and will develop. National and regional tourism organizations and consultancy firms as well as applied oriented universities and colleges top the list in the production of this type of knowledge truth. Economics, psychology, environmental sciences and business studies with their specific discipline proclivities have done a great deal to advance research in this direction. Given the rapid rate of growth, the phenomenal world of Asian tourism is dynamic, with some of the change actually originating from the contributions of this form of ordered knowledge. In view of this, to prioritize emancipatory critical knowledge over technical knowledge would not be a prudent move for Asia. Decoding trends and patterns will remain an important part of knowledge ordering.

Knowledge can also be practical and seeks merely to understand and gain deeper insights into what is happening about the phenomenon on the ground. Interpretive work, especially by anthropologists (Graburn 1983; Picard 1996a), sociologists (Edensor 1998; Erb 2000a) and geographers (Chang 1997; Cartier 1998) that provide rich information about people's lives as they react to and go with the flow of tourism e.g. Dahles and Bras (1999), Carroll (2006) and Nyíri (2006) fill an important gap in knowledge because they throw light on Asian social networks, motivations, societal functions, conditions and behaviors. Delving deeper is necessary because

> studies of tourism have tended to highlight certain practices and subjects in particular (Western) settings and generalise about them to produce meta-theories about tourism and tourists . . . [*But*] non-Western tourists and tourism in non-Western locations may not fit in with these theories and models . . . [Hence, the] range of practices . . . which emerge out of particular cultural locations [need academic attention].
>
> (Edensor 1998: 3)

As such, the contribution that Asian tourism can make to knowledge truths has yet to find its place in knowledge order.

Finally, research can take on an emancipatory intent to expose the relative as well as partial nature of all 'truths.' Discourses about tourism, especially power relations, postcolonialism and embodiment have been the most helpful in exposing and hence challenging 'truth' régimes. Since neoliberalism as an ideology has foregrounded the need for tourism development, critical theory through the discourses discussed in this chapter has the job of ideology critique by asking whose interests are being served. At the end of the day, in raising the issue 'Is it a question of theory?' which is the starting section of this book, one needs to reflect on who and how knowledge is formed as much as what is knowledge. To question whether Asian tourism is an immanent part of/separate from Western tourism is not enough. In prescribing epistemological and ontological directions for tourism studies in Asia, ultimately it is necessary to ask, who does tourism research, for what ends and who supports this research capacity, for these are as important concerns as rethinking tourism theory.

Notes

1 Tribe also talked about the dissemination of knowledge at universities. Some places of learning have an emphasis on teaching and less on research. In Asia, a cursory examination shows the former to be more than the latter but this will constitute another paper to justify this observation. For the purpose of this chapter, the commentary will be confined to research.
2 This is real growth even in spite of India not having the largest number of visitor arrivals in Asia.
3 This is defined by WTTC as personal spending on travel and tourism by residents in the region/country mentioned. It includes services such as lodging, transportation, meals, entertainment, financial services, etc. and durable and non-durable goods used for travel and tourism activities. Spending may occur before, during or after a trip and includes outbound and domestic tourism (WTTC 2006).
4 In reviewing works on Asia, I do not intend to provide a comprehensive literature review of Asian tourism. Instead, the cited works provide support for the importance of certain force-fields in the region.

4   Destination Asia
Rethinking material culture

Tim Winter

Introduction

Today, the legacy of Cambodia's colonial past can still be seen in the country's 'cultural heritage.' Indeed, commonly held prescriptions of an 'authentic' Khmer or Cambodian culture, forged during a period of French colonialism, have been re-invigorated through the cultural logics of a post-conflict international tourism and heritage industry overwhelmingly oriented around the World Heritage Site of Angkor.

Closer examination of tourism in Cambodia today, however, suggests important shifts are now occurring. During the 1990s, North America and Europe dominated Cambodia's arrival statistics. More recently, Northeast Asia and ASEAN countries have become the country's key source markets. Today, over 70 percent of all tourists traveling to Cambodia are from within Asia. This shift in markets holds important consequences for Cambodia's material culture, where a Eurocentric discourse of what is considered as 'traditional' Khmer or Cambodian is now being overlaid, transcended and reconstituted by the aesthetics of a tourism industry linked to Taiwan, Korea and China. Characterized by a multitude of economic and cultural flows, this shift in tourism holds major implications for a country still very much engaged in a task of socio-cultural rehabilitation and identity reconstruction.

An exploration of the recent changes in Cambodia reveals a number of issues and questions that have yet to be adequately addressed in the literature on material culture and tourism. It will be seen that debates in this field have primarily revolved around critiques of commodification, tradition versus modernity, the local versus global, or the paradoxes of staged authenticity. Implicit to these studies has been a monolithic and undifferentiated reading of the tourist as subject. Indeed, as with much of the literature on tourism, the prototypical encounter has been between Westerners – silently gendered as male and ethnically as white – and their host destinations. As a result, less attention has been given to differentiating between tourist audiences and practices, and understanding the consumption of material culture in variegated, culturally divergent terms. In response, this chapter argues the situation in Cambodia demonstrates why more nuanced, less universalist, understandings of aesthetics and taste, and a willingness to rethink how places are being re-scripted and re-packaged for new forms of consumption are urgently required. In offering such an account, the chapter seeks to discuss the aesthetics of material culture in less judgmental terms, and move beyond ideas of high/low culture and quality/mass tourism, by highlighting the cultural positions from which such pronouncements are made.

Approaching material culture

The study of souvenirs within tourism studies stretches back more than two decades. Most broadly, attention has principally focused on the production of handicrafts, craftpieces and indigenous or ethnic arts: the 'primitive arts' of traditional societies. Relatively little attention has been given to mass manufactured plastic or metal items, or what is often referred to as 'kitsch' items on sale in places like New York, Milan, Shanghai or London. The analysis of souvenirs, as forms of material culture, therefore reveals much about the field of tourism studies generally, and the epistemological foundations it rests upon. One of the first scholars to treat souvenirs as a serious field of enquiry back in the mid-1970s was Nelson Graburn. Not surprisingly, the framework for interpreting tourism-related material culture at that time was heavily oriented around the concept of authenticity, an idea that gained a wide following through the writing of Dean MacCannell (1976). As we know, understanding tourism as a quest for the authentic rests upon a structuralist reading of societies, peoples, and cultures conceived as the 'other' of an alienated Western subject. In laying out the foundations for such debates in the context of *ethnic and tourist arts*, Graburn (1976) simultaneously recognized the problems and limitations of conceiving the authentic in relation to ethnicity, tradition, or culturally relative definitions of quality.

Despite such early words of caution, numerous studies conducted subsequently have seen authenticity in more absolutist, positivist terms in order to question processes of commodification and the introduction of mass manufacturing in 'traditional' contexts. Indeed, 24 years after Graburn's observations, a number of authors in the excellent volume *Souvenirs: The Material Culture of Tourism* (Hitchcock and Teague 2000) were at pains to remind readers of the contingent and highly subjective nature of authenticity. As Hitchcock (2000), Dougoud (2000), Mars and Mars (2000), and Wilkinson (2000) show in the volume, souvenirs become prescribed as authentic through their symbolic value as markers of place, as expressions of difference, or as signs of good taste.

Debates concerning processes of commodification, tradition versus modernity, and the paradoxes of staged authenticity have endured over a number of decades largely due to the geographies of research, with a prevailing discourse of 'locally crafted' invariably referring to non-Western, pre-industrial settings. Feest's (1992) typology of *tribal art*, *ethnic art*, *pan-Indian art* and *Indian mainstream art*, for example, has remained influential for a number of subsequent studies (see Evans 1994a, 2000). McNaughton (2006) considers host–guest relations in India as a factor of handicraft production, while Teague (2000) examines handcrafted metalwares in Nepalese villages to ask questions about tourism's impact on tradition and a localized cultural integrity. In their respective studies, Evans (2000) and Graburn (1982, 1987) pursue similar themes, but from a perspective that contemplates the arrival of tourism as an engine of revival. Discussing the case studies of Mexico and Lombok, Evans suggests 'whilst the demise of "tribal" art may be regretted . . . the development of a tourist art and craft market has effectively revitalized indigenous art, and local economies, albeit in Western terms and tastes' (2000: 132).

Clearly, for Evans, a sense of ambivalence arises from the way tourism shapes the very aesthetics of a revival. Such sentiments have been a recurring theme within the literature. Important studies in Cohen's special issue on tourist arts (1993) have illustrated how the lack of tourist knowledge about a place leads producers to change their design, at once both reverting to more archaic styles and simultaneously drawing on Western designs for inspiration. Similarly, Causey (2003) provides us with a richly detailed account of how the 'style' of handicrafts in North Sumatra emerges through an interweaving of tourist perceptions and evolving designs and production techniques. Causey reads the production of handicrafts in terms of market interaction. Likewise, Evans (1994a, 1994b), McNaughton (2006), Sinclair and Tsegaye (1990) and Stanley (2000) all look towards market intermediaries as a pivotal factor in the evolution of styles and designs.

With the vast majority of studies on souvenirs dedicated to non-Western, pre-modern socio-cultural contexts, today's academic gaze continues to revisit and rework many of the themes explored by early anthropologists interested in the 'primitive arts' of traditional societies. Situating this recent scholarship in its nineteenth- and early twentieth-century roots also draws us into the arenas of European colonialism, early approaches to museumology and the travel of objects from colonial territories to metropolitan centers. Europe's fascination with primitive arts at the beginning of the twentieth century would segment and codify masks, carvings, and 'mysterious' sculptures according to Western typologies of art and design, and the exotic and ethnologic.

While authors like Teague and Stanley point towards a need for greater reflexivity concerning the cultural positioning of scholarship on tourism today, ideas like authenticity, tradition and localized cultures remain highly territorialized debates: conversations typically located in the traditional, pre-modern 'third world.' The endurance of these themes has also relied upon a simple distinction between inward and outward audiences, whereby tourists are regarded as external, non-indigenous subjects. It is a binary distinction, however, that presents the tourist in undifferentiated terms, and as a monolithic subject. The Western (authentic-seeking) tourist has come to speak for all tourists, regardless of their ethnicity, location, religion or color. As a consequence, little attention has been given to differentiating between tourist audiences and understanding consumption in variegated, culturally divergent terms. This chapter attempts to address this by examining recent developments in Cambodia.

History repeats itself: revival and restoration

As the 1990s unfolded, Cambodia embarked upon a number of rapid and profound social transformations; from civil war to peace, from a socialist-style authoritarianism to multi-party democracy, and from geographic isolation to a free-market economy. The country would also be recovering from an era of history defined by civil war, genocide and a decade of foreign occupation. A key focal point for these interweaving transitions would be a heritage tourism industry oriented around Angkor. The conservation of Angkor's temples promised the restoration of identity, history, cultural sovereignty and national pride. International tourism promised much-needed socio-economic development. As I have detailed at length elsewhere, Angkorean heritage tourism would thus be pivotal in shaping a broader nationalized discourse of 'revival' (Winter 2007a, 2007b). To fully understand the socio-political dynamics of this language, however, it is helpful to return briefly to the early decades of the century.

The date '1860' stands in Cambodian history as the moment the French botanist, Henri Mouhot, 'discovered' the ruins of Angkor. His diaries, posthumously published across Europe, would inspire numerous travelers and explorers over the coming decades to set off in search of the mysterious, labyrinthine remnants of a lost civilization. Until the turn of the century, such trips from Europe were narrated and written up as voyages of exploration, rather than merely tourism. By 1907, the visitors log for Angkor recorded around 200 names for that year. As the early decades of the century progressed, the Ecole Française d'Extrême-Orient (EFEO) – a research and conservation body established at the turn of the century – made significant advances in clearing and restoring a number of the temple sites (Edwards 2006). Angkor thus became the focal point of a colonial cultural, political dyad, enabling the French to claim sovereignty over Cambodia's vestigial glories and present themselves as gatekeepers to the arts and crafts of a magnificent, but lost ancient culture.

A nascent tourism industry would also deliver an international audience for a burgeoning arts and crafts industry in Cambodia. Deeply concerned about the impact of imported goods from Europe, and the resultant cultural modernization, the historian, artist and archaeologist George Groslier had been working towards a national arts program since the early 1910s. Arguing that Cambodia's traditional arts were in 'crisis' and threatened with 'contamination' from foreign imports, Groslier embarked upon a mission of 'rescuing' the country's culture. In her detailed examination of his diaries and daily records, Muan (2001) traces his description of an artistic essence; one that was fixed in tradition and the 'climate, flora and fauna' of where the Cambodian people lived (cited in 2001: 20). She argues that, for Groslier, the crisis did not involve the end of aesthetic production, but rather a shift towards Westernized art forms that 'did not match the ethno-national portrait of "Cambodian art"' he envisaged.

Some years later, Phnom Penh would see the opening of a new Department of Fine Arts. Under the guidance of Groslier, the Department focused its attention on creating a cultural industry which linked arts training with the city's Musée Khmer, an ancient temple heritage and a steadily growing tourism industry. The School of Cambodian Arts he helped establish would also train teams of craftsmen to work in the ancient traditions, reproducing the intricate carvings and sculptures found in the temples. In stark contrast to the rise of modernism and its various movements in Europe, art in Cambodia was returning to its classical roots. The Angkorean civilization had given this young nation a magnificent cultural heritage, a moment of unsurpassable artistic achievement.

In Groslier's eyes, mimicry and replication were thus natural and honorable aspirations for Cambodians to hold. Cambodian art would be handcrafted, classical designs reproduced on a mass scale. The school helped shape a colonial ideology which transposed a concern for the high art of classical antiquity on to the colonial subject. Tourists from Europe and America would reaffirm this aesthetic régime by giving it an economic validity. Temple paintings or replicas of bas reliefs and Angkorean statuary made ideal souvenirs: supposedly authentically Cambodian and 'tasteful' enough to be proudly displayed in a middle-class European home. In essence, then, Groslier's efforts, along with the work of EFEO and the growing popularity of Angkor as a tourist site elevated the temples into the definitive, and omnipresent, point of reference for a cultural tourism and heritage industry oriented around the notions of revival and restoration.

After more than two decades of violent conflict and civil war, this language of revival would return in the early 1990s. The combination of a multi-billion dollar United Nations assistance program and an economic reorientation towards a Western donor community ensured a discourse of reconstruction was in large part conceived around, and driven by, Western understandings of what constitutes Cambodian culture. The return of EFEO as a key player in a World Heritage framework for Angkor would also mean that conservation and architectural restoration would dominate the country's heritage industry. In effect, the need to protect the temples from a turbulent social environment and re-establish a program of restoration re-solidified a former colonial narrative that firmly prioritized and reified the country's classical antiquities. The reintroduction of a Eurocentric reading of Cambodian culture also meant those cultural forms, both tangible and intangible, indisputably linked to the Angkorean period – and thus indisputably Khmer in heritage – received the bulk of aid and nourishment. One of the most successful organizations in this area was the Siem Reap-based *Chantiers-Ecoles*.

Founded in 1992, the training school was co-funded by the French Foreign Ministry (Ministère Français des Affaires Etrangères) and the European Union. Over the coming years training schools for silk, carving, and lacquering and gilding would open. In 1998, *Artisans d'Angkor* was created with the aim of making the operation entirely self-financed. A year later, the first *Artisans d'Angkor* boutique opened in Siem Reap. Among the principal product lines were wood and stone reproductions of statues, busts and the temple bas-reliefs. Carved in stone, the single most popular tourist souvenir marking a trip to Angkor has been the bust of the famed leader of the Angkorean period, Jayavarman VII. Recalling Meethan's (2001) arguments concerning the need for provenance in the transaction of touristic objects, workshop tours vividly demonstrate to clients that production techniques have 'changed little' since the Angkorean period. As the display for the *Artisan d'Angkor* airport shop presented in Figure 4.1 suggests, Jayavarman VII has been carved tens of thousands of times by those learning and working in their workshops.

In their production of silks, while a range of bags, cushions, and scarves have been designed to suit 'modern' tastes, the organization has made great efforts to research and reclaim traditional production techniques and 'classical' designs. A continual focus on such hand-woven silks, along with wood, lacquer-ware and hand-carved stone reflects the underlying philosophy of the organization. Strongly reminiscent of Groslier's language of restoration, their mission statement declares:

> *Artisans d'Angkor* has renewed interest in the authenticity and value of the strong Khmer cultural identity and stands for upmarket workmanship creativity, a showcase for traditional Cambodian savoir-faire . . . Its activity is centered around the social, economic and professional

Figure 4.1 Artisan d'Angkor airport shop display, Phnom Penh (2005) (Photo by author)

advancement of the artisans, and around promoting quality handicrafts with a strong Khmer identity.

(*Artisans d'Angkor* 2006)

Not surprisingly, this link between community development and the reclamation of a cultural identity has been a recurring theme for a number of other non-governmental organizations (NGOs) working in the country. The town of Siem Reap, for example, is home to the retail outlets of Rehab Craft Cambodia, Joom Noon (Gifts of Hope), Rajana (Design), Tabitha, and Hagar among others.[1] As part of a post-conflict civil society imported from countries like Sweden, the UK, France, Canada, or Belgium, these shops offer a range of handicrafts made from wood, stone, silk, lacquer, cotton, as well as handmade cards, photo albums, wall hangings, paintings and other decorative ornaments. Invariably, such items bear the hallmark of 'Made in Cambodia.' Handed to every tourist that enters the shop, the promotional brochure of the Stung Treng Women's Development Center (SWDC), an organization specializing in the production of 'Mekong Blue' silk, states:

> Through a program of teaching sewing and weaving skills, women learn about the traditional art of Khmer silk, lost after decades of civil war . . . We aim to empower vulnerable women and their children. The weavers learn all stages of the traditional art of Khmer silk weaving from dying the raw silk through spinning and eventually weaving the silk into its finished product. Thus the art of Khmer silk weaving, once common to this province, is kept alive.

(Anonymous 2004: 4)

In the absence of a substantive domestic market for premium products like hand-made silk, the arrival of high spending tourists from abroad presented a vital, and steadily growing, stream of revenue for such organizations. From annual arrival figures of tens of thousands in the early 1990s, tourism would rapidly grow with sustained political stability. Throughout the 1990s, the demographics of Cambodia's tourism industry were dominated by European and North American countries. In 2000, visitors from the USA topped the list of country-by-country statistics, accounting for 14 percent of the 265,000 arrivals. However, while France, the UK and Australia also featured in the top ten, a shift in the geography of source markets was now beginning to occur. As the twenty-first century dawned, it was clear that future growth in Cambodia's tourism industry would come from countries in the ASEAN (Association of Southeast Asian Nations) and Northeast Asian regions.

The arrival of Asian tourism

Initially led by Japan, this growth in intra-regional tourism has continued to gain momentum with ever increasing arrivals from Taiwan, Korea and

China (Ministry of Tourism 2000, 2003). By 2003, nearly 60 percent of the 701,000 tourists entering Cambodia originated from Asia, with around two-thirds of that figure accounted for by countries located in the northeast of the region (Ministry of Tourism 2003). According to the Ministry of Tourism, the fastest growth from the previous year, 2002, came from Korea (141 percent), Malaysia (46 percent) and Thailand (37 percent). The less spectacular, but still notable, increases from China (17 percent) and Taiwan (16 percent) ensured Cambodia and Angkor in particular were entering a new era of tourism (Ministry of Tourism 2003).

Since the late 1990s, the town has witnessed an extremely rapid expansion in the number of businesses catering to the Asian tourist and in particular the Chinese, Korean, Japanese and Taiwanese markets (Winter 2007a). By the end of the decade, a high level of integration had evolved between numerous travel agents, restaurants, souvenir shops and hotels, all targeting markets from Northeast Asia. Rather than aiming at the high-end luxury sector, virtually all the hotels and restaurants have been constructed with the 'mid-range' package tour market in mind. Much of the investment for this infrastructure has come from outside Cambodia. Since the late 1990s, Siem Reap has witnessed a rapid growth in Korean, Japanese and Chinese expatriates operating in its tourism industry. As the second major economic hub of the country, the town is now home to a significant proportion of the estimated 30,000 mainland Chinese living in Cambodia today (Beech 2005). In many cases the investments made by these communities also intersect with Cambodia's well-established, and often wealthy, ethnic Chinese population. By establishing various partnerships, entrepreneurs have been able to secure stakes in a variety of tourism-related products, including hotel rooms, night-time entertainment, catering and even imported alcoholic spirits.

One of the most important industries in terms of revenue generation for this sector has been the sale of souvenirs. Since the late 1990s, a number of large shops targeting the Asian tourist have opened. In response to the rapidly increasing number of tourist arrivals from around the region, these outlets have become larger and larger, with some now employing as many as 60 sales assistants across two or three floors. Nestled in between restaurants, hotels and massage parlors, the shops typically occupy prime retail locations along the two roads connecting the town with the airport and the Angkor Park. For the majority of the year their car parks are full during late afternoon or the minutes either side of sunset with taxis and tour buses making a 'souvenir stop' before returning guests to their hotel. In part, success in the industry has been driven by a system of commissions. Bus, taxi and motorbike drivers, along with tour guides and tour operators, are all given monetary incentives to bring their clients to particular stores. With substantial percentage commissions on sales, buses carrying up to 50 passengers have become lucrative sources of income for the guides and their drivers; an economic system that has contributed significantly to the average length of stay in the country hovering around the two-day level. For guides, tour operators and shop owners alike, securing a souvenir stop every 48 hours has proved far more profitable than having guests visiting a shop once during a four- or five-day stay.

Not surprisingly, tourists entering these shops are immediately faced with an array of Angkorean themed items. However, in both design and materiality, the products offered differ significantly from those at *Artisans d'Angkor* and the other NGO outlets in the region. Jayavarman VII appears once again, but instead of being exclusively carved in stone or wood, he comes in a choice of glass, metal or gold-painted plaster of Paris. While sandstone replicas provide *Artisans'* customers with a tangible connection between the very materiality of Angkor's temples and their future memories, glass reproductions speak of another cultural aesthetic. In place of an 'authenticity' of material, etched and polished glass promises the precision of mass manufacturing, a souvenir that sparkles and looks very 'modern.' Glass is also the material of choice for a range of molded blocks, inside of which sit three-dimensional miniature 'etchings' of Apsara dancers, the central complex of Angkor Wat, the four-faced towers of the Bayon temple, or the words 'Angkor of Cambodia' (or indeed, in some cases, Angkop of Combodia). Once fitted with three AA batteries, a switch at the back turns on the unit's upward-facing Light Emitting Diodes. Best viewed in a darkened room, Jayavarman VII, or the gently leaning Apsara dancers, now flash on and off in vibrant red, green and blue. Similarly, matching Angkorean key chains made from cubes of Perspex flash from the power of watch batteries.

For those customers wondering where such items have been manufactured, the stamp 'Made in China' on the bottom of the plastic pedestals provides the answer. The origins of textile products such as scarves, shoes and skirts, however, are less clear. Casual enquiries to sales staff are met with a default 'Made in Cambodia.' On further probing, they reluctantly admit all the items have been imported, 'mostly from China or Taiwan.' Indeed, in contrast to the subdued, primary colors found elsewhere, these shops offer their clients a choice of 20 to 30 different scarves, many with elaborate designs and multi-colored patterns. Among these are designs that are also commonly found in Laos, Thailand and Vietnam.

This blurring of ethno-cultural and national boundaries also appears in the 'reproductions' of the sculptures and bas reliefs found in Angkor's temples. Plaster casts of Apsara dancers are recomposed and modified to feature musical instruments not depicted anywhere in the actual temples themselves (Figure 4.2). Similarly, a desktop-sized model of a wooden folding screen, perhaps of 'Chinese style,' features figures taken from the Ramayana depicted on scroll paintings of a style commonly found in Thailand. On the panels either side of these images is a brief description of the history of Angkor Wat and a map of Cambodia (Figure 4.3). With their metal hinges, high gloss machine-sculpted wooden panels and raised plastic frontispieces, these items conveniently fold up for travel. But in their design these objects speak little of a Cambodian or Khmer heritage.

Figure 4.2 Plaster reproduction of temple bas-relief (Photo by author)

Figure 4.3 Folding wooden screen (Photo by author)

With an ever growing market of tourists traveling from Northeast Asia, these shops have continued to diversify their range of products. The temples now provide the inspiration for hologram pictures, clocks, bath towels, cutlery, cigarette trays, and even desktop-sized three-dimensional 'watercolors' cast in plaster, complete with model easel (Figure 4.4).

Typically, these Angkorean themed items occupy the front, most prominent, sections of floor-space. Further into the shops, the product lines diverge and appear to have little connection with Cambodia. Tea sets, gold jewelry, jade amulets and belts made from sting-ray 'leather' have been sourced and imported from a variety of countries. The jug and cups set presented in Figure 4.5 are among numerous items that have traveled overland from Bangkok.

More recently, however, one of the town's largest outlets, the *Royal Angkor Shopping Mall*, located in the very prominent 'royal square' in between the *Grand Hotel d'Angkor* and the King's private residence, has turned its ground floor over entirely to precious stones and gems. Sapphire, moonstone, kunzite, amethyst and garnet stones, imported from Thailand, are displayed in rows of glass display cases. Owned by a Taiwanese businessman, the large two-storied shop also stocks an extensive range of metal and glass temple replicas, alcoholic spirits, 'ethnic' clothing and other home decorations. Typical of many of these 'malls' located on the roads to the airport and Angkor park,

Figure 4.4 Angkor Wat on easel (Photo by author)

Figure 4.5 Thai drinks set sold in Cambodia (Photo by author)

the target audience for this business is primarily tourists from China, Korea, Taiwan, Thailand, and the secondary markets of Malaysia and Singapore. Clearly, in aiming at these sectors of the global tourist public, these businesses have brought into play a set of very different aesthetics and cultural logics than those employed by the shops and stalls more reliant upon clientele from Europe and North America. The final section of the chapter situates this shift within the broader context of Cambodia's socio-cultural recovery, and considers how the rise of the Asian tourist poses new challenges and questions concerning the relationship between tourism and material culture.

Implications: rethinking material culture

As countless studies have shown, tourism does not merely sit detached and external from its social context. Indeed, as tourism is performed for an outside world, its definitions and prescriptions of tradition, ethnic identity, or national culture become part of the fabric of the host society. This chapter has considered such issues during a highly charged and emotive moment in a country's history. The recovery of Cambodia's cultural landscape after an era of genocide and prolonged conflict has in part been driven by a rapidly expanding international tourism industry. An analysis of souvenirs reveals how a rapid rise in Asian tourism is bringing new cultural logics and new aesthetics to this recovery process.

By considering how a language of the 'traditional' has historically emerged, Cambodia's culture has been read in socio-political and discursive terms. Rather than pointing towards any notions of 'authenticity' and associated critical assertions concerning loss or commodification, the chapter has examined material culture as evolving and dynamic, and contingent upon particular economic and social relations. Accordingly, parallels between a French colonial period and a post-war era have been cited; historical moments of anxiety and uncertainty within which discourses of reconstruction and restoration have been driven by Eurocentric ascriptions of the country's culture. A brief look at some examples of the material culture imported for a Northeast Asian market, however, suggests that the parameters and contours of Cambodia's post-war revival are now being shaped by a very different set of aesthetic and cultural criteria.

We have seen that, when funded by foundations, governments and NGOs, the production of culture for tourism has been oriented towards a provenance of place and an 'authenticity' derived from the use of locally sourced materials and hand-made manufacturing. In contrast, an entrepreneurial business sector from Northeast Asia applies very different logics to this process in response to the aesthetics of the Asian consumer. In this respect, it can be seen that Asian tourism is opening up the parameters and discourses of a Cambodian cultural 'recovery.' It encourages the absorption of 'modern' techniques and materials, and the integration of eclectic designs and technologies. Seen in a positive light, a more fluid, open and less xenophobic notion of recovery can perhaps emerge from culturally vibrant trans-national connectivities. Asian tourism is also encouraging the 'traditional' to be reconstituted and represented in different ways. Equally, however, it can be validly argued that these current trajectories of tourism pose very real threats to already fragile socio-cultural, ethnic identities and weakened claims of sovereignty. Perhaps most importantly, this brief study suggests the need for further research over the coming years investigating the degree to which such cultural flows are welcomed, absorbed or rejected by Cambodians themselves. Clearly, the shifting nature of tourism in Cambodia poses unfamiliar questions and issues that negate critiques oriented around inside versus outside audiences.

At a broader level, this study suggests Asian tourism demands more critical responses to the aesthetic and cultural shifts accompanying the growth of regionalized economies and consumer audiences. Cheap manufacturing, for example, combined with trans-national business networks reaching across Southeast Asia is reconfiguring, even severing, ties between place and culture. Clearly, the souvenir industry for Korean, Chinese and Taiwanese markets does not rely upon ideas of local provenance. Instead, it appears the most popular souvenirs for such markets only take up temporary residence in Cambodia: imports that in many cases return home to their country of manufacture. In that they speak little of their locality, and that their value does not stem from being 'Made in Cambodia,' these items pose important analytical challenges. As a conceptual category, the 'local' rests upon the idea of a globalized network of locales, where distinction and difference within the network provide the criteria for judgment. Invariably, such difference has been simplistically ascribed along the political and geographical fault lines of the modern nation–state, whereby Cambodian culture, for instance, stands in relation to Thai or Laotian cultural expressions.

The examples cited above suggest the need for a re-conceptualization of the relationship between culture and place in terms of fluidity and cross-border mobility, and a move towards the cultural and social flows within networks over 'local' culture as a static, nodal category. Too often scholarship on material culture privileges an aesthetic truth which is supposedly integral to, and thus retrievable from, the object of attention. The movement of objects promotes fusions of influence. Industrialized manufacturing offers both standardization and modification. To read such aesthetics requires an understanding of traces, of ghosts and of hybridity. I would therefore suggest that cultural artifacts that do not exclaim their provenance should not be dismissed as less valuable or 'authentic' than those that do.

The souvenir industry in Cambodia also poses the challenge of how to develop critiques that retain a sensitivity towards different aesthetic régimes, yet simultaneously recognize gradations of quality. To talk of glass or plastic items made in China as 'kitsch' or 'tacky' demands an understanding of the cultural and subjective bias from which such pronouncements are made. It appears that Asian tourism in Cambodia opens up questions about signification which have yet to be addressed within the literature. What, for example, do the etched glass blocks cited above signify when they contain images of Kuala Lumpur's Petronas Towers, Singapore's Merlion or Shanghai's Oriental Pearl Tower? Does the desire to travel, collect and display such items back home tell us about new or emerging forms of cosmopolitanism or class distinction in Asia? Given the limits of space, I have not pursued an analysis of taste and aesthetics along lines of class or gender here. Clearly, such approaches would provide further clarification and help answer some of these intriguing questions which are posed by a fast-growing Asian tourism industry.

In an attempt to open up such dialogues, this chapter has considered the production and consumption of souvenirs in relation to certain market and economic relations. However, rather than critiquing these relations in terms of their impact on local practices and traditions, or why tourism *per se* introduces new technologies and methods of manufacturing, the chapter has sought to understand how a rise of a non-Western consumer market brings with it new social and institutional contexts within which souvenirs are manufactured, circulated and exchanged. As Gell reminds us in the Introduction to his challenging text, *Art and Agency: An Anthropological Theory*, 'the project of "indigenous aesthetics" is essentially geared . . . to providing a cultural context within which non-Western art objects can be assimilated to categories of Western aesthetic art-appreciation' (1998: 4). He thus concludes that a theory of art production and circulation 'cannot be the study of the aesthetic principles of this or that culture, but of the mobilization of aesthetic principles (or something like them) in the course of social interaction' (ibid.: 4). Accordingly, by focusing on Asian tourism, it has been argued here that new modes of analysis are required, ones that critically engage with new forms of consumption in countries like Cambodia and the socio-economic relations they depend upon.

The challenging and precarious situation in Cambodia has also illustrated why ideas of taste, quality and other aesthetic sensibilities need to be read in relation to their political, even ideological, underpinnings. Accordingly, to what degree do the foundations and developmental aid agencies operating in such countries import Eurocentric notions of culture? Does authenticity remain an orientalist language? Indeed, and as I have shown elsewhere, these same questions are equally applicable to heritage policies put in place for managing more static, larger forms of material culture such as architectural structures (Winter 2007b). As we have seen for Cambodia, the consumption of Asia by Asian tourists is bringing different representations of place, culture and history to the fore. In presenting such arguments, this chapter has attempted to illustrate why Asian tourism challenges us to move beyond analyses predicated on global/local, traditional/modern and foreign/indigenous dichotomies, and instead develop a greater sensitivity towards multiple gazes, cultures of difference and the ways in which emergent economic and social networks are rescripting and repackaging places for consumption.

Note

1 Information about each of the organizations listed here is available at (listed in order):

www.camnet.com.kh/rehabcraft/aboutus.html;
www.cambodiahouse.gpoint.com.au/represent.cfm?pageIndex=joom_noon;
www.rajanacrafts.org/about_Rajana.html;
www.tabithauk.com/About%20Tabitha%20Cambodia.htm; and
www.hagarproject.org/Home/home/default.htm.

For further information about the Artisans Association of Cambodia, an umbrella organization for craft-related non-governmental bodies operating in Cambodia, see www.aac.org.kh

5   Disorganized tourism space

Chinese tourists in an age of Asian tourism

Chan Yuk Wah

Introduction

Outbound Chinese tourists[1] have constituted a powerful presence in the global tourism space in the past decade, and have captured the attention of the international tourism industry and media. The rapid growth in the number of Chinese tourists now traveling has been well documented, including some specifics about their travel behavior and interactions with local communities. However, Chinese travelers, as with other non-Western tourists from the developing world, have generally been ignored in mainstream tourism studies. This chapter calls for greater academic attention on Chinese outbound tourism as well as the study of non-Western tourism more generally, in order to better understand the increasingly diverse trends in global tourism and tourist–host interactions.

I employ the concept of 'disorganized tourism space' to illustrate and analyze the specific global tourism space that accommodates this emerging category of visitors. This tourism space generates stereotypical gazes of the tourists as well as particular ideological and spatial treatment of them. I have selected three different research sites, namely Hong Kong, Singapore and Vietnam, for comparative purposes. All three sites have witnessed a rapidly increasing rate of Chinese tourist arrivals over the past decade. A comparative account of the experiences of and impacts by a single tourist market will help illustrate place-specific host–guest interactions within the 'disorganized tourism space.' By drawing on the tourists' reflections on their outbound experiences, this chapter also analyzes the quest for modernity by the Chinese particularly in the context of the 'inadequate modernity' of their home country.

In terms of fieldwork, I have chosen to focus on the three countries because they are destinations where the Chinese tourists are either the first or second largest market. I had conducted field research in Vietnam for my PhD dissertation; Hong Kong and Singapore were added to my original research as I had access to local tour operators and was able to conduct interviews with locals without any linguistic difficulty. The ethnographic data in this chapter was collected over a span of four years. While the data on Vietnam was collected mainly in 2002 and 2003, research trips to Singapore (accompanying two group tours of Chinese tourists) were organized in August 2005 and June 2006. During these times, I also interviewed four Singapore-based travel agencies. From August 2005 to August 2006, I further conducted 22 interviews with individual travelers and group tourists from mainland China in Hong Kong.

A literature review of Chinese tourists in Asia

The World Tourism Organization (WTO) predicts that in the coming decades, Asia will be the most active tourism region, producing the largest number of tourists and generating the highest tourism growth rate (UNWTO 2005). Within this growth projection, the Chinese tourist will feature prominently. From 1999 to 2006, China's outbound tourism increased over three times, producing 34 million outbound tourists in 2006. China is expected to generate 115 million outbound tourists by 2020 (CLSA 2005: 15). Chinese tourists have already become either the largest or second largest category of visitors in many parts of Asia including Vietnam, Singapore, Thailand, as well as Hong Kong and Macau (Greenlees 2005). Despite their international prominence, many current studies on Chinese tourism focus on domestic development (e.g. Lew and Yu 1995; Oakes 1998; Sofield and Li 1998; Xu 1998; Ghimire and Li 2001; Wen and Tisdell 2001; Lew *et al.* 2003; Nyíri 2006). Some years ago, Lew (2000) and Oppermann (1997) pointed out that more attention should be given to the growth of new generating markets in Asia, especially from China. However, there are few such studies to date. A recent exception by Arlt (2006) provides detailed political, economic and cultural backgrounds for the rise of Chinese outbound tourism, as well as forceful arguments and statistics emphasizing the importance of this trend. Others such as Chan (2006) have focused on host–guest interactions as Chinese travelers relate to local communities. It should be noted, however, that much of the research by mainland Chinese scholars have been published in Chinese and focus on the improvement of tourism services, marketing and tourism policies (see Zhao 2002; Zhang *et al.* 2003; Ma and Kou 2006; Yang 2006).

Since the establishment of the three week-long holidays by the Chinese government in 1999 (namely, the National Day holiday, the Lunar New Year holiday, and Labor Day holiday), Chinese tourism has never subsided. Collectively, the three holidays have come to be known as the 'golden weeks.' At this time, waves of Chinese tourists churn in and out of domestic and international airports in China, and contribute significantly to the Asian tourism landscape. Three decades earlier, Turner and Ash (1976: 11) dubbed the affluent mass Western tourists the 'Golden Horde,' a term suggestive of barbarians in an 'age of leisure' who often flex their economic power in poor Third World countries (see also Mowforth and Munt 1998). Are we now witnessing a new category of the golden horde from China? How are they different from the Western holidaymakers three decades ago?

Many stereotypes of the Chinese tourists have been formed and are transmitted in the transborder tourism space through the media. However, unlike mass Western tourists who are often regarded as culturally and economically superior, the Chinese tourists are stereotyped as country bumpkins lacking in international exposure, and who are too 'poor' to offer monetary tips to locals. This chapter will examine the different stereotypical gazes that hosts hold towards Chinese tourists, and elaborate on the place-specific interactions between tourists and locals. The discussion is premised on the notion that outbound leisure mobility is an expression of Chinese modernity. Before I explain the concept of 'disorganized tourism space,' some statistics on Chinese tourism in the three case sites of Singapore, Vietnam and Hong Kong are presented.

Statistical overview of the Chinese tourism boom

The surge in Chinese tourists visiting Asia can be better appreciated when we look at some statistics. As the case studies deal with Singapore, Vietnam and China, statistics.

Chinese tour groups to Singapore surged in the aftermath of the Asian economic crisis of 1997, when there was a comparative advantage of the *renminbi*. Chinese tourists now constitute the second largest international market in Singapore's arrivals (after Indonesians), and over 60 tour companies cater to Chinese groups. In 2004, more than 850,000 Chinese tourists arrived in Singapore, an increase of 54.8 percent on 2003. The majority visit Singapore either on shopping/sightseeing tours or for business/a convention/an exhibition. Typical shopping/sightseeing itineraries are either for three-day/two-night or four-day/three-night tours. It is also common for Chinese groups to travel on five-day tours covering both Singapore and Malaysia.

Tourists from China constitute the largest single category of visitors in Vietnam numbering over 750,000 in 2005, a dramatic increase from around 62,000 in 1995. Most Chinese travel to Vietnam through border tourism. In 1979, a one-month long border war was fought between the two countries leading to a decade-long border shutdown (Chang 1985). The border was reopened in November 1991 after a series of high-level diplomatic talks (Nguyen 2001: 114–16). As a result of the reopening, border tourism on the Vietnam–China frontier emerged in 1992 with simplified immigration procedures. In the early 1990s, border tourism only allowed tourists from either country to enter border towns but forbade them from visiting interior cities. Since the mid-1990s, however, different border provinces in Vietnam have received Chinese groups in abundance and many cross provincial borders, entering other parts of Vietnam. From 1998 to late 2002, the border province of Lao Cai saw a dramatic upsurge in Chinese visitors due to the opening of routes to many parts of northern Vietnam including Hanoi, Ha Long and Hai Phong.

Lao Cai is a province in northern Vietnam which shares a border with Yunnan Province, China. The number of travel agencies in Lao Cai town, its provincial capital, increased from one in 1994 to over a dozen in 2001. Correspondingly, Chinese tourist numbers have surged in the province from 9,700 in 1996 to over 175,000 in 2002. Typical group tour packages provided by local agencies include a five-day tour of Northern Vietnam, a two-day tour of Sa Pa town (a mountainous region of ethnic minorities), or a one-day tour of Lao Cai town.

Hong Kong began to welcome Chinese visitors in 1983 when the Chinese government allowed tourists to visit their relatives in Hong Kong (Zhang *et al.* 2003). After 20 years of package travel, the mainlanders were allowed to enter Hong Kong on an individual basis under the Individual Travel Scheme (ITS) implemented in July 2003. The scheme was originally launched for residents in four Guangdong province cities, and within a year it was extended to the entire province as well as Beijing, Shanghai, Fuzhou, Xiameng, Quanzhou, Nanjing, Suzhou, Wushi, Hangzhou, Ningbo, Taizhou, Tianjin and Chongqing. These are supposed to be the most prosperous interior cities in China with a population of 158 million. In 2003, there were over 8.4 million Chinese tourists, which is larger than the resident population of Hong Kong. The number swelled to over 13 million in 2006.

Chinese mobility and the quest for modernity in a 'disorganized tourism space'

To understand the increase in Chinese tourism since the post-reform era, one must consider the transformation of Chinese mobility which had long been restricted by the socialist state, on the one hand, and crippled by poverty, on the other. The 1950–1970s were marked by mass population movements instigated by political forces, as the state wanted to distribute workers and talents across the country. Since the economic reforms in the 1980s, Chinese household incomes have increased dramatically and many people began to enjoy greater freedom to travel (Zhang *et al.* 2003). Domestic travel expanded in the early 1990s when the state began promoting tourism as a strategy for economic development (Wen and Tisdell 2001; Lew *et al.* 2003). Besides domestic tourism, outbound tourism also soared as more countries opened up to receive the Chinese. Hong Kong and Macau were the first to welcome them in 1983 and 1984 respectively, in the name of 'family visit.' Thailand opened its doors in 1988 while Singapore and Malaysia did so in 1990, and the Philippines in 1992. China's immediate neighbors including some former states of the USSR, Mongolia, Vietnam, Laos and Myanmar signed agreements with China in the late 1980s and early 1990s to facilitate border tourism. South Korea welcomed Chinese tourists in 1998, with New Zealand and Australia doing so in 1999. Japan began issuing group travel visas for Chinese in 2000 and many European countries followed suit after 2002 (CLSA 2005: 15; see also Zhang, G.R. 1997; Zhang *et al.* 2003; Arlt 2006).

The 1990s saw the 'impetuous fire' of *luyou re* (or 'the craze for travel') (Xiao 2003). The flame '*re*' burned particularly bright during the golden week holidays. In these week-long holidays, tens of millions of Chinese move within the country and abroad. The word '*re*' signifies an earnest desire to 'move.' Amidst the backdrop of restricted movement before the mid-1980s, the newly gained mobility through tourism represents a shake-off of traditional earth-boundedness, poverty, and political control of the post-socialist era. Contemporary Chinese mobility is, however, ideologically loaded. As Liu (2000) noted, Chinese mobility is underlined by an upward-looking mentality. When the Chinese get a chance to move, they prefer to move to more developed sites within the country. '[T]he direction of movement was expected to be from poor localities to rich regions, from rural areas to urban centers, from inland to coastal areas . . . from China to the West. People are not expected to travel in the opposite direction . . . One could hardly be right to travel in a wrong direction' (Liu 2000: 6). The desire to move is closely entwined with the desire for modern experiences. While Liu's comment was not specifically linked to tourism, it highlights a developmentalist principle in Chinese mobility.

During the early years of border tourism development between China and Vietnam, many Chinese from the border provinces were attracted to the idea of '*chuguo luyou*' (traveling abroad). One tour guide from the town of Hekou in Yunnan province told me that although Vietnam was a mere walking distance from Hekou, the very idea of *chuguo* (going abroad) fascinated many Chinese. She added, 'After they go back to China, they can claim that they have *chu guo guo* (have gone abroad)' (personal interview, 15 December 2002).

The ITS in Hong Kong offers further insights into Chinese outbound tourism. For most Chinese, overseas travel is bound to the collectivity of group visas and the prescribed itineraries of collective tours. Though emancipated as tourists, the vast majority of Chinese still move in groups. In the 1980s and 1990s, the term *ap tsai tuen* (duckling tour) was widely used in Hong Kong to refer to group tours in which tourists were herded like ducklings according to a schedule, with very limited personal choices and freedom. In recent years, another term, *chu tsai tuen* (tour groups of piggies), has been applied to the Chinese, implying that the tourists are cheated like pigs by unscrupulous tour operators. The ITS was implemented after 20 years of the *ap tsai tuen* and *chu tsai tuen* experience. In Hong Kong, the ITS is popularly known as 'free walk,' which conveys double meanings for the Chinese tourists. First, it points to the freedom that the Chinese enjoy for the first time, in which they are able to plan their trips independently, no longer bound by collective schedules or subject to the coercive arrangements of travel agencies.

A second interpretation can be made of the term 'free walk' in relation to tourism identity politics. As one woman from Shenzhen explained, 'We are not tourists, we are free walkers' (personal interview, 6 October 2005). To this woman, the term 'tourist' (*luke*) is a demeaning one. 'Free walk' implies an eventual emancipation from the collectivity of packaged tour groups that

Chinese tourists have so long been tied to. No longer in 'groups,' the 'free walker' gains the first taste of being an independent and free individual. 'Free walk' calls for an imagination by the Chinese to shake off age-old collectivity, planting Chinese individuality in a new transborder (tourism) space which allows them to transgress spatial and ideological boundaries. The 'free walk' scheme of Hong Kong indeed provides researchers with a platform for further analysis of the different layers of Chinese mobility as well as the identity politics implicit in the process.

Urry (1990: 2) has suggested that travel is a marker of modern living. Within the disorganized space of outbound tourism, the newly gained tourism mobility of the Chinese is certainly part of the repertoire of their expression of modern experiences. The significance of such freedom and mobility must be understood against the background of decades-long state control on movement. With more Chinese tourists beginning to enjoy non-packaged travel experiences, greater subjectivity and individuality are formed in the transborder tourism space. By comparing their home experiences with what they observe overseas, outbound Chinese tourists often cast a critical gaze upon their own lifestyle in China.

Unlike other researchers who assert that Chinese tourism creates a form of fake modernity (Oakes 1998) or represents the hegemony of state authority (Nyíri 2006), I argue that within the disorganized space of Chinese outbound tourism, the Chinese acquire a taste for mobility and freedom, and this has spurred them on to seek other modern experiences different from those at home. Such a space, I contend, sheds new light on Chinese modernity. For most residents in developing Asia, modernity is a process in the making, and people negotiate between the modern and the pre-modern through their accumulated life experiences. For the Chinese, outbound travel constitutes a key part of their experiences as they aspire towards modernity.

I use the term 'disorganized tourism space' to conceptualize not only the new forms of travel open to novice travelers, but also the ideological and spatial treatment of tourist groups from the developing world, as well as the differentiated host–guest interactions that take place. Such a space also accommodates reflections on the part of the tourist as they venture abroad. I borrow the term from Lash and Urry's (1987) 'disorganized capitalism,' which stresses the emergence of new forms of capital interaction arising from economic restructuring and the emergence of fragmented employment, informal sectors and fragmented interests groups. The disorganized tourism space represents a divergent space different from previously West-dominated global travel space, which catered to middle-class Westerners interacting with poor locals.

Within the emerging global tourism landscape, the allocation of space and power, and the cultural interactions between guests and hosts are often uneven and disruptive. The tourists, especially those from the developing world, are not seen to be 'powerful,' like the tourists elaborated in Urry's tourist gaze thesis (1990, 2002). Instead, it is the tourists who are subjected to unfavorable stereotypical gazes and disciplinary behavioral guidance in the disorganized tourism space. The concept of disorganized tourism space, to be elaborated below, is thus meant to be an overarching concept encompassing new typologies of host–guest interactions, spatial segregation, as well as stereotypical and discriminative gazes by the locals. All these allude to the emergence of a new hierarchical order of tourists in the evolving tourism landscape. In the case of Chinese tourists, they differ markedly from Westerners who seek post-modern authentic experiences (MacCannell 1973, 1976); the Chinese instead aspire to 'a modern way of life,' and visiting 'advanced' and 'developed' destinations is seen as a step towards this goal.

Stereotypes of Chinese tourists

In all three destinations covered in this chapter, I encountered no difficulties in gathering negative stereotypes about Chinese tourists. In Singapore, a manager of a tour agency which mainly handled Japanese visitors said that although the Japanese market has shrunk, her agency has refused to turn to the Chinese market because 'Chinese tourists are like hooligans (*haoxiang liumang yiyang*)' (personal interview, 16 August 2005). Stereotypical comments against the Chinese made by travel providers were summarized in a *Straits Times* report in August 2005 entitled 'The rise of the ugly China tourist' (Chua 2005; see also Arnold 2005). The report tells of the many 'misdeeds' of Chinese tourists including spitting in public places, being rude to salespeople and messing up display items in shops. The report also noted incidents of public protests undertaken by Chinese groups. A notable example is a staged sit-in to protest the delay of a Cathay Pacific departure. Two hundred Chinese tourists refused to disembark the plane until the airline apologized and reimbursed each tourist US$50. Another public protest involved 300 Chinese tourists protesting against the 'pig drawings' on their room key dockets in Genting Highlands, a popular gaming resort in Malaysia.

Throughout the past three to four decades, Hong Kongers have also cast a discriminative gaze on the Chinese mainlanders. 'Ah Chaan' is a stereotypical mainland bumpkin popularized by a television drama in the late 1970s, epitomizing Hong Kongers' distaste of the unfashionable, greedy, lazy and timid village folk from China (Law and Lee 2004). Chinese tourists in the 1980s were nicknamed 'relatives-visiting' groups (*taam tsan tuen*) and stereotyped as poor village folks carrying all manner of unsightly bags containing whatever they can gather from their Hong Kong relatives. Although the ITS scheme boosted Hong Kong's retail economy, many Hong Kongers downplay these contributions, focusing instead on the negative impacts. For example, Chinese tourists were captured by local media squatting in an unsightly manner and their children urinating in public places. Pictures showing Chinese mobs climbing over the gates of Hong Kong's Disneyland during the Lunar New Year holidays in 2006 further perpetuated the unsavory image of the mainlanders.

Negative stereotypes also persist in Vietnam. In the border town of Lao Cai, Chinese tourists are particularly eye-catching during festive holidays such as the Lunar New Year (celebrated by both Chinese and Vietnamese) when they travel in groups wearing colorful caps. They roam the main streets and monumental sites, and bargain fiercely in local markets. Shopkeepers and souvenirs sellers whom I interviewed complain that the Chinese bargain too much, and interacting with them is troublesome and headache-inducing. A shopkeeper noted that Chinese tourists often come into his shop in groups, making a mess of his display items. A gallery manager in Hanoi further noted that Chinese visitors entering her gallery never greet her. Vietnamese tour guides have also criticized Chinese guests for speaking loudly and inconsiderately, failing to tip, and creating all kinds of trouble such as asking for hot water to make tea far too frequently.

With their rapidly increasing number and intensive interactions with locals, the Chinese tourist is increasingly depicted in the media as boorish, rude, rough, loud and aggressive. Such an image is akin to the 'golden horde' of Western holiday-makers some 30 years before. As Westerners become part of the norm in the Asian tourism space, the Chinese are beginning to constitute a new category of 'aliens' for the Asian hosts, to be policed by strict rules and regulations. In Hong Kong's Tsim Sha Tsui subway station, for example, there is a warning message in Mandarin reminding Chinese tourists not to spit onto the side of rubbish bins. In museums in Vietnam, some notice boards are written only in Chinese to ask tourists not to touch the exhibits or step on the grass in the gardens. In Singapore, I note a spatial segregation between Asian tourists from the developing world and Westerners. In one four-star hotel, for example, during the buffet breakfast, waiters and waitresses pool together their effort to fend off Chinese, Indian and Vietnamese guests from Western guests sitting at one end of the café. The Asian tourists, belonging to packaged tour groups, were coerced to sit at the large round tables. Not only are there behavioral codes targeting the Chinese, spatial segregation also exists, signaling a hierarchical order in tourist status and power. Such practices of discrimination on the part of the hosts also extend to tourist–local interactions, and it is to this point that the discussion now turns.

Place-specific host–guest interactions

In this section, I will show that Chinese tourists behave differently in different destinations, and are also subject to different host–guest interactions. All people are situated subjects, and they move with a baggage of historical and cultural imprints which shape their 'situatedness' and condition their interactions with others. Tourists and hosts have differing perceptions and presumptions about 'other' peoples and places, which in turn affect the way they interact and behave in tourism space. Chinese–Vietnamese interaction, for example, is historically and politically sensitive and certain aspects of Vietnam's history are deliberately left out in tourist commentaries. Some Lao Cai travel agencies forbid their tour guides, for example, from mentioning anything pertaining to the 1979 border war and other Vietnam–China conflicts. A tour company manager whom I interviewed told me: 'Nowadays, Vietnam only talks about good relationship with China, no more talk of wars' (personal interview, 22 October 2002). Tour guides also avoid taking the Chinese to places associated with conflict. During a visit to the Military Museum in Hanoi, I was criticized by the Vietnamese tour guide for bringing my Chinese guests to view exhibits showcasing historical conflicts between Chinese and Vietnamese forces. He noted that Vietnamese tour guides with Chinese visitors often avoided that particular hall and instructed me to do likewise in the future.

Vietnamese tour guides have noted that Chinese tourists are particularly chauvinistic and often look down on the Vietnamese for two reasons. First, many Chinese perceive Vietnamese culture as originating from China and is similar to Chinese culture. Second, many Chinese regard Vietnam to be underdeveloped, far lagging behind China. Although the Vietnamese economy has improved tremendously in the past decade, many Chinese comment that Vietnam looks like China in the 1980s. Some have also noted that a visit to Vietnam was like a visit to a minority community in China (Chan 2006). Although Chinese–Vietnamese interactions have existed for centuries, the notion of the Chinese as modern tourists is novel to most Vietnamese. Many in Vietnam have yet to find an appropriate way to receive the ethnocentric Han Chinese visitors. The historical tension overshadowing the Sino-Vietnam relationship in the past also explains the unease many Vietnamese feel towards the Chinese today, as well as the Chinese 'over-lording' behavior with the Vietnamese (Arlt 2007).

On the other hand, Chinese tourists in Hong Kong and Singapore do not act as egocentrically as they do in Vietnam. This is because before they leave for Hong Kong and Singapore, they are well informed that these cities are among the most developed and modern in Asia. Rather than be chauvinistic, Chinese tourists in Hong Kong, I observe, behave timidly (for example, when they are unable to figure out how to use the ticketing machines at subway stations). Chinese tour groups led by guides holding flags stand out most awkwardly in the modern city spaces of Hong Kong and Singapore.

Chinese tourists feel both alienation and familiarity in Hong Kong and Singapore. On the one hand, Hong Kong and Singapore are inhabited by a majority of Chinese, providing them with some sense of cultural assurance. On the other hand, Singaporeans speak mostly English whereas Hong Kongers speak Cantonese. The Chinese are particularly uneasy when they encounter road signs in English. Hong Kong and Singapore are also regarded as far more metropolitan than most Chinese cities. Their highly modern infrastructure and urban order impress the Chinese. A group of tourists from Jiejiang

I spoke with said that they were most struck by Hong Kong's cleanliness, while some Shanxi mine workers told me they marveled at the achievements that British rule had brought to Hong Kong. Another group of Hunan tourists confided that they were unaccustomed to the prohibition of smoking in Hong Kong even though they felt that such a prohibition is 'good for society' and should be implemented in Hunan (personal interview, 10 October 2005). A group of co-workers from Beijing was also impressed by Hong Kong's public transport system, comparing it to the dismal state in traffic-logged Beijing.

'Discoveries' made in outbound travel have produced an imaginative time/space for the Chinese tourists to reflect on their inadequacies back home. As I have elaborated elsewhere, this inadequacy underlines the collective gaze of Chinese tourists in the transnational tourism spaces, in which they feature as swarms of bees busily crossing borders to collect the nectar of 'modern' experiences in order to mend the inadequacy of Chinese modernity back home (Chan 2006). Such outbound travels also fill the people's longing for the modern good life.

Conclusion: disjuncture in the global tourism landscape

Chinese outbound tourism has largely been ignored in the tourism literature. This chapter represents one attempt to focus attention on Chinese outbound travel. It provides comparative data on host–guest interactions within a new tourism space, and analyzes various cultural meanings of Chinese outbound tourism across Asia. By using the concept of 'disorganized tourism space,' I have highlighted a space divergent from previously Western-dominated travel. In such a space, one can find host–guest relations different from the past when Western tourists exerted dominance over the hosts. This disorganized tourism space of Chinese tourists, one of Asia's fastest-growing markets, has generated new typologies of host–guest power relations, as well as a new hierarchical order of tourists in the global travel landscape. Within this tourism space, Chinese tourists are subject to stereotypical gazes and disciplinary behavioral guidance.

I argue that the concept of disorganized tourism space is useful not only for analyzing Chinese outbound travel, but may be productively applied to other tourists and tourism landscapes. It is theoretically meaningful and practically useful for tourism studies, particularly as the world is witnessing an epochal tourism shift with the rapid rise of international tourists from the developing world. With the coming of age of this new wave of tourists, researchers should be prepared to develop new theoretical frameworks for analyzing travel behavior, host–guest interactions and power relations different from the past where middle-class Western tourists predominated. Such readiness on the part of scholars should be prioritized in future tourism research agendas.

Acknowledgements

Part of the data in this chapter was produced in research trips fully financed by research funds of SEARC (Southeast Asia Research Centre), City University of Hong Kong.

Note

1 The term 'Chinese tourists' in this chapter refers to Chinese tourists from mainland China.

Part II

Emerging markets, (re)scripting places

6 Singapore's postcolonial landscape

Boutique hotels as agents

Peggy Teo and T.C. Chang

Introduction

In postcolonial studies, overgeneralizations about the hierarchies of power between former colonial powers and colonies are deliberately avoided. Instead, scholars pay heed to the complexities of different postcolonial contexts and to the complicatedness of their specific interconnections. This is articulated by Nash (2002: 228; emphasis added) who argues that 'understanding colonialism as general and global, *and* particular and local, between the critical engagement with a grand narrative of colonialism, *and* the political implications of complex, untidy, differentiated and ambiguous local stories' actually helps us to appreciate that postcolonialism is a highly contested and provisional term that is constantly in question.

In unraveling the multiple spatialities of colonial discourse, King (2003: 389) singles out the 'physical, spatial, symbolic, visual and material environments . . . [of] *everyday life*' (emphasis added) as needing more attention. He argues that much has been written about the unequal economic relations between the imperial core/metropole and periphery city/colony (King 1990) but the mundane and important cultural ties that bind imperial cities to 'colonial' cities are less understood. Ashcroft *et al.* (1998) exemplify these ties as mimicry in which colonized subjects adopt colonizer's lifestyles, values and habits but are, at the same time, parodying whatever it mimics. Indeed, as Young (1990: 147) argues, '[I]mitation subverts the identity of that which is being represented, and the relation of power, if not altogether reversed, certainly begins to vacillate.' The *relational* identities of colonizer and colonized are also taken up by Bhabha (1994) who argues that colonial domination inevitably results in transcultural hybridization. Mixing, syncretism and cross-fertilization are in fact rearticulated subversions of elements taken from the dominant culture, wherein the outcome is not a mix of X and Y but there exists an X and x (Alsayyad 2001). Hence, the spatial and built forms in cities should be appreciated not only for their symbolic significations of power and control but also for other vital tropes such as 'hybridity' and 'transculturation' which help offer a more nuanced understanding of the postcolonial city.

In this chapter about tourism in contemporary Singapore, we keep an eye on the spectre cast on many Asian societies by previous colonial administrations and their existing legacies but we are also cognizant of post-independence movements aimed at creating nationalist identities. The contemporary city, within which many innovative tourism developments have taken place, provides a fitting backdrop to discuss issues of tourism and post-colonial identity formations. We have chosen an emerging boutique hotel trend to expand upon this theme, with three specific intentions:

1   To uncover the *creative tensions that inform the postcolonial landscape* of Singapore by examining the rationale behind themed designs that constitute the selling point of boutique hotels. As good examples of the convergence of past and present, the material landscapes of these hotels, as well as the contemplations of the owners/operators that preceded their form, help to elucidate the complexity of the 'post' in postcolonial landscapes.[1]
2   As an independent country that appreciates the strong interconnectivities of the past and present, it is important to understand *the state's position on postcolonial identity* even as it tries to capitalize on pre- and existing (neo)colonial connections. At this juncture in Singapore's history,[2] we need to ask what is the state's projection of Singapore's postcolonial (and post-independent) identity? Tied to this account, we will explore how boutique hotels are at once constitutive of and contributive to this identity.
3   As a common outcome of varied encounters in postcolonial cities, the concept of *transculturation* (Karla *et al.* 2005) will be teased out via an examination of the persona behind these global yet local, colonial yet modern establishments. In addition, by examining *who stays in and who patronizes* these boutique hotels, we articulate the postcolonial identity as indeed messy, changeable and highly dynamic.

In geographical explorations of postcolonialism, it has been argued that debates should extend beyond the traditional focus on discourses and representations to engage with '*material* practices, *actual* spaces and *real* politics' (Yeoh 2001: 457; emphasis added). We take on this challenge through our tripartite emphasis on hotel *landscapes* (commercial inventions of new spaces), government *ideologies* (nationalist concerns about development) and social *profiles* (pertaining to hotel guests and owners). We will explore how boutique hotels in heritage precincts offer a useful lens to explore the postcolonial resonances of tourism and contemporary urbanism. In doing so, we argue that as the epicenter of tourist activities shifts to the Asia-Pacific, there is a need to rethink our knowledge about tourism. By deepening our understanding of the contributory roles of society, economy and ideology in *this* part of the world, we hope to define a study of tourism that is relevant for contemporary Asia which will go some way in charting an alternative to Western epistemologies.

For our research, we conducted semi-structured in-depth interviews with eight hoteliers in 2006 on what they thought to be the contributions of their hotels to Singapore's heritage and tourism landscapes. The hotels represented by our interviewees included Tropical Hotel, Inn at Temple Street, Sha Villa, Berjaya Duxton Hotel, Hotel 1929, New Majestic, Scarlet, Royal Peacock, Hotel 81 and Fragrance Hotel. In our fieldwork, we also observed the types of visitors and their activities; we perused hotel brochures, press accounts and media reports; we took photos of the exteriors and interiors; and we undertook guided tours of the rooms and amenities.

Hollinshead's (1998, 2004) summary of Homi Bhabha's (1994) *The Location of Culture* provides the post-structural motivation for our research. Arguing for the importance of ambivalence in cultural formation, Hollinshead challenges tourism researchers to develop a more vigorous interrogation of tourism activities which have tended previously to ethnocentrically essentialize people, places and pasts. By elaborating on how cultures are intertwined, and how places are the complex bundling of diverse cultures, practices and histories, research can demonstrate that the postcolonial condition is affected by multiple influences, some more and some less. For certain, the outcome of such complex cultural intermixing is 'hybridization,' 'transculturation' and 'simultaneity.' Before we substantiate these three tropes with reference to Singapore, we first discuss the boutique hotel as a potential site and signifier of postcolonial possibilities.

Boutique hotels as postcolonial embodiments: promises and possibilities

The emerging popularity of 'small luxury boutique hotels' since the 1980s has often been described as a reaction to the prevailing mass tourism of the 1960/1970s characterized by identically-designed transnational hotel companies, commodified attractions and rigid travel practices of 'old tourism' (Poon 1990). As emblems of 'new tourism' and the postmodern age, boutique hotels exemplify anti-mass principles of small individually-owned and designed businesses catering to niche markets and segmented interests. Boutique establishments running the gamut of stylish townhouse hotels in European cities, to owner-occupied home-cottages and traditional historic inns are characterized by their small size, high staff-to-guest ratio, market segmentation, and an inordinate emphasis on aesthetics, ambience and atmosphere (McIntosh and Siggs 2005). Whereas in the past, hotels played secondary roles in the travel experience, staying in boutique hotels today is very much *the* travel experience. Often travelers understand a city/country and its culture through boutique hotels, just as much as the hotel experience defines the traveler as an individual of discernment and distinction. Boutique properties thus embody a tourism subculture that emphasizes personality, experience and individuality.

In his innovative suggestion that cultures are hybrid and intrinsically inventive, Bhabha prognosticates that postcolonial culture is constantly (re)created, renewed and reinterpreted. This is not to say that cultures have no moorings but as an 'imaginative process . . . given the fast pace by which new ideas . . . are transmitted across seemingly different societies today . . . it ["culture"] need no longer have a *definitive* geographical or pervasive socio-historical context' (Hollinshead 1998: 123, emphasis added). Heavily influenced by postmodern thinkers, Bhabha's concept of hybrid culture parallels postcolonial discourses on the entangled nature of postcolonial identities. Neither spurning colonial culture and its legacies nor rejecting pre-colonial cultural values and ways of life, the postcolonial condition is fashioned from a hybrid combination of past and present, and an ambiguous position of the relative value of the past to the present as well as the multiple influences of the current. With fluidity as a hallmark of the postcolonial condition, the imagination of the 'other,' as well as how each group regards itself, are constantly shifting.

For boutique hotels, this line of thought has immense relevance. In the first instance, the past is drawn upon in a big way to distinguish the hotels from the ubiquitous international establishments that dominate the mass tourism industry. Yet, given the high standards required by today's discerning consumer, these hotels have to modify their interiors and their service to keep ahead of the competition. Put together, boutique hotels provide very good examples to think about the relevance of postcolonial practices in tourism. The trope of hybridization, for example, is particularly useful in exploring the significance of heritage and past architectural styles in providing stylistic distinction for boutique inns. At the same time, the past is entwined with consumer needs of the present to fashion new, innovative landscapes that serve not only as counterfoils to colonial histories, but are reflective of the manifold possibilities of the postcolonial.

Central to the boutique hotel concept is the importance of the touristic experience of place histories and cultural identities. Of particular appeal is the hotel's ability to create 'out-of-the-ordinary' experiences which provide 'extra advice' and insights into a locality's cultural background (McIntosh and Siggs 2005: 77). In the case of ex-colonial countries like Malaysia and Singapore, playful and whimsical hybridities offered by boutique hotels come in the form of staying in historic shophouses – remnants of the colonial era formerly inhabited by indigenous communities – which have now been refurbished into trendy inns. Past indignities of life in dilapidated shophouses are transformed into present-day heritage, and marketed as 'one of a kind' experience to the postcolonial visitor. As Jacobs (1996: 28) elegantly expresses it, such hotels participate in the 'creative remaking of the colonial by the colonized in the service of a postcolonial present/future;' more than just an innocent recall of the past, these hotels practice a 'subversive return to the colonial heart,' marketing this postcolonial stance as a draw to novelty-seeking visitors. As we explore the outcomes of strategic hybridity effected in Singapore's boutique properties, we show that the subaltern identity that emerges from this hybridity does not have only one form but many and is fluid. This is because hybridity is 'empowering' and opens the way to 'conceptualizing an *inter*national culture . . . [where] it is the "inter" . . . that carries the burden of the meaning of culture' (Blunt and Wills 2000: 188–9).

Besides embodying a fluid nature, the hybridity and ambiguity of the postcolonial age are also invariably affected by the 'simultaneity of today' (Bhabha, cited in Hollinshead 1998: 126). Resonating similar thoughts, King (2003) argues that social relations of power can only be understood in terms of the *lived* experiences occurring *every day*. Jacobs (2002) likewise highlighted two important temporal dimensions in postcolonial practice: first, the willingness of people to act upon their cultural politics depends on their multicultural and postcolonial consciousness *operating* at the street level in *everyday life at that moment*; and, second, what happens at any point in time depends on local *contingencies*, people's thoughts and conditions at that postcolonial *moment*. Hence, even as the tyranny of the past is brought to bear in postcolonial consciousness, the importance of the current/present cannot be overemphasized. In many ways, the present provides a window of what the postcolonial society wants to be in the future.

The simultaneity of today is most evident in the urgency with which many postcolonial cities compete with one another for hyper-mobile capital and talent. In an age of the entrepreneurial global city, cultural economies have increasingly become a weapon by which urban areas compete to attract tourists, investments and skilled professionals (Florida 2005). Inasmuch as heritage injects charm to urban locales, cutting-edge activities, events and facilities also provide a strong pull to the discerning consumer. In the competition for high-spending tourists and members of the 'creative class,' innovative place marketing and lifestyle products become absolutely essential, exemplifying the imperative of the 'simultaneity of today.' In the case of Singapore, we argue that boutique hotels represent one of many discursive and material strategies by which the state collaborates with private enterprise in projecting an image of urban creativity and social conviviality. Such hotels, with their emphasis on innovative services and upmarket clientele, underlie Singapore's 'quality of place' and 'quality of life' (Leslie 2005: 404), competitive with other world cities in attracting tourists.

As we contemplate the hybrid identities created by boutique hotels and the socio-economic demands of the present, the concept of transculturation provides a way to understand the strategies currently employed by boutique hoteliers. To Bhabha, transculturation focuses on the *interstitial* spaces of cultural identification. Instead of discrete spatialities where 'them' and 'us' can be found, cultural identities emerge from the 'slipperiness of the[se] spatialities' (Papoulias 2004: 54). More than just the vacillations between colonizer and the colonized in their relational identities to each other, globalization has overturned ideas about cultural, national and racial purity. Yeoh (2001) refers to these interstitial spaces as the intersections between social, ethnic, racial groups in the postcolonial city which offer opportunities for newly emergent practices and social identities to arise. According to Crush (1994), the new *inter*-subjectivities inherent in transculturation personify *changeable* perspectives that are responding to characteristically unfixed and plural inputs and not just the metropolis and the periphery in their pure forms. This pluralism is often positioned by the postcolonial nation as its new *cosmopolitan* identity. In an era where diversity is used as a selling point for tourism, local people in periphery sites often harness these intersections to remake themselves in a manner that is appealing to the tourists yet acceptable to themselves. The idea behind the dialogic interrogation by transecting cultures is to dismantle 'fixed worldviews' in favor of shifting but reflexive ones (Hollinshead 1998: 147).

The spirit of transculturation is certainly exemplified in boutique hotels. As part of the tourism landscape which is locked in time because the buildings are historic, boutique hoteliers also receive multiple intersecting inputs from numerous sources, and they make significant modifications to the interiors as well as create new facilities and services. In various Southeast Asian cities, the boutique hotel environment personifies the cross-cultural influences that characterize the hoteliers themselves. Hotel décor may thus include Peranakan (Chinese and Malay hybrid) aesthetics mixed with Western elements such as the iconic furniture of Philip Starck. In much the same way that the past and present are embraced in a hybrid environment, different cultural practices are also blended to create innovative offerings for new lifestyle needs. These transcultural and transnational influences that find their way into the topography of hotels clearly reveal the postcolonial landscape to be open and discursive. Previous works have shown that many boutique hotels in the USA, the UK, Europe and Australia have used design concepts from Starck and Schrager to re-brand themselves (Rutes *et al.* 2001). While not denying that these studies never predisposed themselves to a postcolonial lens, we argue that the complex influences in Singapore yield interesting and enlightening insights on cultural hybridity from a postcolonial context to which we now address.

Postcolonial landscapes: hybridization and alterity

Singapore received 8.9 million visitors in 2005 who spent 10.4 million room nights in hotel accommodation.[3] The earnings reported were US$1.2 billion and the average occupancy rate was 84 percent (Singapore Tourism Board (STB) 2005). While the lion's share of room nights still goes to big hotels, boutique hotels have survived the competitive environment and most report a healthy occupancy rate of between 80 to 90 percent (interview materials).

Characteristically small and owned by individual business operators, boutique hotels are often located in buildings of the colonial era. Some are monumental buildings. Peleggi (2005: 264) discusses iconic buildings like Raffles and Fullerton Hotels in Singapore and the Metropole in Vietnam that appeal to nostalgia-seeking Western tourists because they offer 'physically tangible' pasts and a 'spectacle' which the wealthy and not-so-wealthy can consume. These 'mnemonic sites' serve as catalysts for remembrance of a grand colonial era in the collective memory of the colonizers as well as colonized.

While not quite the scale of such monumental hotels, the boutique hotels we study are also significations of Singapore's postcolonial landscape, and are in fact *multiple* representations of the postcolonial identity. This, we infer from the multiple and varied themes we found in the boutique hotels.

The first theme we came across was the Peranakan theme. Well known for ornate work on tile designs, doors, furniture, crockery and apparel, it is a popular theme that features the intermarriage of the Malay and Chinese heritages which is only apparent in Southeast Asia. The Royal Peacock Hotel (Figure 6.1), the Inn at Temple Street and Sha Villa use this theme in an attempt to reinstate an important local identity that is fast disappearing. This theme has particular appeal to tourists from the richer North (and Oceania):

> When we planned the hotel, . . . we choose something that is backward [*sic*: read 'old']. Most of the hotels they are modernized [but w]e choose Peranakan type of design, something that is *unique*. It takes us a bit of time to go and hunt down all those old wardrobes, those old . . . everything [which] Caucasians like it very much.
>
> (Inn at Temple Street)

Figure 6.1 Indigenous Peranakan shophouse style of the Royal Peacock Hotel (Photo by authors)

After independence, rapid development had brought about a modern sky-line that challenged core–periphery notions inherent in postcolonialism. The revival of a disappearing culture in the boutique hotel landscape represents yet another way to distinguish contemporary vibrant Singapore from colonial Singapore. As much as Western nations draw upon the past (Ashworth and Tunbridge 2000) to capture the global tourism market, so does an ex-colony. This is, however, only one signification of Singapore's postcolonial identity. We discovered that there are many other ways of expressing alterity.

In our interviews, it came across that there is actually a conscious inten-tion to interpret the past in a novel, cosmopolitan and subversive way. Boutique hotel owners are well aware of the fields of care and sense of place historical vernacular buildings have for Singaporeans. Yet, as subaltern voices desir-ing to offer a different and distinct postcolonial identity, the developers of boutique hotels choose to mix the new with the old to create distinctive environments. Thus the second theme, 'eclectic' describes the New Majestic (Figure 6.2) and Hotel 1929 (Figure 6.3) where the façades have been tedi-ously conserved but the interiors have been hybridized to incorporate what is trendily new. For instance, the color themes are bold (lime green, splashes

Figure 6.2 The New Majestic (Photo by authors)

Figure 6.3 Hotel 1929 (Photo by authors)

of red) at the New Majestic and Hotel 1929. Lifestyle options such as a jacuzzi in an open deck, expensive goose-down bedding and Kiehl toiletries, and *haute* dining are some examples of modern-day indulgences. They do not, however, detract from the traditional window and balcony fittings or the historic photographs of Singapore in the common corridors. The New Majestic's lobby even has its ceiling stripped bare of plaster to reveal its cracks and original details (Figure 6.4). As the hotelier explains:

> Old ceilings . . . we have left exposed [so that] people can really see the . . . architectural details of this typical shophouse . . . It is difficult to do that because . . . [we had to] scrape away a lot of decorative layers and really exposed [the unpainted skeletal rafters]. [We] took a lot of care . . . to show the uniqueness of those architectural details . . . [We] left that [pointing to ceiling], . . . the cracks . . . and things like . . . the original details.

This gritty interpretation of the old has given New Majestic a distinct form which has made it a conversation piece in Singapore's urban, tourism and design landscape (*The Straits Times* 2006a).

Similarly housed in a row of 15 converted shophouses built in 1868, the Scarlet Hotel is bold and brash. Describing itself as a 'boudoir,' heavily accented

Figure 6.4 The New Majestic's lobby (Photo by authors)

by dark red walls, plush dark purple carpets, gilt trimmings and impressive chandeliers, Scarlet proclaims itself as 'glamorous' and 'shamelessly uninhibited' (*The Straits Times* 2006b: S4). The hotelier actually worked on the design for over a year because he wanted the hotel to have a 'huge personality' (*The New Paper* 2006: 24). With each room having its own unique design, Scarlet plays up its decadent theme with abandon. Its suites suggestively named – Passion, Opulence, Lavish, Splendour and Swank – are 'veritable palaces' with their jacuzzi, marble floors, four-poster beds, and black, aubergine and emerald color themes (Scarlet's brochure). On the exterior, the all important heritage architecture has been carefully preserved and given a bright color befitting its namesake (Figure 6.5). The building was the 2005 URA (Urban Redevelopment Authority) Architectural Heritage Award winner.

The last theme of alterity may be called the 'shallow' theme. Here, the co-existence of the past and the present is singularly superficial. Hotel 81 at Joo Chiat has a conserved Peranakan façade that is spectacular enough to win it the 1996 URA Architectural Heritage Award but the past is confined only to the building exterior. Inside, the rooms are standard rooms since the owner is only concerned with 'economies of scale' and the 'bottom line' (personal interview). An 'accidental conservationist,' the postmodern hybrid look

Figure 6.5 The main entrance to the Scarlet hotel (Photo by authors)

is very different from the innovative tongue-in-cheek representations of the other hotels (personal interview).

When all the hotel themes are taken *en masse*, the landscape is manifestly a postmodern pastiche, underscoring the notion that the postcolonial landscape is an assortment of subaltern identities existing cheek by jowl with each other. The boutique hotels obviously draw inspiration from all types of localities and times, both intimate and far away. As 'intertextual' and 'inter-spatial' (Edensor and Kothari 2004: 198), the landscape is a geographical and historical *mélange*, yet there is a sense of going forward which we will now discuss.

Envisioning postcolonial futures: innovative hotels and the creative economy

As much as the postcolonial landscape demonstrates hybridization, it also responds to the 'here and now' of political-economic imperatives (Hollinshead 1998: 126). Competition in the global economy requires political and economic practises that will inevitably give rise to inequalities between countries. Singapore is not exempt from this challenge. The embrace of a creative sector is actually positioned by the government as the 'next phase of development' where imaginative and creative capacity is essential for future economic growth (Ministry of Information, Communications and the Arts 2002). Since this initiative, a path has been paved for a more eclectic landscape to set the nation apart not only from other destinations but also as a way to nurture a new national identity that citizens will be proud to share.

As the governing body in charge of urban conservation, the URA has been trying to protect historic landscapes since 1984. It prescribes guidelines on what can/cannot be done to conserved buildings and what type of land use historic buildings can be put to. Boutique hotels have creatively taken advantage of this to inject vibrancy, novelty and identity to Singapore's landscape. First, they use the distinct architecture of vernacular shophouses as a selling point to attract tourists and to give Singaporeans 'something that people will remember' (personal interview). Rather than discarding/disparaging the old, the gentrification of historic precincts give Singaporeans and foreign visitors a chance to appreciate the richness of lost traditions and hopefully, find creative inspiration from it. The irony of crossing the past with the present is not lost on Singaporeans. According to one hotelier, 'You will be sitting in this *very classy* lobby and suddenly, some guy with singlet and shorts [strolls by]' (personal interview). This stark contrast is but one example of the contradictory but yet complementary styles that will hopefully bolster imagination and underscore diversity in the creative environment.

To facilitate the burgeoning of the creative industry, new environmental features are constantly added to the landscape mix. The government has tried to be more accommodating to the evolving demands of trendsetters and lifestyle impresarios. As agents of the creative industry, boutique hoteliers constantly push the design boundaries and the URA has to adapt its conservation and land use regulations to cater to new design dictates. Such demands include, for example, having a swimming pool or jacuzzi in a historic environment, creative use of rooftops and back alleys, as well as garden landscaping in the public five-foot pathways. Speaking on his negotiations with various state agencies, one respondent speaks of the 'educational process' that the government is subjected to by creative hoteliers:

> [For] Hotel 1929 we have [*sic*] more issues [with] . . . URA because things like doing a Jacuzzi, the RC roof at the back.[4] . . . I was like, 'What were the alternatives that you want me to do, a zinc roof?' Surely that is not better. Why don't you just put a garden there? . . . So they [URA] puzzled . . . for a while . . . [T]hey finally allowed us . . . [after] four appeals.

A 'different' choice is exactly what Singapore needs to become a creative metropolis. Greater flexibility and support from the state are essential if 'Uniquely Singapore' is to emerge among the ranks of global cultural capitals.

In thinking about the 'simultaneity of the present,' the significance of policy shifts cannot be emphasized enough. The government's willingness to negotiate in the present provides a voyeuristic window into what it aspires for the future – a city distinguished by charm, novelty and openness. Indeed, if urban cultural economies are to be the weapon by which cities vie for tourists, investments and skilled professionals, cutting-edge activities and a more liberal governance are needed to project Singapore as liveable, 'visitable' and 'investable.' Boutique hotels, by virtue of their architectural quaintness and global media exposure (the New Majestic has been featured in *Condé Nast Traveler*), represent a discursive and material strategy by which Singapore projects an image of urban creativity and social conviviality.

Trendies and tourists: transculturation and personal identities

In this section, we revisit Bhabha's claim that transnational encounters actually foster indeterminacy in cultures and create forms of signification that resist discursive closure. In writing about transnational meetings in tourism, Lanfant *et al.* (1995: ix) assert that the phenomenon actually 'compels local societies to become aware and to question the identities they offer to the foreigners as well as the prior images that are imposed on them.' In doing so, personal identities are therefore always in reformulation, and it is a constant struggle for those involved. We now outline the process of reworking identity among Singapore's boutique hoteliers and its clientele base of Asian tourists and local people.

Although the owners and designers of Singapore's boutique hotels are an eclectic group, they share a common bond through their transnational backgrounds and diverse training. We attribute the hybridity of the hotels to creative Singaporeans who draw from their cosmopolitan experiences and multicultural/multidisciplinary encounters to create novel environments. The epitome of such a cosmopolitan hotelier is the owner of New Majestic and Hotel 1929, a Singaporean trained abroad who is extremely well traveled and who considers, as his design inspiration, American hotelier Ian Schrager.

Returning to his roots, he hopes to introduce 'design-forward' concepts and landscapes to Singapore (*The New Paper* 2006: 24).

The New Majestic building was built in 1928 and refurbished at a cost of S$3 million (*The Straits Times* 2006a). A fashion designer, graphic designer, theater director, furniture designer and fashion show producer (all Singaporeans) were invited to design a room each. They were deliberately hired for their 'experimental' views and 'out of the ordinary' insights (personal interview). Even the overall coordinating designer of the New Majestic claims he was brought in because the owner 'wanted someone who had no preconceived notion of what a hotel room should look like' (*The Straits Times* 2005: 30).

The eclectic boutique landscape is also very much a personal landscape, reflecting the values and outlook of the owners. Unlike large hotels, the boutique environment is an extension of the owner's *persona*. This is illustrated by the owner's personal collection of vintage furniture and memorabilia used in the lobbies/rooms of both the New Majestic and Hotel 1929. His 'idiosyncratic' hobby had yielded a collection far larger than he anticipated; hence it was 'the most natural thing' to redeploy his collection of chairs, lamps and other furniture to his hotels (personal interview).

Not only do the entrepreneurs hail from different design worlds and cultural perspectives, their target clientele are likewise eclectic. At Hotel 1929 and New Majestic, for example, the niche market is a 'lifestyle and design focused' person, in his/her twenties/thirties rather than the typical 'international audience' (aged fifty/sixties) content with traditional 'comforts of a colonial residence' (personal interview). Their trendy cosmopolitan clients like the quirky landscaping and furniture. People working in advertisement and design agencies, television production, as well as bankers and financial workers form the motley crowd at the hotels' rooms and restaurants:

> Singaporeans have come a long way and they are well traveled now and they seem to accept this [waves his hand in acknowledgement of the hotel surroundings] product very confidently and they love this product . . . the Asian market is big, for example . . . Hong Kong . . . they seem to understand us better. Because they have a lot of boutique restaurants, so when they see this [referencing Scarlet], they can relate very easily.

Transculturation – the interaction of the colonizers, the colonized, and others – results in a grappling of disparate cultures. This mixing is also evident in the hotel guests. In terms of cultural predilection, the clientele base of Singaporeans and international tourists embody a state of transcultural in-betweenness. Pritchard and Morgan (2006) argue that hotel spaces can be liminal sites of transition and transgression which we argue includes that of national identity. Since as many as 70 percent of the clientele of the hotels we interviewed are Singaporeans, these boutique spaces can serve as in-between performative spaces where Singaporeans rediscover their self, not as an oversimplified coupling of 'colonial' and 'anti-colonial,' but a much more fluid and ambiguous reality (Sidaway 2002).

This emphasis on the 'local' does not discount the presence of a colonial or western mentality which resonates strongly in a number of properties. For example, at the Berjaya Duxton Hotel, British, Australian and American clients are 'very comfortable' about the colonial theme (personal interview). Nonetheless, the possibilities for transculturation are ever present. For instance, SHA Villa's representative mentioned that its clients would find the hotel more appealing *if* the hotel was 'modernized . . . a bit more' to look more like the 'building[s] in Shanghai' (personal interview). Victorian-style buildings of Shanghai are grand, evoking the heady days of capitalist penetration by the West but inflected by a distinctly Chinese presence. This opinion runs parallel to Hollinshead's (1998: 143) point that instead of a melting pot to describe cosmopolitan cities of both the core North and peripheral South, a 'chowder pot' is more appropriate because, in truth, the bits are still distinguishable.

Transculturation has an extensive reach beyond space and time. Boutique hotels recreate heritage for the current post-independence/postcolonial (1965) generation of decolonized Singapore who want to 'remember and treasure' the past, according to one hotelier. Another hotelier confides that many of his guests are 'overseas Chinese . . . [who come] back to visit their own relatives' (personal interview). Just like the 'stretched out' geographies of economic activity in today's transnational world (Radcliffe 2005), Singaporeans who live and work overseas delight in returning to heritage hotels to share in this reconstituted identity. Hotel 81 in Chinatown is extremely popular with Indonesian Chinese tourists because, according to its representative, many visitors re-enact historical bonds with past Chinese immigrants in Singapore who lived, worked and played mainly in the confines of Chinatown (personal interview). Strong historical place associations are evoked, giving the overseas Chinese visitors an imagined sense of familiarity which transcends nationality. This example entangles postcolonial Chinese identities into a transcultural entity that clearly defies history and geography.

To summarize this section, the entrepreneurs behind the boutique hotels are the products of transcultural hybridization. Neither the 'Orientalist Other' nor 'Colonial Self,' they occupy an in-between ambivalent space of contact between the colonizers and the colonized by virtue of their date of birth, multi-disciplinary training and globe-trotting travels. Instead of an exclusive nationalist identity, these entrepreneurs have appropriated elements of dominant cultures about the colonized and subverted them. At the same time, they also have infused encounters with other cultures disassociated with their historical heritage, and incorporated these as part of their transcultural identity. This multi-cultural identity is similarly reflected in the clientele base.

Conclusion: boutique hotels in postcolonial Singapore

Given the many works that point to the imperialist tendencies of tourism and the 'positional superiority of western forms of consciousness at the helm of the industry' (Meethan 2001, cited in Hollinshead 2004: 31), colonial accounts of our received pasts and lived presents seem inevitable. Since Said's (1978) groundbreaking work, however, counter-stories that emphasize the voices of the colonized have emerged. We argue that the counter-textualities of the boutique hotel landscape in Singapore constitute an important post-colonial project to challenge Western epistemology embedded within tourism studies. The counter-narratives of the rich Peranakan décor theme as well as the shallow theme that only emphasizes the exterior provide anchors for locals and overseas Singaporeans seeking nostalgic pasts while still indulging in the comforts of a modern inn. A second account of postcoloniality appears in the cross-textualities of the eclectic theme wherein a postmodern aesthetic incorporating hybrid global influences imbibed from foreign travels and/or education of the owners/proprietors are inscribed onto the landscape.

If Singaporeans are willing to pay S$800 a night to be immersed in a created hybridity where old textualities about place-ness are conjoined with new imaginary essences, then certainly the 'declarative agency' Hollinshead (2004) says is responsible for re- or de-making the world exists in Singapore. Through tourism, they have helped subjugated/de-colonized populations realize alternative narrations of meaning, identity and becoming.

Finally, the chapter has given substance to the notion that indeed, Asia has moved from 'hosts' to 'guests.' More affluent Singaporeans and Asian tourists are contributing to new tourism landscapes. Yet, upon further reflection, we can also see that spaces are not mutually exclusive – what is center and margin, inside and outside, host and guest – are epistemological and onto-logical dualisms that can be undermined. It is in such discursiveness that we hope a more analytical edge may be given to future tourism studies.

Notes

1　Although not the focus of this chapter, colonial architecture with modern interiors provide support that the postcolonial can also be postmodern. For cross-references between postcolonialism and postmodernism, refer to Simon (1998).
2　Postcolonial literature recognizes that the postcolonial identity does not have a fixed form. It imbibes and responds to influences around it. Further discussion of the importance of what Bhabha (1994) refers to as 'simultaneity of today' will be provided in a later part of the chapter.
3　There are over 36,000 gazetted and 6,000 non-gazetted rooms in Singapore (STB 2005).
4　The RC referred to here is a reinforced concrete flat roof which the proprietor wanted to convert into a garden with a jacuzzi. URA's hesitancy had to do with the load-bearing issue of such a proposal.

7 The rebirth of the hospital

Heterotopia and medical tourism in Asia

Audrey Bochaton and Bertrand Lefebvre

Introduction

'Hospital is the new destination' (*Globe Health Tours* 2006: n.p.), and 'A little sightseeing, a little face-lift' (Doheny 2006: n.p.) are some of the sensational newspaper headlines that illustrate that medical tourism has become an important component of the tourism industry in recent years. There is wide media coverage of its escalation and much of it reports medical tourism as a positive development for the countries involved. This chapter looks at its growth in Thailand and India, particularly how healthcare is promoted as a 'unique experience', and assesses the significance of the Asian traveler for its expansion and subsequent consequences on local populations. Connell (2006: 1093) in presenting medical tourism as a combination of 'sea, sun, sand and surgery' argues that it is *the* answer for patients from developed countries who have to deal with long waiting lists and high costs. This Western-centric point of view does not tell us much about the Asian medical tourists' motives and expectations. In this chapter, we focus on the Asian experience of medical tourism.

We approach the topic by examining the hospital and its transformations. Medical tourism is definitely giving birth to new places of care, e.g., new international patient wards. Hospitals designed for foreign patients have been planned in India, Middle East and Southeast Asia. In fact, hospital architecture, design and organization are being rethought through this prism of medical tourism. These hospitals face a dilemma of trying to meet local healthcare needs as well as the expectations of a tourism industry standard. Hence we find it relevant to investigate the services such hospitals provide and precisely how the 'new' patients' demands are being met. Foucault's (1967) theoretical concept of heterotopia will be employed to analyze the 'distinctive experience' of healthcare proffered in medical tourism. The main actors of medical tourism always stress the 'unique' experience it can offer patients coming from abroad. Only positive elements are emphasized and the medical treatment offered is said to be near to perfection. The whole experience emulates 'a realized utopia.'

For this research, we conducted fieldwork mainly in Bangkok, Thailand, and had extensive interviews with five top managers and health professionals from two corporate hospitals (Bangkok International Hospital (BIH) and Bumrungrad International) as well as officials from the health and tourism ministries in 2006 (see Bochaton and Lefebvre 2006). Thailand was selected as it is a pioneer in medical tourism in Asia and currently leads the way in terms of the number of foreign patients treated each year. In addition, we also draw limited information gathered from fieldwork in India which provides a good contrast as the country entered the medical tourism sector much later. In the main, our analysis will focus on the two biggest private hospitals in Bangkok – Bumrungrad International and BIH. We will discuss Indian hospitals (e.g., Apollo Hospital Delhi) to elucidate our discussions.

The chapter is divided into two sections. The first introduces medical tourism in the Thai–Indian contexts. The second section provides a presentation of the concept of heterotopia and an analysis of medical tourism through it.

Of Asian origins: the true face of medical tourists in Asia

If the links between healthcare and tourism are relatively new, the nexus between health and tourism is far older. In the past, some forms of tourism were already set out to, directly or indirectly, increase health and well-being. In India, the hill stations (e.g., Mussoorie, Shimla) that are now so popular among the Indian middle class, were settled from the middle of the nineteenth century by the British administration for medical reasons (Harrison 1999). In India, religious pilgrimages allow people an opportunity to be 'cured' of their ailments (Sébastia 2002). In Thailand, a tradition of spas and massages has existed for centuries. Today, massage schools are specifically created for the purpose of teaching traditional techniques to foreigners. Hill or coastal resorts remain popular with Thais e.g., Hua Hin, seeking rejuvenation.

As the link between healthcare and tourism becomes increasingly common, it is easy to forget that the expression 'medical tourism' is based on a contradiction which combines the notions of leisure and pleasure with those of disease, suffering and treatment. The union of these two words suggests that healthcare is now associated with ubiquitous consumerism. Some of the promoters of medical tourism have been uncomfortable with the expression 'medical tourism.' At its 2005 Health Summit, the Confederation of Indian Industry (CII), one of the most active promoters of medical tourism in India, proposed to replace the term with 'medical value travel.' In Thailand, the Thai Authority for Tourism (TAT) is marketing medical tourism more as the euphemistic 'wellness tourism' through spas, naturopathy and relaxation therapies rather than serious ailments.

As discussed by Connell (2006), it is difficult to assess the exact number of patients involved in medical tourism. Hospitals and national health authorities differentiate in their statistics between national and foreign patients. Mostly the 'foreign patient' category remains extremely vague and often overemphasizes the real extent of medical tourism. Figures from the Department of Export Promotion (2002) in Thailand show that in 2002,

60 percent of foreign patients were expatriates living in Thailand or neighboring countries; 10 percent were tourists falling ill during their holidays and 30 percent made the trip specifically for healthcare. In our opinion, expatriates and sick tourists cannot be considered medical tourists since their use of medical facilities is not directly related to travel. For the purposes of this chapter, we understand the term medical tourism to be the phenomenon involving patients traveling overseas especially for an operation or medical treatment – 'where tourism is deliberately linked to direct medical interventions' (Connell 2006: 1094) and medical screening. Similar problems in defining what a tourist is are not confined to medical tourism but occur in many other forms of niche tourism (Equipe MIT 2002). This is why all the figures presented should be used with caution.

Regardless of this problem, the number of foreign patients is on the rise in India and Thailand. In Thailand, the number of foreign patients has risen from 470,000 in 2001 (Pachanee and Wibulpolprasert 2006: 313) to an unexpected 1.4 million patients in 2006 (interview material). In India, it is believed that the number rose from 10,000 in 2000 to 175,000 in 2006 (interview material). Those figures could quite possibly be exaggerating the weight of medical tourism. As we have seen previously, such figures combine expatriates, tourists who fall sick during their vacation as well as those who come purely for the purpose of receiving medical treatment. The statistical system is weak and incomplete and some private hospitals are reluctant to divulge their figures. It is only now that public authorities have started to implement some tools to measure the phenomenon. In Thailand, before entering the country a traveler can specify whether or not they are coming for medical purposes. In 2005, India launched medical visas for foreign patients.

If we analyze in detail the figures in Table 7.1, we find that in 2004, more than 58 percent of the total number of foreign patients coming to Thailand were from Asia, including Australia. Japan was the top ranked country with almost 250,000 Japanese patients. At BIH, more than 90 percent of Japanese patients are expatriates working in the region. Between 2002 and 2004, Asian patients accounted for 80 percent of the total growth of foreign patients in Thailand. The growth between 2003 and 2004 was far more important for most Asian countries (ASEAN countries: +155 percent, Middle East: +105 percent, South Korea: +60 percent) compared to North American (+39 percent on average) or European countries (+17.5 percent on average).

One of the important milestones in the story of medical tourism are events that took place on 11 September 2001 (collectively called the 9/11 attacks). Patients from the Middle East who used to travel to Europe (e.g., the UK) and the USA for medical treatment are now going to Thailand, India and other Asian countries. Visa constraints, coupled with a suspicious climate, have pushed them away from Western medical systems. BIH has seen the number of Emiratis increase by 318 percent from 2005 to 2006. In the Bumrungrad International Hospital, the number of Middle Eastern patients has multiplied 14 times between 2000 and 2005 to reach the 70,000 mark. This growth

Table 7.1 Foreign patients in Thailand (2002–2004)

Country/Region of origin	Number of patients			2004 (%)	Growth 2003–2004 (%)
	2002	2003	2004		
Japan	131,584	162,909	247,238	22	52
South Asia	47,555	69,574	107,627	10	55
ASEAN	–	36,708	93,516	8	155
Middle East	20,004	34,704	71,051	6	105
Taiwan & PRC	27,438	46,624	57,051	5	22
Australia	16,479	24,228	35,092	3	45
South Korea	14,877	19,588	31,303	3	60
Asia	**257,937**	**394,335**	**642,878**	**58**	**63**
Britain	41,599	74,856	95,941	9	28
Germany	18,923	37,055	40,180	4	8
France	17,679	25,582	32,409	3	27
Scandinavia	–	19,851	20,990	2	6
Europe	**78,201**	**157,344**	**189,520**	**17**	**20**
U.S.A.	59,402	85,292	118,771	11	39
Canada	–	12,909	18,144	2	41
North America	**59,402**	**98,201**	**136,915**	**12**	**39**
Others	**234,460**	**323,652**	**133,782**	**12**	**−59**
TOTAL	**630,000**	**973,532**	**1,103,095**	**100**	**13**

Source: Compiled from TAT 2005

is likely to accelerate in the future with the signing of numerous Memorandums of Understanding between the big private Thai hospitals and some public bodies (army, government departments) from the Middle East.

In India, it is difficult to obtain an equally detailed picture of medical tourism. Following interviews in Delhi, it appears that foreign patients come mainly from other South Asian countries (Bangladesh, Nepal, and Afghanistan). East Africa, the Middle East and increasingly Central Asia can be considered as secondary zones. The truth remains that the typical medical tourist in India is a non-resident Indian (NRI) living abroad (usually a developed country) who travels for medical treatment to his/her 'homeland' during his/her holidays. According to the Indian medical professionals we interviewed, NRIs come largely for health checks and plastic surgery. As such, it would not be presumptuous to say that Indian medical tourism has some elements of 'Asians on tour.'

Foreign patients now account for more than 40 percent of the patients in the Bumrungrad International and BIH in Bangkok. The increasing presence of medical tourists in these facilities, combined with the drive of private hospital groups to attract more medical tourists, creates a major makeover in the organization and the architecture of the hospitals, to which we now turn.

Medical tourism as a heterotopia

The concept of heterotopia

In *Of Other Spaces*, Foucault (1967: n.p.) explains heterotopia:

> First there are the utopias. Utopias are sites with no real place . . . There
> are also, probably in every culture, in every civilization, real places . . .
> which are something like counter-sites, a kind of effectively enacted utopia
> . . . Places of this kind are outside of all places, even though it may be
> possible to indicate their location in reality. Because these places are
> absolutely different from all the sites that they reflect and speak about,
> I shall call them, by way of contrast to utopias, heterotopias.

Foucault presents six principles in order to qualify the heterotopias: heterotopias arise around points of crisis; their nature changes according to the
era considered; they are capable of juxtaposing in a single real place several
spaces; heterotopias function with unconventional time; they 'always presuppose a system of opening and closing that both isolates them and makes
them penetrable;' finally, 'their role is to create a space that is other, another
real space, as perfect, as meticulous, as well arranged as ours is messy, ill
constructed, and jumbled.'

Some geographers have made interesting use of heterotopia to study gated
communities (Hook and Vrdoljak 2002) and tourist practices (Shackley 2002;
Bartling 2006). We employ the same concept because we noticed that hospitals involved in medical tourism insist on presenting themselves as very different compared to normal hospitals. They are special from the environment
they present, the time taken to give treatment, the type of recovery options,
and so forth.

The perfect medical experience

Heterotopia of crisis

According to Foucault, we find heterotopias in every society through two
different categories. First, there are the heterotopias of crisis which are
'privileged or sacred or forbidden places, reserved for individuals who are,
in relation to society and to the human environment in which they live, in
a state of crisis: adolescents, menstruating women, pregnant women, the elderly,
etc.' (Foucault 1967: n.p.). Then there is the heterotopia of deviation 'in which
individuals whose behavior is deviant in relation to the required mean or
norm are placed' (ibid.: n.p.).

Nowadays, medical tourism concerns all patients who are sick and cannot
find a solution in their own country. These people are still in a crisis stage:
a crisis linked to the disease and all the ensuing physical and mental suffering

plus a crisis linked to inappropriate healthcare systems in the country of origin – a crisis of the patient in relation to his society. The milestone in medical tourism came at some point in the mid-1990s. Some patients started to travel to Thailand, India, Singapore and other Asian countries because of long waiting lists in the British National Health Service, an increasing number of Americans without medical insurance, and the stress on health systems trying to cope with a shortage of care and an aging population such as in Japan and Taiwan. It is easy to understand that it is financially worthwhile for patients who are not covered by health insurance to go abroad even when airfares are included. While in 2004 open-heart surgery cost US$30,000 in the USA, the price was US$14,250 in Thailand and US$5–7,000 in India (Bartling 2006). We find in medical tourism, an important characteristic of heterotopia: 'that in many ways it is a spatial answer to a social problem' (Hook and Vrdoljak 2002: 211). Medical tourism provides the solution to many a social crisis.

In the aftermath of the 1997 financial and economic crisis of Southeast Asia, Thai private hospitals saw the middle class fleeing from their infrastructures. The proportion of patients using the public infrastructure rose from 25.4 percent to 48.5 percent between 1996 and 2001, while the proportion using private hospitals and clinics decreased from 26.9 percent to 17.7 percent during the same period (Pachanee and Wibulpolprasert 2006: 312). As one manager from BIH explained to us, the hospital was forced to change its strategy. The hospitals argue that since Bangkok is an international tourist hub, it should attract foreign patients. The hospital first tried to encourage patients from the expatriate community in Bangkok and from the rest of the Southeast Asia region through targeted marketing campaigns and community-oriented schemes. Later expatriates from the rest of the region (Laos, Cambodia, Burma, Vietnam), who were looking for quality care, became the target of their marketing efforts. Eventually, the local and rich population of these countries also became the target. The Bumrungrad Hospital in Bangkok took a similar step at the same time. Similarly, in India, we can consider the sudden upsurge in medical tourism as a supply-driven phenomenon. Low health insurance coverage in the Indian population has been, along with other factors, one of the major constraints on the development of corporate hospitals. In 2002, the CII asked the audit agency McKinsey to prepare a report on the future of Indian healthcare (*Healthcare in India: The Road Ahead*). The report highlighted the role that medical tourism could play in ensuring comfortable profits to finance and to feed the development of private hospitals. Following this report, the phrase 'medical tourism' became a buzzword among corporate hospitals and later in government circles.

Time control

'The heterotopia begins to function at full capacity when men arrive at a sort of absolute break with their traditional time' (Foucault 1967: n.p.).

Foucault demonstrates how the cemetery or the museum are highly hetero-topic places by being a place of loss of life and quasi-eternity on one side, or by accumulating time with 'the will to enclose in one place all times, all epochs, all forms, all tastes . . . in an immobile place' (ibid.: n.p.).

Medical treatment time is generally divided into different stages, with consultations, then treatment/operation and later the recovery spread over time. Medical tourism proposes to go beyond this notion of time and to accelerate it. No time is wasted during the experience abroad. Time is under control from the first appointment to the recovery period. Both BIH and Bumrungrad Hospital present well-designed websites to inform international patients, still thousands of miles away, of the specialities delivered. Patients can get information about specialists, medical staff training, languages spoken and thus make an appointment via email with the doctor who seems best suited to the specific patient health problem.

BIH has also developed a network of referral centers in many Asian countries. The patients can approach the hospital from a familiar and reassuring entry-point and first meet local doctors before traveling to Bangkok. Once first contact is made and an appointment arranged, the patient can book an international flight and be in the hospital within a few days. Then comes the first consultation and very quickly, if required, the operation. This is one of the main sources of pride in these hospitals: to be available and efficient in a short time for patients. Information technology (IT) is a key factor in providing foreign patients with easy access to the treatment Thai and Indian private hospitals can offer. Patient management within the hospital is increasingly IT-intensive, with medical records being stored in data servers. This plays a crucial role in time reduction.

The existence of package tours including flight tickets, medical treatment and recovery also helps the acceleration of time. Time is under control and the patient is in a cocoon throughout his/her stay. Medical tourism also gives the patient the ability to control the course of his/her medical experience and to regain freedom of choice. By establishing a rupture with the classic medical time, the experience of medical tourism is therefore a heterotopic one in the sense defined by Foucault.

The standard of excellence

> The last trait of heterotopias is that they have a function in relation to all the space that remains . . . Their role is to create a space that is other, another real space, as perfect, as meticulous, as well arranged as ours is messy, ill constructed, and jumbled.
>
> (Foucault 1967: n.p.)

Foucault calls this a heterotopia of compensation and medical tourism clearly includes this function in the sense that the main actors pose as the perfect response to the dysfunction of the healthcare system in other countries. Though for Western medical tourists, time is of importance, the issue of quality care is also paramount.

Quality is a common key standard in both tourism and healthcare sectors. In the medical field, quality refers first to skilled and well-trained medical staff. Thai and Indian hospitals involved in medical tourism therefore recruit doctors who were trained in Europe, Japan and North America. In the Bumrungrad Hospital, most of the doctors are certified by an American medical board (e.g., American Board of Pediatrics). Quality of care also means getting the best medical equipment and ensuring medical and security standards are as high as possible. Both hospitals have invested a lot of money in medical electronic equipment which ensure the latest technologies are accessed. If this equipment is bought for diagnostic or treatment purposes, it is also used as a selling point in hospital brochures and marketing material. In order to get recognition for their efforts in providing quality and to sign profitable deals with insurance companies, growing numbers of Asian hospitals are rushing to get US Joint Commission International (JCI) accreditation. In 2002, the Bumrungrad Hospital became the first hospital in Asia to get accreditation. The medical excellence factor attracts obviously both Asian and Western patients, but for many Asian patients this issue really matters. Some rare therapies are available in developed countries but are far beyond their means. Bumrungrad and BIH bring these treatments to Asian patients at a more affordable price.

Quality in the medical tourism sector is also about how patients are welcomed and cared for during their stay in hospital. Bumrungrad stipulates that medical staff must be fluent in English. Translators are also on hand to help and/or accompany patients. From the concierge who can pander to almost any whim, to the design of the furniture or the van that will bring the patients from the airport to the hospital, everything is done to ensure the patients' time in the hospital is a truly exceptional experience. The chance to recover in a resort or a hospital near the beach transforms the patient's stay into a pleasant, near perfect experience. Relying on its large hospital network, the Bangkok Hospitals group offers its patients the opportunity to rehabilitate after surgery in one of its hospitals in Pattaya or in Phuket.

Rejuvenating the hospital

The redefinition of the hospital

The hospital traditionally carries a 'heavy' message to patients: suffering, death, treatment, hygiene, isolation. All these elements are present in hospital architecture and the atmosphere prevailing in them has helped carry negative perceptions of hospitals throughout history. In a modernist post-Second World War period, the hospital appeared as a functional space rather than a living space (Gillespie 2002).

One of the strengths of Foucault's analytics of heterotopia is 'that a society, as its history unfolds, can make an existing heterotopia function in a very different fashion' (Foucault 1967: n.p.). In our case, through medical tourism, the function and the design of the place 'hospital' are completely renewed. Its functions have diversified and evolved; medical tourism has intensified in Indian and Thai hospitals the need to make patients feel comfortable. The patient is of course primarily at the hospital for his/her health but having made such a long trip, the hospital cannot afford to disappoint the patient: a lot of attention is given to patient well-being. Like any tourist, the patient is also consuming the space he/she is surrounded by. With this is in mind, private hospitals are inspired by five-star hotels (Figure 7.1). Even the expression 'five-star hospital' is often used by managers to describe their hospitals.

When you enter the BIH, a hostess greets you and guides you to the reception or the concierge. In the same building, the ground floor consists of a central lobby containing plants, bamboo and fountains which create a pleasant ambience. All the furniture – chairs, desks, sofas – are made from good-quality wood and the natural light coming through the windows creates a comfortable place. It is now common for the patient to have his/her own private room where he/she may accommodate some guests for the night.

Figure 7.1 The main entrance of Bumrungrad Hospital is similar to any five-star hotel (Photo by authors)

Some hospitals in India and Thailand are now even proposing suites with attached kitchen and living room. The reproduction of a hotel atmosphere in hospitals can be seen from the rooms' design and furniture. As explained on the Bangkok Hospital website (http://www.bangkokhospital.com/eng/Room_Facilities.aspx), all rooms at Bangkok Hospital include the following: electrically adjustable beds, cable television including Thai, English and foreign language programs, a personal nurse call system, microwave oven, refrigerator, guest sofa-bed, telephone for local and international calls, individually controlled air conditioning, premium bathroom amenities and personal safe.

The food has also improved. In 2005, Bumrungrad International Hospital launched its Great Chefs Program and invited top chefs from leading hotels, and restaurants to cook dishes for its patients. Hospitals can no longer afford to offer foreign medical tourists, who are far from home, the same food they would offer local patients. Following this trend, Apollo Hospital in Delhi has adjusted its menus to suit the taste of its increasing number of foreign patients.

Juxtaposition of realities

One consequence of this reorientation is that the hospital is no longer just a hospital or medical place, but combines several realities. Foucault's criterion of 'juxtaposed realities' makes for useful application here. This criterion usefully draws attention to the ways in which the hospitals are a paradoxical balance of medical, consumerist and leisure space. As a headline from the *Guardian* emphasizes: 'Is it a hotel? Is it a trendy bar? No, it's a hospital' (Purvis 2001: 14). This trend of diversification is also taking place in private hospitals globally: 'Late twentieth century hospital architecture has increasingly embraced the open space model of the shopping mall, housing commercial spaces such as shops, banks and restaurants which came to embody the power of commercialism' (Brandt and Stone 1999, cited in Gillespie 2002: 213). Medical tourism pushes this diversification logic to the limit. The example of the Bumrungrad International Hospital is enlightening. We can find a huge food court similar to any found in shopping centers. There are now seven restaurants, ranging from McDonald's and Starbucks to Italian and Japanese restaurants. The Bumrungrad International Hospital has also a small supermarket, hair salon, flower shop, bookshop and two medical suppliers. Within the medical ward itself, there is now an immigration service desk where patients can renew their visas.

New forms of segregation

Finally, Foucault's last criterion of heterotopia is the idea of a strict and characteristic system of admission. 'Heterotopias always presuppose a system of opening and closing that both isolates them and makes them penetrable'

(Foucault 1967: n.p.). Historically, the hospital perfectly adheres to this definition. We find necessary segregation according to the different types of care required or the contagiousness of diseases. The gatekeepers at the reception desks simultaneously ensure access to patients while also acting as a barrier to protect this 'closed' world. 'Everyone can enter into these heterotopic sites, but in fact that is only an illusion – we think we enter where we are, by the very fact that we enter, excluded' (ibid.: n.p.).

With medical tourism, the rules of segregation are changing and the spatial organization within the hospital is also undergoing a transformation. While many Indian hospitals continue accommodating the medical tourists along with local patients, in Thailand, some hospitals have adapted their infrastructure to this new foreign population. On the Bangkok Hospital campus, the BIH is dedicated exclusively to international patients. Thai patients have no reason to go to the international building or consult doctors working there because they have a building dedicated to local healthcare. Medical tourism thus creates in this case a space integrated in the classic medical fabric but functioning as a closed world. It is interesting to note here that the international building of BIH features internal divisions of space: indeed, three types of wards can be found: an 'Arab ward' for Middle Eastern patients, a 'Japanese ward' and 'a global international ward' for the other nationalities. Each ward is different from the others in the interior design, spatial arrangements, food services, prayer rooms, translator services and so forth. Such segregation is also the answer to some complaints about the experience of sharing the premises with patients from another nationality. This process creates a closer proximity for each type of patient according to their culture, religion and language but at the same time it creates a compartmentalized space and a model of segregation. Interestingly, the Bumrungrad International Hospital prefers to treat all patients equally, regardless of where they have come from.

Conclusion

Most of the time, a heterotopia is an 'other space' integrated within the social space when deviant behavior or a crisis appears. However one singularity of medical tourism lies in the fact that this heterotopia functions at an international scale. The 'crisis' (dysfunction of the healthcare system) takes place at some Western or Asian countries and medical tourism as a response (as a possible answer to this crisis from the point of view of the patients) occurs in another part of the world. In this sense, there is a spatial move from the origin of the problem to the location where it is resolved. In this context, the issues of impacts are important to consider insomuch as they act at two scales: on the national healthcare system of 'host countries' and more globally on the conceptions of health and healthcare linked to globalization.

It may be too early to judge whether medical tourism is having a positive or negative impact on local health systems. We can be sceptical when looking at the future. If medical tourism helps in part to reverse the brain drain in the medical profession, with for example, many NRI doctors returning to India, it is also possible that medical tourism could exacerbate the brain drain between the public and private sector. The salary, better working conditions and the possibility of continuous training offered by the private hospitals are understandably appealing and are leading to a concentration of medical excellence in a small group of private hospitals. In order to minimize criticism, and to reassess their local roots, hospitals are involved in many charitable and community-oriented schemes, ranging from free health camps, to health awareness campaigns or the sponsorship of non-governmental organizations or social activities. Some hospital insiders explained to us that these efforts were largely cosmetic, designed to minimize criticism. Charitable activity helps to legitimate hospital activity and thus medical tourism in the host country.

Heterotopia is a valuable concept with which to study and follow the various transformations hospitals undergo when faced with the pressures of medical tourism. Nonetheless, conclusions about the impacts on medical tourism brought about by Asians on tour remain uncertain. Medical tourism's first asset remains the quality of care, a realm where you have to standardize medical procedures for safety reasons. Therefore, all the patients are equally treated. As many doctors in Thailand and in India kept telling us, they first face patients who are suffering. The nationality, the religion or the gender of the patients are secondary considerations to them. If the Asian medical tourists make an impact in terms of number compared to Western ones, the surveyed hospitals seemed to have largely ignored such categorizations in their functioning. Bumrungrad Hospital still mixes local and foreign patients. Hospitals are keen on offering tailor-made non-medical services to their patients. The creation of specific wards for foreigners in BIH was not based on an Asian/non-Asian distinction but on market sensitivity to the Japanese and the Middle Eastern patients who form the majority of foreign patients in this hospital. Following this trend, the next step for the biggest players of this market is to settle a network of hospitals in different parts of Asia in order to increase their patient pool. Bumrungrad International Hospital is due to open one new hospital in 2008 – with partly Thai staff and using Thai traditional architecture pastiche – in the Middle East. The objective seems not to make Arab patients to feel at home, but instead to recreate in Dubai the exotic atmosphere of a Thai hospital. If there is no Asian medical tourist, *per se*, medical tourism is accelerating the formation of an Asian hospital care market and pan-Asian hospital chains.

Acknowledgements

We would like to thank Professor Bernard Elissalde, Dr. Vincent Coëffé, Professor Peggy Teo, Dr. Tim Winter, Dr. Shalini Panjabi, Rajeshree Sisodia and Lorraine Bramwell for their input and reviews at various stages.

8 Affective sites

Hur Jin-Ho's cinema and film-induced tourism in Korea

Youngmin Choe

Introduction

The regional governments in Korea invest heavily to entice film and television dramas to film in their provinces. Between 2000 and 2005, some 31 film sets were built in 25 cities and counties, with the investment of regional governments totaling 49 billion Korean won (approximately US$52 million) (Ministry of Culture and Tourism 2006). Many of the provinces have the prospects of tourism in mind. Faced with a dismaying decline in inbound tourism due to SARS, the Iraq War and the ongoing North Korean nuclear controversy, the Korean tourism industry had launched an aggressive campaign exploiting the unexpected popularity of Korean popular culture in Asia known as *hallyu* or the 'Korea Wave.' By March of 2005, when Japan re-ignited latent postcolonial hostilities by voicing territorial claims over Takeshima, an uninhabitable island known to Koreans as Tokto, elation over the unforeseen success of *hallyu* tourism to Korea, in particular to Kangwŏn province, was at an all-time high. Amidst the mood of heightened nationalism and political anxiety, the controversy threatened to stall the momentum gained from events born of the reconciliatory spirit between the two nations such as the 'Visit Korea–Japan Year,' 'Visit Kangwŏn Province Year,' and the Korean Wave Tourism Campaign, organized by the Ministry of Culture and Tourism in cooperation with the state-run Korea Tourism Organization (KTO). And at first glance, it would appear that it did.

Compared to 2004, the overall tourism figures in 2005 dropped. Yet, as the KTO would surprisingly report in its *2005 White Papers* released at the end of the year, the number of inbound tourists reached 6 million, of which an estimated 1.2 million were tourists whose prime destinations were film sets, up from the 1.12 million recorded in 2004 (Ministry of Culture and Tourism 2006). Figures for particular locations in Kangwŏn province where films were made reveal much more astounding numbers. Tourism to the city of Samchŏk, for example, where Korean director Hur Jin-ho's *April Snow* was filmed, had by the end of 2005 recorded an unprecedented 298.9 percent increase compared to the year 2004. Kangwŏn province recorded a 10.2 percent increase of tourists from the previous year 2004. And as with foreign tourists, Kangwŏn province also saw a 10.4 percent hike in domestic tourists, bolstered by the increased popularity of themed tour destinations, such as film-induced tour sites, in contrast to the decline or stagnancy seen in the case of the usual tourist destinations such as beach resorts (Kangwŏn Provincial Government Tourism Policy Department 2006a, 2006b). Regional political tensions did little to curb the enthusiastic foreign and domestic touristic flows generated by film.

This chapter concerns the intersection of film and film-induced tourism in the Northeast Asian market and how it works towards creating new 'structures of feeling' that potentially override conflicting regional political tensions, thereby participating, interrogating and redefining the new Asian order. As a highly concentrated point of attraction for tourists from all over Asia and closely associated with *hallyu*, by definition, an Asian phenomena around Korean popular culture, the filming locations in Kangwŏn province can be seen as constituting Asian sites within Korea. In that particular context, Korean tourism to these sites, although domestic, could also be seen as partaking in a form of Asian experience. The continued and heightened appeal of these film sites to both domestic and foreign tourists in spite of contradicting political tension points to a need for analyses aligned not with the interests of tourism institutions and their marketing strategies, but motivated by identifying the critical underlying factors that potentially allow for a consumption of these sites that suspends or is removed from dominant political tendencies.

In order to conceptualize a preliminary approach that emphasizes the genre-specificity and emotional experience of film spectatorship as inherent in some forms of film-induced tourism, I draw on theories of cinematic affect and affectation to examine the domestic and foreign tourism generated by the Asian films of Korean melodrama director Hur Jin-ho, and the complicity of film and tour sites. Through an intertextual approach combining close readings of the films, supplementary footage documenting tourists at film-induced tour sites, and analyses gathered from on-site observation methods, I show how the film is implicated in its film-induced tour site, thus attempting to *move* the film spectator-cum-tourist in both senses of the word, emotionally and physically, beyond conventional spaces of cinema spectatorship into the actual spaces of the film at the tour sites, consequently collapsing the distinctions between filmic gaze and tourist gaze, filmic experience and tourist experience. Scholarship on film-induced tourism has attempted to negotiate the relationship between film and tourism in terms of place marketing and community tourism development (e.g. Riley *et al.* 1998); impact on destination image (Kim and Richardson 2003); authenticity and inauthenticity (Rojek 1997; Torchin 2002); the relationship between the filmic and tourist gaze (Rojek 1997; Jackson 2005); and psychoanalytically (Jackson 2005). Where previous studies of film-induced tourism generally viewed TV shows or films as flat images providing a series of locations, I view media images at the film location as emanating from a particular filmic genre rather than as a homogenous and static category. Accordingly, the tourist at film-induced tour sites is regarded not simply as a consumer of a series of images, but as bringing their experience as a film spectator with them to the touristic experience.

I focus on two melodramatic films by Korean director Hur Jin-ho: *One Fine Spring Day* (*Pomnalŭn Kanda* 2001) and *April Snow* (*Oech'ul* 2005) that were hugely popular in Asia. *One Fine Spring Day* (henceforth *Spring Day*), filmed in the city of Tonghe on the northeast coastal region of Kangwŏn Province in South Korea, is a joint production between Korea, Japan, and Hong Kong. It follows a divorced radio journalist (Lee Young-ae) and a younger recording specialist as they start a relationship while producing a program on nature sounds in Kangwŏn Province. Hur Jin-ho's *April Snow* (starring Bae Yong-jun and Son Ye-jin) was filmed in the city of Samchŏk, also a popular coastal tourist destination in Kangwŏn Province, and tells the story of the attraction between a man and a woman who meet at a local hospital where their adulterous spouses lie in a coma after a car accident while in Kangwŏn Province for an illicit weekend together.

The tourism-inducing factors of Hur's melodramas can be said to be its reliance on *affect* over effect and *bodies* over words. Drawing on cultural geographer and film scholar Giuliana Bruno, I treat the visual medium of film not just as 'the manifestation of fixed structures' but as 'an expression of restless energies' involving 'the position and movement of body in space,' and in which the spectator is seen, not merely as a '*voyeur*, but a *voy(ag)eur*' (Bruno 2002). I suggest that in this case, film sites function to motivate film-induced tourists to re-elicit the almost involuntary, embodied affective experience of corporeal intensity gained while viewing a film by spatially traversing the film locations and thus argue that the tourist gaze in such cases be considered a kind of belated filmic gaze.

Affect, emotion, feelings and heart

Hallyu star Bae Yong-jun, known to his Japanese stars as 'Yonsama,' recognized early the 'affect-ionate' role of film-induced tourism in Asia and its potential during times of political conflict. When pressed by irate local critics to take a stance on the Tokto/Takeshima issue in March 2005, Bae, at the time filming *April Snow* in Samchŏk, released a statement on his website:

Tokto is Korean territory, which I think calls all the more for a rational response.

There is also a need to consider from a remove[d standpoint] what actually gets changed as a result of arguing about the territorial rights over Tokto, and whether this contributes to finding a real solution. It is my earnest desire that people from both countries do not get hurt by letting their *feelings* [*kamchong*] get involved, thus allowing relations to worsen . . . If there is a role for me, I wonder if it is not in connecting the *hearts* [*maŭm*] and minds of an Asian family, rather than drawing territorial lines with mere words. As it has been up to now, my heart's [*maŭm*] desire to accomplish something good with our family in Asia remains unchanged. Therefore, I will try to return the undeserved love I have received thus far as an even greater love.

(Bae 2005: n.p.)

Bae resorted to the discourse of emotion to appease his Korean critics, making an interesting distinction between 'feeling' and 'heart' in the context of cultural tourism and their role in creating an Asian community. Feeling (*kamchong*) has negative connotations of irrationality that threaten political reconciliation. Nationalism that can give rise to anti-Japanese or anti-Korean sentiments is associated with this sentiment. The bodily heart (*maŭm*), however, is perceived as distinct from nationalist sentiment and able to overcome political relations and territorial claims. His role, as he sees it as a Korean *hallyu* star and tourist attraction, is in connecting hearts in Asia to create a community.

In Korean domestic screen tourism, emotion (*kamtong*) is seen as a primary motivator for film-induced tourism. Emotion (*kamtong*) is distinguished from feeling (*kamchong*) and heart (*maŭm*), in that it entails the sensation of being able to move or be moved, by acting upon, or impinging upon, another body an intense emotion. As such, the word 'affect' might be a better translation for the Korean word *kamtong* elicited by cinema spectatorship. To get a sense of how these terms are used in the context of film-induced tourism, take writer Kim Sun-kŭn's popular guide *Screen Tours* (2002). According to Kim, *kamchŏng* differs from person to person at the majority of tour sites. In contrast, literary, filmic, dramatic, and historical memorial sites enable tourists to remember how they were moved. The emotion (*kamtong*) felt at these sites,

> is a kind of 'organized emotion,' thus making literary, film and drama-induced tour destinations different from other tourist destinations. Even though it may be a destination you have been to several times, historical events, drama and film locations have an additional 'spice' that still gives it a sense of novelty and difference every time. If we are to seek a tourist destination more than once, there must be something that moves you.

(Kim S.K. 2002: Preface)

Feelings (*kamchong*) at tour sites differ depending on the tourist. The emotion (*kamtong*) at film sites, on the other hand, is described as outside of personal experience, that is pre-personal, affecting all tourists in an organized manner, and as moving and intense. These aspects of this definition of the term *kamtong* resonate with the term 'affect' used in Western philosophical discourses of emotion that make distinctions between feeling, emotion and affect. To dwell on affect theory would detract from the focus of the chapter, namely to explore how affect works in popular film-induced tourism and its relation to contradictory political contexts. Instead, I simply outline the fundamental conceptual elements, enough to show how an affective focus and analysis can make sense of this phenomenon of continuous touristic flows in sites of political tensions, by mobilizing Deleuze and Guattari's definition of affect by way of Brian Massumi (2002). Massumi's way of distinguishing between emotions, feelings and affect is very useful here. Emotion is differentiated from affect (or 'intensities' to use Massumi's term), in that it designates feeling given 'function and meaning':

> An emotion is a subjective content, the sociolinguistic fixing of the quality of an experience which is from that point onward defined as personal. Emotion is qualified intensity, the conventional, consensual point of insertion of intensity into semantically and semiotically formed progressions, into narrativizable action-reaction circuits, into function and meaning.
>
> (Massumi 2002: 28)

Thus, emotions are genuine or contrived feelings that conform to social convention and consensus. Feelings are personal, drawn from a set of previous experiences distinct from person to person. In contrast, affect is difficult to represent in linguistic terms and lies before and outside of consciousness, thus making it the most abstract of the three terms. According to Massumi (1996: 237), affect is 'unformed and unstructured, but is nevertheless highly organized and effectively analyzable (it is not entirely containable in knowledge, but is analyzable in effect, as effect),' that is, registered corporeally and not necessarily linguistically. Affect, then, is a bodily function, defined in the broadest sense to include the mental and ideal bodies, and arises within the energies of a particular situated context; it 'doesn't just absorb pulses or discrete stimulations; it infolds contexts' (Massumi 2002: 30). This corporeality of affect is perceived as being easily aroused, but difficult to control. Most crucially, affect determines sensation, giving feelings their intensity.

Where cultural studies scholars working on affect have often drawn from Deleuze and Guattari (1983, 1987) and Massumi (1996, 2002), Linda Williams is a critical figure in film studies of cinematic affect. While pairing these two traditions may seem odd, both share a focus on physical effects at the corporeal level, and seek to enable understandings of cultural texts and phenomena, such as film, in structured terms beyond linguistic signification. This pairing enables us to pursue an integrated analysis of film-induced tourism and film texts that seeks to specify affective characteristics in so far as they explain the complicity between film text and tour site in inducing affect in the spectator-cum-tourists in such a way that also specifies the affect occurring not only, or necessarily, between the characters onscreen and the film-induced tourists but also between the affective tourists themselves at the site.

In the following analysis, I suggest that domestic screen tourists to the sites of Hur Jin-ho's weepies in Kangwŏn Province do not necessarily seek authenticity, simulacra or proximity to celebrities, but this affective experience. By way of discourses of cinematic affect, I show how film text and tour site are complicit in producing what I call *affective tourism*. What moves the tourists and that which they seek at film locations is not content or the meaning derived from the visual, but the intense sensation and emotions acted and impinged upon the body while viewing the film, which they hope to re-embody by traversing the palpable space of film, spatially at the location. What drives affective tourism is not necessarily the successful attainment of affect, which is fundamentally abstract, but the *hope* of affect.

Body genres, cinematic affect, and affective tourism

Hur Jin-ho's *April Snow* relies on body over words, and *Spring Day* silences words in favor of sounds. This emphasis on extra-lingual and bodily expressiveness calls attention to Hur's attempt to transmit affect. Both films belong to what Linda Williams (1991) in film theorization on cinematic affect has called 'body genres' of excess. Aspects of this work, in so far as it pertains to understanding the film-induced tourist as a body and not just a gaze, are significant for the analysis of film-induced tourism. According to Williams, the three 'body genres' – horror, melodrama and pornography – are conducive to spectatorial embodiment and thus elicit a bodily response from spectators. In body genres, there is first 'the spectacle of a body caught in the grip of intense sensation or emotion.' Like the portrayal of the orgasm in pornography or of violence and terror in horror, the body spectacle is featured in melodrama through the portrayal of weeping. Second, they are marked visually by 'a quality of uncontrollable convulsion or spasm – of the body "beside itself" with sexual pleasure, fear and terror, or overpowering sadness' and aurally by 'recourse not to the coded articulations of language but to inarticulate cries of pleasure in porn, screams of fear in horror, and sobs of anguish in melodrama.' Third, they share the perception that 'the body of the spectator is caught up in an almost involuntary mimicry of the emotion or sensation of the body on the screen.' The audience lacks any 'proper aesthetic distance between the spectator and the representation' (Williams 1991: 4–5).

From the very first moment of *April Snow*, we are gripped by wordless images of the body gripped by intense sensation. In-su's heavy breathing and immobility, registering physical shock as he stands backstage at a rock music concert, is followed by Sŏ-yŏng's anxious wringing of hands while rocking catatonically. According to Eric Shouse (2005), 'every form of communication where facial expressions, respiration, tone of voice, and posture are perceptible can transmit affect,' and Hur's staged images use precisely these measures. Through a parallel development between the living characters and their comatose spouses to whom they have to tend at the hospital, Hur Jin-ho lures the spectator into the gradual process of the awakening of the characters' sensory capacity as they start an affair of their own, which occurs through a delayed mimicry of the intimate images and words of passion left behind by their cheating spouses on their cameras and on their hand phones. The comatose bodies inflict physical responses from both In-su and Sŏ-yŏng. Each scene of dating at a popular tour site is punctuated by a visit to their spouse's body, next to which they sit as they wait for some sign of life. They are in turn shocked, disgusted, and ironically, taught by the bodies. The images of their spouses on the road and in bed together, which initially cause bodily revulsion, are later mimicked by In-su and Sŏ-yŏng in their own affair. But where the bodies in the video image are experiencing pleasure and joy in each other's company, In-su and Sŏ-yŏng's relationship is mostly physical, and their mimicry of their spouses' acts lacks genuine attraction.

This repeated relationship between images depicting the feelings others have and the affect that these images have upon the viewer is not limited to the familiar images of their spouses that elicit intense feelings, but applies also to general images. In one scene, Sŏ-yŏng lies in her room flicking through TV channels, lingering a moment on a pornography channel. Turning it off, she then turns to the window where she sees In-su, and heads out seeking his company. We see her reflected in the window watching him from the room, yet the camera position has the window pane containing both of their reflections, relegating the viewer to an unsettled position that is neither inside nor outside. Captured in this space, marking the transition from the transmission of affect from the TV screen to Sŏ-yŏng to the possible transmission of affect from the film screen to the spectator, is that moment of belated cinematic affect. In a scene where In-su cleans his wife's naked body with a towel, he begins to talk to her. Where he had wished he could replace his body with hers in the beginning, he now wishes her dead. Through the affect their spouses' comatose bodies have on them, In-su and Sŏ-yŏng slowly come to realize what makes them feel. In effect, Hur's depiction of the affective relationship In-su and Sŏ-yŏng have with the images of their spouses and the visual and aural media replicates the relationship film spectators are to have with the embodied images of Hur's film.

April Snow and *Spring Day*, along with Hur's *Christmas in August*, about a terminally-ill photographer who falls in love, are sometimes referred to as a trilogy (Kim S.Y. 2005). They all experiment with lighting, sounds, and photo-imaging, respectively, as narrative vehicles and affective cinematic techniques. The tendency towards long, slow shots emphasizes the sensory expressions. In *Spring Day*, director Hur fills the space of his screen with the palpability of aurality. Throughout the film, sound recorder Yi Sang-u attunes radio producer Han Ŭn-su to the rhythms and sounds of nature, creating associations between places of nature with sound with stages in their relationship. Images of still bodies enraptured by sound stand in contrast to sounds, for example, at the Donghae bamboo forest where they stand quietly listening to the sounds of swaying leaves. Later, they go to Maengbang beach to record the lapping of waves which surround them in that moment of aural experience. Like the sound of the waves that crash then recede, their affair which seemed to weld so well in winter begins to melt, showing cracks. Before spring has passed, Sang-woo is forced to resort to his recordings to re-elicit the body memory of the emotions contained in them. Music and sounds are central to the film, and are a critical factor in impinging intense sensations upon the body. The act of conversing, on the other hand, is lingual and therefore seen either as hindering access to the more sensual sounds of nature, as in *Spring Day*, or extending awkward situations, as in *April Snow*.

By *affective sites*, I mean the destinations of screen tourism induced by melodramas, in which tourists are moved by certain film scenes to travel to the sites in hopes of recapturing, through mimicry, the bodily emotional sensations prompted by the film. This notion draws on Anne Rutherford's concept of 'affective space,' which are characterized by corporeal intensity. Not only would such space be 'inscribed with a palpable cinematic image . . . with traces of the forces that play around the body in space,' and be a site in which 'mimicry of the physical movement or a simulation of motion perspective' occurs, it would be able to 'transport, the possibility of the spectator's dissolution, or loss in the movement' (Rutherford 2003: 11). Rutherford's concept is particularly useful in understanding the relationship between cinematic affect and tourism, because unlike Williams' aesthetics of cinematic embodiment which relies 'on the presence of the human body on the screen,' Rutherford proposes an aesthetics of embodiment in which 'the tensions and dynamism of the surface of the image can effect a bodily agitation' just as well (ibid.: 5). Affective tourism, exemplified here by the *April Snow* and *Spring Day* tours, operates within a slippage between both aesthetics of cinematic embodiment, that is, with and without the body. Each site is marked by a cinematic image from the film on a sign depicting the characters caught in a moment of experience. Entering and touring the site, in which the characters are not always inscribed, thereafter becomes for the tourist a moment of mimicry of the physical movement.

Even though Hur Jin-ho's films may not be produced with the tourist enterprise in mind, they can nevertheless be said to have been imagined in touristic terms. Hur is famous for eschewing the constructed film set, opting instead for real places where, as in both *April Snow* and *Spring Day*, he barely alters the location. Filming actors in a real space, he has said, elicits distinct natural and unexpected elements enabled by that space, which he aspires to capture with his camera (Kim H.R. 2005). Hur seeks out the affective energies of a particular place. His followers have said in order to appreciate his films, one must view them not with the eyes, but with the heart (*maŭm*). The success of Hur's films depends on a critical relationship between the bodies of the actors 'infolding' the space within which they work. Furthermore, these places, selected by Hur, are intentionally not the carefully engineered urban centers or tourist sites. On the contrary, they are places like Samchŏk or Tonghe that maintain what he calls a 'junk style,' meaning that they contain the traces of time and change that a place has undergone naturally. Just as Hur expects these disembodied places to elicit certain bodily responses from the actors, so we can expect images of these sites without the bodies on screen of the characters to elicit affect from spectator-tourists.

Affect and affectation

There are three ways in which these sites arouse in a tourist the embodied affect of the spectator. First, as in the finished film product, there cannot be a differentiation between exterior and interior film locations, which can obstruct the necessary elimination of aesthetic distanciation. The affective tourism of *April Snow* and *Spring Day* works because the films are mapped almost in their entirety onto the city and/or region, and it is possible to tour most of the locations of one particular film. Film location tours in Manhattan, Hawaii, or Los Angeles, in contrast, often guide tourists to the film locations of several movies, because in most cases, although the exterior shots of the city are shot on location, the interior shots are usually filmed on sets elsewhere. Rather than seeing an exterior of a particular shot from a scene as detached from the effect of the film, film spectators here 'view' the film again on tour, reconstructing narrative and bodily traversing the cinematic space of the narrative because the movie and the emotions it conveyed is laid out across the city and region, film here acting as an emotional map. The tour is not so much of where the film was made, but rather into the world of the film itself.

The affective tourist is drawn into the scene and the moment of experience by way of a cinematic image that activates the memory of the palpable emotion and energies conveyed through the body of the depicted characters. The film *April Snow* is reproduced spatio-visually onto the city of Samchŏk by way of strategically situated maps and signs throughout the city that direct walking tourists to the various sites, which are numbered and sequenced to correspond to certain scenes and stages of emotional development in the film (Figure 8.1). The whole tour takes about three hours (a little longer than the film itself) if the tourist walks (the main characters list walking as one of their favorite activities). The entrance to each site along the tour is inscribed with a matching still from the film, as in the sign outside Somang Pharmacy (Figure 8.2). The maps and tour guides, on the other hand, present the sites as void of bodies, presenting them only structurally and spatially. For example, the Samhŭng hotel, one of the locations, is pictured on a photo in free tour maps that guide tourists from one destination to the other. Pictured in the upper right-hand corner in a photo-within-a-photo is the hallway on the second floor of the motel. Both images do not have any bodies in the photos, and depict only the place as it is. The inserted photo in the lower right-hand corner, however, is a frame captured from the film itself, picturing an intimate exchange between the two lovers that takes place in the room pictured above in the hallway.

The cinematic image corresponding to the locations and inscribed at the site is placed so that it always follows the tourist's encounter with a generic

Figure 8.1 One of many signposts for *April Snow* film sites in the city of Samchŏk (Photo by author)

photo of the location. That is, first, the spectator views the film. Second, at the filming locations, the spectator-cum-tourist reads the map and views the photos of the destinations. Third, at the destination, the tourist encounters the cinematic image that links the space to the tourist's memory of the relevant scene in the film. The sites are inscribed with the cinematic image in such a way that it evokes the particular scenes at a particular moment. For example, the hallway in the photo, as in Figure 8.3, is marked at the site with a photo of Sŏ-yŏng and In-su meeting in the hallway.

If we consider the precise location and function of the cinematic image in the film-induced tourist experience here, as well as the nature of its content, it is possible to discern a tourist experience closely linked to the experiences of cinema spectatorship. Take, for instance, the photo in Figure 8.4. A number of scenes in the film take place in room number 205, thus many parts of the room are marked with the corresponding scenes framed and hung near the relevant places, sometimes even referencing related scenes that help the tourist to make the emotional connections. The film image superimposed onto the hotel's picture on the tour map can be seen in Figure 8.3 above the window seat by the TV where the depicted scene in which In-su brushes Sŏ-yŏng hair aside and takes her hands into his takes place. Narratively, the

Figure 8.2 Somang Pharmacy (Photo by author)

scene prefigures a turning psychological point in the film – In-su and Sŏ-yŏng suddenly realize the illicitness of their relationship and the emotional pain they will potentially inflict upon each other when In-su's father-in-law suddenly knocks on the door. In-su grabs Sŏ-yŏng and shoves her into the bathroom

Figure 8.3 A scene from *April Snow* hangs in the pictured hotel hallway (Photo by author)

Figure 8.4 The hotel room (Photo by author)

to hide her. The urgency of this scene, especially after the director had just lingered on the shot of them having fruit and touching together, is agitating. The inscription of cinematic images into the bathroom space resonates with Sŏ-yŏng's initial shock and fear as the door closes on her, the relief when In-su returns after shaking off his father-in-law to help her out, and the tenderness and gratitude he expresses towards her as she forgives him. The tactility in this scene functions to produce a sense of spatiality by occurring not in the actual space but in the mirror reflection of the image. The bodily experience, it suggests, is perceivable only in the relationship between real space and image. At the site, when one looks into the tiny bathroom, the tourist's position at the doorway looks directly onto the cinematic inscription and the poster reflected in the mirror (Figure 8.5). Looking in the mirror, one might almost feel that the characters were in the bathroom as bodies, not as images on a poster. The spatiality of the two-dimensional image in which Sŏ-yŏng is doubled in the mirror, reflected again in the bathroom's real mirror, creates a three-dimensionality that 'infolds' the spectator-cum-tourist into the bathroom scene and the emotional energies it acted upon the spectator.

The bathroom scene and site in Figure 8.5 are an example of how cinematic image and site are complicit in producing a distinct film-induced tourist experience that involves the body in space, not just the gaze, in eliciting cinematic affect, or the hope of this embodied affect at the tour site. *Spring Day* is marked less obviously as the sites are natural sites set further apart from one another. However, large prints from the film can be found on the local highways with arrows pointing to the locations. The stages of Sang-u and Ŭn-su's relationship are marked by the seasons and the changes nature goes through. They meet in winter, when Ŭn-su senses the sensuality of sounds for the first time. And on one fine spring day, while at Maengbang beach recording the sounds of the waves, Sang-u suddenly realizes that the waves that hit the shoreline and recede so abruptly foreshadow his relationship with Ŭn-su.

Second, the involuntary mimicry of corporeal sensation is sought through voluntary imitation of the physical movements on-site, to the extent possible. Affect sites evoke affectation. Like the double structure of *April Snow* in which In-su and Sŏ-yŏng mimic the images of their cheating spouses, tourists mimic the movements in hopes of retrieving that body memory of the embodied affect elicited during viewing. For example, in Samchŏk, tourists can sleep in the same room, eat the same foods, sip coffee at the same table, and walk the same streets. And on the *Spring Day* tour, visitors to the bamboo forest pictured in Figures 8.6 and 8.7 at the base of the mountain go past the side of the elderly couple's house to stand in the forest, just like the characters did.

Third, embodied affect is auratized at affective sites. Samhŭng Motel's room number 205 and 210 and Palace Hotel's room number 1407 used to be available to tourists wishing to stay there. Since then, it has been closed to overnight guests, and is open for tours only. The rooms have preserved

Figure 8.5 The bathroom (Photo by author)

everything down to the clothes In-su and Sŏ-yŏng wore, to the bags they carried, even the hairspray and lotions she used in the scenes beside frame by frame images of the scenes as they played out in the room next to the precise location (Figure 8.8). The set of Somang Pharmacy, provided for the purposes of the film by the city, has also been preserved.

Figure 8.6 The bamboo forest of *One Fine Spring Day* (Photo by author)

봄날은 간다

대나무 숲 200m →

Figure 8.7 A sign marks the turn to the film location (Photo by author)

Figure 8.8 Sŏ-yŏng's coat is preserved in the same place as in the film (Photo by author)

In the case of *Spring Day*, it is conflated with religious aura, as at the Silla Koch'al Sinhŭngsa Temple in Samchŏk, where Sang-u and Ŭn-su went to record the fall of snow. This process of musealization and enshrining is counterproductive to the production of affect at tour sites, and can be seen as a sign that a film location is beginning to lose its appeal and effect as affective site.

Conclusion

By designating domestic screen tourism to *hallyu* film locations as affective tourism, I have attempted to show a different dimension to film sites that goes beyond the exclusive focus on the gaze to include the body and the way it is moved. In the interest of analyzing the potential of affective tourism induced by cinema as not merely passive response, but as somehow participating, interrogating and redefining structures of feeling in Asia, can we speak of a 'transmission of affect' occurring at such sites of cinematic affect? If we recall Massumi's (2002) definition of affect, he defined it not only as the ability to affect, but also to be affected. One body's experiential state can be passed to another, inducing that body's capacity to act. His notion of *affection* is closely related to the transmission of affect and refers to the state when the affected body encounters a second affecting body and a transmission process of 'infolding intensities' occurs. This transmission of affect can occur because affect, unlike feeling and emotion, is unformed, unstructured, and ubiquitous. If we consider these sites as affective sites, where the hope of re-experiencing affect motivates tourists to seek the destinations, perhaps it is not too far-fetched to suggest that a transmission of affect may occur at these film-induced sites. In terms of film-induced tourism as a potential mode for resisting dominant political hostilities and promoting reconciliation, an empirical study assessing the relationship between film-induced tourists from various locations at such sites removed from political hostilities would be beneficial.

Clearly, further empirical research would complement the argument for a politically relevant transmission of affect occurring at film-induced sites. This empirical research might methodically assess the emotional experiences of tourists specifically as it relates to their prior experiences as film spectators of the particular films, as well as their political views. In this study, I have focused primarily on conceptualizing affective tourism through a study of melodramatic film-induced tour sites and on broadening existing categories and methodologies in film-induced tourism to consider more closely the intricate associations with the filmic experience. Other factors that have emerged during the course of this study but merited further study outside of the scope of this brief chapter are the ways in which Asian celebrity fan culture and related tourism would differ from that in non-Asian countries, as well as the role of gender in Asian film-induced tourism. Last but not least, the study focuses on Korean and Asian tourists to an Asian site, but it should be acknowledged that any study of widespread 'Asian' cultural phenomena can only be but a contribution to a larger picture and that studies that approach the examined phenomena from positions of expertise situated elsewhere in Asia would be beneficial.

9 Renewing bonds in an age of Asian travel

Indian tourists in Bali

K. Thirumaran

Introduction

The rise of Indian tourists in Southeast Asia raises new perspectives on travel choices and destination attractions in Asia. Today Indian tourism is revitalizing bonds established many centuries ago. This chapter examines Indian tourism in Bali in order to question the 'exotic-difference' paradigm and its applicability to Asians on tour. In this regard, the chapter explores Indian tourists as a case where affinity appears as a key factor in the practices of Indian tourists. An understanding of the choices Indian tourists make in terms of attractions allows us to conceive an alternative view to the exotic-attraction paradigm. Accordingly, the chapter considers specific choices of Indian tourists in Bali as a way to think about consumption of the familiar or shared heritage, and how this may tell us about tourism experiences that deviate from the more common cases involving unique or different experiences. To date, Bali has been a popular destination for Australians, Americans and Europeans. A recent increase in the number of Hindu Indians traveling to the island, however, alerts us to the different dynamics and encounters. As we shall see, for the Indian visitor the exotic paradigm is less relevant than a sense of 'cultural affinity,' which occurs between the visitor and the travel destination.

Tracing the exotic

The field of tourism studies has a long tradition of understanding other places and cultures in terms of difference and the exotic. Scholars such as Urry (1990), Boniface (1995), Yamashita, Din and Eades (1997), Rojek (1998), Brown (2000), Franklin (2003), Bochner (2003), and Hall and Tucker (2004) all consider tourism in relation to the search for 'otherness' or 'difference.' For example, Chang and Huang (2004: 223) suggest that 'tourists are lured by distinctive cultures and sceneries' and destination areas accentuate 'local uniqueness' for this very purpose. In the marketing of places like Bali as 'paradise on earth' or 'the exotic east,' we see confirmation of Chang and Huang's analysis. Bruner (1995: 224) goes further: 'tourism thrives on differences; why should the tourists travel thousands of miles and spend thousands of dollars to view a third world culture essentially similar to their own?' Bruner considers difference as a key to the motivation for traveling from the 'first to third world.' Only a decade later did he partially alter this account and acknowledge that familiarity plays a role in touristic consumption (Bruner 2005: 10). To this end, he studies Tobak Bataks visiting Taman Mini and gazing at Tobak Batak house replicas, and American tourists visiting Abraham Lincoln's heritage site in New Salem who 'reinforce their own sense of American history,' so Bruner (2005: 11) claims, 'difference and similarity depend on position and perspective.' That is, individuals on domestic travel may indulge in the similar and familiar. However, as we can see, Bruner's study is limited to domestic tourism.

In contrast, Western scholarship on Bali continues to discuss the island as an exotic place with a strong focus on the idealization of paradise. This is understandable because historical encounters between Europe and the island have been instrumental in forging a limited number of themes and narratives, as evidenced in a number of early travel writings. According to Howe (2005: 26), by 1914, tourist brochures were promoting Bali as a 'gem of the Lesser Sunda Isles.' At this time, as Picard (1996b) points out, the initial guidebooks did not mention anything about dance as an attraction. Until the 1930s, Bali was still in its nascent stage of tourism development, a situation that contrasted with the far more popular island of Java. As part of his study on the history of tourism in Bali, Vickers (1989: 98) calls this period an 'era of bare breasts,' where Western men were most interested in Balinese women. Bali gradually became a romantic stop as the 'dancing girl images' (ibid.) of the performances gained worldwide publicity. Rickover (1975: 4) writes, 'at issue was the exposed upper half of the Balinese women which the government and KPM wished to keep that way in the interest of the tourist trade.' In other words, during a period of Dutch colonization Bali became synonymous with notions of landscape beauty, religious traditions and sexuality (Powell 1921; Belfrage 1937; Rickover 1975; Baranay 1994; Shavit 2003). Gorer, an anthropologist, for example, expressed his deep admiration for Bali: 'I left wholly unwillingly, convinced that I had seen the nearest approach to Utopia that I am ever likely to see' (1936: 52). Academics like Margaret Mead, Geoffrey Bateson and the famous German painter Walter Spies, inventor of the *Kecak* dance, and many others who visited Bali were also 'wowed' by the images and cultural practices they saw. This created both excitement and interest in Bali and inspired others to travel in search of the 'exotic paradise' with its 'charming' Hindu practices.

Travel exhibitions overseas, news feature articles and word of mouth all exposed potential travelers to Bali's exotic feel (Prunieres 1931; McPhee 1946; Belo 1970). Prunieres (1931: 8) was very impressed with the Balinese traveling dance-drama troupes composed of amateurs, remarking that 'we have still a great deal to learn about the ancient Asiatic civilizations, and if we can rid ourselves of prejudice, we can obtain from them artistic experiences of a rare quality.' In other words, Westerners still considered these performances spectacular and exotic but lacking civilized value in terms of their art form. In addition, Western movies, American cruise ship stops and the colonial exposition held in 1931 all added Bali to the list of desirable travel spots (Morand 1932; Covarrubias 1937). Films like *The Isle of Paradise* (1932) produced by Charles Tillyer Trego and *Man's Paradise* (1938) by Grace Goodhue Huntington further elevated Bali's heavenly status (Shavit 2003).

As Vickers (1989), Howe (2005) and others have shown, these framings and themes remain entrenched, and continue to shape how the island is represented and marketed as a tourism destination today. For the European, Australian and American tourist industries, Bali remains the quintessential exotic, and idyllic lost paradise. An analysis of Indian tourism, however, forces us to head in different directions. As tourism from India to Southeast Asia grows, it is becoming increasingly apparent that heritage sites offer a major attraction. But as we shall see, to understand this phenomenon, we have to look towards ideas of shared heritage, and cultural familiarity, rather than the exotic other.

Historical ties

To better understand the dynamics of Indian tourism in Bali today we need to situate it within its wider historical context. The two countries of Indonesia and India have had ties dating as far back as the height of the Chola kingdom in India (seventh to thirteenth centuries) and the Srivijaya Empire of Southeast Asia (ninth to thirteenth centuries). However, the first signs of Indian and Hindu influence in Southeast Asia have been traced back to the first century (Holt 1967). Colonization, intermarriage between Indian and local royalties, trade settlements and the widespread use of Sanskrit are some of the factors highlighted when tracing the early spread of Hinduism across the Indonesian archipelago (Basham 1959; Holt 1967; Leur 1967; Yadav 2004). At the beginning of the twentieth century, ties between Bali and India were strengthened once again through the establishment of a Dutch colonial territory. The Dutch government in the 1920s pursued a systematic policy of 'rebalinization' by officially reinstituting the princes and eventually recognizing them as *rajahs*, or kings, in 1938 (Picard 1999: 21). To protect and preserve Balinese Hinduism, the colonial policy aimed to contain Javanese Islam and Christian proselytization in Bali (Picard 1999; Ramstedt 2004a; Howe 2005). At this time, Balinese intellectuals also established contact with Indian centers of learning and worship.

Further contact came with the formation of the Indonesian state in 1947. Because the national constitution recognized only three main religions – Islam, Catholicism and Protestantism – those not adhering to these religions were considered 'heathens' and subject to conversion by officially recognized religious organizations (Ramstedt 2004a). Reacting to the possible loss of local religious traditions, the Balinese provincial government in 1952 declared itself as an 'autonomous religious area.' In 1962, the Indonesian state recognized Hinduism as an official religion after Balinese intellectuals and the religious order made vigorous attempts to textualize and consolidate Balinese Hinduism into a form similar to that of Indian Hinduism through the standardization of rituals and religious books. Nonetheless, Picard (1999) and Widana (2001) argue that *Agama Hindu Bali* (Balinese Hinduism) is not an equivalent to Hinduism as practiced in India. According to Widana (2001), even though both entities share the same source of Vedas, rituals and many celebrations follow local Balinese customs and practices.

In recent times, a variety of economic and political developments have ensured such ties are sustained between the Balinese (and Indonesians at large) and India. In India, the government has pursued a series of policies which have helped foster a burgeoning middle class that is interested in traveling (*The Times of India* 2004). The rise of Hindu nationalism in India has also added the idea that the cultures of East and Southeast Asia represent an extension of Indian culture (Ramstedt 2004b). The Balinese themselves have also responded to such developments in India, recognizing the new political climate and economic outlook in Indian national thought. Accordingly, in October 2004, a new era of official relations between the two commenced with the opening of the India Cultural Centre in the heart of Bali's capital, Denpasar. Modern travel connections, the establishment of numerous Hindu organizations of Indian origins and the many religious dialogues that take place among Balinese themselves create awareness of India as a source of their religion. From the élites of Balinese society consisting of priests and officials to ordinary people, there exists an awareness of India's religious and philosophical contribution to their religion. In this brief historical overview, then, it is evident that the links between Bali and India are long and complex. Crucially though, and as we shall see shortly, these cultural, political, religious and trade histories continue to inform and shape Indian tourism to the island today.

Indian tourists in Bali

When referring to the flow of Indian tourists, the annual handbook on Balinese tourism (Dinas Pariwisata Provinsi Bali 2004: 9) reads, 'the cultural similarity to Bali (Hinduism) needs to be paid attention to.' Aside from their interest in buying souvenirs and making commercial purchases, the Indian tourists are also interested in Balinese heritage, that part which is common (ibid.). This reference to 'cultural similarity' between Indians and Balinese is a bold public admission by a tourism authority that normally emphasizes uniqueness and distinction to tourists-generating markets.

When traveling to Bali, upon arrival, Indians receive a visa for three days for US$10 and for 30 days for US$25. The peak periods of Indian tourists are from May to September and December. The flow of Indian tourists into Bali has steadily increased in the past decade. Exceptions here include the years 2002 and 2003 when the Bali bombing and Severe Acute Respiratory Sickness (SARS) had a tremendous impact on tourist arrivals to Indonesia and Southeast Asia as a whole (*The Straits Times* 2004). In 1999, almost 4,000 Indian tourists traveled to the island, with this figure rising to almost 7,000 by 2005. But a combination of factors, including Balinese promotions and a new visa upon arrival policy, helped the arrivals figure exceed 10,000 in 2006 (Dinas Pariwisata Provinsi Bali 2004).

A variety of factors have contributed to this growth. In part, it is due to the annual marketing efforts by the Balinese Tourism Office's Indian missions, an expanding industry connection between Balinese and Indian travel agents and the increasing number of flights between the 'stop-over' cities of Singapore, Bangkok and Kuala Lumpur. Previously, many Indian tourists have not traveled to Bali as a popular destination mainly due to a lack of information and the poor visibility of the Balinese tourism industry in India (Yadav 2004). Only recently have representatives from the Balinese tourism industry begun regular marketing tours, bringing along their cultural dance-drama troupes to help sell Bali and popularize the island. In India, travel agents market Bali as part of a multi-stop destination, with trips often including destinations in Singapore, Malaysia, Thailand, and Indonesia. The profile of Indian tourists visiting Bali is various; characterized as family, groups and honeymoon couples. Among these travelers, the majority are Hindus and mostly vegetarians. Against an average tourist length of stay in Bali of 10 days, Indian tourists stay around 6 days, somewhat higher than Indonesia's national average (excluding Bali) of 4.2 days. Indian tourists spend about Indonesian Rupiah (Rp) 475,000 per day; an amount slightly more than half of the total average of Rp800,000 per tourist expenditure in 2004 (Dinas Pariwisata Provinsi Bali 2004: 51, 53). It is relatively common for tourists to pre-arrange their itinerary. In such cases, requests are made for Indian food, often vegetarian, temple tours and a cultural performance or two.

Shared heritage and bonds

In order to show the significance of affinities and the gravitation to attractions that are familiar or similar, I examine the relationship of the tourists and host at the point of consumption to draw a sense of a shared Indian, Hindu heritage. In addition to looking at language, temple practices and styles of worship, I consider the performance and consumption of dance-dramas. There are three key reasons for approaching the subject through dance-dramas. First, dance performances often reflect the color, vibrancy, tradition and values of a culture. In Bali, some cultural performances for tourists resemble India's own cultural practices while there are others that have a strong local Balinese content. Second, these scheduled performances require prior planning and commitment by the audience-tourists. As a site of research, they offer a high degree of predictability and reliability. Third, there are normally a number of performances to choose from in a given day. Given that only some of the titles of these performances contain words that allude to an Indian/Hindu heritage, it is apparent that particular choices are being made. Thus, the attendances of Indian tourists at performance sites with Hinduistic themes suggest specific cultural gravitations, planning and alternative choice considerations.

It is generally safe to assume that Indian tourists have at least a rudimentary knowledge of the epics in *Mahabharata* and *Ramayana*. These two words alone are familiar to most Indians. Therefore, performances such as *Legong Mahabharata* and *Kecak Dance* with *Ramayana* themes provide a reference to an Indian and Hindu heritage as much as a Balinese one. Whereas, although performances with titles like *Barong* or *Lion Dance* may also carry local Balinese themes or themes of Indian origins as well, their names conceal their Hindu links, meaning that tourists have no way of telling anything about such origins prior to the performance.

In some Balinese dance-dramas for tourists, for example, in the *Ramayana Ballet* performance, the storyline is similar to those performed in India. *Rahwana* kidnaps *Rama*'s consort, *Sita*. *Rama*, with the help of the Monkey God, helps secure *Sita* and kills *Rahwana* – a triumph of good over evil. But of course this dance performance has its own Balinese uniqueness. The dance performance presented for tourists does not contain only an entertainment value to Indians. Such performances have wider religious and cultural meanings. The dance styles and choreography may vary but the general storyline and representations of them provide the solid structures of recognition to the Indian audiences present. A few of those interviewed did mention that the eye movements in the *Legong of Mahabharata* were very similar to *Kathakali* and *Bharatnatyam* but emphasized that this was an impression rather than an expert's opinion. All the Indian audiences I interviewed indicated that the name of the show was what attracted them to the performance. The two performances were full of gestures and of these, the hand gestures, or *mudras*, were most prominent to those I interviewed. Movements and their meanings in dance-dramas are not new to Indian tourists. To many Indians, such movements are a norm that is easily interpretable and understood, given that Indian dances and dramas are full of gestures coded with meanings. The Balinese music and gestures often include brief narratives in Balinese. It is common for this narrative to be inaudible or unclear. Like the Indian art of dance-drama, Balinese performances typically involve the whole body for codified messages. Many of the Balinese dance-drama performances consist of *mudras* in the classical traditions of Indian dances such as *Kathakali* and *Bharatnatyam* (see also Zoete and Spies 1970). Another dance style from Orissa is called the *Tribhanga* position (three bands). In this position, the performer adopts an 'S' curve as shown in Figure 9.1. The dance styles shares another similar feature to a performance called *Odissi*, which is also found in temple rituals in Orissa (Kolanad 2005).

Beyond the dance-dramas or stories, it is difficult to judge whether the setting has much to do with cultural similarity or familiarity. The backdrop

Figure 9.1 Balinese dancer in 'S' like position in a *Ramayana* ballet (Photo by author)

of the stage is normally an ancient temple complex or palace, which in itself radiates a magnificent scheme of antiquity and shades of darkness set in an ambience of modern, strategically placed lighting. As the performing troupes take position at the gamelan instruments, a priest or a senior member of the troupe sprinkles water and flowers over the stage in a traditional ritual blessing. The gong signals and the performance begins with the group of dancers smiling in two rows as they make an entrance to tell the tale of *Ramayana*. The costumes are well pressed and vibrant in colors, and the movement of eyes and body are intended to captivate the audience. In another performance, at the Pura Dalem located in the village of Ubud, a full moon overhead helps create a highly evocative atmosphere in the grounds of a temple. Carvings of Balinese gargoyles and statutes further contribute to the aura of a ritual dance that may entail human sacrifice. But it was not to be that way; the *Kecak* dance is an almost non-stop chanting of a ritual performance of the *Ramayana* epic. With over 50 topless men chanting 'Kecak-Kecak-Kecak' endlessly, the performance seems both ancient and real.

When it comes to selecting a cultural performance, the words *Ramayana* or *Mahabharata* resonate well. This is more than just a choice of convenience when there are opportunities for attending other performances, including the *Rangda-Barong* dance, which relates to a fight between a prince and demonic lion. The choice is clear as one Indian tourist, Lal Patel who was traveling with his new bride, explained:

> It would be good to know what these people here know about our traditions. I have been told by my travel agent in India about Bali being a Hindu place, but I came to learn about this particular performance here only . . . I wanted to see how they tell the story and the evening suited our schedule.

At one of the temples, I interviewed an elderly gentleman and his family of four who were touring Tanah Lot. A retiree from the state of Tamil Nadu, Jayaram was on his first overseas trip. As someone who is very familiar with the Hindu traditions, and in particular the *Ramayana* and *Mahabharata* epics he remarked:

> We have not attended the performances yet. Maybe you could recommend to us . . . ya, ya, my wife and daughters thought that we should either watch the *Legong Mahabharata* or the one with the furry lion dance [a reference to the Barong Dance] . . . if we choose to go to the *Mahabharata*, I hope my daughters don't fall asleep . . . it could be too boring for them . . . they have seen it before in India . . . ya, ya, we have this at home too, this is all from India.

At this point, his elder daughter, Santhini interjected: 'But it may be different here since it is only a short show.'

In a subsequent conversation, Santhini responded that her family had visited the Barong performance due to schedule and the risk of rain. They missed the *Legong Mahabharata* because it had rained the night of the performance, and as a result they opted for the Barong dance held the following day. Their choices suggest a preference for attending cultural performances with a story line that is familiar to them. Similarly, a woman in her mid-forties, traveling with an American female companion, claimed that she was attracted to the performances despite regularly turning off *Ramayana* performance shows that are broadcast on Indian television. She explained that she has been familiar with the story since she was 5 years old, as her mother told her stories and she has watched it countless times on television. Born in Rajasthan, Punjam said that she was thus 'curious' about how Balinese dances would interpret their Hindu themes:

> After all, what is visiting Bali without witnessing at least a cultural performance? . . . I chose this *Kecak* performance because I heard from the hotelier that this is an all-man performance (laughing) . . . but no . . . truly because of the storyline . . . well, I am familiar . . . I want to see whether it is the same as in India. After all, it is only two hours or less, in India the stage performances could go on and on and on.

She also added that she could better relate the familiar story to her American friend traveling with her. Summarizing how she felt seeing the performance, she explained:

> I never expected this performance to be so beautiful with the men chanting 'Kecak Kecak' all the way. The story of *Rama* and *Sita*'s rescue from the *Rahwana* is quite similar to ours. I was thinking about our formats of presentation and theirs. This is different and may be more exciting but didn't quite understand the words they used in this performance, I wish I did . . . I love it.

Similar sentiments of familiarity, yet confusion, were expressed by further interviewees. Having watched a *Kecak* dance, Meesha recounts:

> Yeah, I liked the performance . . . had a little difficulty understanding the play but soon figured out the story as I related it to my experiences of watching Indian *Ramayanas*. I had read previously from the program brochure and knew that this story was about *Ramayana*. But the costuming and music are a bit different. So, I initially could not quite figure it who was the *Krishna* and his consort . . . but was able to follow as the drama unfolded. Well, you can say that I am happy and proud that the people here follow our traditions in their art and culture. I see that they do it in their own ways also.

I would thus suggest that, in Bali, religion offers a medium through which the Balinese and Indian visitors culturally interface, and where performances of *Mahabharata* and *Ramayana* are concerned, an emotion of shared heritage validates the attraction. In those fleeting moments of looks and gazes, an exchange beyond monetary transaction takes place. At the height of such a moment, there exists meanings and emotions that transpire between the performers and guest. For Indian tourists, the Balinese dance-dramas communicate history, religion and a shared history.

Indian visitors feel a sense of pride and comfort that their 'national' culture has spread geographically and has long been appreciated by the Balinese people. For the Balinese musicians and performers, there is an emotional connection with an Indian audience that is different from other audiences. As two performers explained:

> Indian tourists normally approach us after the shows. They talk to us. We like to take pictures with them and have them send to us. They are our brothers and sisters. I want to exchange views and experiences about our religion . . . We also like to talk to Australian tourists and Japanese tourists. But Indian tourists share our same religion with us, so I feel special because they know our Gods. Our ancestors had connections to India and to see them visiting Bali makes us feel

happy because they are interested in our Hindu culture and they are my brothers.

(Interview with Suarka, December 2004)

Yes, some of our performances have India Hindu stories and dance styles. We would like to have chances to exchange dance styles with Indian groups if have the opportunity. These days there are indeed many Indian tourists who see our performances. They take a lot of pictures and once in a while they come to us to talk about the story or style . . . here are two name cards they gave me.

(Interview with Sujapta, January 2005)

In other words, Balinese performers feel a special affinity with the Indian tourists because of their common religion and an awareness of a long-standing relationship between the Balinese and India. There is also a keen sense that Indian tourists are part of their larger community of families, as many of them interviewed also referred to Indians as 'brothers' and 'sisters.' The interest and idea that Indian dance styles can be learned and exchanged through cross-country visitations adds to the suggestion that Balinese share a deep affinity and gravitations towards Indian culture. Equally, the fact that Indian tourists connect with the Balinese to discuss their religion and attend a cultural performance with which they are already familiar is an indication of the interest of the visitor as much as the host. The Balinese view of the Indian tourists is not so much as the 'other,' but more as 'one of us.'

Conclusion: thinking of bonds

The ongoing rise of Asia, and the resultant generation of a class of affluent travelers are creating a new wave of interactions within the region. This chapter has examined the premise of an exotic paradigm against the idea of tourists traveling to destinations where similar or familiar sights connect tourists to the place and people. Instead of using the traditional analytical context of seeking differences and uniqueness in terms of cultures of the other, I have looked at the similar and familiar as a motivating force for travel. This paradigm helps us to learn about Asians on tour derived from a perspective that emerges from the way places and culture are consumed, particularly where visitors and hosts share some common cultural traits. Adopting such a paradigm in the context of Bali reveals how dance performances with themes drawn from the Indian religious epics resonate strongly with Indian tourists. Despite being familiar with the stories, they were drawn to watch the performance.

As we have seen, Bali has been in the Hindu axis for many centuries and has preserved many of the traditions and beliefs that originated from India. These Hindu practices, as manifested in dance performances, bear a close resemblance to a contemporary Indian culture that is quite familiar to the Indian tourists visiting Bali. This eclectic exchange between the hosts and guests creates meaningful encounters between audience and performer. Embedded in these encounters are deep-seated emotions of pride and a sense of connectedness. In this sense, today's tourism is renewing lingering ideas of an ancient cultural and religious bond.

Naturally, Indians are not the only tourists who may gravitate to cultural performances that have familiar themes in an overseas destination. Further research will no doubt highlight other examples of encounters based on shared heritage and cultural familiarity in Asia. Such research reminds us then that the pull of specific attractions in a destination is not necessarily premised on the exotic-difference paradigm but may be based on affinities. I would suggest that a bond that speaks of shared heritage among Asians from different countries will undoubtedly be an engine of tourism growth across the region in the future.

10 Ayurvedic tourism in Kerala

Local identities and global markets

Denise Spitzer

Introduction

Global ethnoscapes, the flow of ideas, people and material between different parts of the globe that characterize transnational passages in our contemporary world allow for the creation of hybrid and syncretic forms of knowledge as well as the shaping of desires marked by 'authentic' identities (Appadurai 1996). Within this mélange of crossings, former colonies have seized opportunities to redefine their pasts and recreate national futures.

Tourism, one of the largest industries in the world (Wood 1997), serves as a major field where national and local identities can be played out, played upon and projected to a global audience. The state has often been engaged in working with or building on the efforts of tourist professionals to create enticing images and products for the tourist gaze (Reid 2003; Mathew 2004). As Harrison (2003: 185) notes, tourists seek to 'visit places still connected to an imagined past, a purer time, before other tourists got there, and somehow outside time-space compression.'

Growing interest in cultural tourism where visitors are guaranteed exposure to the exotic other has been taken up by many countries who must both provide a sufficiently culturally distant experience for the cultural tourist in search of 'authenticity' as well as adequately familiar surroundings in which to enjoy them. While this form of tourism can reinforce cultural boundaries and an essentialized, Orientalist view of the other, the presence of tourists seeking these experiences can be read by the local populace as evidence of their success in retaining their authentic cultural identity (Wood 1997). Cultural tourism is predicated also on the view that culture is quite literally grounded in territory such that people are required to be transported to another place to experience 'difference.' This localization of culture invariably ignores both cultural diversity and transnational border crossings that trouble the notion of indisputable boundaries and the dichotomies of 'us' and 'other' (Gupta and Ferguson 1997). Under conditions of globalization, the boundaries of nation–states that have given way to de-territorialized flows allow for the reconfiguration of notions of space and give rise to new power differentials and to variant identities (Berking 2003). In this chapter, I examine the ways in which Ayurveda, a South Asian medical tradition, is being deployed by stakeholders of Asian origin as an identity marker of the Indian nation–state and as an economic, symbolic and socially charged tourist activity in the context of globalization.

Tourism in India

In 2002, 2.2 million foreigners visited India; those numbers increased by 20 percent the following year (Mathew 2004). Tourist literature produced by the Indian government portrays India as a country rooted in tradition yet sufficiently modern to offer Western-style amenities (Bandyopadhyay and Morais 2005). Additional images of Indian society as a place of ancient mysteries where transformation can take place through personal enlightenment or healing are offered up for those interested in pursuing a personal as well as physical journey.

Ayurveda, one of the major medical traditions of the subcontinent, is employed as a key element in the construction of India's postcolonial identity and as a cornerstone of its tourism market. Ayurvedic tourism is being marketed as part of the worldwide explosion in health tourism spurred on by global trends including aging populations, high rates of stress and increased interest in health and self-care, particularly among more affluent sectors of society (Messerli and Oyama 2004). Ayurvedic tourism attracts Westerners exploring the ancient art and science of the exotic other as well as citizens of Southeast Asia, West Asia, and members of the global South Asian diaspora of 20 million persons who reside in 70 countries (Sahoo 2006). In the southwestern Indian state of Kerala, Ayurvedic tourists also visit from northern regions of the country.

Tourist literature describes Ayurveda as a gentle system of holistic healing that is grounded in centuries-old tradition while evincing a modern and professionalized stance supported by scientific research and grounded in the rigorous training of practitioners at officially recognized Ayurvedic colleges. This dual representation of Ayurveda within the context of tradition and modernity may be regarded a way in which Ayurvedic practitioners have responded to postcolonialism and globalization.

The study

I undertook fieldwork from January to April 2005 throughout the state of Kerala on the southwestern coast of India to explore the practices, meanings and representations of Ayurveda with Ayurvedic physicians who work with foreign clientele, entrepreneurs who foster health tourism, and foreigners who have sought out Ayurvedic treatment in India. Using standard anthropological methods, I engaged in participant observation and conducted semi-structured interviews with 18 Ayurvedic physicians, five professors of Ayurvedic medicine, two resort owners and 12 foreigners who were in-patients at various Ayurvedic treatment facilities in the state. After consent was obtained from informants, interviews were taped and transcribed verbatim and subject to content and theme analysis. For the purposes of this chapter, I focus on the responses of informants of Asian origin.

Ayurveda: a brief overview

Ayurveda has existed in South Asia for thousands of years. Grounded in Hinduism and Vedic texts dating back 3,500 years or more, Ayurveda, literally knowledge or science of life, represents a sophisticated system of healing that offers a holistic approach to living based on the balance and nurturance of mind, body and spirit (Shroff 2000; Gaur 2002). Within the world-view of Ayurveda, human beings are comprised of *panchamahabuta* (five elements) – earth, air, water, fire, and ether – that combine to form seven tissues or *dhatus* that are further nourished by food (Sundar 1998; Shroff 2000; Gaur 2002). As a person is comprised of the same elements as the universe, the relationships between individuals and their environments are embodied in both physical (Zimmerman 1988; Trawick 1995) and social landscapes such that Ayurveda has a role to play not only in healing and maintaining balance at the level of the self and the physical environment, but the body politic as well (Nordstrom 1989). The five elements also combine to form three *doshas* – *vata*, *pitta* and *kapha* – regarded as the embodiment of wind, fire and rain. A person's *dosha* profile, *prakruthi* (literally 'natural or original form') is established at birth and determines an individual's constitution (Sundar 1998). Ideally treatments – the form of which is related to its mode of activity (Bannerjee 2002) – are uniquely devised for each individual. The focus on individuality and the attention to the patient's relationship to the environment foster a unique relationship between patients and practitioners. Ayurvedic physicians, *vaidyas*, and their patients are bonded through a shared world-view and moral code that is medico-religious in nature (Nichter 1996a).

After over a century of deliberate marginalization and repression by colonial powers (Langford 2002), the Indian independence movement became interested in reinvigorating the status and practice of Ayurveda (Shroff 2000). Although Gandhi himself was relatively unenthusiastic about Ayurvedic medicine, his focus on diet and frequent fasts, similarly recommended in Ayurveda, linked bodily discipline and health measures with nationalism (Alter 2000). In recent years this association of health and nationalism has been reinforced as the recovery of Ayurvedic knowledge and practice is seen as the recovery of 'Indian culture' (Shroff 2000). An increasing number of Indians have been turning or returning to Ayurveda, particularly older persons and Hindu revivalists who, believing Ayurveda to have been passed on through a pantheon of Hindu gods to celestial physicians (Dash 1999), have encouraged the uptake and retention of Ayurveda as a political project. Indeed, some employ 'Ayurvedic medicine as a means of an identity reconstruction which entails the embodiment of "Hindu" values' (Nichter 1981, cited in Nichter 1996b: 212).

Ayurvedic medical companies are expanding their consumer base from among the rural poor to include increasing numbers of urban wage earners who value indigenous knowledge and are influenced by the holistic health movement imported from the West (Jordan 1999; Bannerjee 2002). Fully three-quarters of the Indian population is reported to use Ayurvedic medicine if even occasionally and the demand for Ayurvedic products is increasing (Jordan 1999).

While the legacy of colonial education and its disdain for indigenous knowledge lingers (Sharma 2001), the government relies on the tropes of both tradition and modernity to lend support to Ayurveda and other healing traditions. They established a department for Indian Systems of Medicine and Homeopathy, known as Ayush (Ayurveda, Yoga, Unani, Sidha, and Homeopathy), whose mandate is to promote indigenous medicines, grant approval to pharmaceutical companies to extract, test and market drugs based on traditional knowledge (Kumars 1999) and establish laboratories to evaluate the efficacy and safety of Ayurvedic medicine (Patwardhan *et al.* 2005). Firms which position themselves as 'modern companies selling tradition' are expanding their product lines to include a growing number of personal care products which they claim are influenced by traditional formulations (Bannerjee 2002). While there is a concerted effort to capitalize on India's medicinal heritage by standardizing and manufacturing herbal products for export, problems with adulterated products and mishandling of plant materials have contributed to a loss of consumer trust and subsequent decline in sales in the herbal pharmaceutical industry (Dubey *et al.* 2004).

Ayurvedic tourism in Kerala

The migration of Indian workers, many from Kerala, to the Gulf region (Osella and Osella 2000), the escalating interest in Ayurveda in the West due to the popularity of New Age gurus such as the Maharishi Mahesh Yogi and Deepak Chopra (Baer 2003), its association with Indian nationalism, and the willingness of the government to support such enterprises, have contributed to the intensified growth of an Ayurvedic industry. Ayurvedic pharmaceutical shops and clinics have opened up to serve diasporic communities in a number of countries (Shyam 2004) and clinics throughout South Asia have developed residential health resort programs to offer overseas clients and those from northern India, treatment in comfortable (and often costly) settings (Johnson 2002).

The southern Indian state of Kerala has become a popular destination for both Indian and foreign tourists interested in partaking in Ayurvedic treatments for either rejuvenation or the treatment of a serious ailment. The state is renowned for its high level of health and social indicators that rival many other developed countries (Osella and Osella 2000). Investment in healthcare and education, public distribution of housing and food, and the implementation of land reform have all helped improve the standard of living for many of Kerala's 32 million inhabitants – although not uniformly so (Osella and Osella 2000; Nabae 2003). Its largely literate population has benefited from a series of state governments that have invested in education, healthcare and indigenous knowledge (Sankar 2001; Menon 2004). Since the late 1800s, the ruling class in the region have supported Ayurveda both as a cornerstone of health and wellness and as a practice that could transcend caste and community boundaries. In 1917, a government department of Ayurvedic medicine was established along with Ayurvedic medical schools (Nair 2001; Jeffrey 2003). In addition, local maharajahs made healthcare, which included biomedicine, homeopathy and Ayurveda, a priority for the populace (Nabae 2003). Ayurveda remains a popular choice among Kerala families for many health conditions and is, therefore a stronghold of Ayurvedic practice in India (Kurup 2004) as further evidenced by the Ayurvedic clinics and hospitals that in some regions outnumber biomedical facilities (Sankar 2001).

As Kerala's economy began to decline in the 1990s, it turned to tourism and the marketing of Kerala as 'God's Own Country' (Sreekumar and Parayil 2002). The state spent Rs742 million (approximately US$18.8 million) in 2003–4 on its tourism campaign and Ayurvedic tourism is now reported to account for almost 40 percent of its tourism revenues (Neogi 2004). By 2012, health tourism is estimated to contribute US$1 billion to the Indian economy (Messerli and Oyama 2004). Tourists generally seek help at bona fide clinics; however, there are concerns about unscrupulous individuals and organizations who offer Ayurvedic treatment without qualified personnel and who leave unwitting clients with the impression that massage with warm oil constitutes Ayurveda in its totality (Mathew 2004).

Despite its economic benefits, Ayurvedic tourism poses a variety of challenges to the various stakeholders who are engaged in both Ayurvedic practice and the tourism industry. I explored the perspectives of resort managers, professors at Ayurvedic medical schools, tourists availing themselves of Ayurvedic treatment, and Ayurvedic practitioners treating foreign patients in a variety of settings from state and private hospitals to clinics and resorts. What emerges in this examination is a highly charged debate about the meaning of Ayurvedic medicine, its grounding in local conditions and its place in a globalized world, that has raised questions regarding its suitability for export, its relevance to the South Asian diaspora, the commodification of traditional knowledge, and the impact of increased demand on human and botanical resources, among others.

Marketing Ayurvedic tourism in a global world

State officials working with private industry have shaped the growth of Ayurvedic tourism and supported its marketing to regional, national and international audiences. The owners and managers of resorts who offer

Ayurvedic treatment packages are vital players in the Ayurvedic tourism industry responsible for establishing the parameters of Ayurvedic care in their facilities, from the quality of the infrastructure, the hiring and supervision of personnel, to establishing prices and selecting their market audience. Ayurvedic tourism is regarded as way of promoting economic growth by highlighting the living heritage of India. Resort managers emphasized their own allegiance to Ayurvedic medicine as Keralites who grew up using or at minimum respecting Ayurveda as part of the Indian, but, more importantly, a Kerala legacy. While distancing themselves from unscrupulous and unregulated facilities that they viewed as harming its reputation, resort managers regarded their efforts to market Ayurveda as beneficial to the physical, mental and spiritual health of their clients as well as the financial health of resort owners and others who benefit from the tourism industry.

Resort personnel tapped into a worldwide interest in holistic medicine spurred on by a growing distrust of biomedicine that produced too many untoward effects and offered little resolution to chronic problems. Ayurvedic packages that focused on stress reduction, rejuvenation, skin treatment and weight loss were marketed in major tourism exhibitions worldwide. Resorts which offered a range of Ayurvedic treatments marketed therapeutic programs to individuals who wished to undergo prolonged treatment for specific complaints in a more comfortable environment than could be found in an austere hospital setting. Dr Bhaskaran (all informants are pseudonyms) who operates a well-respected and popular clinic with a variety of clientele that include Indians, non-resident Indians (NRIs) and other foreigners observed that people from various parts of the country and the world have different expectations for treatments as well as services; these observations may influence regional advertising campaigns:

> So the expectation of non-resident Indians, and north Indian patients, are the same because they are also coming from a lot of other treatments and [are] very chronic people . . . they come to Kerala and they get . . . *podikizhi* [powder pouch massage] and other special Ayurvedic treatments. Also, they come for very specific reasons: that is *panchakarma* [purification] treatment. The Kerala people are not like specific, sometimes they take *kashayam* [medicinal concoction]. But the north Indian people they come not to drink *kashayam*, they want *panchakarma*. That is a difference; that is a *real* difference. Kerala people we can admit and we give treatment, but for them, after contacting us, the expectation is getting some specific treatment, *pizhichil*, Kerala *pizhichil*, [medicated oil massage] . . . for that they are coming. One hundred percent of non-resident Indian people . . . their expectations are to recharge their batteries. That means after heavy work in Europe or America or Dubai or places like that, they come here and have an Ayurvedic treatment as purification or for detoxification. And for a segment, these foreigners, people outside India, come here for the same purpose as these NRIs.

Ayurvedic tourism is also becoming linked with other forms of health tourism as hospitals in major urban Indian centers who sell biomedical and surgical services to patients abroad sometimes offer bonus trips to Ayurvedic centers during patients' recovery periods (Mudur 2004).

The geography of Kerala was also a prominent feature of the tourism strategy. Kerala was presented not only as a tropical paradise, but one that contrasted with the rest of India due to its literate and healthy population. The Kerala tradition of Ayurveda was also heralded for the rich, relatively unpolluted, fertile land where a large variety of healing herbs can be grown. For Indians from other parts of the country and the South Asian diaspora, this image may have been particularly potent as evidenced by the advertisements for Kerala-style Ayurveda and Kerala-trained personnel in other parts of the country.

Impact of tourism on Ayurvedic practice

What is the impact of the marketing of Ayurveda and the burgeoning Ayurvedic tourism industry on Ayurvedic practice? There are more than 190 Ayurvedic colleges in India, graduating an estimated 7,000 students annually. Students enrolled in a Bachelor of Ayurvedic Medicine and Surgery (BAMS) program that takes over five years to complete (Kurup 2004), must be well versed in sciences and Sanskrit in order to study the iconic texts that are the foundation for Ayurvedic practice. Professors of Ayurvedic medicine are well positioned to observe the changes in attitudes towards Ayurvedic medicine, the motivations of medical college students, and their placements upon graduation. The professors were highly critical of marketing strategies that equated Ayurveda with massage and relaxation rather than representing it as a highly complex system of diagnosis and healing. One professor, however, noted that when traditional Chinese medicine was introduced to the West, it was reduced to the singular technique of acupuncture whereas in recent years a more holistic set of practices has come to be accepted. In this vein, Ayurvedic 'massage' could open doors for the complete practice of Ayurveda to become acceptable in different parts of the world. Of more immediate concern to professors, however, is that their best students were being recruited by resort facilities where they could earn substantially larger salaries, but where, from their perspective, their protégées' talents were being wasted as they treated predominantly wealthy clientele who were not truly ill. Dr Menon who was working at a premier resort concurred:

> [Working here] was not my choice actually . . . I was a good student when I was in my college and it was not my dream to work in a resort; my dream is in work in clinical practice, but I studied with education long and all . . . I was working with [prominent company] and all, I was getting a small salary, but it was just meeting my needs and all those things, but to fill my loans I wanted to get another opportunity.

The professors also noted that even though the cadre of Ayurvedic physicians is growing, rural areas remained underserved and public facilities are increasingly bereft of trained physicians as more medical graduates gravitate towards private practice (Menon 2004).

Physicians presented varied attitudes about Ayurvedic tourism and the interest of foreigners in Ayurvedic practice. Some respondents credited the South Asian diaspora, particularly the movement of workers from Kerala to West Asia and elsewhere, with stimulating interest in Ayurveda among their new neighbors. As foreigners came to Kerala to seek out Ayurvedic treatment, so too did numbers of NRIs who wanted to avail themselves of detoxification after working overseas. Furthermore, the influx of foreigners coming to India for Ayurveda has inspired, or reinspired, local interest and usage as well.

Burgeoning interest in Ayurvedic medicine remains problematic. The explosion in the numbers of centers that advertise Ayurvedic massage or who offer a broader range of treatments without qualified personnel has been distressing for all of the physicians, regardless of their type of employment. They fear that irregular practitioners will give an incorrect or improper impression of Ayurveda, or even harm the patient. Clientele who are unfamiliar with Ayurveda are unable to adjudicate whether a facility is bona-fide despite a government program to accredit centers (two tiers of accreditation are available: for further information, see http://www.keralatourism.org/php/business/data/AyurvedaClassification.html#Criteria).

Despite their influence in revitalizing interest in Ayurvedic medicine and contributing to the Kerala economy, foreign patients, regardless of country of origin or heritage, were also regarded with ambivalence. For instance, local hospitals have altered in-patient facilities both to meet the demands and to attract foreign patients, including among them those who had been born in Kerala, but whose experiences abroad had altered their expectations of healthcare facilities. I was assured that foreigners, including non-resident Indians, 'don't like to mingle' so they were housed in private cottages away from the main building complex. In one public hospital, a separate wing with private rooms was being designed for foreign patients, the profits from which will help to offset the costs of constructing new public wards to replace the overcrowded ones that currently housed local patients. While these facilities have the potential to add to the coffers of these institutions, when unused, they can as readily be regarded as siphoning resources from core services.

Individuals who sought Ayurvedic treatment in clinics in an effort to address chronic conditions were regarded as serious patients; however, those who opted for a 'taste' of Ayurveda while on holidays or who chose to obtain treatment at a resort clinic were viewed dismissively by some physicians. Indeed, physicians who worked at these facilities were also regarded with disdain by some physicians in public or private clinical practice who felt that these individuals were apt to compromise Ayurvedic practice and principles. Conversely, others commented that people introduced to Ayurveda through resort massage centers and clinics would turn to it when more serious problems arose.

Some physicians working in resort clinics acknowledge that they compromise prescribed treatments to please both clients and hotel managers who may resist restrictions placed on activities or consumption. Others maintain they provide appropriate therapy to persons whose standards of cleanliness and comfort might not be met in most hospital settings. The relative wealth of resort clients also disturbed some of the informants working in the resort field. Dr Rao often treated in his words 'rich people from the north' (referring to northern India) remarking that: 'Ayurveda is not the property of the rich man.' Dr Balakrishna now works at a resort registered as a hospital that features luxurious accommodation, but which offers 'Ayurveda without compromise' meaning strict individualized diet and no activities besides yoga and prescribed treatments. She described working at another resort where compromise was expected:

> If you are taking internal medicines . . . it's not good to be outside in the sun and the wind . . . Actually in Ayurvedic treatment, it's prohibited . . . Then we should be a little bit flexible . . . because the management needs money. If you're strict, then the patients won't come, they will go to a place where is not strict . . . we are forced to do like that.

Practitioners in hospitals and clinics who treat Ayurvedic tourists revealed their own strategies for working with often more demanding clientele who have invested both time and money in their trip and treatment plan. Physicians felt that it their responsibility to gain their patients' confidence and trust to convince them of the necessity of undergoing certain therapies even if they caused momentary discomfort. Some clients find it unpleasant to consume an emetic or have an enema inserted although these are standard techniques used to cleanse the body. If a patient appeared too distressed about a particular therapy, alternatives were sought that were appropriately grounded in the ancient texts.

Physicians also raised concerns about the pressure that increasing interest in Ayurveda may have on dwindling botanical resources. The rush to harvest plants for use in manufactured herbal preparations without plans for replenishing the stock may have deleterious consequences. The efforts of transnational corporations to patent materials such as tumeric and neem have raised the alarm about the potential threats to Ayurvedic medicine and have prompted initiatives to ensure that the textual evidence that supports Ayurveda's claim to this medical knowledge is widely disseminated (Traditional Knowledge Digital Library 2006; see also Shiva 1996).

Ayurvedic tourism and Indian identity: global and local intersections

For all of the informants, Ayurveda was clearly grounded in Indian – more accurately Hindu – heritage, understood only through the archaic tongue of Sanskrit, and Indian – again more accurately Hindu – habits, such as a vegetarian diet, as well as the Indian landscape where healing herbs can be grown, and the warm Indian climate that enables people to function and heal. Furthermore, the environment of Kerala was particularly important to Ayurveda as the herbal preparations described in the *Ashtanga Hridaya*, the basic Ayurvedic text employed by physicians trained in the Kerala tradition, are all available.

The association of Ayurveda and the Indian environment is reinforced by physicians who insist that Ayurveda cannot be transplanted to other environs. Some also ponder whether it can even be relevant to non-South Asians who travel to South Asia for treatment. Ayurveda, Dr Prakash asserted, 'is constructed in such a way that only Indians, the constitution of our body, the whole things are just written for the constitution of the Indian person's body.' Others insisted that Ayurvedic medicine is predicated on understanding the complaints and context of the individual whose constitution, food habits and living environment call for unique interventions. While diagnosis and treatment may be more challenging, the general principles that underlie the practice ensure that Ayurveda is not the sole domain of South Asian bodies especially as those bodies are changed by living abroad in a different environment, different diet and different life-style. Dr George explained:

> Ayurveda can be used by foreign country persons, but these medicines must be changed. That has to be according to the climatic conditions and not only that, it may depend on the dietetic conditions of the patients, if they are using more non-vegetarian food, then we have to give some other type of food. 'Other' means the ingredients must be different . . . So Ayurveda itself can be given, but it should be given according to the diet as well as the climate, the economic status as well as everything, all has to be considered.

Clients of South and West Asian heritage who came to Kerala for Ayurvedic treatment were also seeking 'authentic' treatment grounded in the soil and tradition of southwestern India. Two of the four Kerala-born informants now residing in Canada and the United Arab Emirates recall frequent use of Ayurvedic medicine in their households while growing up. For both Meera and Nora, their early memories of Ayurvedic medicine were imbued with a sensual nostalgia of the smells, tastes and sounds associated with joyful family gatherings during summer holidays and bitter tonics swallowed under the watch of an elder during the monsoon season. Both women were immensely proud of their Kerala heritage, and had confidence in Ayurvedic practitioners who were raised in this practice. Like the other patients, these informants were reassured by the routine practices that integrated what they assumed to be centuries-old tradition such as the prayers offered by practitioners prior to treatments and use of modern devices and techniques such as blood pressure cuffs, X-rays and MRI reports to aid in diagnosis and to monitor their progress on a regular basis.

Two of the other Kerala-born patients did not use Ayurvedic medicine when they were growing up. Talia and Suresh, now in their thirties, became interested in trying it after hearing about other Canadians who had traveled to India for treatment of their chronic conditions. Suresh, who suffers from severe arthritis, was greatly relieved by his treatment. Now they return regularly. Talia undergoes a relatively routine *panchakarma* (purification) treatment to maintain her health while Suresh ensures that his condition does not deteriorate. Suresh's encounter with Ayurveda made him realize that: 'Yes. I am part of the tradition, the Ayurvedic tradition . . . I was born in Kerala and I'm proud to be born here.'

Reflecting the trend noted by physician informants, Abdi had learned about Ayurvedic medicine from South Asian friends in Bahrain. With a long-standing interest in herbal medicine and meditation, his experience undergoing treatment at an Ayurvedic center in Kerala has altered his view of India that in his estimation has raced to embrace Western ideas to the detriment of its own significant heritage. Echoing the observations of the physicians, he believes that foreign interest in herbal medicine and meditation is prompting renewed embrace of Ayurveda.

Conclusion

Globalization engenders linkages and invariably tensions between various local and global interests. In the tumult of shifting boundaries, changing political allegiances, and the migration of peoples and ideas, postcolonial nations have been attempting to deploy identities that may embody a unique and glorious past yet situate it within the realm of the postmodern present. Tourism offers a powerful venue through which Ayurvedic medicine as a key symbol of India's past and present can be asserted. A strategy through which the ills of the West can be healed, Ayurvedic tourism is also directed towards local and regional markets and the networks of South Asians that span the globe. Stakeholders in the Ayurvedic tourism industry, from resort operators and patients – those who make a deliberate visit to Ayurvedic facilities for treatment and those who opt to 'taste' Ayurveda as part of a holiday experience – to physicians and those who train them all collaborate in reconfiguring Ayurveda.

For resort operators, the industry can be regarded as an extension of Kerala's innovation, creating markets for healing strategies that build on trade networks for spices and other products that have existed for hundreds of years. The exotic mysticism of India and the image of Kerala as a clean, tropical paradise are now coupled with images of India as a center for high-tech industry proffering a safe and modern site for medical treatment for tourists from the region who have come to be introduced to or to rediscover Ayurvedic treatment.

The literal and symbolic grounding of this medical system in the land, particularly Kerala, draws both tourists who hope to journey to the pre-colonial past (Bruner 2005) and those nostalgic for the landscapes of their youth. In India, Ayurvedic medicine is a decidedly Indian body of knowledge and practice that has weathered the onslaught of history to heal the wounds of individuals and society. In recent years, it has been reinvigorated by members of the South Asian diaspora, by Westerners who have tired of the reductionism of biomedicine, by members of Indian society who have linked the practice to the health of both individuals, and the nation and by those who have continued to favor this tradition through generations. Ayurveda too is born of Indian gods, nurtured by Hindu philosophy, shaped by history, and reliant on the natural substances that heal the sick. So too are ideas of Indian nationhood a 'shared living landscape with all of its cultural and regional complexity' (Eck 1998: 168). For those global nomads who are members of the South Asian diaspora, traveling to Kerala for Ayurvedic treatment connects or reconnects them with a personal and communal past, uniting or re-uniting them in the body politic. The sensuality of Ayurveda suggests that we must pay attention to the way in which the body is inscribed by treatments and the way in which experiences are embodied, interpreted and expressed.

The impact of Ayurvedic tourism on practice is being felt in various sectors. As Berking (2003: 255) notes: 'The global circulation of cultural artifacts is leading to a permanent de- and recontextualization of spatially bound cultural knowledge, lifestyles, etc.' As intervention modalities change to meet the needs and desires of diverse patients and the demands of resort operators, the activity of treatments and the knowledge gained from the observation of these interactions will change as well (Bannerjee 2002).

Physicians and professors eager to perpetuate this long-standing medical system that is one among the pluralist system in India play a vital role in reconditioning Ayurveda in the current economic context. Ayurvedic medicine as the tonic of the East is offered as a balm for those infected by the stressful lifestyle of the West with its fractured kinship ties and rampant consumerism. Indeed, the contemporary predicament wherein individuals as consumers and workers are bombarded with competing messages of consumption and control is embodied in one of the dilemmas of Ayurvedic tourism where consumerism and the desire and capacity for travel, so often hedonistic, are tempered by the bodily discipline demanded by Ayurveda. As physicians interpret Ayurveda's ancient texts to meet contemporary needs and heal the ills of the increasingly diverse group of patients who present themselves today, India and Kerala similarly navigate the imaginings of their pasts to create local identities that can be both marketed to and are capable of withstanding global forces that may operate to threaten their identity status under globalization.

Acknowledgments

I would like to express my heartfelt thanks to all the people who kindly shared their time and their stories with me; special gratitude to Dr Kutty and his family, Dr Abram and Ali.

Part III
National imaginings and tourism development

11 Between encouragement and control

Tourism, modernity and discipline in China

Pál Nyíri

Introduction

As late as the mid-1990s, the issue of whether China should support or discourage domestic tourism was contentious within government circles. Its opponents argued that tourism bred immoral behavior, wasted resources and distracted the population from productive activities. The precipitous decision, in 1998, to designate tourism a 'new key growth area of the national economy' and, in the following year, to create three weeks of public holidays, giving the Chinese people unprecedented stretches of leisure, was triggered by the 'Asian financial crisis,' as the government faced an urgent need to increase domestic consumer demand. The measures resulted in a dramatic transformation of urban Chinese lifestyles, not only creating a domestic leisure economy but also sending foreign governments scrambling for the Chinese tourist, predicted by the World Tourism Organization to dominate the global tourism market by 2020. In 1990, based on bilateral government agreements, Singapore, Malaysia and Thailand became the first countries to receive Approved Destination Status (ADS) from China, meaning that Chinese citizens could legally travel there as tourists. In the 2000s, this program has been expanded to a wide range of countries, including the European Union and Australia. The introduction of on-arrival visas in some Southeast Asian countries of the region and the arrival of low-fare airline Air Asia in the mid-2000s have meant further incentives to travel. According to official statistics, 30 million Chinese citizens traveled abroad in 2005, continuing a steady exponential rise.

Tourism as 'spiritual modernization'

Though the decision to promote domestic tourism was an emergency measure, it fit the logic with which China has gradually liberalized and encouraged various forms of spontaneous population movement. Before 1978, most population movement (except for the hunger migrations of the 1950s) was state-planned; much of it was involuntary. As for tourism, which in any case lacked any significant domestic tradition, it was regarded as part of the bourgeois lifestyle and, as such, taboo. After the beginning of Deng Xiaoping's reforms, however, the official view of population movement changed, and mobility came to signify modernization in ways that display striking parallels between internal migration and tourism.

The encouragement of rural migration to towns had the direct economic rationales of fostering the labor-intensive consumer goods industries and alleviating rural unemployment, and later of providing a cheap and flexible labor force for continuing industrial growth. But mobility was clearly more than just a means to accelerate economic modernization: it was also supposed to help the rural population develop qualities compatible with the transition to market economy. Rachel Murphy (2002: 45) quotes Chinese authors as suggesting 'out-migration and return as development strategies by using migrant experience as an inexpensive substitute for education.' Murphy goes on (2002: 124–43) to point out that the Chinese state envisages a role for returned migrants in diffusing an awareness of civilized manners, hygiene, law, and modern culture into the countryside. The influx of urbanites from the more economically developed eastern seaboard to newly developed areas of western China is also positively evaluated as a harbinger of investment and 'advanced ways of life' (Ma Ping 2001).

After the government adopted a policy of encouraging domestic tourism, the ideological arguments made in its support were very similar to those promoting rural–urban migration. Authors pointed out that, beyond the economic growth that tourism can bring, it can also make 'residents of scenic areas improve and elevate their manners and politeness, speech and bearing, habits of hygiene, thinking and outlook' through 'imitation and learning' from tourists (Jin Hua 1994). Despite increasing concerns over the erosion of local cultures and environmental damage caused by mass tourism, most Chinese authors continue to maintain that 'the development of the tourism industry helps raise the civilization level (*wenming de chengdu*) of poor regions' (Li Zhushun 2003: 49). In 2001, the State Council proposed 'closely connect[ing] the development of tourism with the construction of socialist spiritual civilization; cultivat[ing] superior national culture through tourist activities; [and] strengthen[ing] patriotic education' in tourism.[1] An article on CNTA's website goes as far as saying: 'Scenic spots are a front of propaganda for thought work. Sites of patriotic education . . . may not be turned into places of leisure and entertainment.'[2] Since 1994, many tourist destinations have been designated 'patriotic education sites,' and schoolchildren are required to visit 40 of them before they graduate from secondary school (Guo 2004: 26) (Figure 11.1).

Thus, unlike migration, tourism is seen as a two-way civilizing tool, capable of producing positive change in tourists as well as 'tourees.' Moreover, unlike migrants, tourists are a 'captive audience,' and – unlike in many other situations – are generally willing consumers of narratives prepared for them. Therefore, beyond encouraging domestic spending, tourism is central to the development of 'leisure culture' (a concept that had first emerged in 1995,

Figure 11.1 Sign in the newly touristified town of Weishan, Yunnan Province, 2006
(Photo by author)

when China switched to a five-day working week). The idea of a 'leisure culture' is, in the words of a Chinese researcher, for 'the broad masses to learn to . . . create scientific, healthy and civilized leisure lifestyles' (Ma Huidi 2004a: 4). In this way, 'leisure culture' is to constitute another strand in the state's ambition to modernize the thinking and way of life of the Chinese people, seen as part and parcel of the country's overall modernization strategy. But the dictum that 'tourism synthesizes material civilization and spiritual civilization' first appeared in official texts much earlier, in the State Council's 1981 resolution on developing tourism (*Renmin Ribao* 1981). The ideal of a 'socialist spiritual civilization' has been the overall framework of the government's idea of a desirable citizenry since the early years of reform. It entails a broad range of – sometimes contradictory – ideals, combining love of the Fatherland and the Party with 'traditional' virtues such as industry, frugality, and respect for elders and a modern, scientific, open-minded and entrepreneurial outlook. Tourism is seen as a particularly promising vehicle of 'constructing spiritual civilization' as it both 'improves the physical quality of tourists' and 'provides them with more new ideas, which is the foundation of improving national quality' (Liu Fei 1998: 62).

Tourists are of course unlikely to identify with these ideological prescriptions. But they do perceive travel as a quintessentially modern experience.

In *Scenic Spots* (Nyíri 2006), I showed how Chinese backpackers explicitly reflect on the modern nature of their pursuit even as they eschew 'scenic spots,' as mainstream tourist attractions, with their standardized gates, tour guides and visual experiences, are known in China. As for group tourists who visit 'scenic spots' and theme parks – and they are the majority – their expectation for the site/sight to have been 'developed' (*kaifa*) is rather more explicit than that of Western tourists, who tend to value 'authenticity' and would prefer to forget the hardware that goes into 'staging' it for their benefit (MacCannell 1976). The experience of the modern – in accommodation, infrastructure or entertainment – appears as an explicitly articulated, central desire in mainstream Chinese tourism, reflected in the popularity of theme parks but also in the bounded and performative nature of sites that are based on nature or tradition, or the preference for glass-and-marble hotels. Even the experience of 'eco-tourism' has to do with modernity, rather than just the protection of nature: as Wei Xiaoan (2003: 398) notes, tourists are willing to obey no-littering and no-smoking rules in 'green' scenic spots, which they would consider a nuisance in other areas, because 'they feel like they have also improved their own quality in the process.' The touristic refurbishment of 'old towns,' which – as we will see in more detail below – typically involves the widening and repaving of public spaces conforming to an urban standard and the erection of patriotic statuary, works to attract more Chinese tourist groups. Abroad, Chinese tourists often comment on the levels of urban modernity with disappointment (see survey on Europe by Schwandner and Gu 2005) or self-satisfaction, as in the blog of a young woman who visited Vietnam: 'After arriving in Hanoi, my first impression was that it was crowded and messy, lacking the grandeur and luxury of our capital Peking. There are very few tall buildings' (Wanshui Yifang 2006).[3]

To what extent do Chinese 'tourees' identify tourism with modernization? Recent research confirms Oakes' earlier finding that locals, especially younger and more urbane ones, positively evaluate the spatial and cultural changes brought by tourism (with the exception of government directives that force residents to keep to 'traditional' building materials and styles, preventing them from building 'modern' new houses). This appears to hold true even in ethnic Tibetan areas, where one might expect to see resistance to Chinese-led development. Well-known Tibetologist Toni Huber, writing about the Songpan area in northern Sichuan, notes, for example, that:

> as far as decline or loss of religious tradition goes, I found nobody in Shar khog [i.e. the Songpan area] who expressed the slightest regret about this fact, although they did express regret about a lot of other things that happened as a result of recent Chinese rule.
>
> (Huber 2006: 19–21)

It is particularly interesting that, when asked about the benefits of tourism development in 2005, my respondents in Songpan emphasized not the increased prosperity it had brought but that it had improved the 'quality (*suzhi*) of the people' – a phrase that is central to the government discourse on 'spiritual civilization' – by making the place cleaner and organizing communal activities such as dancing in the new main square.[4]

In sum, mobility in China is now seen as part and parcel of the market economy: internal migration advances economic growth by increasing, rationalizing, and reducing the cost of production; international migration – another form of movement strongly associated with modernization – generates foreign currency and attracts investment; and tourism contributes to domestic consumption, reducing overly high saving rates. In equal measure, however, mobility serves a function of *embourgeoisement*. As in nineteenth- and twentieth-century European nationalisms, tourism is an instrument of getting to know one's nation and situating oneself within it as a citizen. At the same time, and more particularly to the contemporary Chinese case, learning proper forms of consumption (or 'healthy forms of leisure,' *jiankang de xiuxian fangshi*), experiencing modern infrastructure, witnessing 'advanced ways of life' (*xianjin de shenghuo fangshi*) and learning 'modern methods of entrepreneurship' are seen as contributing to the improvement of 'population quality.' Both the migrant and the tourist spread 'civilization,' particularly to the 'backward' countryside, characterized by an anemic 'small peasant consciousness' (*xiaonong yishi*) and 'feudal superstition' (*fengjian mixin*). The former does so primarily by becoming a better producer; the latter, by demonstrating better ways of consumption.

Disciplining the traveler

Even as the government began promoting tourism, its misgivings about negative consequences for travelers' morality remained, particularly when it came to trips abroad. In an early speech on developing border tourism, the vice-director of the National Tourism Authority (CNTA) praised its contribution to the 'construction of spiritual civilization' in border areas through the exposure of tour groups to 'positive phenomena in Russia and North Korea such as clean cities, orderly traffic, civilized and courteous residents.' In the same speech, however, he also emphasized the need to 'strengthen propaganda and education of tour participants, make them . . . obtain healthy and correct benefits from participating in the tour' (He Guangwei 1992).

In addition to concern with what ideas tourists might get from their experiences across the border, the authorities were also worried what ideas about China they might project to the locals. For the government, tourists, like anyone else going abroad, were representatives of the nation because their behavior reflected on China itself. Regulations concerning the behavior of Chinese citizens going abroad displayed, in particular, great concern with the bodily and mental temptations individuals may be subject to abroad. Party members who patronize prostitutes while abroad were to be expelled; those who sought 'entertainment at lewd and obscene venues,' 'have inappropriate relations with foreigners of the opposite sex,' or gamble were to be relieved of their Party positions; and those who repeatedly watched or perused 'lewd films, books or pictures' were to be reprimanded.[5]

Manuals published for people going abroad reflected similar concerns. They contained chapters on etiquette: 'How to deal with foreigners' customs and habits,' 'How to greet foreigners,' 'How to talk with foreigners in public places,' 'Ways of drinking beer, coffee and tea' (State Statistics Bureau 2002: 25–7). More surprisingly, some of the books included sections on how to avoid disclosing state secrets or voicing inappropriate opinions in interaction with foreigners. They portrayed foreign countries as dangerous terrain, where 'foreign intelligence agencies and other enemy forces' waged a 'battle for hearts and minds' by engaging in 'reactionary propaganda to topple the leaders of the Chinese Communist Party and our country's socialist system and to split the Fatherland' (Zhang and Guo 2002: 154). The authors of this particular book warned travelers against splitting off from their group and advised them to exercise caution when dealing with foreigners: 'Do not actively bring up or directly promote our political views; do not enter into discussions of political issues of your host country.' By contrast, if an 'attack' on China took place at a public venue, travelers should protest vocally and, if necessary, leave the event. Any opinions expressed about China should 'follow the line of the Center's foreign propaganda' (ibid.: 151). In addition, travelers were 'not allowed to look at, read, or buy pornographic videos and books, to enter inappropriate entertainment venues' and should not go to casinos or 'black markets' (ibid.: 159).

When tourism to the three Southeast Asian countries started in 1990, tour groups were supposed to undergo 'education in patriotism, internationalism and diplomatic protocol . . . in order to avoid international incidents.'[6] After the opening of Western destinations to Chinese group tourism, CNTA took renewed measures to counter what it perceived to be an unflattering impression left by these tourists. Thus, in 2003, the government conducted 'a campaign to curb the unsocial [*sic*] behavior of Chinese abroad, which has seriously marred China's international reputation' (*People's Daily Online* 2003). This included enlisting the cooperation of travel agencies, which introduced 'special courses on habits and customs in destinations before going abroad.' Three years later, the Spiritual Civilization Commission (SCC) and the National Tourism Administration released an 'Action Plan to Raise the Civilizational Quality of Chinese Tourists,' which called for regulating tourists' norms of behavior through the media; monitoring travel agencies to ensure they carry out 'civilization education work' among tourists; making tour guides personally responsible for tourists' misbehavior; and awarding titles such as 'Civilized Tour Guide,' 'Civilized Travel Agency,' and 'Civilized Tourist.'[7] Subsequently, SCC and CNTA published a *Guide to Chinese Tourists' Civilized Behavior Abroad* and a 'Civilized Behavior Convention of Chinese Domestic Tourists.' The former compressed the manners to be observed by Chinese citizens traveling abroad (for example, 'respect time,' 'queue up in an orderly way,' 'ladies first,' 'eat in silence,' 'reject gambling and salacious activities') into an eight-line nursery rhyme.[8] While these attracted little attention, the government's announcement of its intention not to renew the passports of those 'whose behavior has been proven to harm the image of Chinese tourists' triggered much debate. To date, however, there is no evidence of this threat having been carried out, and attempts to firm up cadres' ideological training before traveling abroad are often met with ridicule. Before a delegation of county-level officials from Yunnan Province left for an 'inspection' tour of Australia and New Zealand in 2006, they were summoned to Peking and given a two-day training on 'Three represents Important thought,' one of the core components of the Party's ideology. They were told to apply it to everything they see and experience, and write a report on it when they come back. But the participants quietly ignored this; as one of them told anthropologist Zhang Juan, he did not know what to write because 'China lags far behind Australia, so what can Threerepresents represent?'[9]

What is noteworthy is not the official's reaction but that efforts to order and direct citizens' exposure to foreign countries continue despite their obvious inefficiency and even quaintness. These efforts are akin to the emphasis on 'civilizing' migrant workers in the cities or contract workers going abroad by such means as organizing classes on hygiene or political awareness (see Murphy 2002: 45). But because tourism, more than other forms of mobility, almost invariably involves some self-conscious form of cultural consumption, it is a sphere of life where examples of cultural control are particularly plentiful. Back in 1988 – years before the emergence of mass tourism – the *Pocket Tourism Encyclopedia* admonished tourists-to-be to adopt 'the attitude of the healthy and optimistic observer; photographing the backward, unsanitary, or impoverished should be resolutely avoided' (Shandong 1988: 494). As I will discuss in more detail below, the heavy involvement of the state as both owner and regulator in tourism development ensures that scenic spots function as tools of patriotic education and modernization and transmit a 'healthy and optimistic' message that locates tourists within a uniform national narrative.

Tourism as 'indoctritainment'

China's new tourist geography spans a rapidly growing network of 'scenic spots' that include ethnic villages, 'old towns,' nature sites, temples, historical sites, and theme parks. Despite their varying content, these sites typically include some common features: a ticketing gate, a shopping street offering largely similar souvenirs, an accommodation area suitable for tourist groups, cultural performances (usually involving ethnic minorities or else reenactments of supposedly historical ceremonies) and an elaborate narrative on the history of the site that is repeated in a more or less unchanged way by tour guides and in brochures. Tim Oakes has noted the synergy in the new tourist economy between the state wishing to 'fix the boundaries of a unique and essential China' and the desire of Chinese capitalists from outside China to invest in 'tourist landscapes that symbolize a traditional Chinese cultural core for the new Pacific Century' (Oakes 1998: 48). Scenic spots, as well as theme parks, with their celebration of China as a harmonious multiethnic community with a glorious history, are a form of 'indoctritainment' (Sun 2002: 191). As Ann Anagnost (1997: 174) wrote, citing Benedict Anderson in her analysis of the theme park Splendid China, the 'quotidian reproducibility' of what Anderson had called the state's 'regalia' by the desirability of the consumption of iconic sites collected in one place in one's leisure time revealed the 'real power of the state' (Anderson 1983: 183, quoted in Anagnost 1997: 174). Splendid China's endorsement by the state, indeed, came from the highest level: Chairman Jiang Zemin visited it in 1992 and praised its 'patriotic message' (Oakes 1998: 51). Of the estimated 2,000–2,500 amusement and theme parks subsequently opened in China, most showcase Chinese history and ethnic 'folk customs,' and many are explicitly modeled on Splendid China (Ap 2003: 195–7) (Figure 11.2).

Figure 11.2 Mi Building in Zhouzhuang, a popular tourist destination near Shanghai. Revolutionary memories are added to a 'scenic spot' dedicated to the traditional culture of imperial China (Photo by author)

Chinese authors have interpreted the spatial transformation of touristified villages and towns as a result of the intrusion of the global market whose inexorable force locals are unable, but also often unwilling, to resist (Duan and Yang 2001). No doubt, such transformations are undertaken in part because they correspond to tourists' expectations. But how are those expectations formed? In supporting particular kinds of touristic transformations, the government deploys the rhetoric of civilizing 'backward' places, and there is evidence to suggest that such 'civilizing' has real consequences beyond the expansion of the market economy (Figure 11.3).

Take the example of Songpan, which until 2004 had not been on the Chinese tourist map but was a somewhat popular hideout for Western backpackers who liked its atmospheric ethnic mix. Then, at the initiative of the city government, the old town was sequestered from the rest of the place by a reconstructed wall, and the distinction between mundane and touristic space was ritualized through gates and pedestals (Figure 11.4). Several ceremonial spaces – one of them vaguely reminiscent of Tiananmen Square in Peking – and a monument celebrating Han–Tibetan friendship were erected, identifying Songpan with the Chinese nation and used for the 'healthy' activities of photo-taking and dancing. In Zhongdian, the center of a Tibetan area in

Figure 11.3 The gate of Zhujiajiao, an "old town" (*guzhen*) near Shanghai (Photo by author)

Figure 11.4 A town officer points to the plan of the new square and rebuilt town
wall in Songpan (Photo by author)

the northwest of Yunnan province that has been rapidly developing as a tourist
destination since having been renamed 'Shangri-la,' very similar plans have
been drawn up for a new main street and a Mandala Square, to be completed by 2020 (Kolås 2006: 287).

Advocating greater state attention to 'leisure culture,' Chinese researcher
Ma Huidi recently wrote that 'the state's governance and control (of society;
zhili yu tiaokong) requires not only economic, administrative, scientific, technological and legal means; even more, it requires the workings of cultural
guidance' (*wenhua yindao*; Ma Huidi 2004b: 170). She was no doubt attuned
to the interest the new leadership of Chairman Hu Jintao was taking in
engineering a 'cultural turn' in governance by focusing on 'community
building' (*shequ jianshe*), meaning the creation of local communities of citizens
actively engaged in mutual education and surveillance in order to attain a
'harmonious society' (*hexie shehui*), which is 'healthy,' morally correct, well
mannered, educated and politically loyal.

Travel and displacement heighten people's susceptibility to new ideas and
interpretations of the world; they also relax the boundaries of the socially
acceptable. Therefore, they often serve as a laboratory of new social practices.
Mobility in China, simultaneously encouraged and limited by the state, is
an arena where the shift to cultural forms of control is both, from the state's
standpoint, necessary – in order to counteract the loosening of administrative

control and to control the interpretation of new impressions – and promising, because travelers are sensitized and exposed to cultural representations (in the form of performances, displays, and explanations). Tourism is an arena with the potential to both civilize the 'tourees' and respond to officials' calls for the 'propagation of correct notions of leisure.'

The Chinese state – as many others over the course of history – sees the correctly framed consumption of places as an instrument of strengthening national consciousness. No site is allowed to escape the 'totalizing view' applied to monuments (Spakowski 1997: 291) and can mean something ambiguous, purely local, or purely playful. At first sight, the remodeled 'old towns,' like the 'water towns' or Pingyao in Anhui, appear to be akin to Stratford-upon-Avon or Rothenburg ob der Tauber. Their 'developers' seem to wish to communicate, as their European colleagues, an extraordinariness that lies in the towns' quaint charm, not in any larger significance. But Anagnost (1997: 166) suggests that the function of old towns is to reconstruct 'the antiquity of the nation in the very process of its commodification.' What they contribute to the nation is a visual sense of continuity: a tenet parroted incessantly in the indoctritainment theme of the 'five-thousand-year-old superior culture.' Songpan's transformation into a scenic spot has necessarily entailed the conversion of spontaneously evolving local ways of consuming space into national spaces of civilization. As Zhang Gu, Deputy Director of the Sichuan Tourism Bureau declared:

> The construction of scenic spots and scenic areas must both fully reflect modern material civilization and fully display the positive and advancing spiritual civilization of the Chinese race (Zhonghua minzu). Indeed, this is what distinguishes the socialist tourism industry with Chinese characteristics from the Western capitalist tourism industry.
>
> (Zhang Gu 2000: 121)

What has enabled the Chinese state to carry through this agenda more successfully than some other states have is that – as I have discussed in more detail elsewhere (Nyíri 2006) – government bodies (mostly at the county, prefecture, or provincial level) are present as both stakeholders (co-owners) *and* regulators in every tourism development project. Although ownership and management rights of scenic spots are notoriously confusing and usually subject to squabbles among government departments, and although the priority for all of them is to make a profit, officials – similarly to their colleagues in the publishing and film industries – will usually take care not to expose themselves to charges of 'unpatriotic' or 'unhealthy' tendencies on the part of their superiors. Moreover, despite the ostensible 'separation between government and enterprise' (*zhengqi fenkai*) carried out in the 1990s, most tour operators and larger travel agencies are affiliated with government departments and often headed by former or current officials (the Sichuan branch of China Travel Service has not even moved out of the building it shares with the Sichuan Province Tourism Administration). Smaller agencies are typically subcontractors of larger ones, as CNTA keeps a tight control on the number of licenses, no doubt to limit its own affiliated agencies' exposure to competition. Furthermore, the Tourism Administration must approve tour routes and issue 'tourist village' labels before a place begins to receive tourists: again, an exercise that may be serving its economic benefits more than anything else, but nonetheless makes explicit deviation from the accepted canon of representing places unlikely. The embedding of tourism development in the organizational and discursive spaces of government bureaucracy thus enforces a kind of narrative uniformity, ensuring that the affective and sensual experiences of the places as well as their narratives of history and geography conform to the state-endorsed 'structure of feeling' (Williams 1961). This mechanism further amplifies the homogeneity of tourism development projects, which in any case often are crash copycat developments by entrepreneurs and municipalities desirous of rapid profits from the tourism boom.

Nowhere is the state's desire to control the perception of tourist sites clearer than in the effort to regulate the commentary produced by tour guides. Because of the prevalence of group tourism in China, the vast majority of tourists will be accompanied by guides. An article on the CNTA website warns, therefore, that:

> In introducing scenic spots, [guides] must display their love for the homeland, the nation, the people, and the native place . . . While [talking about] a natural landscape, they should take care to introduce China's long and outstanding history, the nation's ancient and outstanding culture; to introduce the Chinese people's fine tradition of hard work and frugality, national unity and harmony.[10]

A genre peculiar to Chinese tourism management is the publication of guides' talks, used as teaching material in the training of tour guides at universities, colleges, and vocational secondary schools. For example, concerned that 'in recent years, some guides have revealed content that was primitive, superstitious or even contrary to state . . . policy' (*Overview* volume [*zonghe juan*], p. 2), the National Tourism Administration published a five-volume collection of guides' talks, *Zoubian Zhongguo* (Across China) in order to

> strengthen the construction of spiritual civilization in the tourism industry . . . to foster the patriotic sentiment of all cadres and employees in the tourism profession; to raise the guiding level (jiangdao shuiping) of guide personnel; to regulate (guifan) guide language.
>
> (Overview, p. 1)

CNTA's guidelines for the licensing of tour guides stipulate that they must 'love socialism and the Fatherland.' *The Guidelines of Tourism Management of the Tibet Autonomous Region*, published in 2003, are particularly detailed on this subject: they specify that tour guides – who must be 'patriotic, with an unwavering political stance, protective of the fatherland's unity, opposed to splittism' [*sic*] – must also 'talk according to unified standards' (Articles 26–28 of the Guidelines).[11] In 2002, Hu Jintao – soon to become the Party's Secretary-General – mentioned the necessity of including the training of tour guides in the national program of 'aid' for Tibet. In 2005, the National Tourism Administration's Party committee explained that this task was of a 'political' nature: it was to 'contribute to the stability of Tibet and the unity of the peoples' (National Tourism Administration 2005).

In many places, guides are required to undergo training administered by the local Tourism Bureau. In Shangri-La County, guides 'are trained and tested about the essential characteristics of ethnic minorities' as well as:

> what is considered politically appropriate behavior on the part of the guides. If, for example, they are asked about the importance of the Dalai Lama to Tibetans, they are instructed to answer that they do not know about such things.
>
> (Hillman 2003: 187)

Such guidelines may be particularly strict in Tibetan areas, but they exist all around the country. The Hubei Province Tourism Development Master Plan (2003) also envisages the standardization (*guifan*) of guides' explanations and signs (*lüyou jieshuo*) and the unification (*tongyi*) of guides' talks in the main scenic areas (ibid.: 135).

How tourists respond

Several authors, beginning with Oakes (1998), have observed that Chinese tourists realize they are being shown staged performances and yet appreciate, even expect, them. But unlike the 'post-tourists' of Western literature – who have stopped pursuing the 'authentic' because they have realized that everything is fake anyway and that they might as well have a good time – Chinese tourists seem to 'play along' because they consider participating in performances of the nation serious business. As Woronov reminds us, appropriate behavior at tourist sites is part of what the school teaches: school visits to national historic sites are occasions not simply of edification but of rehearsing exemplary discipline and solemnity (Woronov 2004: 306).

> Children are supposed to see and then appreciate China's history and aesthetics in specific ways ... the attempt always exists on the part of all pedagogues (parents, teachers, state textbook writers) to make the experience 'right' by appreciating the site.
>
> (ibid.: 307)

Ku Ming-chun's ethnography of tourists at historical sites in Western China (2006) demonstrates the success of such state-led pedagogy among participants of tour groups. One of the richest sites of Buddhist art in China, the Mogao Caves at Dunhuang is included in UNESCO's World Cultural Heritage. The caves acquired their renown in the early years of the twentieth century, after a British expedition led by Sir Aurel Stein. Since many of the statues and frescoes of the cave were subsequently shipped to London, Paris, and St Petersburg, Dunhuang is a perfect site to represent not only the splendors of China's cultural history but also the depredations perpetrated by foreign powers in a China that, before the Communists took power, was weak and humiliated. Accordingly, Dunhuang is not only a popular tourist site – marketed above all with the World Heritage brand – but also a key patriotic education site. 'Nationalist terminology – for example "national treasures stolen by foreigners" . . . constantly surfaced in my interviews with other domestic tourists in Dunhuang,' writes Ku. Even as the tour guide focused on Dunhuang as a World Heritage site, visitors, all too aware of Dunhuang's significance in the broader national discourse of history:

> would constantly issue . . . comments that reached beyond the framework of the introduction. For example, a domestic tourist may broach the topic of how foreigners stole the treasure of the Mogao Caves, and immediately the other tourists would add their own comments to this topic . . . The staff guide had no way to stop the tour group, which turned into something like a forum of patriotism and nationalism.
>
> (Ku 2006: n.p.)

Another site Ku visited was Yan'an, the centre of the Communist Party's legendary 'liberated area' before it had taken national power in 1949. Learning that Ku was from Taiwan, a fellow tourist undertook to tell her the story of Yan'an with a flair that

> made me wonder whether he had lived in Yan'an in the 1930s and the 1940s. The answer was no. He told me that he had familiarized himself with these stories by reading books, watching movies, and listening to the radio.
>
> (ibid.: n.p.)

In both Dunhuang and Yan'an, Ku's respondents behaved in a way foreseen by dominant, state-endorsed or state-imposed interpretations of places.

Chris Rojek (1997: 53) describes the endowment of tourist sites with a set of cultural references as 'indexing.' He defines it as the creation of 'an index of representations; that is, a range of signs, images and symbols which make the site familiar to us in ordinary culture' (ibid.: 54). Tourists and tourism developers can consciously or unconsciously create new tourist sites by 'dragging' 'images, symbols and associations' through 'advertising, cinematic use of key sights and travelers' tales' into new indices of representations. Rojek illustrates this process by the construction of Kazimierz as 'the Jewish quarter of Krakow' following the 1994 release of the film *Schindler's List*, whose story takes place in that neighborhood, then long ago cleansed of any relics of a Jewish past but today studded with klezmer bars and 'Jewish' curio shops.

But, in today's Western tourism, 'dragging' rarely occurs at 'heritage' sites, and even when it does (such as St. Augustine or Plymouth Rock in the United States), it represents only one of many readings of the landscape, as indexing and dragging practices in the media are multiple and contested. This is because – despite criticism of the concept – authenticity remains central in Western heritage tourism for governments, the tourism industry, and tourists alike. Few Westerners are prepared to challenge the deeply rooted tourist stigma ('the tourist is the other fellow,' Evelyn Waugh's words), overtly to play the 'post-tourist,' give up on seeking the unstaged, the 'everyday,' the still-as-it-used-to-be – no matter how much staging has gone into it behind the scenes – and to enjoy the openly commercialized without embarrassment. Commodification must take place in a carefully concealed fashion and correspond to ideas of authenticity. The development of Hill Top, the home of Beatrix Potter in the Lake District whose mainstream index is related to Wordsworth and 'English heritage,' into a Peter Rabbit site has largely been the result of massive interest from Japanese tourists, and it has encountered resistance from both the National Trust, which owns the house (Rea 2000: 640), and local residents. On the other hand, as Edensor (2001: 64–78) points out, 'carefully stage-managed spaces may be transformed by the presence of tourists who adhere to different norms' and by the varying nature of performances staged on them, some of which may be improvisatory, nonconformist, ironic, cynical, or resistant, such as cross-dressing by French tourists taking part in a costumed 'Village Night.' In addition, it is a common occurrence for Western tourists to refuse to remain within the enshrined site altogether and instead wander off into adjacent areas 'where performances without parameters can be entertained' (ibid.: 77). In China, one sees little of that subversion, and this, I suggest, has to do with the seriousness of their 'play.' Just as tourist enclaves in China are not separated from but play an important role in the national body, just as consumption is not just play but an act of partaking in modernity, the experience of performances and participation in play at these sites is not an ironic postmodern distancing of the self from 'reality' by acting out a fantasy; on the contrary, it is partaking in the rehearsal of a high modern hegemonic discourse. Each tourist site has only one index of representations – constructed from 'objectively documented,' internationally unique or superior natural features, from names of great persons or events in the canon of Chinese history, or from the exoticism of its ethnic groups – which is then inserted in the flow of visual representations of the nation, in which images of Tiananmen Square, the Great Wall, and sunrise on Mount Tai are so familiar that television audiences know what kind of music matches each.

China's tourism industry – consistent with its post-revolutionary origins as a propaganda tool to showcase the achievements of 'socialism' to 'foreign friends' – functions as a mass cultural industry. Most of the new Chinese traveling class became familiar with 'scenic spots' again through publications in the 1980s after the hiatus of the Cultural Revolution and was trained in tourist behavior at school trips to 'patriotic education sites' and through the vicarious experience of theme parks in the 1990s. For them, consuming scenic spots is quite naturally an exercise in recognizing canonical representations of the nation while enjoying the modernity of hotels and the evening entertainment of ethnic dance shows. The tourism industry remains heavily enmeshed with the state, and therefore – like publishing and television – follows market logic only up to a point defined by both the 'hard' factors of government ownership and licensing and, more importantly, the 'soft' influence of informal supervision, managers socialized in government organizations, and self-censorship. In today's early stage of Chinese tourism development, when the largest market segment still consists of people who have never been tourists before, product differentiation is not a priority for all but the most farsighted agencies, and there is little incentive for operators to try too hard to wiggle their way out of state ownership or risk trouble by deviating from established scripts.

Conclusion

This chapter has pointed to two important discursive tropes that underlie the rapid development of Chinese tourism: its association – like that of other forms of human mobility – with modernization, placing it in line with the state's vision of creating a new national citizenry; and, at the same time, its view as threatening to that very project by virtue of the uncontrollable encounters and interpretations that travel gives rise to. These threaten the state's grip on representations of the nation, on which much of the Communist Party's legitimacy and power rests (Guo 2004). Having reviewed the techniques employed by the state to ensure that tourists behave and view sites in the desired way, I suggested that such efforts are aided both by the state's economic and discursive control over tourism development and by the revived tradition of Chinese literati tourism that focuses on canonical representations of places rather than seeking 'authenticity' (more on this in Nyíri 2006). The dual effort to encourage but discipline tourism is likely to persist for some time to come, and group tourism that is its main object is bound to remain dominant as a large reserve of first-time tourists enters the market.

Maintaining hegemony of state-endorsed representations is bound to be an uphill battle, especially as individual travel within China and abroad becomes common and gives rise to a range of alternative narratives. How these narratives can spread on the Internet is illustrated, for domestic backpackers, in the chapter by Francis Lim in this volume. Even so, this chapter should serve as a reminder that even as seemingly globalized practices of tourism become incorporated into the lifestyle of the emerging middle classes in China and elsewhere, the state continues to play an important role in shaping them.

Acknowledgments

This chapter benefited from discussions with Sanjay Srivastava and Antonella Diana.

Notes

1 'Guanyu jin yi bu jiakuai lüyouye fazhan de tongzhi' (Notice on further accelerating the development of the tourism industry), 11 April 2001.
2 www.cnta.gov.cn/21-wxzw/2j/zrj-3.asp (accessed 10 December 2004).
3 Thanks to Zhang Juan for pointing out this post.
4 I conducted field research on the touristic transformation of Songpan in 2003 and 2005.
5 Article 12 of 'Gongchandangyuan zai shewai huodong zhong weifan jilü dangji chufen de zanxing guiding' (Temporary regulations on punishments for Communist Party members who violate discipline and Party rules while dealing with foreigners), issued by the CCP's Discipline and Investigation Commission (Jilü Jiancha Weiyuanhui) on 23 May 1988.
6 China National Tourism Administration, 'Guanyu zuzhi wo guo gongmin fu Dongnanya san guo lüyou de zanxing guanli banfa' (Temporary management procedures for organizing the travel of our citizens to the three Southeast Asian countries), 5 December 1990.
7 *Tisheng Zhongguo gongmin lüyou wenming suzhi xingdong jihua*, www.cnta.gov.cn/ Upfiles/200681784098.doc, 8 August 2006 (accessed 6 October 2006).
8 *Zhongguo gongmin chujing lüyou wenming xingwei zhinan*, http://www.chinanews. com.cn/cj/xftd/news/2006/10-02/799335.shtml, published 2 October 2006 (accessed 6 October 2006).
9 Zhang Juan, personal communication, February 2007.
10 www.cnta.gov.cn/21-wxzw/2j/zrj-3.asp (accessed 10 December 2004).
11 Xizang Zizhiqu lüyou guanli tiaolie, http://www.cnta.gov.cn/22-zcfg/2j/lydy-2003-3-1.htm (accessed 10 December 2004).

12 Tourism as glitter

Re-examining domestic tourism in Indonesia

Maribeth Erb

Introduction

In the recent decades of emerging growth and affluence in Asian economies, travel is increasingly regarded as a necessary pleasure. Despite the growth of massive movements of Asian tourists within Asia, however, there has been a tendency until recently to still think of tourists in the region's developing countries as coming from the West, with domestic tourism largely ignored. Indeed, in a paper on domestic tourism on the island of South Sulawesi, Kathleen Adams (1998) pointed out a fact that many people who had written about tourism in Indonesia had been overlooking. She argues that the greater number of tourists in Indonesia were actually domestic, despite the fact that the 'dreams' and plans about tourism in Indonesia had often been centered on foreigners.[1] This observation about Indonesia was shown to be generally true in the 'South;' in a collection of essays on 'native tourists,' Ghimire (2001a; 2001b: 2–3) pointed out that the ignoring of domestic tourists was common in lesser developed nations, and policies have always been directed towards international tourism. Given the increasing numbers of domestic tourists in the 'South,' and the likelihood that they have different needs and wants, and affect places differently than foreign visitors, this is a major oversight. In this chapter, then, I intend to examine the question of how officials plan for foreign and domestic tourism. Since 2003, there has been an increasing attempt at the national level in Indonesia to recognize and cultivate domestic tourism; however, I have found that at the local level the way tourism is envisioned varies. My intention here is to examine this variation in ideas about tourism planning in two neighboring (and at one time united) regencies in eastern Indonesia, with specific reference to the differences in developing domestic tourism.

The literature on domestic tourism in Asia raises the question of differences between domestic and foreign tourists. Both Graburn (1983: 60–2) on Japan and Adams (1998: 77) on Indonesia, have suggested that domestic tourists are more interested in reaffirming their national and smaller group identity, as opposed to Western tourists who tend to try to distinguish, as well as discover, themselves as individuals through travel. Adams in particular, sees domestic tourism as a form of 'nation-building,' an idea that other writers such as Edensor (1998) in his examination of Indian tourists at the Taj Mahal, Oakes (1998) in the case of Chinese tourists in reconstructed folk villages, and Dahles (2001) in her discussion of '*pancasila* tourism' in Central Java, also argue. Other studies have pushed the implications of these ideas and comparisons further, by pointing out how domestic and international tourists can react differently to what they find in various locations, such as Alneng's suggestion that Dalat, an ex-colonial hill station in Vietnam, was read by Vietnamese tourists as the epitome of the 'exotic,' while foreign tourists found it excessively boring and 'total kitsch' (2002: 131–2). These differences in terms of feelings of national pride, as well as divergences in taste and expectation, may lead to attractions being shaped for varying audiences in strikingly diverse ways. This is what Bruner (2001) argued about displays of Maasai culture in East Africa, where in one site it was presented as 'folk heritage' for domestic tourists, while in others it became 'primitive culture' for foreign visitors. Indeed, one of my concerns here is to see what happens when planners 'misread' their audience, something more likely to happen in developing countries, if planners focus their hopes of developing tourism exclusively around a foreign audience.

One of the reasons for government planning around international tourism is the perceived higher spending ability of foreign visitors, as opposed to local or domestic ones. An important role that tourism plays in a developing country, however, apart from generating financial benefit, is the way planning for visitors becomes an excuse to re-shape local cultures and places. This is indeed part of what Dahles meant by '*pancasila* tourism' in Indonesia (2001: 26–52), *pancasila* being the five principles that form the backbone of Indonesian political and social ideology.[2] Although as a political philosophy *pancasila* fostered 'unity in diversity' and tolerance of difference, it was also used as a means of indoctrinating a 'national culture' and standardizing the way local culture was presented in Indonesia during the New Order period (1966–98). A number of authors have argued that the New Order government re-shaped 'culture' as an item of display according to a touristic template (Acciaioli 1985; Kipp 1993; Picard 1997; Hitchcock 1998; Erb 2001), and similar arguments have been made about other Asian governments that have actively forged palatable cultural and natural offerings for both tourism and 'nation building' (see especially the chapters in Picard and Wood 1997). One can argue that this was part of what Adrian Franklin meant when he talked about tourism as a kind of 'ordering.' In fact, Franklin suggests that tourism developments were historically an intricate and necessary part of the 'ordering' of the modern world as modern states took shape (2004: 287–91). He shows how historically tourism pioneers, such as Thomas Cook, helped to create the expectation that places were 'knowable' and 'visible,' shaped the networks that made it possible and pleasurable to travel, and persuaded communities to open themselves to strangers (Franklin 2004: 293).

This process of 'ordering the world' through creating tourists, tourist desires and 'tourist-oriented' communities, has an important affinity, I suggest, with Norbert Elias' (1994) idea of 'the civilizing process,' a gradual spread of ideas of mannerly and appropriate behavior that Elias suggests was related to the rise of powerful states in European history. One can argue that the rise of tourism was a later part of that process, and continues to be a part of that process today; governments urge people to 'clean up' their country for tourists (see Leong 1989), but also encourage them as tourists to be on their best behavior when they are away from their homeland. In this respect tourism is a form of management and control (Franklin 2004: 285) and is both a 'civilizing' and an 'ordering' process.

My intention in this discussion is to trace these processes within tourism planning in two regencies located in the western part of the island of Flores in eastern Indonesia (Figure 12.1). I want to suggest that tourism has come to play a significant role in the 'ordering' of these two districts as they moved into a new economic and political era that has emerged in Indonesia in the past decade. These regencies, of Manggarai and West Manggarai, were one united administrative unit until 2003, when following new decentralization regulations in Indonesia, they were split into two. Tourism planners in West Manggarai district, the home of the 'Komodo dragon,' tend to recognize only foreigners, particularly Westerners, as tourists. Therefore their policy and planning are often at odds with the reality of numerous domestic travelers going through and to the regency. Tourism planners in Manggarai regency, on the other hand, where international attention was focused in 2004 on the discovery of the 'hobbit' (*Homo Floresensis*), have been more concerned with shaping leisure attractions for domestic visitors. The comparison of the plans and visions for tourism developments in these two districts helps to illustrate what happens when planners misread their audiences. These cases

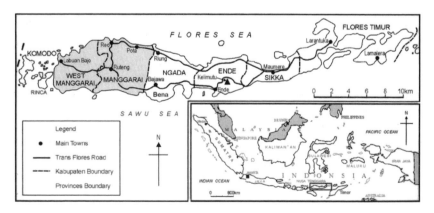

Figure 12.1 Map of Flores, post-2003. Note that Manggarai is now two districts: West Manggarai and Manggarai

will also trace how tourism developments can 'order' ideas about nature and culture in local communities, and encourage a 'civilizing process' in domestic tourism audiences.

Discovering the 'glitter' of domestic tourism in Indonesia

During the New Order period in Indonesia, as suggested earlier, although domestic tourism was seen as important for educating citizens, and forging national pride, it was not seen to be as important economically as international tourism. In this way, as in other developing countries, plans for tourism tended to be made with foreigners in mind. Recently, however, the domestic tourist has been 'discovered' by the Ministry of Tourism and Culture, which starting in 2003 began mounting exhibitions called '*Gebyar Wisata*' (translated as 'Archipelagic Tourism Glitter,' http://www.kbri-bangkok.com/about_indonesia/economy_trade_13.html), or 'Shining Tourism of the Archipelago' (*Jakarta Post* 2003), highlighting domestic tourism in Indonesia. This was partially because of the belated recognition that the numbers of domestic travelers in Indonesia were far greater than foreign ones: over 110 million domestic travelers in 2003, compared to about 4.5 million international visitors (Departemen Kebudayaan dan Pariwisata Indonesia 2006a, 2006b). An equally important factor in the 'discovery' of the domestic tourist in Indonesia, however, relates to a point made by Ghimire (2001b: 5): domestic tourism is less sensitive to political instability, terrorism and natural disasters, which tend to frighten away international visitors. Since 1998 and the fall of ex-President Suharto, Indonesian tourism has been repeatedly hit by political turmoil; more severely the bombings in Bali and Jakarta in 2002 and fears of SARS (Severe Acute Respiratory Syndrome) in 2003, greatly inhibited efforts for recovery. The hopes of those who mounted the tourism exhibitions were to encourage all levels of the population to become involved in the revival and development of Indonesian tourism, especially until foreigners started to return in full force. However, since 2003, recurrent disasters have continued to plague Indonesian tourism – with the catastrophic tsunami of December 2004 in Sumatra, and the second Bali bombing of October 2005, topping the list of tragic calamities. One Florenese acquaintance, long involved in the tourism industry, stated the situation most succinctly: given the gravity of the situation in Indonesia, domestic tourism had to be pushed equally, if not more, than international tourism, simply for the survival of tourism businesses (personal interview, 24 July 2006).

In the *Gebyar Wisata* of 2006, the emphasis shifted more strongly to recognizing and promoting domestic tourism. The Minister of Culture and Tourism quoted statistics showing that well over 112 million people made over 1.95 visits (a total of 219 million domestic arrivals) in 2005; this compares with about 5 million international visitors that year. In his statement he wrote: 'These movements give a positive picture of domestic tourism development and pushes us to make domestic tourist movements our primary agenda in the development of national tourism in the years to come' (*Gebyar Wisata Program* 2006, unpaged; translation by author). The important hope of the 2006 *Gebyar* was 'to encourage domestic tourist visits to every corner of our country, to raise the feeling of love for our country, and to strengthen the feeling of unity as a nation' (ibid.). A specific logo was also designed for the first time to represent this special emphasis on domestic tourism, with the phrase 'Know your country, love your country,' featuring icons of famous leisure and heritage sites. Although nation-building has continued to be a theme of domestic tourism (Adams 1998), the important economic potential of the domestic tourist has also been discovered.

Misrecognition in West Manggaraian tourism

Unlike the national statistics which indicate the numbers of domestic visitors far outnumbering foreign ones, the statistics gathered by the Western Manggaraian Tourism Board, located in Labuan Bajo on the western coast of Flores, have always shown international tourist visits to be much higher. In this section I will discuss why I think this is so, and how these figures have led to a 'misrecognition' or 'misreading' of the picture of travel and tourism in Flores, and a consequent misfit between the activities and plans of the tourism board in and around Labuan Bajo, in relation to the reality of visitors to this town and the surrounding areas (Erb 2005).

The town of Labuan Bajo was planned in the 1980s as a gateway for tourism to the Komodo National Park, declared a national park in 1980, and a World Heritage Site in 1986. Previously a congeries of fishing communities, vast numbers of immigrants flocked to the town over the interceding decades, many seeking to profit from tourism. The focus of attention of both residents and the government tourism board has always been international tourists (in fact the term '*turis*' in Labuan Bajo is synonymous with 'white' Westerner; see Erb 2000c), and the tourism statistics explain this emphasis. Up until 2003, the numbers of foreign tourists was much higher than domestic tourists, at which time the domestic figures jumped rather dramatically (compare Tables 12.1 and 12.2). The reason for this can be explained in several ways. Until recently, the figures that had been used for tourism statistics came exclusively from the National Park entry points located on the two major islands of Komodo and Rinca (refer to Figure 12.1). Visiting this national park is a highpoint of a trip to eastern Indonesia for an international tourist, and in the 1990s many cruise ships visited the park, but did not land on the island of Flores. Similarly smaller boats would bring tourists to visit Komodo Island from other islands (Bali, Lombok, Sumbawa), but not to Flores. Hence the figures for foreign tourists give an exaggerated picture of international tourism in the town of Labuan Bajo, and the island of Flores more generally. Conversely, domestic tourists found it quite difficult and expensive to travel to the park, since one needed to be

Table 12.1 Data on tourist visits to Manggarai Regency (1989–2003)

Year	International	Domestic	Total
1989	7,870	991	8,861
1990	11,840	1,080	12,920
1991	15,071	969	16,040
1992	16,553	678	17,231
1993	15,338	1,090	16,428
1994	20,421	2,000	22,421
1995	26,034	2,241	28,275
1996	29,040	1,790	30,830
1997	29,841	2,477	32,318
1998	21,547	2,977	24,524
1999	15,806	2,049	17,855
2000	11,137	1,313	12,450
2001	12,342	1,272	13,614
2002	12,938	2,320	13,803
2003	11,084	1,402	12,486

Source: Compiled by the Tourist Board of Manggarai, Labuan Bajo, based on information gathered from the National Park Service

Table 12.2 Data on tourist visits to Manggarai and West Manggarai Regencies after the 2003 split

Year	Manggarai Regency			West Manggarai Regency		
	Int'l	Domestic	Total	Int'l	Domestic	Total
2004	1,022	6,666	7,688	16,648	10,707	27,355
2005	488	3,911	4,399	19,137	13,549	32,686
2006	96 (Jan to April)	2,203	2,299	5082 (Jan–May)	Not yet available	Not yet available

Source: Compiled by Tourism Boards, Manggarai and West Manggarai regencies

on a cruise or chartered boat. Domestic tourist visits to the island of Flores, however, were not counted, until recently, because figures for Manggarai tourism until 2003 were captured only from the National Park. In 2003, when the national interest in domestic tourism intensified, additional sources of visitors, such as hotels and local attractions, were tapped to enhance the domestic tourism statistics. In mid-2003, the district of Manggarai was split into two separate districts (see Tables 12.1 and 12.2 comparing data from before and after the split). The statistics for domestic visitors to West Manggarai in 2004 rose rather dramatically after these occurrences, but the planning for tourism in the regency has continued to focus almost exclusively on foreign tourists.

The neglect of domestic tourism became evident to me when, in July 2006, I went to the Tourism Board in Labuan Bajo to ask about the matter. At first, I drew a bit of a blank from the Head of the tourism section when I asked, 'Are there domestic tourists?' and 'Where do they come from?' They had the absolute numbers, but no other information. When the Head started to ponder, however, on the movements of local people, he admitted that domestic travelers through Labuan Bajo contributed a great deal to the everyday activities of the town. Daily ferries took hundreds of passengers to and from Sumbawa Island to the west; weekly thousands of people passed through the town, boarding or disembarking from large ships going to and from Makassar on Sulawesi to the north, or Bali and Surabaya to the west. Often family would accompany passengers, and people would await the boats for several days. Even if these people did not stay in hotels or homestays, they ate in restaurants, or their relatives had to buy extra food to feed them; clearly these travelers had a large impact on the economy of the town. There were also many local groups from west Flores who chartered trucks for pilgrimages to nearby shrines for the Virgin Mary (with many devotees on this Catholic island), and then afterwards would picnic at beaches and caves outside of the town that were noted tourist attractions. Many middle-class residents of the chilly mountain town of Ruteng, capital of Manggarai district like to 'weekend' in Labuan Bajo to swim, relax and visit the surrounding islands; all in all, Labuan Bajo is a very popular local leisure haunt. These types of visitors, however, usually do not get captured in the statistics of tourism, nor do they figure in the plans that the Labuan Bajo Tourism office has for development and promotion.

This tendency for the tourism board to recognize only foreign tourists is evident in the way it organizes tourism promotion events. My first experience of the mismatch between reality and plans was at a major Labuan Bajo tourism promotion festival in 2000. Plans for canoe and cross-country races, cultural displays, and a big *rama tama* (friendly gathering) dinner, were made in hopes of attracting young foreign tourists to the town. Despite advertisements in Lombok and Bali, and a massive prize offered for the winner of the cross-country race in hopes of drawing people to Flores, very few foreign tourists showed up for any of the events at the three-day festival. In the end, only two tourists took part in the cross-country race, the rest of the participants being local guides pressured into participating by the organizing committee. Due to the low level of tourist attendance, the government did not take the affair entirely seriously; everything started late, and not according to the times nor places indicated on the program. The few tourists who did show up for scheduled events left in disgust after a long wait. Additionally, even though activities were organized specifically for tourists, no announcements were made in English. When the rules were read for the cross-country race, no one was designated to tell the two tourists involved what was going on. At the final *rama tama* dinner, one of the organizers invited two Westerners who were staying at his hotel to attend; no other tourists were present. They left before the food was served, since they did not understand what was going on and did not realize that they were being honored for their presence at the event. The government officials gave speeches (in Indonesian) about the great hopes they had for tourism, but had no way of dealing with the actual tourists in their midst. They talked about the abstract notion of 'tourist attractions,' but had no sense of actually how to attract, or make an event attractive to, tourists.

These kinds of events have been replicated over and over again in the intervening years. Since July 2004, the first anniversary of the new district of West Manggarai, cultural festivals have been held in Labuan Bajo every year. The first festival was planned at the provincial level as a cultural festival for the whole of Flores Island, and cultural groups from across the island came to perform. It was touted as a tourism festival because of Labuan Bajo's role as the 'premiere' tourism town in East Nusa Tenggara province and was posted on Internet sites and advertised in hotels and homestays throughout the town. At the first day's activities, however, very few foreigners attended. One of the organizers personally went into the town and combed the hotels to bring tourists to the festival, eventually finding about ten. The crowd of locals was enormous, so the organizers cleared seats near the front to let the tourists sit down. One of the reasons no tourists had initially showed up, was that the promotion posters were in Indonesian; tourists would not have known about the events unless they had been informed. However, guides, who work on commission, saw no profit in bringing their 'guests' to a festival where no money exchanged hands. One French family I spoke to after the first day's events was very disappointed that their guide had taken them to Komodo Island on that day, instead of telling them about the festival. Tourist numbers were low anyway; perhaps 20–30 foreigners attended over the three days. The affair was, however, well patronized by local people, who found the show extremely entertaining. Attempts to give some explanations in English were made, but most of the explanations were in Indonesian.

In July 2006, I attended the third such festival in Labuan Bajo. This one was of a more modest scale, and only celebrated the various 'cultures' in Western Manggarai itself. On this occasion as well, there were few tourists; most of the crowd was local. Various officials gave speeches (in the Indonesian and Manggaraian languages), enthusiastically talking about how tourism has helped preserve local culture. Performances were offered exhibiting the diversity of cultural groups in Labuan Bajo; Makassarese performed songs sung at weddings, Manggaraians showed how a harvest was done and marriages negotiated. Halting attempts were made in English to give some explanation, but most of the descriptions were in Indonesian. At the end of the evening, by which time the tourists had long returned to their hotels, the regent, who had actually been attending a wedding party nearby, showed up to give the closing speech, reiterating the importance of tourism in the economy of Labuan Bajo. 'We need more investors to build hotels,' he said.

'The tourists will come and they need places to stay.' Before his speech was over, most locals also had gone home.

After the festival I went to visit one of the organizers and told him I was confused about the aims of the festival. The speeches and most of the explanations were in the Indonesian or Manggaraian languages and could not be understood by foreigners, yet the event was touted as a big tourism festival. The festival did not seem designed to really interest tourists, who might prefer simulations of real village ritual events, as well as something they could participate in. On one of the nights a few tourists had spontaneously gotten up on stage and danced with a local band when they played a western song; it was an amusing sight for the locals, and the tourists really enjoyed it. However, there was too little for them to get involved with; the cultural shows went on for five or six hours, there weren't any accessible toilets, nor places to get food and drink, and the whole event was organized in a very formal way. So what were the intentions of this festival? His answer surprised me. The event was less for preserving culture or promoting tourism, he said, than it was for politics, a showcase for the district head. 'Tourism promotion' in Labuan Bajo was not about tourism, but about creating 'projects' to get money from the central government. The tourism board would propose a festival and get funding from Jakarta, which they could siphon off in various ways. The festivals, in fact, were not generating any money for the economy, since no entrance fees were paid.

Other people involved in the tourism industry have also complained about the West Manggarai government turning tourism into a money-extracting project. In particular, many were upset about the building of a luxury hotel by the government on a prime spot overlooking the sea. Although the regent said Labuan Bajo needed more hotels, this hotel had never been finished, and still is empty today. The money that the local government had received from the central government to build the hotel had run out before it was finished. They were waiting, so people said, for an opportunity to ask for a 'renovation project' for this hotel, and hence get more money from the central government to finish it. Given this particular idea about tourism as a 'government project,' it is not surprising that domestic tourists had no particular interest for them, since it was not really about the tourists or tourism itself, at all. According to these cynics, tourism planning was about extracting money from the central government. From this point of view, the mismatch between the audience and the planning of tourism events can be understood; the planning was not really done with the audience in mind.

Tourism as an ordering

Franklin's claim that tourism is part of the 'ordering' of the modern world, and a way states have come to 'manage' populations, is supported by some of the discussion above. The cultural festivals, put on in the name of tourist promotion, pigeonhole different ethnic groups and encourage not only their ordering as particular groups, Makassarese, Manggaraians, etc., but also particular aspects of their life (e.g., 'This is a Makassarese wedding ceremony;' 'This is how Manggaraians plant their fields'). Distinctive aspects of life are laid out in an organized manner and people are encouraged to interpret their own lives and activities in this way. But the ordering of modern states, and particularly tourism's role in this, goes much further. Franklin suggested that the journeys that Cook discovered and packaged, laid out space in a particular manner; journeys were imagined as a spatial movement to see certain places – 'attractions.' In this way, a tourist journey was a cataloguing of national attractions; and people were encouraged to journey to 'get to know' their country.

The first time I sought information about tourism developments from the Tourism Board in Labuan Bajo in 1996, they presented the picture of tourism in Western Flores precisely as a catalogued 'ordering.' 'Manggarai has 128 attractions, most of them are "natural attractions",' I was told. Tourism Board officers had been scouring the regency, seeking out things that might be of interest to foreign tourists, while realizing that most of the places were hopelessly inaccessible for the average tourist. What was important to them was the idea of 'tourism potential;' how could the regency be developed with this 'potential' in mind. In this way, tourism would be not only an impetus to the development of infrastructure (as various 'projects'), which would connect places with one another, but would also be the lens by which the places were seen and shaped (a 'tourist gaze,' as it were, as per Urry 1990). This shaping, however, was done specifically with foreign tourist tastes in mind.

Shortly after the regencies split in 2003, a Tourism Board opened in the town of Ruteng. Ruteng had been the administrative center of Manggarai district since the first years of the Dutch administration of Flores, beginning in the early twentieth century. Unlike Labuan Bajo, Ruteng has long been an urban center associated with education and progress, the home of the educated and political élite (see Erb 2000b). In 2003, I went to visit the newly appointed Head of the Tourism Board, Mr. Marsel Timbul, who had previously been the Head of the Department of Information, and long interested in cultural diversity in Manggarai. As Head of the Ruteng Tourism Board, he expressed an interest in developing more tourism facilities for local tourists, not surprisingly at that time, since Ruteng had been losing out over the previous decades to Labuan Bajo as a focus of interest for foreign tourists (Erb 2000c). However, when I went to visit him again in July 2006, international interest in the Ruteng area had increased, due to the discovery of 'hobbits' (a.k.a. *Homo Floresensis*; Brown *et al.* 2004), the small, apparently unique hominids, that were found in a cave about 15 kilometers from Ruteng town. This new spectacular discovery had not, however, changed Mr. Timbul's mind about the directions he wanted to take in developing Manggaraian tourism. 'Travel is a new necessity,' he had written, 'something that all people enjoy' (Timbul 2006). In his mind 'the tourist' was not a foreigner, but his fellow Manggaraians. The newly elected regent of Manggarai district (who started his term in 2005) agreed with the direction of Mr. Timbul's plans, saying: '500 international visits a year is enough for Manggarai, we want to focus on domestic visitors.'

Mr. Timbul shared with me his grand vision for tourism in Manggarai; his main concern was not creating spectacles of cultural display, but instead identifying sites of leisure that could both satisfy as well as cultivate local tastes. He saw Bali as a model, not in terms of their splendid culture or their fancy hotels (as Labuan Bajo Tourism Board people tended to do, see Erb 2005), but in terms of how tourism had been integrated into the lives of the local people. He was very concerned with building and maintaining facilities that would 'civilize' the domestic visitor, such as proper and abundant toilet facilities, and playgrounds for children. His pet project was the beach at Cepi Watu on the south coast, where he had designed a park-like landscape for the enjoyment of local urban dwellers. Only six foreigners had ever been there, he said, but the number of local visitors had been growing every year. He often visited Cepi Watu, and encouraged the nearby communities to perceive local visitors, not just foreigners, as 'tourists,' that is as sources of income. Mr. Timbul was thus the epitome of a modern-day Thomas Cook; not only did he have long-term master plans to shape and manage places as tourism sites, getting communities to open up and integrate themselves into a touristic context, but he also, in a way that was very different from the Labuan Bajo Tourism Board, felt it was important to cater to and manage local people as tourists, cultivating 'civilized' tastes and behaviors.

Mr. Timbul is not the only person in Manggarai who is thinking about Manggarai as a domestic tourism site and Manggaraian people as tourists. While I was sitting with him, a local musician, long resident in Jakarta, asked for his endorsement for a concert that he was planning to mount, with funding from a new cigarette company. This musician wanted to write songs that sang of the glory of his homeland, the beautiful mountains and the green valleys. He envisioned this concert being for the enjoyment of the people of Manggarai, with songs that praised their homeland, but also as a means to attract other Indonesians to visit. Similarly, some long-time friends, who own a hotel in Ruteng, were interested in my conversations with Mr. Timbul, and mused about what they could do to attract domestic tourists. For some time they had been making plans to convert some family land about 15 km from Ruteng, into a picnic area/weekend retreat for town dwellers. Another Ruteng resident, long involved in guiding tourists, confided that the younger generation in Ruteng thinks differently about leisure than their parents. His son, for example, longed to take a holiday and go for a weekend to Labuan Bajo, something that members of his generation never contemplated when they were young. He suggested that travel was becoming, for the contemporary, younger generation, a taken-for-granted expectation. Mr. Timbul thus understood societal changes well, and was attempting to do his part to shape the direction of these changes in attitude towards travel and leisure among Manggaraian urban, as well as rural, dwellers.

Conclusion: glitter dreams and domestic tourism

Ideas about tourism in Indonesia have been changing over the years. Although Indonesians have been on the move for a long time for various reasons (see Charras 2005), the idea of Indonesians as tourists is rather recent. The massive movements of Indonesians across the archipelago is now being interpreted in this new light by the Ministry of Tourism, which hopes to put this to advantage to keep the tourism industry alive, in the face of the sensitivity of international visitations to political, natural and social upheavals.

I have tried to show in this chapter that the idea of Indonesians as tourists has been unevenly accepted, promoted and planned for in different places in the archipelago. In the contrast between two districts in Western Flores, I have shown a different orientation towards the movements of people in these districts, and how the statistics on these movements are gathered, interpreted, and acted on. Tourism thus 'glitters' in different ways in the plans and policies of the Ministry of Tourism and different tourism boards. The West Manggarai Tourism Board focuses on the international tourist, thought to be the epitome of what a tourist is; the 'glitter' of tourism is its potential to generate wealth and power. The dream of attracting tourists and foreign currency that has traditionally been part of the Indonesian tourism planning, has not only continued there, but has taken on a life of its own. Foreign tourists are part of a plan, an illustration of the possibilities of growth and prosperity in the town; but much of the money that actually comes into the town in the name of tourism comes in through projects aimed at foreign tourists. These projects, however, have not been well planned to actually attract foreigners. In the minds of the people who have constructed them, perhaps they do not need to be, since of themselves these projects have become a source of money for those who have instigated them.

On the other hand, the Manggarai Tourism Board in Ruteng sees tourism as a leisure pursuit that needs to be designed and facilitated for the enjoyment of the local recreation seeker. With this idea in mind, the local landscape is being reorganized to appeal to the leisure pursuits of local urban dwellers, but also to shape their behavior as 'civilized' visitors, who learn to utilize places in particular ways. In this way tourism 'glitters' with a different kind of promise, of pride in self and homeland, of becoming equally as 'cultured' as foreigners, and of learning to be a tourist to better know oneself, one's country, and the world.

Acknowledgments

Research on tourism in Flores was formally initiated in July–October 2000 and May–July 2001 under the auspices of LIPI (Lembaga Ilmu Pengetahun Indonesia, The Indonesian Council of Sciences) with the sponsorship of Universitas Nusa Cendana in Kupang, and with funding from the National University of Singapore grant # R111-000-022-112/007 and continued with affiliation with the Department of Anthropology at the University of Indonesia in 2003, and with the Centre for Local Politics and Regional Autonomy in Gadja Mada University in 2007. Many thanks to all these institutions for their support and affiliation. My sincerest gratitude also goes to the staff in the Tourism Boards in Labuan Bajo and Ruteng for their assistance, especially the late Mr. Marsel Timbul, a real Thomas Cook of Manggaraian tourism.

Notes

1 Wall (1997: 140) in a paper published slightly before Adams, in fact, states that substantial numbers of domestic tourists were traveling in Indonesia in the 1990s, but at the time there was no means by which to systematically monitor them.
2 The five '*sila*' are: belief in one God, humanitarianism, unity, consensus and social justice (Dahles 2001: 50).

13 Openings and limits

Domestic tourism in Japan

Nelson Graburn

Introduction

This chapter focuses on the recent internationalization of Japanese domestic tourism, a powerful trend alongside the growth of Japanese international tourism. This phenomenon has added to but not replaced the two previous forms of domestic tourism, namely, modern religious and secular tourism at urban and historical sites and, second, tourism that has recently expanded to cultural and natural hinterlands. In the 'consumption of foreignness,' a basic theme in the internationalization of domestic tourism, sites of foreignness within Japan are being discovered and/or constructed, and these are providing arenas in which the tourist population can experiment, play and learn about foreignness in a safe environment. It is argued that this consumption of foreignness is producing a cosmopolitan middle-class population in Japan, and their ability to consume foreign cultures within a safe domestic environment helps in stimulating creative cultural growth, thereby allowing for the expansion of what being 'Japanese' means today.

Tourism in Japan began hundreds of years ago when the Buddhist temples attempted to gather new adherents (Ishimori 1995). The following patterned sequence is the prototype of all Japanese pilgrimage and most forms of traditional tourism: someone (or a few people) travels as a representative for the family or the home community or group, using its money (*sendatsu*), with an experienced leader; spends money (and assuages sins) at a religious site; gets souvenir proofs (*omiyage*) of arrival, and/or worship, religious mementos and cleansing in exchange for money spent; and travels home with return gifts to rejoin the group. Modern, secular group tourism to famous sites follows the same pattern, except for the growing popularity of small groups of families and individuals among Japan's younger tourists today. The prevalence of this paradigm for sacred and secular journeying provided the title for my book on Japanese tourism, *To Pray, Pay and Play* (Graburn 1983).

My original idea that modern tourism is analogous to or a replacement of traditional ritual journeying (Graburn 1989) was formulated before my research in Japan illustrated this claim. Modern non-pilgrimage travel, which often includes tourism to the same sites visited by religious travelers, is rarely completely bereft of 'ritual' practices. Even going to themes parks or urban wonders, for example, can include cleansing practices at the entrance, bowing or purchasing spiritually meaningful souvenirs.

To the countryside

Here, I shall consider the factors in contemporary Japan, not unlike in the West a few decades earlier, which have impelled the urban and suburban populations into rural recreation and tourism. Using the model of recreation and tourism as a ritual of reversal, we infer that rural attractions may include such 'pull-factors' as offering relief or liminal compensation (Graburn 1983, 1989) whereas 'push factors' might include stressful contemporary urban living. Advertising and publicity systems (Ivy 1995: 29–65) also increase tourists' awareness of the potential rewards and pleasures to be enjoyed in the countryside, as well as the pain (or guilt) engendered by city life such as not tending to family graves back in the *furusato* or 'old home village.'

Kelly (1986) suggested that contemporary urban populations feel an ever-decreasing experience of 'Japanese-ness' as valued in both nature and culture. Many harried white-collar workers live in cramped city apartments and hanker for the spacious facilities and leisurely pace of rural or foreign holidays. There is a gendered dimension to this urban malaise (Graburn 1995b), whereby the man leaves the family and goes out to battle the modern (Western-style) world, while the wife, even with a part-time job, takes care of the home and the child(ren) and provides traditional security.

The 1964 Tokyo Olympics attracted many foreigners and coincided with the relaxation of restrictions on Japanese travel abroad. Japanese tourists went abroad in increasing numbers, itself a willingly self-imposed 'internationalization' (*kokusaika*) for the wealthier and more adventurous; however, the vast majority did not go abroad. *Kokusaika* became a more insistent national policy by the 1970s. However, Lebra noted (1993: 13) that *kokusaika* is a phenomenon that many Japanese felt was thrust upon them, causing anxiety (perhaps paralleling the feelings of many white Americans about 'affirmative action').

The Japanese National Railway (JNR), in collaboration with Dentsu, the world's largest advertising agency, began the 'Discover Japan' campaign in 1970. The campaign urged urbanites to travel back to their *furusato*, the villages and small towns from which they or their families had migrated. *Furusato*, is an inherently nostalgic concept implying contemporary alienation. Ivy points out that the idea of *furusato-mairi*, or going back to the old/home village, parallels the common appellation of the Discover Japan campaign – *Nihon no saihakken* – which literally means 'Rediscover Japan.'

For those who maintain contact with relatives 'back home,' there are at least two annual occasions when they should return home for family/ritual purposes. These are *Oshōgatsu*, the week starting with the New Year's Eve visit to the local Shinto Shrine, and *Obon*, the Buddhist mid-summer 'All

Souls Day.' Family members are supposed to pray for blessings for the new year, and also to care for the graves of their ancestors on these occasions. In reality, as the annual pilgrimage 'home' has become less compelling or has been replaced by the desire to go elsewhere (even abroad), the metaphor of *furusato* itself has broadened. Today, *furusato* is being promoted as a cultural conception devoid of 'real' historical or genealogical links. Trips out of the city may be aimed at '*furusato*-like' places – sites which look and feel 'homey' to the urban middle classes.

The 'Discover Japan' campaign was replaced by 'Exotic Japan' (Ivy 1995: 48), perhaps at a time when the possibility of having a 'real' *furusato* faded and was replaced by a multiplicity of socially constructed *furusato*s; for example, the countryside had become 'foreign' and exotic rather than 'home' for a majority of urban Japanese. It became a place to explore, just like a foreign country, according to multitudes of promotional television programs. This idea that rural/*furusato* is somehow 'foreign' to younger, urban Japanese, is strengthened by Rea's discussion (2000) of the significance that at least two foreign rural places have been labeled *furusato* – Anne of Green Gables' (*Akage no Ann*) 'home' country in Prince Edward Island, Canada; and Hill Top Farm in the Lake District, the former abode of Beatrix Potter, the writer of 'rural' children's books and founder of the National Trust in England. The thousands of Japanese tourists who go to these places show that for many, the 'real' nostalgic moral center no longer lies in the Japanese countryside but in someone else's.

The ideology of *furusato* reached its peak when Prime Minister Takeshita (in 1987) loosened it from its rural moorings, and declared that every place in Japan – cities, suburbs, small towns and villages – should become *furusato*, i.e., communities with sentimental relationships of long-term loyalty based on face-to-face interactions. Increasingly, recreational travel reached places that were previously too bucolic, too remote or previously unmarked on tourist maps. If these displacements result from urban alienation, what do the attractions of the countryside mean? It cannot be just the rice paddies, but the whole imaginary rural way of life that provides the antidote to urban civilization (Ohnuki-Tierney 1993).

There was a further tipping of the moral hierarchy, ironically instigated by the Western-influenced Romantic intellectuals such as Yanagita, Yanagi and Hamada, which involved an ideological shift from rich city/poor village, to poor city/rich village (Knight 1993: 211). This ascendancy in things rural representing 'tradition,' coincided with a parallel valuing of 'natural' foods and drink, in 'greenery' (e.g., Flower Expo' 90 in Osaka), and the emphasis on fresh locally available 'organic' foods such as *sansai* (mountain vegetables, often wild).

Communities of foreignness

At the dawn of recorded history, the Japanese had already traveled to Korea and China and returned, along with numerous Chinese and Koreans, to introduce much of what is today known as 'Japanese civilization.' Such elements of civilization include literacy related to Buddhism, systems of socio-political organization and stratification, monetary commerce, weapons of war, city planning and architecture, and forms of clothing and recreation. This discussion will focus on three examples of 'foreignness' in present-day Japan and they include ancient immigrant sites, contemporary landscapes of alien cultures (e.g., Chinatowns), and foreign 'theme' villages.

Ancient immigrants and sites of foreignness

In contemporary Japan, many central aspects of assimilated Chineseness and Koreanness are not recognized as 'foreign' except in the analytical sense. Foreignness consists of *historical* incursions and borrowings from the outside world. Until the Shogun closed Japan in 1640, Japanese were often involved in trade (or at war) with overseas civilizations, and the Japanese country-side, especially northern Kyushu, is marked with sites and memories of these contacts. These historically remembered events or sites are part of the fabric of today's Japan. Most places in Japan have special events or prod-ucts, allegedly unique characteristics or *meibutsu* (things to be famous for), which are their contribution to being 'Japanese' and which are also key tourist attractions, *even if they are non-Japanese.* The uniqueness of a place is its particular part in 'making Japan.'

Kyushu, the southern island, 'is unique' for its multiple non-Japanese historical events and characteristics, including Nagasaki's *ekizochishizumu* (exoticism); 'Kyushu has always been a window on other cultures,' for domestic tourists, according to Japan Travel Bureau's (JTB) guidebook (1999: 18); the island's 'near foreignness' is its *meibutsu* within the Japanese system. This is particularly true of the Shimazu family domain, the Satsuma *daimyo*-ship (feudal domain, centered on Kyushu's southernmost prefecture, Kagoshima) that is famous not only for spearheading the Meiji restoration in 1868, but also for its long history of foreign contacts. The people of Kagoshima today are proud to say that they were so far from Tokyo that their *Daimyo* (feudal lord) could get away with things that other Japanese could not.

Among the historical evidences of foreignness and hence the sources of many 'foreign attractions' are: the century-long spread of Christianity (and trade) from the Portuguese Jesuits starting in the 1540s, the long history of trade with and the eighteenth-century incorporation of the Ryukyuan kingdom of Okinawa, a direct source of trade and products from China and Southeast Asia, and the Imjin War when Shogun Toyotomi Hideyoshi invaded Korea in 1591–98. The 17th Lord Shimazu Yoshihiro of Kagoshima accompanied him and had 80 Korean potters brought back and set up in three towns with suitable clays and minerals to produce superior porcelain and pottery, known as *Satsumayaki.*

The town of Miyama (Beautiful Mountain) west of Kagoshima City is famous for the manufacture of Satsumayaki-ware in its 14 working kilns. In one compound of old wooden houses stands the enterprise that has been run by the Chin Ju Kan (Shim Su-Kwan in Korean) family for 400 years. Publicity materials tell tourists of the sixteenth-century Korean origin of the pottery and the prowess of the Shimazu family. Though most tourists are domestic Japanese, the Shim family and their traditions have also been major news in Korea. This mixed tradition is visited by international exchange students as something 'uniquely Japanese' and by domestic tourists as something 'not quite Japanese.' Japanese guidebooks have increasingly played up the Korean connection and recognize Satsumayaki as an 'improved' form of Korean pottery. On the 400th anniversary of Miyama in 1996, the town was unusually bustling; a Korean reproduction of a sixteenth-century ship brought 'fire' from Korean kilns, and Shim Su Kwan XIV was invited to Korea and has been regularly invited since then.

Another celebration of Korean civilization in Japan takes place in the village of Nango in Miyazaki-ken, the prefecture next to Kagoshima, at the south-east extremity of Kyushu Island. The arrival of the royal family of Paekche in AD 664 is promoted and museumized in recently built village structures known as *Kudara no Sato* ('The village of Kudara,' which is the Japanese name for the ancient Korean kingdom of Paekche). Legend has it that the royal family fled defeated by the combined forces of Silla and the Tang dynasty, and sailed round Kyushu until they were given land in the ancient province of Hyuga (now Miyazaki-ken) about 30 km inland of the present port town of Hyuga. Legends, archaeological remains, and unique *matsuri* (festival) processions, and the discovery of 30 royal bronze mirrors (of Chinese design) in the local Mikado *Jinja* (shrine) are highlighted. An exact replica of the ancient Shosoin (royal storage house) of Nara has been constructed to contain the royal mirrors and to present the evidence for the settlement of Paekche royalty. An imposing replica of one pavilion of the long-destroyed Paekche royal palace contains a souvenir store, more evidence of the Korean presence, and a unique museum demonstrating that much Japanese cultural paraphernalia – castle and defense plans, houses, agricultural implements, and even Shinto shrines, all derive from Korea. There are Korean syllabic *hangul* road signs on the road from Hyuga and in the village, where a Korean is employed to handle translation and publicity. *Kudara no Sato* also attracts Koreans, who come to admire a lost facet of their domestic civilization through overseas tourism.

Modern guides to Kyushu point out Christian sites and major attractions (Japan Travel Bureau 1999) including the oldest church in Japan (built in 1597), places of the expulsion or martyrdom of Christians, and the sites (villages, caves, shrines) where *Kakure Kirishtan* 'Hidden Christians' lived (Turnbull 1998). Though most places are historical *lieux de mémoire* of the former short-lived successes of Christianity, some Christians survived until the twentieth century. Newspapers and magazines report on Hirado Island near Nagasaki, the Goto Islands as well as Kuroshima, where 'Christmas was still celebrated' and 'pure' versions of Christianity, often disguised as Buddhism, survived amongst older residents. 'In Hirado today, tourists come to visit the city's beautiful Catholic churches . . . surrounded by Buddhist temples. The view, which mingles East with West, is the only reminder of the city's unusual past' (Nagai 2001: 10). Nagasaki itself is infused with memorials of both early historical and recent Christianity, including the 1945 atom bomb death of 15,000 Korean forced laborers; this is particularly poignant as Christianity was the mainstay of Korean resistance towards Japanese colonialism.

Living communities of foreignness

There are a number of sizable 'foreign communities' in contemporary Japan. Many of the immigrants have suffered discrimination as 'racial minorities' as did 'native minorities' such as the Ryukyuans of Okinawa and the Ainu of Hokkaido (who were only recognized as a separate ethnic minority in 1995). Aside from the Korean potters, the oldest of the ghetto-like communities are the Chinatowns. Chinese had lived in Nagasaki because of the Dutch trade there, and more arrived when Westerners forced Japan to open up to foreign trade by treaty in 1853. No provisions for them had been foreseen and they had to live on the edge of 'white' communities in Kobe and Yokohama. Kobe's Chinatown today forms part of the unique *ekizochishizumu* of that treaty port. Previously a marginal community, it has undergone a transformation in recent years (see Tsu 1999). Like other Chinatowns in Japan, it is mainly known as a place for Chinese food; somewhat similar to Chinatowns in the West, it is also a site for familiar as well as inexpensive food, artifacts and festive celebrations. This positive reading has been strengthened recently both by the number of Chinese coming to Japan as descendants of Japanese left behind after the war, and also for reasons of education and business. After the massive Kobe earthquake, Chinatown was quickly rebuilt as a prestigious community, which in turn further attracted more Chinese.

While historical Korean-ness (such as in Miyama and Nango) is associated with high cultural borrowings, twentieth-century Korean-ness was constructed through colonial domination, Korean labor immigration and Japanese attempts to erase Korean cultural practices (Ryang 2000). A total of 600,000 Koreans inhabit the cities of Osaka, Tokyo and elsewhere, and there is gradual opening of social relations and respect for Koreans as well as the Chinese. In some mixed communities in Osaka, the majority and minority work together in business and for local ward purposes, and cooperate in staging festivals such as the Korean Shitennoji Wasso parade, which has become a gala spectacle for all (Hester 1999).

Korean street markets and colorful shops and restaurants are also 'international' tourist attractions for Japanese domestic tourists, Korean-Japanese domestic visitors, as well as foreign Korean tourists (the latter numbers more than two million annually). Smaller foreign communities within Japan include refugees from Vietnam, migrant Japanese-Brazilians and Peruvians, and foreign workers from Middle Eastern, East, Southeast, and South

Asian countries. These communities are to be found in industrial areas such as Osaka, Hamamatsu and parts of Tokyo, but their enclaves have yet to become major tourist attractions. However, there are concerted efforts to promote 'multiculturalism' for its own sake. For example, in 2000, *Tabunka Takentai* (multicultural exploration teams) held more than 70 events in Tokyo aimed at promoting understanding among people of various cultures (Yuginuma 2000; Shoji 2004). I argue that these foreign enclaves are greatly welcomed and will eventually become tourist attractions, strengthening *kokunai kokusaika* or 'domestic internationalism.'

The 1.8 million *gaijin* (meaning foreigners, most often connoting Westerners) in Japan are, to most Japanese, living examples of *kokusaika* ('international-ness'), with features both admired and despised ever since their arrival in 1853. The Japanese are used to the foreign presence not only in big cities, military bases, universities and international tourist sites, but also in smaller towns and villages via the JET ('Exchange Teachers') program. In their regular non-touristic lives, the Japanese absorb enormous amounts of Western technology, popular culture and foreign words into their language, adapting them for their own needs (Tobin 1992). Yet, most Japanese are still curious about various aspects of Western ways of life, cuisines, clothing, music, sports, and even personal aspects such as an individual's size, smell, posture and habits.

Areas within large cities, such as Roppongi and Hiroo in Tokyo, are known for their Western presences in terms of embassies and nightclubs, as well as residences, shops and restaurants. There are similar smaller areas in other cities, where bold young Japanese can frequently practice their English as well as make new contacts and friends. The longest-standing *gaijin* community is the American military, largely based in Tokyo, Kanagawa (Yokohama) and Okinawa. For young people, their 'attractions' include the military gear, American dance and music.

The double 'foreignness' of the Ryukyuan people and the American military makes Okinawa the most 'foreign place' in Japan. Although inhabited 'ethnologically' by Ryukyuan peoples whose original language is unintelligible to Japanese, for many touristic purposes Okinawa's 'ethnicity' is 'American.' As the Americans landed on Okinawa during World War II and administered it until 1972 (it still maintain large bases there), Okinawa is almost entirely 'foreign' as a domestic Japanese tourist site. However, a subtle distinction must be made between the 'otherness' of Okinawa (Nugaido 1997: 16), expressed as *ikoku* (literally 'a different kind of country') as opposed to *gaikoku* ('outside country,' usually reserved for Westerners).

Guidebooks and websites stress not only Okinawa's tropical nature, but also its 'international' feeling. According to Nugaido (1997: 20) 'Japan has always been a closed country but not Okinawa . . . people are more open minded when they meet others from different countries [as they did Chinese and Americans]. They have something more than Japanese.' One of the main attractions of Okinawa is Kokusaidori (International Street) where

American military gear and athletic shoes, backpacks, etc. are the best-selling souvenirs sold to Japanese to take 'home' to Japan. Koza City is known for its 'foreign' atmosphere, particularly in its stores and nightclubs. Western cultural attractions are played up for tourists: restaurants, parks with Arizona cacti, another park called 'Sala Banda' with Mexican cultural and natural items, 'American-style' products, a Fourth of July American Festival (in which people are invited to the military bases). There is a Peaceful Love Rock Festival, and historical attractions include graveyards and memorials to English, American, and Germans who were shipwrecked and died in Japan. Other 'foreign' cultural contacts are highlighted too, some lending a 'Southeast Asian' atmosphere such as Chinese architecture and ruins, and museums relating to Asian historical contacts. Emulating its main rival, Hawaii, one resort greets guests with staff wearing grass skirts and holding spears and shields (Nugaido 1997: 71).

Gaikoku Mura – *foreign villages*

Japan is replete with all kinds of theme parks, dominant of which is the 'Japanized' Tokyo Disneyland (Raz 1999), opened in 1983, which attracts about 16 million tourists a year (about the same number of Japanese go abroad every year). There are also more than thirty *Gaikoku Mura* or 'foreign country villages' in Japan (Hendry 2000, 2005). These villages are representations of foreign places now extant, such that Japanese tourists would recognize the 'real thing' abroad after visiting the imitation. The National Anthropology Museum 'Little World' (located in a park near Nagoya; Figure 13.1), opened in 1983 with authentic imported 'villages,' probably served as a model for subsequent foreign villages. Most *gaikoku mura* pay attention to authentic detail, bringing in foreign workmen and materials but, like Disneyland, they are specifically commercial and were designed to attract paying visitors. We will not examine each in detail (see Talmadge 1996; Hamilton-Oerhl 1998; Hendry 2005, for details) but we should note some major features.

Most villages represent countries that the Japanese admire and might visit as tourists, with the more 'popular' built earliest and largest, mostly before the economic 'bubble' burst of 1991. Foreign villages include Glucks Königreich ('Lucky Kingdom,' Germany, 1989), Oranda Mura (Holland Village, 1983) which developed into Huis ten Bosch ('House in the Woods,' est. 1988–92), Spain-mura (Parque España, 1988), and Canadian World, located in Hokkaido (1990). While Disneyland (1983) represents a fantasy culture of the United States, other theme parks represent 'real' parts of Britain, Denmark, Italy, Korea, Mongolia, New Zealand, Russia, Scotland, Spain, Switzerland and Turkey. In Spring 2001, the French conglomerate Vivendi developed an Osaka version of 'Universal Studios' in order to provide a 'genuine American experience' to visitors (Taniwaka 2001). Created at a cost of US$1.16 billion, the theme park hopes to attract at least 8 million Japanese a year and compete directly with Tokyo Disneyland.

Figure 13.1 Japanese families dining at the Apulia Restaurant in Little World Museum (Photo by author)

Regarding the foreign villages, Joy Hendry is correct to state that most of them share common features including 'an extraordinary degree of attention to detail and an internal idea of authenticity;' in fact, these parks 'try to create a space that will induce the visitors to feel that they have actually entered the foreign country featured' (Hendry 2000: 20). Nearly all the villages have buildings that are faithful reproductions of foreign originals, and these reproductions are either built abroad or from imported materials by foreign workers. Some are famous landmarks such as the Royal Palace in Amsterdam and the Domtoren of Utrecht at Huis Ten Bosch (Appelgren 2007), cottages from Stratford-on-Avon (Shakespeare County Park), Buckeberg Castle (Glucks Königreich), and so on. Also like the Little World Museum, nearly all the European villages have churches or chapels. Often these are rented by Japanese couples who prefer to get married 'in white' in a church, as a fashion statement; Western-style weddings are seen by Japanese to be 'modern' rather than 'Christian' (Goldstein-Goldini 1997).

Again, like Little World, nearly all the villages employ foreigners from their 'original' countries as performers or interpreters. Many of the entertainers play characteristic music, be it classical or folk, belonging to their countries. This is the case for Parque España, Glucks Königreich, Russian Village, as well as the Turkish Culture Village where belly dancing is performed (Talmadge 1996). Most of the entertainers are dressed in what the Japanese consider typical for the people from that country. In fact, some guests were disappointed at the Canadian Village when they were told 'Canadians wear T-shirts at home' (Urashima 1991). Above all, the numerous visitors like to interact with the foreigners in a situation where they are in the majority and their attempts at the language will not be mocked. The Japanese also love to be photographed with 'typically' dressed attendants. This follows the Japanese tradition of *kinen shashin* (Graburn 1983) whereby Japanese tourists like to have photographs *of themselves at the place* or with the personnel as proof that they were in a particular site.

Enhancing the 'foreign' experience are the chances to eat and drink the cuisine of the country, sometimes with menus in foreign languages and decorative table settings. Yet, the food is often modified to Japanese tastes. Drinking in beer halls at Glucks Königreich and the Bavarian Village at Little World, and the pub at British Hills, are seen to substitute for overseas tourist opportunities. Shopping for characteristic goods – wines and pâtés at the French Village, beers and cuckoo clocks at the German town, porcelain at the Danish parks, and rugs at the Turkish Village – teaches the visitors what the *meibutsu* ('famous things') are that they, as tourists, would be expected to buy for *omiyage* (souvenirs).

Most Japanese visitors have *not* already been abroad, so the attractiveness of the villages depends on their appearing to be authentic to the visitors. It should be noted, however, that all judgments of authenticity by neophytes are *mediated*, i.e., they are judged against media-driven images acquired through education, in *manga* (comic books, mainly for adults), books, television, films and videos, as well as hearsay, friends' experiences and photographs, and even *omiyage* received from those who have traveled abroad. Japanese culture stereotypes the icons of place as *meibutsu* – famous things, people or images which can be condensed into *omiyage*. It is therefore not surprising that most *gaikoku mura* feature famous writers or their fictional characters who are well-known 'brand names' to Japanese. Thus Denmark is represented by Hans Christian Anderson (a statue at Nixe Danish castle), Britain by Shakespeare, and Don Quixote at Parque España. Outdoing these is Glucks Königreich which reproduced parts of Bavaria's Märchen Straße devoted to the Brothers Grimm, whose characters and dwellings are reproduced or named throughout. Canadian World takes advantage of the open spaces of Hokkaido to reproduce the fictional landscape associated with 'Anne of Green Gables' of Prince Edward Island. Indeed, like the original locale, the topographical contextualization of the fictional character is symbolized by the house of the author Lucy Maude Montgomery, which many Japanese have visited (Fawcett 1998; Rea 2000).

In addition to the commercial aspects, many parks also express strong moral values, sometimes reflecting the vision of their founder or more general values such as 'peace' and 'understanding.' Huis Ten Bosch grew from the founder's admiration for the 'ecologically benign' way that the Dutch have reclaimed land from the sea. It is designed for 'co-existence of ecology and economy' by recycling water and all waste products, co-generating power as well as housing efficiency, especially for the thousands of Japanese who live on the site. The housing scheme uses the best Japanese technology and was built at a cost of over US$2.2 billion (Huis Ten Bosch 2000; Appelgren 2007). In addition, Huis Ten Bosch, situated near Nagasaki, symbolizes the Japanese 'special relationship' with the Dutch who inhabited the restricted island of Deshima in Nagasaki when all other foreigners were kept out of Japan for nearly 250 years. Spain-mura/Parque España's establishment was partly responsible for the 1986 meeting of the *Associación Japonesa de Hispanistas* which founded the Academic/Friendship Association, CANELA. Now associated with Nanzan University, it holds its annual 'Congresos' at Parque España where its members get preferential rates at the hotel. Somewhat more commercial is British Hills outside of Tokyo which provides a manor house, guest houses, and a pub reminiscent of 'medieval British lifestyle.' Guests also get to mingle with the foreign staff and learn English and other cross-cultural communications skills. On the other hand, there are also some strictly commercial enterprises associated with the theme parks. For example, Canadian Village and the popularity of 'Red-haired Ann' inspired a consortium of 36 builders in Canada's employment-hungry Atlantic provinces to export prefabricated 'Green Gables-style' houses which could be erected in Japanese suburbs for about US$300,000 each (Whyte 1998).

Discussion

Since the Meiji restoration, Western residential, recreational and industrial paraphernalia have become objects of interest and tourism. Since World War II, political and popular interest in the foreign has accelerated so that *kokunai kokusaika*, interest in the international *within* Japan, has kept up with *kokusaika*, or internationalization through overseas tourism. Japan, as with most other Asian countries, sends abroad a very small proportion of its population (about 17 million a year, or 13 percent of the population) compared with many wealthy European nations. It is probable that domestic 'international tourism' attracts a larger proportion of the population. However, those who do go abroad are important sources of information for those who do not, and they are often nostalgic and rarely critical when they do visit sites of foreignness within Japan.

We have identified the expansion of Japanese domestic tourism from the traditional and urban attractions, outwards in time and space with recent emphases on three particular touristic 'foreign within.' These are: (1) archaeological and historical remains, such as *Kudara no Sato, Kakure Kristan*; (2) foreign communities, both historical and recent, such as Korean Miyama, Korean and Chinatowns, American military bases; and (3) constructed foreignness including foreign restaurants, anthropology museums and *gaikoku mura*.

These tourist attractions are some of the many forms of the contemporary 'consumption of foreignness' in Japan. Many adapted forms of Western culture are popularly consumed, in films, games and television, from clothes to cakes, with the increasing focus not only on foreign cuisines but also on non-standard Japanese foods such as Okinawan and Nagasaki *champuru* (literally a 'mixture'). Notorious is the recent *Itaria bumu* (or 'Italian boom'), expressed not only in tourist visits to Italy, but the proliferation of Italian simulacra, evidenced at Little World and Villagio Italia near Nagoya and the reproduction of historic Italy at DisneySea in Tokyo. These are accompanied by a crescendo of Italian restaurants and a serious specialization in the production and consumption of *ita-meshi* (Italian food) at home.

Another recent 'foreign' cultural boom connected to tourism, is the Korean Wave *hallyu*. This started in 2003 with the broadcast of a dubbed Korean *junrei* ('pure love') television drama about a young couple who parted with a misunderstanding and discovered each other when it was too late ('Winter Sonata' or '*Fuyu Son*'). The drama series attracted large audiences, particularly middle-aged women, and the bashful male protagonist 'Yonsama' became a superstar. Other dramas and films from this fount of Korean creativity tap a market for nostalgia and attract audiences from all over East Asia, stimulating a burst of tourism from Japan (and China) to visit the actual places where the dramas were filmed, causing a cascade of international location-drama-filming contracts (see Choe's chapter in this volume). It has also stimulated a genuine boom among Japanese for Korean culture, food and language. Many Japanese, especially women, love the *hallyu* productions because they portray Korea as a place of simpler, purer human relationships, akin to the Japan of their youth. Thus, like the *furusato*-seeking tourism of younger Japanese, forays to *hallyu* sites represent a nostalgic 'virtual' domestic tourism to a Japan that no longer exists.

A recent *New York Times* article entitled 'For curious Japanese: nibbles of foreign cultures' questioned the authenticity of *gaikoku mura* (Kitamura 2006). Late capitalism ever more minutely differentiates products in order to stimulate consumption; we can thus say that these various forms of foreignness consumed at home are more than mere simulacra of foreign tastes and styles, made accessible and superficially different. These attractions are consumed in different ways, as social spaces for the family by some, and the opportunity to 'play foreign' for a time being by others, and to learn about a foreign culture by yet others. Japan's campaign to 'internationalize' has at last been internalized by its citizens. This version of 'cosmopolitanism' has become part of 'being Japanese' for the middle class, especially women (in much the same way that many Americans now consume table wines with their meals). Although this consumption of the foreign is molded to Japanese tastes, particularly in the visual authenticity of attractions and their consumed appurtenances, it is also a Japanese claim on an international cosmopolitanism, in which they see themselves as leading other Asian nations in catching up with and 'overtaking' the West.

The overall argument of this chapter is thus – under modern conditions of globalization and exploration of the past, the cultural and spatial dimensions of 'domestic' and 'foreign' tourism are no longer isomorphic. Japanese are finding aspects of Korean and other foreign cultures and peoples at home, while the Koreans are finding aspects of their past abroad in Japan. Similarly, younger and middle-aged Japanese are searching for lost aspects of their recent past abroad, while consuming more and more aspects of foreignness in their own lives at home. Cosmopolitanism has become a status marker, especially among women, and the Japanese are entertaining and training themselves, both playfully and seriously in consuming conspicuous foreignness at home and abroad.

Acknowledgments

I am particularly grateful to Director Umesao Tadao and Professor Ishimori Shuzo for their hospitality at the National Museum of Ethnology ('Minpaku') during visits in 1978–79 and 1989–90 and to Professor Matsubara during my sabbatical at the Research Centre for Korean Studies, National University of Kyushu, Fukuoka, in 2005. I am also grateful to the Center for Japanese Studies and to colleagues and students at the University of California, Berkeley, and to the Yaguchi, Ono, Sakou and Matsumoto families, for their encouragement, support and assistance.

14 Disruptions of a dialectic and a stereotypical response

The case of the Ho Chi Minh City, Vietnam, tourism industry

Jamie Gillen

Introduction

In Vietnam, there is a well-known phrase among Vietnamese called '*nguoi tay*.' Literally translated, it means 'person West,' or 'Western person,' and has numerous meanings and contexts. Its historical origins, according to one respondent I interviewed, are from French colonial times. It was used by Vietnamese to describe the French colonizer and is sometimes used today in slightly demeaning terms to describe all Western people. In the current era, Vietnam has witnessed a radical shift in its economic landscape with the advent of *doi moi* ('new change' or 'renovation'), a policy established by the Vietnamese government in 1986 that has opened the country to foreign investment, allowed more privatization opportunities to entrepreneurs, and made promises to deregulate the monopolies of state-owned enterprises (SOEs) in all economic sectors.[1] These shifts in the Vietnamese economy have broadened definitions of the term '*nguoi tay*' to reflect the economic and social habits of foreign investors, new residents, and overseas tourists. In Vietnam's cities, especially in Ho Chi Minh City (HCMC), other meanings can be explained as follows: '*nguoi tay*' can be used when Vietnamese discuss marriage between a Westerner and a Vietnamese (as in '*lay nguoi tay roi*,' literally 'he/she takes a Western spouse'), it is used in jokes to capture some of the strange behaviors and tendencies non-Vietnamese display, and it is used to call attention to a potential customer in a store or on the streets of Vietnam's cities.[2] As these examples attest, there is a direct correlation between these discursive understandings of 'Western people' and consumption patterns in Vietnam. Indeed, if one takes the historical trajectory of '*nguoi tay*' from the period of French colonization in the 1800s, the term's consumptive tendencies carry much historical baggage and thus may incorporate the consumption of people, livelihoods, and identities as much as material or symbolic goods. In research conducted on how actors in the HCMC tourism industry give explanatory voice to '*nguoi tay*,' I have learned that these 'outsiders' are coveted for their spending power, compliance and generosity in giving to the disabled and poor, intrigue of Vietnamese socio-economic character, and generally easy-going dispositions. The quintessential tourist consumer is the '*nguoi tay*,' for he/she symbolizes wealth, status, openness, 'outsideness,' and a certain gullibility that is laden within these identities.

'*Nguoi tay*,' however, only composes a fraction of Vietnam's consumers and investors. A new Vietnamese middle class (and the growing upper class) has emerged which now regularly tours Vietnam, taking in the sites and sounds once reserved and constructed for Westerners by Vietnamese. While the domestic percentage of Vietnam's total tourism market is unreliable,[3] a recent Vietnam state news agency reported that Vietnam had 17.5 million domestic tourists in 2006, and the number is predicted to increase to 18.5 million in 2007.[4] The exponential increases in domestic tourists disrupts the dialectic in Vietnam between 'outside' consumers and 'inside' residents, between those who have the ability to consume Vietnam and who are in the business of embodying Vietnam to these actors. Trevor Barnes states that a dialectic is 'defined as an opposition that propels change' (Barnes 2006: 38) and dialectics have historically been employed as a method for analysis by Marxist scholars. However, because it is a 'productive' method rather than a form of scientific verification (ibid.: 37), it is increasingly being used in other aspects of the social sciences, including as a framework for identity-building (see Castree and Gregory 2006, and Dixon and Jones III 2004, to show how Marxists in geography, especially Harvey, have grappled with dialectical thought; and Mitchell 2002, who uses a dialectical framework to critique work in landscapes and identity).

With the dialectical oppositional categories of the foreign tourist 'outside' and the national 'inside' as the theoretical basis for this chapter, I ask the following question: how do local HCMC tourism operators stabilize the insider/outsider dialectic in the face of increased Vietnamese consumerism in the city? HCMC has been at the forefront of the country's economic changes, so it may be legitimate at least at the onset to retort, why can't both Vietnamese and Western identities have a consumerist dimension to them? The point that I hope to make in this chapter is that both do, but that they are substantially different in scope and tenor, with Vietnamese tourists consuming from the 'inside' and Westerners consuming from a vantage point outside Vietnam, causing friction and contradiction among tourism operators over the identity of the tourist. The tension between an imagined stability of the insider/outsider dialectic, the work to preserve this stable opposition on the part of HCMC tourism players, and paradoxically the blurring of these categories as Vietnam experiences striking socio-economic changes lies at the heart of this chapter. Using data collected from 126 one-on-one interviews with managers and executives in the HCMC private tourism industry over the course of one year of fieldwork, and with comments verified by these respondents, this chapter seeks to examine the changing face of Vietnamese identity in the midst of a shifting national class structure.

How do employees in the HCMC tourism industry arrange Vietnamese national identities given that some of its own residents now have the same spending power as the '*nguoi tay*?' The answer lies in the creation of stereotypes of Vietnam's burgeoning middle-upper and upper-classes as infringers on the tourism landscape. The Vietnamese middle and upper-classes – the body of Vietnamese who have the ability to conceive of Vietnam as 'travelable' – are seen as adversely tampering with Vietnamese identity and lacking in respect and interest in recreating the performances that Western tourists display in Vietnam. Western tourists have created the tourism landscape of HCMC and thus are 'changeable' in ways that Vietnamese tourists are not. Vietnamese tourists are placed then in a doubly privileged and isolating position: they are seen as tampering with both the 'outside' and the 'inside' and thus disrupt the stability of this oppositional dialectic that is communicated by the actors in the HCMC tourism industry. Circulating stereotypes of Vietnamese consumers enacted by HCMC tourism actors do something to resolve the contradictions that Vietnamese tourist consumers have placed on the state's tourism industry. I offer three 'stereotypical' examples – that of the 'uncategorizability' of the Vietnamese tourist, their unrelenting demands, and their spendthrift nature – used by HCMC tourism employees in order to re-solidify the categories of Vietnamese 'insider' and foreign 'outsider.'

A brief conclusion will focus on the implications of these changing identities on category generation and upkeep. Interviews with a series of HCMC tourism industry actors find that the grounded realities of the changing tourist socio-demographics in HCMC muddy the distinction between the categories of 'Vietnamese' and 'Westerners.' Categories of insiders and outsiders in the HCMC tourism industry, therefore, emerge out of practices and discourses among actors such as the ones in the tourism industry rather than existing as stable categories in which identities can neatly be placed.

Utilizing stereotypes in the HCMC tourism industry to reconnect broken categories

Vietnamese tourists are a new phenomenon in the collective mindset of the HCMC tourism industry. Recent changes to the national economic landscape now allow increased domestic travel opportunities, upsetting foundational categories tour operators use as they shape and understand Vietnamese and foreign identities. Prior to the opening up of the country to foreign investment, deregulation, and private entrepreneurial opportunities, the categories of 'inside' Vietnamese and 'outside' foreign tourist were firmly entrenched in the HCMC tourism industry. In fact, the insider category has both a strong historical and political precedent. Before *doi moi* was enacted, Vietnam's state-run tourism companies had one particular task: they issued travel permits to Vietnamese residents if they wanted to visit another area of Vietnam (interview material, Phuc, male tourism director, July 2006). Because state-owned enterprises were largely without private competition in the years before *doi moi*, the only possible way to travel was by issuing a formal appeal to the state. This imposing rule – in place for over 20 years – assisted in defining the boundaries of Vietnamese 'insider' and foreign 'outsider' in stark terms.

Moreover, the travel permit rule was only applied to civilians and was waived for Vietnamese government officials, war heroes, and their families. Foreign tourists, though regulated through a lengthy visa process, in many senses could conceive of Vietnam as 'travelable' in ways that the Vietnamese could not. Foreigners need only pay a visa fee and fill out an application to be welcomed to most every part of the country. For most Vietnamese nationals the roadblocks to travel were more diverse than a simple monetary payment and written application process (although the monetary function was certainly important in the form of bribes). The obvious power and political authority over human movements that the state tourism operators had under these conditions notwithstanding, this sort of 'offering' is not typical of most tourism operators throughout the world. State-run companies no longer offer permits to Vietnamese residents, but the historical context of having to ask state-run tourism companies for permission to travel – let alone to travel for leisure and consumption purposes – still exists in the mindsets of Vietnamese people and its historical significance has contributed to the idea of the Vietnamese resident as an insider lacking in the mobile capabilities of their Western counterparts.

The dismissal of the Vietnamese tourist segment

The extent to which a person travels often contributes, fairly or not, to the idea that that person is 'progressive.' 'Travel is life' is a common slogan in much of the West, and it is a term appropriated to suggest a higher form of life than non-travelers enjoy. These meanings have seeped in to constructions of Vietnamese and foreign identities in the HCMC tourism industry and indeed have served to further partition the categories of 'insider' and 'outsider.' Middle- and upper-class Vietnamese now take advantage of HCMC's tourism opportunities but are resistant to and easily bored with HCMC's established tourism performances, performances that center on the exceptionality of Vietnam and its culture. Moreover, for many Vietnamese tourists, HCMC tourism programs are offensive: their primary promotional approach reproduces the Vietnamese Communist Party's long-standing ideological program centering on the distinctiveness of Vietnamese culture (Pelley 2002), which delegitimizes the HCMC tourism sector as yet another of the Party's mouthpieces. More generally, a sustained presentational cadence of the distinctiveness of 'Vietnamese culture' insinuates that Vietnamese tourists lack accurate knowledge of Vietnamese culture.

The HCMC tourism players interviewed respond to Vietnamese behavior by repeatedly saying that Vietnamese residents do not have the characteristics of a progressive tourist desiring to consume Vietnam. In fact, they do not have any characteristics. A tourism operator who only caters to a Western clientele refuses to deal with the Vietnamese segment of the HCMC tourism market. In Tai's words: 'Vietnamese tourists are a growing segment but in Vietnam they are not categorized yet. The segment is very small. The segment creates a lot of headaches and is difficult to deal with correctly' (interview material, Tai, male independent tour guide, May 2006).

The tension between Vietnamese tourists infringing on the tourism landscape – constructed and driven by outsiders – and their small, disruptive, as-yet-uncategorizable form provides a window into the ways in which the contemporary Vietnamese tourist has disrupted the dialectical opposition between insider and outsider. Tai presents the Vietnamese tourist as uncategorizable, and this explanation fits with the chapter's theoretical premise. How can the Vietnamese tourist be categorized as a cosmopolitan tourist consumer when he/she is already categorically stabilized as a resident? Tai has imbued meaning into the category of Vietnamese tourist by rendering it a non-category, one not desired or allowed to be placed within the stable distinctive category of tourist outsider.

Another respondent, an independent tour guide named Bac, echoed Tai's statements:

> They [the Vietnamese] drink all the time. Even on the bus! They drink all day long. It is so hard to keep the drunks on the bus and in order. They have to go to the bathroom, want more beer. We never make it to the destination and when we do they don't even look at it . . . they sit and drink together.
>
> (Interview, Bac, independent tour guide, June 2006)

In Bac's case, the Vietnamese tourist is an outsider in the local tourism industry. Drunkenness and alcohol consumption are not behaviors that Bac associates with the consumption of the cultural landscape and it is apparent in his incredulity that this behavior is perverse in the realm of the tourist. In our discussion that morning Bac's tone was one of discomfort, but not of a sinister nature. Rather, it was a perspective revealing his astonishment, as if his conceptions of who tourists are, how they are served, and what their practices include are dramatically upset every time he takes domestic tourists on a trip. We did not discuss much about domestic tourists after his initial explanation to me despite repeated attempts to bring the interview back to Vietnamese tourists. His answer was repeated verbatim: 'They drink so much!' and it seemed that it was difficult for him to fill out the answer much further. This limited response suggests that he is not yet ready to form a perspective on local tourists but that their performances disrupt the categories of tourism and consumption that he has set up and sustains through his work. Tai's and Bac's responses are the narratives behind the changing dynamics of the Vietnamese tourism industry. Their positions as workers in the construction, repair, and presentation of the inside/outside dialectic in the HCMC tourism industry in part facilitate definitions of who Vietnamese tourists are and how their actions are understood. As Vietnamese are becoming more upwardly mobile and travel more frequently, tourism employees such as Tai and Bac are employing stereotypes to reinforce the scaffolding that constructs who resides in the inside and outside categories of tourist consumption.

Stereotyping domestic consumer demands to repair the insider/outsider dialectic

The stereotype of the Vietnamese tourist as 'difficult to deal with' is a device that tourism operators in HCMC utilize to resolve the tensions that arise when an insider to Vietnam develops the financial capital and social status to become a national tourist consumer. Thuan, the director of another long-established tourism company in HCMC, eschews setting up contracts for tours with Vietnamese residents. For him, there is 'no incentive to have Vietnamese (on a tour), they are too demanding' (interview, Thuan, tourism company director, July 2006). One can surmise that the Vietnamese tourists Thuan is speaking of are directing their demands toward the local tourism industry's primary supplier of Vietnamese identity, the tour guide. Vietnamese tour guides are archetypal identity producers because they are the 'face' of Vietnam for consumers and thus are the physical representations of a consumable Vietnam that has been constructed for tourists. Moreover, they are more than a representation of Vietnam: they embody the country in their mannerisms, their ability to 'bridge cultures' between Vietnam and the tourist, and tap their own knowledge and impart it to the consumer. Local tour guides' ability to bridge cultures means they are also able to bridge the insider and outsider categories. While they ostensibly embody Vietnam through their actions, their foreign language skills, high income levels, and cosmopolitan flair suggest a sympathy for, if not an outright placement in the foreign outsider category. Local HCMC tour guides are thus at the center of the construction of Vietnamese and foreign identities in HCMC, deciding what consumer traits and characteristics fit into which categories and which – like domestic tourist demands – are deviants. The clashes between the construction of local and foreign identities with the new Vietnamese middle class challenges tour guides' understandings of the very categories they have contributed to creating.

Thus, a stereotype employed by HCMC tourism actors is that the Vietnamese tourists are more difficult for their guides than Western tourists. Guides in HCMC present a defensive position when they relay their interactions with Vietnamese tourists to me. Thuan told me a story. One of his tour guides had taken a small tour out from HCMC to the Mekong Delta. It was a Sunday during the summer months, considered the low period in HCMC tourism. This also coincides with the period when Vietnamese – whose children are on summer holiday and who have vacation time available – take their holidays. Sundays are the most frequent rest day in Vietnam. It is a day when HCMC tour guides hate working for there are numerous get-togethers, parties, and family events that provide a chance of release from work. They also happen to be the easiest day for Vietnamese tourists to get off work. As we see from the following interview excerpt, the obvious problems emerge:

Thuan: We had a situation a few years ago where we couldn't get guides to work on Sundays unless they were doing a tour with Westerners. Guides don't like to work with other Vietnamese anyway . . .

Author: I was under the impression that the guides have some sort of a contractual agreement with you.

Thuan: Not really. All of our contracted guides were out that day because they have the Australians and other foreigners first. The Vietnamese tourists were left over without anyone to take them to the (Mekong) Delta.

Author: Was it because the guides didn't want to work or because they didn't want to work with Vietnamese?

Thuan: Guides sometimes say no to work when it involves other Vietnamese.

Author: Why?

Thuan: Vietnamese tourists don't normally like the guides. Don't think they are necessary. Everyone knows everything already, in their minds. So the guides don't get tips, they have to go buy food, wine, and run around for them. Most guides would rather stay home on Sunday anyway.

(Interview, Thuan, tourism company director, July 2006)

The Vietnamese tour guide is the embodiment of traditional Vietnamese identity and economic success. He/she is well dressed, well spoken and well versed in the English language, business-like in their approach to consumers, diligent, and practiced in relation to persons of other cultures and perspectives. This description could easily be of a cosmopolitan businessperson in the global economy. On the other hand, it is the work of the Vietnamese tour guide to offer Vietnam 'traditions' to the tourist, whether by taking the group to a community market, to watch coconut candy made or farmers tending to their paddies, to listen to traditional Vietnamese music or a storyteller remark on the importance of family life, and so on. The Vietnamese tour guide captures the twin ideas of economic fluidity and insider fixity in his/her practices and thus is an embodiment of the insider/outsider dialectic. This dialectical opposition collapses when the tour guide must face citizens who themselves blur these distinctions. In these situations, Vietnamese tour guides cannot call upon either their knowledge of a foreign language (as an 'outsider') or their gift of storytelling and speaking in irony when describing Vietnam's past (as an 'insider'). Thuan's way of resolving the destruction of this neat opposition is to claim that the guides under his direction are not treated well by their fellow Vietnamese citizens.

Vietnamese spendthrifts and reckless financial behavior

Hy V. Luong argues that wealth differences in HCMC are historically greater than in Vietnam's capital, Hanoi. He goes on to say that there is 'hidden wealth' in HCMC (Luong 2003: 85). Although he does not go in to detail about this comment, it leads one to question who is doing the hiding, who is not aware of the revenue, and who is conscious of southern Vietnam wealth. From Luong's statement we can argue that Vietnamese residents living and working in HCMC would have the greatest knowledge about these financial disparities, the depth and breadth of wealth in their city, and the means by which to best access it. Moreover, Luong's comment suggests that there are wealth differences in Hanoi too, but without the extremes that exist in HCMC.[5] The interviews I conducted with tourism operators produce stories which have become formalized into a stereotype of Vietnamese tourists spending copious amounts of money on tourism excursions. These narratives inform Luong's argument that HCMC residents have greater discretionary income than their compatriots in the north, but the narratives take Luong's position further: HCMC residents spend this excess capital frivolously and illegitimately. In contrast, Western tourists are explained as fiscally conscious and refined in their purchasing choices. These stereotypes provide a collective lens into the changing nature of the insider/outsider dialectic and reinforce the need for the members of the HCMC tourism industry to continually structure their worlds around this stable dialectic.

It was the end of May in HCMC. The high season for international tourism to HCMC was coming to an end and the dreaded 'low season' was rapidly approaching. With it was to come more sporadic and shorter-term employment (for instance, half-day trips rather than week-long ventures) and because money was going to be tight for tour guides like Bac and his family throughout the summer, he was about to cycle to his second job: teaching English at a local high school in the evenings. He was clearly displeased as he discussed with me these circumstances. I asked him how many tours he could reasonably expect to lead during the summer. This question spurred him on to a sour lament:

Bac: Who can be sure? Some people [tour guides] never get a tour throughout the summer. The Vietnamese travel domestically. You know something about them? The Vietnamese spend all of their money when they go on holiday. Incredible! They save their money for a long time and then they spend it on their holiday. Every bit of it!

Author: Why is that?

Bac: They have a bad way of keeping their money. Instead of buying a better motorbike or spending money on education, they spend it at the beach, drinking. No one cares.

Author: Do they spend money on the trips?

Bac: (hesitating) Not really, because they know where to get things more cheaply. There is not much that they buy on the trip.

Author: So they have more money to pay you better tips then?

Bac: (with incredulous laughter) Of course not!

Author: Does this happen throughout the country? (suggesting outside of HCMC as well)

Bac: Of course!

(Interview, Bac, independent tour guide, May 2006)

I have repeatedly come across this complaint, from tour guides, executives, desk employees, even Vietnamese college students majoring in tourism studies. Why would such a notion about Vietnamese tourists be so pervasive, and why? There are certainly emotive considerations to take into account on the part of the tourism industry collective. Jealousy, desire, and pettiness spring to mind. However, emotions have a tendency to vary widely in their style and substance and in the interviews and participant observations there has been a repetitive, distanced uniformity during our discussions of Vietnamese tourists' lack of frugality. Increased and varied personal expenditures are a correlate to a country's financial growth, so this aspect can be (at least partially) dismissed in the analysis. Who wouldn't want to spend their money if they are making more of it? Which brings us to the cultural aspects of tourism, and it is at this point that it can again be argued that complaints about overspending are a veil for the disturbance of the Vietnamese cultural project. Newly minted Vietnamese tourists are not purchasing the cultural trinkets at stands littered along their prescribed paths at inflated prices, they are not lauding Vietnamese cultural sites, and they are not tipping their guides, drivers, or tour operator support staff. In sum, they are not replaying the culturally specific performances that their non-Vietnamese tourist counterparts do, who are the segment of tourists who have helped to define the boundaries between insider and outsider through these actions. Purchases on tourism routes have special significance for the Vietnamese tour guide: he/she usually gets a portion of the sellers' take on an informal commission basis. And there is a satisfaction from all parties (buyers, sellers, and guides) that the purchase will allow tourists to keep their 'Vietnamese' experience long after their trip is over through locally made foods like coconut candy, or handicrafts like chopsticks, glassware, or artwork. Instead, Vietnamese tourists are following *some* of their non-Vietnamese tourist spending habits: they are buying alcohol, upgrading their meals, staying in higher-end hotels, traveling to more destinations, and securing more days per year for travel. Certain consumption trends fall into the culturally unaware yet financially sound 'outsider' category (desiring high-end hotels rather than those with 'history,' for instance) while others continue to inform the Vietnamese insider perspective (like the refusal to tip individuals for their work). Thus the need for stereotypical language when invoking the Vietnamese tourist; the borders between insider and outsider have been tarnished through the practices of this new, strange body of consumer.

Conclusion

In this chapter, I have explained that a new segment of tourist has entered the HCMC tourism industry ill-equipped with the understandings and perceptions that foreign tourists carry. Foreign tourists and their Vietnamese support have been successful in constructing distinctive boundaries around their identities: the Vietnamese the knowledgeable, stable 'insider' and the foreign (usually Western) rich, culturally hungry 'outsider.' These oppositional categories have done the work of propelling the HCMC tourism industry forward since the advent of *doi moi*. I discussed three separate stereotypes by HCMC tourism employees about their fellow citizens in order to show how the categories of insider and outsider are unbalanced and unstable, which is not how the tourism practitioners would like things to be.

The instability in this dialectic has consequences for Vietnamese identity. In scaling out to form a more theoretically informed conclusion, there appear two ways to go about assessing these consequences: (1) the oppositional boundaries I have drawn around 'insider' and 'outsider' are not limits, but are regulated, permeable passageways; or, conversely, (2) that the boundaries themselves are not as much at stake as what flows through them or accumulates in them (Mueggler 2001: 224). It is my hope that my argument suggests the former, although the latter is a useful way to look at changes in the HCMC tourism industry as well.[6] These boundaries in part have been created by HCMC tourism players, players who regard Vietnamese identity as a definitive, coherent body to be maintained throughout the dramatic economic transformations the country's residents are experiencing. This chapter shows HCMC tourism actors' attempts to make sense of and perpetuate the categories they themselves have built while the tourism industry is welcoming increased numbers of domestic tourists.

While HCMC tourism players have certainly developed a façade of stability in the form of stereotypical language, there are doubtless incredible changes occurring within this dialectic. As I have shown, the categories of insider and outsider – seemingly so easily defined – are, in truth, the opposite; in flux, made and remade, collapsed, redefined, and seeping into each other in myriad ways. The categories are constructed from properties that are the scaffolding for the (re)formulation of Vietnamese and tourist identities. As the scaffolding collapses, so the categories follow. As this analysis shows, Vietnamese tourism actors – with an important hand in category creation and upkeep – are working hard to understand these changes with an eye toward an imagined coherency. In this way, the categories acquire a strange dimension, imagined as stable yet pulled and tugged in innumerable directions. The categories of insider and outsider, then, do include a hint of permanence despite their unstable underpinnings.

Notes

1 There is not space in this chapter to explain the preconditions for Vietnam's economic shift, nor the impact of the *doi moi* policies themselves. For discussion of these subjects, see Ronnas and Sjoberg (1990); Leipziger (1992); Turley and Seldon (1993); Fforde and De Vylder (1996); Chan *et al.* (1999); Forbes *et al.* (1999); Boothroyd and Pham (2000); Kleinen (2001); and Werner and Belanger (2002).

2 I am not aware of all of the meanings of '*nguoi tay*,' but it is remarkable to hear the term coined in the variant contexts I have cited.

3 This is due in part to the Vietnamese Communist Party's preference for promoting monthly and annual increases in foreign visitors over domestic gains. There is also some difficulty in accessing accurate numbers in either the domestic and international tourist marketplace because the Party has historically considered overseas Vietnamese to be part of the domestic market.

4 Website available: http://english.people.com.cn/90001/90778/6256406.html. accessed 15 September 2007.

5 Although numbers are never very reliable, best guesses say that the HCMC area has around eight million residents and Hanoi about three-and-a-half. This is 13 percent of the country's population in a Vietnam that still makes great claims to its rural character.

6 I think a long ethnography would be more suitable for the latter line of thinking. Besides, my focus at the outset has been on the fuzziness of the categories themselves, which have been informed by stories that flow through the categories.

15 The internal expansion of China

Tourism and the production of distance

Jenny Chio

Introduction

The Big Bang theory postulates that an explosion of matter and energy set off the expansion of the universe. The universe was created by this explosion, and it continues to grow. This phenomenon is called Hubble's Expansion, named after Edwin Hubble who observed in 1929 that galaxies in the universe are moving away from us. This factual observation – that galaxies are moving – implies that the universe itself is expanding. Cosmological research aside, the concept of expansion can help us use changes at the micro-level to deduce what 'bigger picture,' macro-level shifts might be occurring. Approached metaphorically, expansion can refer to both geographical distances and social differences. Expansion is a conceptual model to understand how groups simultaneously reinforce differences, or move away from each other, while continuing to be connected to each other as part of an interdependent system. The distances between groups can be categorized as physical, social, psychological, political, economic, or imagined differences.

This chapter examines tourism in rural China through the critical lens provided by the concept of expansion. Tourism is one such contemporary practice which engages, maintains, and produces distance. I use observed ethnographic data on social change and tourism development in two rural Chinese villages to argue that tourism, and domestic tourism especially, can effect an expansion conceptually akin to the Big Bang. With improved roads and new airports, people in China are moving closer to one another more frequently and meeting in what James Clifford (1997) has called 'contact zones.' But, while actual travel times are shortened, social distances are growing as the real conditions of life in urban spaces and rural places change at different speeds. The relationship between decreased distances as a result of more travel opportunities may inversely stimulate the expansion of perceived socio-economic and cultural distances between groups and communities.

Whether prompted by economic development or notions of heritage preservation, tourist villages now abound in rural, ethnic minority regions of Southwest China (cf. Tan *et al.* 2001). In this chapter, I am concerned with the ways in which local residents of tourist villages manage and manipulate their social and cultural lives in response to or in anticipation of tourists. By examining the way tourism is given meaning by those who are invested in its sustainability, my analysis engages with the conditions engendered and occluded by opportunities for movement and travel. While the cases presented are specific to contemporary China, the production of distance proposed in the concept of expansion is, I argue, relevant to tourism in other countries, especially when tourism is engaged in development work for poverty alleviation, income enhancement or cultural preservation. It is critical to understand tourism development as a process of laying roots in local contexts and conditions, thereby changing the very nature of the social relations involved, rather than as an 'added-value' project laid on top of static, pre-existing communities.

A clarification of terms will help situate my argument. 'Expansion' is used as an umbrella concept through which I approach the study of tourism development and its consequences. Therefore, in this chapter, I consider the terms 'difference' and 'distance' to be mutually interchangeable. My reason for equating distance with difference is to propose that contexts brushed aside as simply 'different' can reveal more complicated truths when we consider certain situations as 'distant' from one another, but not altogether unrelated. Distances can both separate and connect.

The production of distance is a critical part of understanding how differences are mobilized. Through the following case studies of rural, ethnic minorities in China today, it is hoped that we will be able to reconceptualize our understandings of how the practice of tourism not only brings people in contact with one another, but also constructs, divides, and differentiates communities in accordance with supposed tourist demands and actual economic realities.

Tourism and mobility studies in China

The study of tourism, in the social sciences especially, has tended to view travel as an outgrowth of a distinctly Western and modern condition (Graburn 1995b; Alneng 2002). However, formulaic classifications of tourist experiences (e.g., Cohen 1979; Wang 1999) often fall short when examining 'other,' non-Western tourisms (Graburn 1983; Lew and Yu 1995; Alneng 2002). Recent works have called for a historical sensitivity to ideas of heritage, culture, and the subject position of a traveler. An anthropological study of tourism must contend with pre-existing understandings and structures in order to determine contemporary social meanings of tourism and travel (Sofield and Li 1998). For example, the practice of landscape painting coupled with poetic inscriptions continues to inform contemporary travel and ideas of 'being there' in Chinese tourism practices (Petersen 1995).

In a country that has aimed to control the movement of its population (cf. Wang, F. 2005), tourist travel within the People's Republic of China is an under-explored analytical counterpoint to internal migration (Huang and

Zhao 2005) and the Chinese diaspora (Ong 1999; Sun 2002; Nyíri 2005a, 2005b). Nowadays, tourism travel illuminates another side of the myriad forces propelling internal migration in China.[1] The 'internal expansion' of China, as evidenced through the lives and social conditions of rural families in tourist villages, is one consequence of the increasing mobility of Chinese citizens for labor and for leisure.

For residents of rural tourist villages in China, tourism and migration have become ways of envisioning and mediating current economic and social circumstances. Therefore, I approach the concept of mobility, and tourism, as constitutive of social life, rather than as a disruption to an otherwise stable, static condition (Greenblatt 2004). This idea has been established in research on tourist motivations. From the perspective of the tourist, the idea that touristic mobility (i.e., the ability to be a tourist, or at least to imagine being one) can be an integral part of one's life even when not touring, as demonstrated in Julia Harrison's study (2003) of tourism in the lives of Canadians. What remains to be studied is how tourism is integrated into life expectations for toured communities.

Tourism is no longer just about the tourist's search for the other (cf. Cohen 1979; MacCannell 1999). Instead, contemporary domestic tourism in China sheds new light on how the process of defining the 'other' happens within toured communities. This chapter takes tourism research one step further by considering not only the distances between the tourist and the toured, but also the distances produced by participation in tourism industries.

Two ethnographic case studies

The ethnographic research for this chapter took place in two rural villages in the neighboring regions of Guizhou Province and the Guangxi Zhuang Autonomous Region (Figure 15.1). Sites were chosen for their current participation in tourism industries and tourism-based development programs, and their population composition (residents officially recognized by the Chinese state as belonging to ethnic minority groups).[2]

Ping'an, Guangxi Zhuang Autonomous Region

Ping'an village in northern Guangxi is located within the Longji Terraces Scenic Area. It has a population of about 850 residents, the overwhelming majority of whom identify as members of the Zhuang minority group, and is one of 13 villages within the designated scenic area. The village was visited as early as 1978 by local officials who seized upon the tourism potential of the dramatic terraced fields surrounding the village and the Zhuang cultural customs of the villagers. In the 1980s, two village cadres started the first local guesthouse. Occupying a privileged position within local political spheres, these cadres were 'tipped off' by the government early on. According to Wen (2002: 27), the cadres regularly attended county government

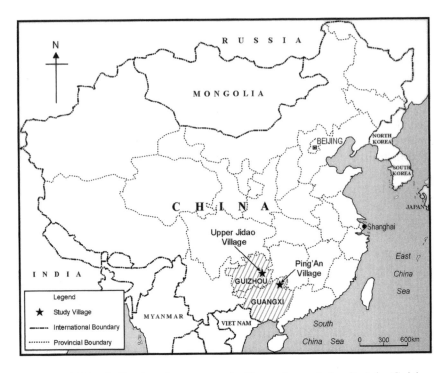

Figure 15.1 Map indicating the two rural villages (case study sites) in Guizhou Province and Guangxi Zhuang Autonomous Region

meetings where they learned of the government's priorities in building up the tourism industry. In the mid-1990s, the county government gradually joined forces with a private management company. This company invested heavily in the region and assumed operational responsibilities for the entire scenic area in return for profits from ticket sales. Tickets in 2007 cost RMB50 (approximately US$6.60)[3] for entry to the entire area.

In one sense, tourism to Ping'an is successful in that many people have returned to the village from work or study elsewhere. Currently, business in Ping'an concentrates around family-run guesthouses and shops. As of April 2007, Ping'an had 82 hotels, the majority owned and operated by villagers, although in recent years a number of hotels have been built by non-local businesses. This means that about half of the 180 households in Ping'an ran hotels at home, but there are many more individual villagers working as porters, sedan chair carriers and guides. One could say that this exemplifies the idea that being successful in tourism is not being mobile, and this is a belief that permeates throughout development programs in rural China. The idea that successful tourism development equates with an opportunity to stay in one's home posits mobility in a negative light, and correlates almost too neatly with the notion of rural to urban migration as undesirable or dangerous.

What makes Ping'an an interesting case study of rural tourism is its relatively long engagement with tourism and tourists, both domestic and international, and the consequences of this on social relations in and around the village. Chinese folklorist Xu (2005) points out that Ping'an residents have gone through an enormous psychological shift in the past 30 years. From being called poor and backwards in the discourse of Chinese national development in the 1960s, by the 1980s, Ping'an was celebrated for its authentic ethnic customs and unpolluted natural environment, which became the base of its tourism industry (Xu 2005: 197–8). The very features of the village itself, from the terraced fields to the wooden houses to the bamboo forests, have been assigned a new value in tourism, and villagers necessarily adopted and embraced this new system of values and meanings associated with their daily lives. Living in the village has become doubly valuable as an example of a rural, ethnic minority cultural group and as a product in the tourism marketplace with a price tag.

Residents of Ping'an not only are adopting the tourists' value systems towards ethnic cultures and landscapes, they are also shaping their lives in reaction to the privileges and priorities introduced by urban tourists. Tourism exposes urban living habits to the villagers, who must constantly reassure the city folk that their food is clean and the water potable. By so doing, they implicitly evoke the developmental discourse that the rural is 'backward' (dirty, unsanitary) and the urban is 'modern' (clean, safe). At a policy level in China, the urban–rural gap in living standards is being addressed through the New Socialist Countryside program, a national policy for rural development introduced in the 11th five-year plan in 2006. As a part of the construction of the New Socialist Countryside, tourism development is promoted as a way towards the 'urbanization' and 'modernization' of rural regions (Zhao 2007). Furthermore, because tourism literally puts urban and rural Chinese in contact with one another, the result is often a shift in villagers' own aspirations (in 2007, for example, computers and motorcycles were hotly desired commodities), and a heightened awareness of the gap between their desires and the current conditions of their everyday lives. It is noted that the average annual per capita income in Ping'an reported in 2006, about RMB3,000 (US$400), is roughly one-third of the 2005 urban per capita income in Guangxi, RMB8,917 (US$1,189).[4]

My ethnographic research in Ping'an revealed complicated layers of social inequalities and corresponding feelings of discontent, spurred by competition and changing resident perceptions of what constitutes progress, wealth and poverty. During the household surveys I conducted, villagers pointed out that tourism has brought about the negative consequence of increasing wealth disparities between families. Although the majority of residents do participate in tourism, the distribution of wealth is highly unequal. Families who can afford to build hotels do so; families who cannot obtain a loan to invest in materials and labor to construct a guesthouse are consigned to small sales or, increasingly, work as staff at another family's business. A

30-year-old female owner of a hotel popular with photography groups and the head of the Ping'an dance troupe put it plainly, saying: 'Now that there's tourism, everyone is in competition with each other, right?' (personal interview, 8 March 2007.) Another 28-year-old man, whose family runs a relatively busy guesthouse, explained it this way: 'Some have gotten rich . . . and there's a bit of selfishness; it's very difficult to manage this – everyone thinks about themselves, and no one thinks about everyone' (personal interview, 4 March 2007). The inference is that in Ping'an a sense of community has been displaced by a feeling of estrangement due to competition in the tourism industry.

Ping'an residents framed their comments around three sets of socio-economic distances that shape their community, their opportunities, and their assessment of what constitutes a good life. There is the distance between the tourists and the locals, whose material differences the government is trying to address; there are the distances between households in Ping'an where neighbors are in direct competition with neighbors; and there are differences between the quality of life in Ping'an versus that in other villages nearby. In the last case, within the region, Ping'an is a social and economic hub. Residents of other villages, near and far, migrate to Ping'an to work as laborers, shopkeepers and hotel staff. A half-hour away by foot lies the village of Longji, which now serves as a reminder to Ping'an of just how far they have come. Longji residents chose not to give up land for a road and as a result, the village is far less accessible and far less visited than Ping'an. Longji's complete name has even been changed to 'Longji Ancient Zhuang Village,' a fitting descriptor which emphasizes the relative modernity of Ping'an. The rise of tourism in Ping'an has expanded the gulf between these two villages to the point that one is by name relegated to the past, while its neighbor faces the new future of the Chinese countryside. Despite geographic proximity, the material differences between the villages are stark; there are no gift shops, no computers, and no wages in Longji. While disparities in incomes and wealth have jarred relationships in Ping'an, opinions about the relationship between Longji and Ping'an are unanimous: Longji is far from Ping'an, developmentally, materially, and economically. Taken together, the case of Ping'an demonstrates that while policy and public attention typically is given to the urban–rural disparities when discussing the merits of rural tourism development, actual conditions at the regional, village level reveal how tourism is driving distances between those whose lives are perhaps most at stake in the success, or failure, of the tourism industries.

Upper Jidao, Guizhou Province

Upper Jidao in Guizhou Province is one of seven villages selected in 2002 to comprise the Bala River Miao Minority Village Tourism Area, which is part of a provincial program for poverty alleviation through tourism development (Guizhou Tourism Bureau 2006). Tourism to the Bala River area capitalizes on the minority customs and crafts of the region's ethnic Miao population; this had already been established by the success of other villages along the Bala River such as Langde (officially opened to tourism in the mid-1980s; Oakes 1998; Zhou 2000) and Nanhua (opened in 1997). I conducted research in what is known as Upper Jidao village. Administratively, Upper and Lower Jidao villages are considered one unit, but as natural villages they maintain separate intra-village leadership associations.[5]

The emerging circumstances of tourism development and community relations between Upper and Lower Jidao closely resemble the situation between Ping'an and Longji, as described in the previous section. The bulk of government financial support for tourism is earmarked for projects which will involve Upper Jidao. When asked why Lower Jidao is not a bigger part of the tourism development plans, most people (government officials and villagers alike) told me that Upper Jidao is 'more beautiful' and 'more suited' for tourists than Lower Jidao. When asked how this was decided, it was explained to me that experts hired by the government and the World Bank came to Jidao in 2004 and declared that Upper Jidao was better for tourism. The latest plans for Upper Jidao are implemented under the New Socialist Countryside program (Figure 15.2). This five-year plan includes the

Figure 15.2 A highway billboard in Guizhou Province reads, 'Develop rural tourism, build the new socialist countryside' (Photo by author)

construction of a cultural center with guestrooms and a performance space. Money for the reconstruction of the village into a suitable tourist destination comes from local as well as national poverty alleviation sources, with a large fund from the city of Ningbo in the wealthy east coast province of Zhejiang. Together, Upper and Lower Jidao receive approximately RMB500,000 (about US$66,700) each year from Ningbo. According to village leaders in Upper Jidao, 80 percent of Ningbo funds are allotted to tourism-related projects in Upper Jidao. Growing discontent among Lower Jidao residents has materialized in the form of strained relations between the upper and lower village associations and isolated cases of damage, ranging from advertisement posters being ripped apart to the road to Upper Jidao being blocked by sandbags on the night of the first day of the October National Holiday week in 2006.

Upper Jidao itself is quite small, with 105 households and a population of 424, although villagers tell me the actual number of people living in the village is usually around 250–300. The majority of able-bodied people have left to find work elsewhere. Many villagers also told me that if tourism were a sustainable enterprise, family members would be willing to return. For the time being, however, among the few younger people who have stayed, there is a real feeling that many would rather have left to pursue opportunities elsewhere. In 2006, tourist arrivals were low; village leaders estimated about 2,000 tourists that year. The tourists I observed spent less than an hour sightseeing in the village. Very few stayed long enough to eat, let alone spend the night with a local family.

In the household surveys I conducted, villagers overwhelmingly agreed that they were interested in developing tourism in Upper Jidao for the income that tourism is thought to generate. When it came to what kind of tourism or tourism activities they considered most suitable to the village, people expressed a desire to distance themselves from the tourism models employed in Langde and Nanhua, both of which are within 5 km of Jidao and which rely on pre-arranged dance performances to attract income (the two villages charge RMB300–500, or US$40–65, to each visiting tour group). Upper Jidao should not become a song-and-dance village like Langde or Nanhua, I was told repeatedly, because there is no need for another such tourist village within the Bala River region. According to a paper prepared by the Vice-Governor for Southeast Guizhou Li Zai-yong (2005), the Bala River project clearly specifies unique tourism 'characteristics' for each of the seven villages involved, as indicated in Table 15.1.

Aside from its content, Table 15.1 is a visual reminder of how villages are to be kept separate, different, and distant from each other. By separating the seven villages and identifying 'characteristics' for each, the tourism development plan renders the kilometer between Upper Jidao and Langde into a much greater distance.

However, finding and developing the necessary distance and difference between these villages may be easier said than done. An official in Maomaohe,

Table 15.1 Tourism development plans for the Bala River Valley in Guizhou

Name of the Village	Characteristics	Work Division and Positioning
Huai'enbao	Ancient postal road built in late Ming and early Qing Dynasties and located at the entrance to the Demonstration Project Area	Providing comprehensive tourism services
Nanhua	Miao songs and dances	Displays of the Miao songs and dances
[Upper] Jidao	Ancient building structures, history and culture	Showing tourists the Hundred-year Granary and the Hundred-year Path; performance of ancient (hundred-year) songs
Langde	Miao songs and dances; ancient building complex; liquor-drinking customs	Showing tourists the ancient traditional Miao buildings; performances of the Miao songs and dances
Jiaomeng	The Miao Copper Drum Dance; Specialty agriculture; Water-buffalo fights; cockfights, bird fights	Specialty agriculture for sightseeing; services at the spots along the hiking route of Maomao–Liaomeng–Nanmeng–Langde
Nanmeng	Homeland of Lusheng art	Performances of *lusheng*; services at the spots along the hiking route of Jiaomeng–Nanmeng–Langde
Maomaohe	A village nation-wide famous for its good sanitation; the entrance to the Demonstration Area	Exhibition of Miao embroideries; leisure tours and holiday making; comprehensive supporting services

Source: Compiled from http://www.gz-travel.net/zhuanban/xiangcun/eblh.asp, accessed 22 August 2006

for example, said that tourism to their village has decreased since 2002. When asked why, he said it was because seven villages were too many; 'We are all the same,' the official said, 'so why would any tourist go to seven of the same places? Historically, socially, culturally, we are all the same Miao!' (personal interview, 16 June 2006). In an interview with Party Secretary Wang Qiao of the Kaili Municipal Tourism Bureau, Wang repeatedly emphasized that the Bala River villages must not be the same (personal interview, 15 December 2006). Even national level tourism officials have pointed out the 'problems' of same-ness. In a paper given at the 2004 International Forum on Guizhou Rural Tourism by Xiao Qianhui from *China Tourism News* explained:

When we came to Guizhou, we found there were too many common points existing between different ethnic villages and different ethnic groups here ... The greatest threat to our rural tourism would be the sameness in a thousand villages. If all the villages ... have the same face, it is unnecessary for tourists to visit them one by one.

(Xiao 2005: 212)

In an interesting twist, being recognizably the same as your neighbors becomes a burden within the tourism worldview, where difference, between this village and the one down the road, demands a distancing of self from the other.

For Ping'an and Upper Jidao, tourism brings not only new enterprises and economies, but also new ways of thinking about community and the future. While in Ping'an, the relative success of tourism has introduced psychological distances between families and neighbors, Upper Jidao and the Bala River Miao Minority Tourism Area demonstrate that a certain kind of distance must be programmed into tourism development. What matters now is not only that villagers express a sense of distance from their neighbors or their ethnic communities, but more importantly that these perceived distances have real implications for village lives, livelihoods, and conceptualizations of belonging within the Chinese nation.

Thinking about an 'other'

My argument about perceived distances as a result of tourism rotates around three primary axes of difference: rural–urban, ethnic minority–ethnic majority, poor–rich. Of course, these binaries are not unique to China, but they are being adopted for promoting tourism. Increasingly, tourism is incorporated into domestic rural development programs in China (Zhao 2007). To coincide with the New Socialist Countryside program, 2006 was named the 'Year of Rural Tourism' by the China National Tourism Administration. This official attention to rural tourism suggests that something much greater than market expansion is occurring – alongside the market, there are subsequent expansions in the socio-economic and political ramifications of tourism. Within the villages, differences and senses of distance are often expressed as feelings of envy or dismissal (in Ping'an) or as a desire and need to 'be different' (in Upper Jidao).

The production of distance between communities (rural–urban, poor–rich, minority–majority) is sometimes grounded in tourist behaviors. Not only do locals find tourists to be different, but tourists themselves are finding the differences they encounter to be somewhat uncomfortable. Studies such as Laxson's (1991) research on tourist perceptions of Native Americans show how too much contact can be undesirable to tourists. According to Laxson, some tourists admitted to feeling more comfortable at a distance: a young woman at the Pueblo Cultural Center in Albuquerque, New Mexico, told her: 'The only way I feel comfortable learning about it [Pueblo culture] or knowing about it is through something like [novels by Tony Hillerman]. Something that lets you keep your distance' (Laxson 1991: 367). This woman's admission reminds us of the presence of distance in tourism and that this space can have real consequences for parties on either side of the equation.

In Ping'an, a luxury hotel owned by a Chinese-American businessman from Seattle opened in 2006 to much fanfare amongst the village residents, who were excited to see for themselves what US$180/night looked like. Unfortunately for the people of Ping'an, the hotel came complete with a buzzer-activated front gate, security cameras, and an elevated construction that allowed guests inside a sweeping view of the terraced fields but those outside only a glimpse of the stone railing around the balcony. Within a few months of opening, villagers told me no one except the staff (only one of whom was a local woman) and guests could enter; the porters who carried luggage up from the parking lot were allowed only as far as the front door. The physical distance created by the hotel's construction reinforced for the villagers the socio-economic differences between them and the tourists (and the non-local entrepreneurs who have come to Ping'an). Furthermore, by offering such an exclusive, secluded space for tourists in a village as small as Ping'an, the inference is that perhaps rural, Zhuang minority life is best experienced from a distance, from a walled balcony.

Growing socio-economic distances are expanding between tourists and the toured. The effects of this are not only constructed into the built environment, such as the luxury hotel in Ping'an, but also worn on the physical bodies of the village residents. In the big picture of Chinese society and politics, the residents of Ping'an and Upper Jidao are officially recognized by the state as ethnic minority populations, and the cultural traditions of each village are heavily promoted as part of the tourism experience in each place. Ethnicity becomes an integral component of tourism, ostensibly for the benefit of the destination communities. As a result, they must be different, if not culturally, then visually or aesthetically, in order to meet certain expected tourist demands. These expectations are internalized by the toured communities as a part of new value systems introduced by tourism. Often this impulse emerges when a camera is present; in Upper Jidao, a television crew from the international news agency Reuters came to shoot a story about rural tourism (on 4 February 2007). As the cameraman set up the shot for an on-camera interview with a local woman, she turned to me and asked: 'Shall I change into Miao clothes and put my hair in a topknot?' I replied: 'If you like, but it's not necessary, is it?' The woman thought for a moment, and then turned to rush back to her house to change. 'It's more representative [if she dressed in Miao clothes and not her everyday clothes],' she said, by way of explanation. She reappeared moments later in a black top with a colored, embroidered piece in the middle (which the villagers referred to simply as 'Miao clothes'), and her hair wound on top of her head and decorated with a silver comb in back and a fabric flower in front. By choosing to look different for the international television crew, she staked a claim in the significance of the Miao ethnic minority as being an 'other.'

Tourism development demands that the Bala River villages, once considered as cut of the same Miao ethnic minority cloth, now have to emphasize differences between themselves and majority, non-Miao society as well as create differences between themselves and other Miao villages in order to reap the rewards of tourism. So much is clear in the statements made by the government officials in Maomaohe and Kaili, who worried that too much sameness between the Miao villages of the Bala River would ultimately be a disadvantage. Ironically, then, whereas being a recognizable part of a mainstream ethnic minority group is still important for political representation in a centralized state system that maintains an exact count and decisive role in naming the nation's constituent minority communities, on the ground, tourism development in Upper Jidao requires a negotiation of difference. The axis of difference created by categories such as minority and majority is complicated when it comes to promoting ethnicity within tourism; indeed, just as economic development demands that we consider the terms 'rich' and 'poor' relative to local circumstances, the minority–majority relationship is also challenged in certain tourism situations.

Whether it is residents of Ping'an talking about wealth and poverty or government officials and residents of the Bala River region wondering how to increase tourist flows to all seven villages, their comments reflect a shift in senses of community and belonging for rural, ethnic minority populations in China. Whereas during China's nationalities identification project of the 1950s the purpose of distinguishing between ethnic minority groups was to integrate all groups into a seamless map of progress and social development, nowadays difference is needed to keep communities apart for purposes of economic growth via tourism. This shift reveals how differences, whether ethnic or economic, are instrumentalized and used in certain contexts. Indeed, difference, like distance, can connect or separate; of the development of the natural sciences in Europe, Foucault writes, 'in 17th, 18th centuries, difference was to find a way to connect all species together; by 19th it was to turn inwards to internal logics, eminently multiple/multipliable, integrative only with itself' (1994: 272). In the Chinese construction of 'rural' today, the 'other' – the rural villagers of Ping'an and Jidao – is supposed to be closely connected to, even similar, to the culture of the tourists: modern and economically well off. These are the progressive goals of national development efforts such as the New Socialist Countryside program. Nonetheless, in tourism development, villagers must also remain distant enough from the national mainstream in order to render culture in the form of 'unique performances' and 'distinctive handicrafts' that might interest tourists.

Domestic tourism in China continues to seek out and codify the internal other. For tourist village residents, the process of tourism development is in understanding why tourists come to a rural, ethnic minority village, and negotiating what happens when tourism benefits this village, but perhaps not that one. The result is the internal expansion of China: the experience of increased distances between communities as a result of concrete social, economic and political changes.

Conclusion

In both Ping'an and Upper Jidao, socio-economic development has meant opportunities to not stay in the village, or at least to imagine a life elsewhere in China. With this, the ability to be mobile takes on increasingly significant resonances. Therefore, what we are dealing with here is what Appadurai has called 'the cultural economy of distance,' which he argues is 'the driving force of merchants, trades, and commodities, especially of the luxury variety' (1996: 71). For tourism studies, the cultural economy of distance is the way physical distances and socio-economic differences interact to affect how individuals come to understand themselves and their communities through activities such as tourism. Tourism travel in/to rural China continues to be a luxury form of mobility, and the counterpart movement of travel from rural China remains mostly for purposes of labor and wage-earning. The internal expansion of China means that the residents of Ping'an and Upper Jidao have more places to go and more ways to get there, but further distances to cross in order to arrive.

This chapter has explored how tourism becomes constitutive of a socially meaningful experience for those whose livelihoods depend upon its industrial and structural existence. The complexity of tourism lies in the fact that, as Urry noted, 'mobility creates new inequalities of access' (2003: 5). In order to examine these new inequalities, a conceptual approach to the idea of expansion can help us to understand how various socio-cultural phenomena are interlinked. It is hoped that this chapter may help illuminate the socio-economic ramifications of tourism development, so that future policy measures can take into greater consideration the effects of such programs.

Notes

1 In 2003, the number of people not registered in their place of residence in China was 140 million, and 114 million 'participated in internal migration' (Huang and Zhao 2005: 2). Comparatively, in 2004 there were 1.1 billion domestic tourism trips made in China, totaling 84.8 percent of the population.

2 Official Chinese documents commonly refer to China as 'a united multi-ethnic nation of 56 ethnic groups' (http://www.china.org.cn/english/features/38107.htm, accessed 1 February 2007). This position is based upon research conducted in China during the 1950s and 1960s under the auspices of the 'nationalities identification project.'

3 Prices here are given in Chinese RMB, with US equivalents, at 7.5 RMB to US$1 (in October 2007).

4 Data from Sha *et al.* (2007) and http://www.china.org.cn/english/features/ ProvinceView/167754.htm (accessed 7 September 2007).
5 In China, the distinction between natural and administrative villages is as follows: 'a natural village occurs when households cluster together, forming a small community. An administrative village is a region consisting of several villages designated by the state as a unit for administrative purposes' (Xing *et al.* 2006: viii) Thus, in the case of Jidao, Jidao is the administrative village name of two natural villages, known simply as Upper Jidao and Lower Jidao.

Part IV

Revis(it)ing heritage

Dissonance or harmony?

16 From the center to the margin

Tourism and conflict in Kashmir

Shalini Panjabi

Introduction

Most literature on tourism in conflict areas has focused on aspects of 'dark tourism.' Studying tourism in Kashmir – where a violent conflict has endured for more than a decade – however, introduces a variant perspective. With the return of some 'normalcy' in the region, domestic tourists from India are returning there in large numbers – but the return is to sites of scenic beauty rather than of bombings and incarceration. Even though the conflict has – and continues to leave – physical reminders, the Kashmiris and the tourists, the hosts and the guests, both seem to largely ignore this. Their return is based not on remembering the violent past, but rather on evading it. Though with the valley swarming with security forces and other physical reminders of the conflict which cannot be ignored, the tourists and the hosts seek to make it as marginal as possible. None of the sites of violence are specifically visited or highlighted, and all attempts are made to make it appear as though these intervening years of violence have not changed the valley, and it remains simply the paradise it always was. However, this denial – of the conflict and thus also of the aspirations of the Kashmiris – creates peculiar situations, ambivalences and paradoxes, which I discuss in this chapter.

To date, much of the dark tourism literature has been about specific sites of death and tragedy; places that memorialize or signify a violent past (Lennon and Foley 2000; Strange and Kempa 2003; Stone 2005; Macdonald 2006). Tourism in areas where a political conflict is still active is treated as a sub-genre within dark tourism. The few studies of 'danger zone tourism' or 'conflict tourism' as it has been called, have focused on experiences of Western travelers 'who are drawn to areas of political turmoil' (Adams 2006: 208). These places are presumed to be 'interesting for reasons of political disputes' (Warner 1999: 10), and the tourists who go there are seen as 'adventure tourists' of a sort, enjoying the thrills of courting danger (Swarbrooke *et al.* 2003). Visits to these areas are thus always conceived of as 'alternate' forms of tourism,[1] and studies of tourism in conflict areas have rarely gone beyond this paradigm.

However, studying tourism in Kashmir today leads us to a different perspective. As a premier tourist destination for domestic tourists before the conflict erupted, the decade of violence in Kashmir is seen within India as an unwelcome interlude. In terms of the numbers it attracts today Kashmir might be a minor destination, but it is definitely not a niche market for dark tourism – most tourists are middle-class Indian families and pilgrims. They go to Kashmir to experience its scenic beauty and visit the holy sites, not to dwell on the violence and the dangers lurking therein. However, the situation is difficult and the experiences and movements of both the hosts and the guests are constrained by the continuing tensions. A different frame thus needs to be adopted here, a frame that moves beyond 'dark tourism' and seeks to present a more comprehensive picture of the various complexities around tourism in a conflict zone. The dominant mode of analysis of tourism in conflict zones, by discussing only the thrills apparently experienced by small groups of international travelers, offers only a partial perspective on the various issues involved. I seek instead to study issues around tourism in a troubled region by focusing on domestic tourism and the experiences of the hosts. Tourism in Kashmir today cannot be seen as distinct from the conflict, even though the tourists and many Kashmiris themselves would like to imagine it so. For the conflict stems from issues of sovereignty, and attempts to bypass it imply also a concomitant denial of issues that are critical for Kashmiris. The government's aim in promoting tourism is also political, even as it seeks to aid economic reconstruction of the valley. Domestic tourism in Kashmir today cannot be considered distinct from the political conflict, the two are enmeshed together, and it is this complex and its effects and implications that are the focus of this chapter.

The centrality of Kashmir in Indian tourism

Kashmir, as popularly understood in India, refers to the 'valley of Kashmir' (often called just 'the Valley'). This demarcation excludes the areas of Jammu and Ladakh from the larger province in India, and also the areas of Kashmir that are administered by Pakistan. The 'vale of Kashmir' is a scenic valley in the Himalayas, with Srinagar as its political and geographical center. The emblematic description of Kashmir as a 'paradise on earth' epitomizes its allure, and the desire of many Indians to visit Kashmir now – despite frequent incidences of violence – is indicative of its strong appeal. The centrality of Kashmir in the Indian imagination, as a destination for tourism, cannot be exaggerated. The boom in domestic tourism in India is a recent phenomenon. However, even at a time when relatively few people traveled for leisure – from the 1950s through the 1980s – Kashmir was the imagined iconic holiday location. Indeed, for those with the money and any inclination to travel, Kashmir remained the favored destination.[2]

Various factors lead to this fascination of middle- and upper-class Indians with Kashmir. One, of course, is the cool, temperate, climate of the valley, set at an average altitude of 1,524 m. Encircled by the high mountains, with green meadows, fruit orchards, and crisscrossing rivers and lakes, it represents tranquility for those living in the hot, dusty plains. This vision was fueled by the countless song sequences of Hindi movies shot in the valley. The valley's association with the Mughals has also always added to its allure. For the Mughal rulers of the sixteenth and seventeenth centuries, Kashmir was a beautiful valley, and they constructed more than 700 gardens and monuments there (Petruccioli 1991: 69; Gole 1993: 156). The Mughal gardens were distinguished by terraced waterways, pavilions and grand *chinar* (Oriental Plane) trees set against the backdrop of the mountains. Though now barely a dozen of those gardens remain, yet three of them in and around Srinagar (Chasm-e-Shahi, Nishat and Shalimar), are mandatory stops on any tourist itinerary. The popularity of Kashmiri handicrafts – shawls, carpets and woodcarving – is also partially owed to their association with the Mughals (Scollay 2000). Furthermore, the horticultural produce, dry fruits and saffron from Kashmir are highly valued, and have contributed to the vision of a 'wondrous' Kashmir.

However, it is important to emphasize here that this fascination for the land has not extended to its inhabitants, the Kashmiris, with whom the engagement of tourists has always been minimal; rarely extending much beyond posing for snapshots in Kashmiri dresses in the Mughal gardens. Indeed, while it is a situation that is not too different from many other tourist sites across the world, in the case of Kashmir it stands in deep contrast to the great desire for the land and its material products. This exclusion of the Kashmiris from the imagination of the Indian tourist has only heightened after the conflict, as we shall see shortly.

In addition to being a popular destination for leisure travelers, the Kashmir region has also been an important destination for pilgrims. Predominantly Hindu, these pilgrims undertake an annual pilgrimage, or *yatra*, to the holy cave of Amarnath, located at a height of 4,115 m. While some prominent Muslim shrines and mosques in the valley also attract pilgrims from other parts of India, the numbers are not very large, and are never enumerated separately. In contrast, the estimates and analyses of the Amarnath pilgrimage are always separated from leisure tourism in the valley, even though there has always been some overlap between the two, for many pilgrims would spend a few additional days holidaying in the valley before returning home. Prior to the period of militancy, the proportion of Amarnath pilgrims within the annual number of visitors to the region remained low. However, with the onset of violence a major shift occurred, with pilgrims far outnumbering tourists. In 1989, of the 653,000 tourists to the valley, 95,000 were Amarnath pilgrims. The next year, 1990, was the worst for tourism, and only 16,000 people traveled to Kashmir, of which 5,000 were Amarnath pilgrims. In 1996, 120,000 of the total 130,000 tourists were pilgrims. By 1999, the figures had begun to change again, and that year of the 331,000 tourists, 217,000 came for leisure and 114,000 as pilgrims (all figures, Dewan and Manzar 2000: 66).

Over the course of the period of militancy, pilgrims were sporadically targeted, and with a number of fatalities their levels declined. Perhaps not surprisingly, there was a more significant drop in the number of leisure tourists after the violence erupted, despite the fact that 'tourists' had not been attacked at any point in the conflict. Peaceful conditions are obviously an imperative for those traveling for pleasure – and it is the recognition of this imperative that leads to the denial of the conflict by the government, the tourists and the hosts themselves.

The militancy retraced

The struggle that has ensued in Kashmir since independence in 1947 has been characterized as an 'ethno-religious conflict' (Ganguly 1996). In 1989, every-day life in the valley was transformed when the conflict took a violent turn. Kashmir was suddenly displaced from the tourism map of the country, and is now struggling to regain its position. To trace the contours of this journey, we will begin with a brief recapitulation of the history of the conflict.[3]

The modern state of Jammu and Kashmir was created in 1846 through a treaty signed by the East India Company and the Dogras, the rulers of Jammu. The Dogras were Hindus, and they discriminated against the majority Muslim population of Kashmir. By the 1930s, the movement against this régime had begun to gather force, but it was brutally suppressed. In 1947, the Dogra ruler Hari Singh initially vacillated in his decision to join either the inde-pendent dominions of India or Pakistan. Later under duress he acceded to India in October that year. This decision was never fully accepted by many Kashmiris – and by Pakistan – and forms the kernel of the conflict. Pakistan's case has been that as a Muslim majority state, Kashmir rightly should have joined Pakistan, while Kashmiris have also nurtured the hope of forming an independent state.

From the beginning, the armed forces of both India and Pakistan have been involved in the dispute. A ceasefire in 1949 left Kashmir partitioned.[4] With Pakistan-supported guerrilla groups becoming increasingly active, and India continually reneging on even its limited offers of autonomy, protests against Indian rule grew in the ensuing decades. Elections to the provincial assembly in 1987, that were widely perceived as having been heavily rigged, formed the trigger for widespread protests that turned increasingly violent with grenade attacks, bomb blasts and assassinations. The first half of the 1990s was violent and traumatic for Kashmiris. In the first couple of years, the militants had the backing of large sections of Kashmiri Muslims. Life in the valley was totally disrupted in those years, as calls for strikes and marches would get thousands of people onto the streets. Often these protests would turn violent and bloody, as the government responded by firing at unarmed civilians. The militants too intensified their violent campaign. In an effort to control the situation, the Indian government called in the army in huge num-bers, and employed force disproportionately. The period of intense violence receded when the Indian government began to accept that force would not control the Kashmiris. Gradually, talks and negotiations were initiated and the political process was reintroduced. The power that the militants wielded also corrupted many, and they became preoccupied with kidnappings and extortions and various illegal trades. By the mid-1990s, most Kashmiris were exhausted with the spiral of brutal violence and anomie in the valley, and the support for the militants began to wane. Coupled with the political initiatives of the government, it led to a situation whereby the past five years have seen a gradual return to a more stable life in the valley, though violent attacks still continue.

To get a sense of everyday life in the valley over the past 18 years, it must be recognized that, unlike some other insurgencies, this is a conflict that has involved all sections of society. The movement initially received support from a large section of Kashmiri Muslims, and the young men who joined in came from across the spectrum. Subsequently, the crackdown by the Indian security forces also affected many. The extortions and kidnappings by the militants seem to have cut across the board. No one could remain unaffected by the complete disruption of life in the valley. Offices, businesses, schools, agriculture, all endured various breaks and stoppages – as years were lost. Tragically though, while the Kashmiris have endured enormous suffering through this period, they have achieved no political gains.[5]

The frustration with Indian rule has still not disappeared, though it is now tempered by the realization – as a number of local residents I interviewed indicated – that neither India nor Pakistan would ever give up Kashmir. The disillusionment with Pakistan has only partially eased the anger against India. As Indian security forces stay on in the valley in large numbers, subjecting all Kashmiris to daily security checks and constant humiliations, the acceptance does not come easy. In such a situation, both the regional and the central governments have been very keen to herald a return to 'normalcy.' The promotion of tourism is an important component of this process. As the source of livelihood for a large number of Kashmiris, tourism is also emblematic of the valley. Horticulture and handicrafts may be earning more revenue now, but it is the image of the *shikaras* (small boats) on Dal Lake that most typifies the vale of Kashmir.

'Tourism for peace'

Positioning tourism as the backbone of the state economy, both the central and the state governments have accorded it a pivotal role in the economic reconstruction of the valley. As can be expected, the conflict has had a detrimental impact on Kashmir's economy. Detailed economic figures about Kashmir are difficult to find as conditions in the valley have curtailed official surveys, but some basic statistics are indicative of the situation. Figures from the Economic Survey 2006–07 for Jammu and Kashmir indicate that the *per capita* gross income of the state at constant price grew from Rupees 8,644 in 2000–1 to just Rupees 9,553 in 2004–5 (all-India: from Rupees 18,113 to Rupees 21,806) (Navlakha 2007: 4034). The unemployment rate in Jammu and Kashmir at 4.21 percent is also higher than the national average of 3.09 percent. Further, wage employees in Jammu and Kashmir account for nearly 61 percent against 52.4 percent at an all-India level, indicating a paucity of economic opportunities (ibid.). The government's plans to boost Kashmir's economy though are aimed at more than an improvement of these figures. For the government, economic reconstruction is essential in its long-term strategy 'to ensure conflict resolution and prevention, and peace' (ibid.). The promotion of tourism, and the concomitant effort to 'normalize' the situation, are important components of this plan.

As noted, the conflict has severely affected the tourism industry in the valley. Non-Kashmiris are not allowed to buy and own immovable property in Kashmir.[6] As a result of this law, and the conditions of the past two decades, there is barely any private investment from outside in Kashmir's tourism industry. The ownership and control of nearly all hotels, restaurants, houseboats and transport services are in Kashmiri hands. Many of these are single-owner, small operations, which were all hard-hit when tourism dried up in the 1990s. As mentioned earlier, the figures for that period are quite startling: the number of visitors dropped from 650,000 in 1989 to just 16,000 in 1990, and only after 1998 was there a substantive improvement (Dewan and Manzar 2000: 66). Kashmiris dependent on tourism thus went through almost a decade with very little earnings. Traveling in and around Srinagar today, one hears various stories about those difficult years. Stories of prosperous houseboat owners having to work as laborers, of traders and taxi drivers migrating to other towns in the country, of artisans and service staff either going to neighboring states as laborers or returning to their villages where they subsisted on some agricultural income and also undertook labor work for the army. Many people became vendors of small goods in pushcarts. Until recently, security forces occupied many hotels, especially in central areas of Srinagar. Even though they were paying (discounted) room rents to the owners, often the damage they caused to the property nullified the income generated.

In the past few years, the security forces have been made to vacate all hotels and most government guesthouses (Ahmed 2004). To help revive the tourism sector the government has also initiated a number of measures including the provision of loans to small tour operators, houseboat owners, and those driving motorized rickshaws. Owners of houses, especially around the Dal Lake, have also been encouraged to convert their residences into guesthouses with some financial assistance.[7]

While the government claims its motivations are primarily economic, its promotion of tourism – at the expense of other sectors of the economy – is seen equally as a political move to deny a conflict exists (Ganai 2007; Greater Kashmir 2007: 6). Tourism clearly cannot be seen apart from the conflict, the politics, in the valley that permeates every sphere of life. However, the government's endeavors to revive tourism seem to deny this link.[8] In its bid to breathe new life into the industry the government has also focused on the tourists themselves, primarily through policies that attempt to ensure their security in the volatile valley. Over the past five years, they have been exhorting people across the country to visit Kashmir. There have also been various advertising campaigns in the media funded by the Jammu and Kashmir Tourism Department. For example, advertisements issued in two popular magazines suggest: 'The enchantment never ends. In the dream called Kashmir' (*Outlook Traveller* 2003: 49) and 'Your senses say it's paradise, your spirit reaffirms it' (*India Today* 2006: 9). Naturally, in a narrative extolling 'paradise on earth' the conflict is not mentioned.

Living with the conflict: curtailed mobility in the valley

Yet the prevailing conditions for the visitors and residents are quite different, as everyday life in the valley is still affected by the conflict. For the visitor, the tension of the unresolved conflict is evident soon after leaving Jammu, on the Jammu–Srinagar highway.[9] At very regular intervals are bunkers and stacks of sandbags, behind which the security personnel are always alert, rifles in hand. Many of them are posted as sentries at high points on the mountainous road, and they often look nervously around for the conflict is still violent. On the long and winding road to Srinagar, the military presence is even more evident. Often military personnel in trucks and jeeps can be seen, moving in convoys for additional security (Figure 16.1).

Figure 16.1 An armed convoy moving along the National Highway (Photo by author)

Srinagar, as can be expected, is populated with security forces. They often stop vehicles at random, check inside, and question the occupants. Most of the security personnel are non-Kashmiris. Tourists often get the privilege of a comprehending nod, outsiders comforted by the presence of other outsiders. The Kashmiris, in contrast, are dealt with brusquely. On 'sensitive' roads in central Srinagar, no vehicle is allowed to slow down and stop. If unsure of directions, people still have to keep moving. After dark, there seems to be an unofficial curfew in the town. As shops down their shutters, and people prefer to remain indoors, there is barely any traffic on the roads. There are still periodic calls for strikes, and any violence in the city can lead to a sudden shutdown for a few hours.

The possibility of movement outside Srinagar too is heavily restricted. Almost all the tourists move only inside the small, fixed tourist itinerary, as they are told by the staff at the Tourism Reception Centre, the hotel owners and even taxi drivers that the other areas are still 'unsafe.' The 'safe' area consists primarily of the three small towns of Gulmarg, Pahalgam and Sonamarg, where tourist facilities are well established, and more crucially there are enough measures in place to ensure the safety of tourists. In fact, even in Srinagar, the residents often do not seem comfortable with tourists visiting the older parts of their city, with its closely packed houses and narrow by-lanes, and the few visitors are usually advised to leave the area quickly (Figure 16.2). So barely any tourists visit the historic old city, with its medieval wooden houses, bridges and mosques. Thus, even in Srinagar, the mobility for tourists is limited. Tourism in the city is focused primarily on the Dal Lake, the central shopping areas, and the Mughal Gardens, as other important sites are left out.

Figure 16.2 The old city of Srinagar, built along the River Jhelum (Photo by Tim Winter)

Further, even in areas where tourists are officially encouraged, the actual access is restricted. This can be illustrated with an example from Dachigam, a National Park just 20 km away from Srinagar. A dense tract of forest that was the hunting preserve of the rulers, Dachigam was declared a protected, reserved forest after independence. As the last existing habitat for the endangered *Hangul* deer, it attracted many wildlife enthusiasts until 1989. During the conflict it has become a preserve for politicians, the bureaucracy and the army. As an isolated, demarcated and guarded area it has been used as a venue for various consultative meetings and retreats. The families of the officers too have enjoyed holidays here. The park is now open to the public, though written permission from the Office of the Chief Wildlife Warden in Srinagar is required. Nisar, a forest guide and guard, has grown up in the adjoining village of Harwan. He has known and loved this forest since childhood, and now after the long decade of isolation, Nisar repeatedly expresses his happiness that visitors can once again come and experience the beauty of his forest. Yet a junior army officer denies permission for a tourist group led by Nisar to go beyond the second barrier because he claims an 'encounter with militants is going on.' However, even as the army officer is speaking, an army car with women and screeching children whizzes past, and Nisar looks a very frustrated and angry man. As an employee of the forest department, and with a written directive from the seniormost wildlife officer in the state, he still has barely any power in his own domain. Without autonomy to ensure tourists can move freely in the park, the whole exercise seems a bit meaningless, and is frustrating for both the tourists and the Kashmiris.

With the conflict over sovereignty remaining unresolved, the writ of the armed forces prevails and even the concerns of Kashmiris involved in tourism are ignored. Various other factors too restrain the development of tourism in Kashmir today.

Tourism: an embattled industry

The government offers financial incentives for tourism, but these are limited and the situation is complicated. Deprivation of a livelihood for a decade creates not only financial problems, but also undermines confidence and hope for the future. The situation facing the Dewans, a Hindu family whose forefathers held high administrative posts before independence, provides a case in point. Despite being wealthy and a family well established in the community, the Dewans were forced to flee the city in 1992, closing the guest-house they had run for a number of years behind them. After returning in 1998, they would have to wait a further two years before reopening their guesthouse business. Gradually, most of their staff too would return from their villages and rejoin them. It is a family business built on hard work and a concern for planned futures. Nonetheless, as conversations with them revealed, it is now marked by uncertainty and apprehension of the future.

With the conflict not yet over, and with regular incidents of violence in the city, there is no certainty about the prospects of business. There also still remains the fear that the situation will worsen again, and so the Dewans have asked one of their sons to stay and work outside Kashmir, thus maintaining an optional site of residence. The precarious situation in the valley thus restricts people from making long-terms plans and investment in their businesses.

Future prospects are even more limited for many others in the tourism business, like the taxi drivers. Most of the taxi drivers are young men, and none of those I interviewed were owners of their cars. They are driving cars owned by their fathers or uncles, and are living in small, cramped family houses though they are married with children. With limited earnings over the past 17 years, this generation has not been able to create their assets and economic opportunities, nor is there hope in the near future. Many young men in Kashmir will have to continue living off their fathers' and grandfathers' assets, and they repeatedly express their frustration at the situation.

Another group of people largely dependent on tourism are the lake dwellers, the inhabitants of Dal Lake. The lake is home to a large community of people, residing in houseboats and in wooden shanties built along the margins of the lake. Many of these houseboats also function as hotels. The Dal Lake – with houseboats, floating gardens and flower sellers and numerous other vendors on boats – is *the* center for tourism in the valley. Most visitors to Srinagar like to experience living in a houseboat at least for a part of their stay.[10] The lake, however, is part of a sensitive ecological system, and the conflict has had a detrimental effect on Kashmir's ecology in various ways. This is a crucial shift given the dependency of Kashmir's economy on 'a sensitive and organized use of its ecology' (Mahapatra 2003: 27). The lake has suffered substantially in the conflict. The sewage and drainage discharge by the inhabitants of the lake increased with a growing population, as did the spread of algae and weeds. The conflict did not allow the time and money required for a cleanup. More troubling were the deliberate encroachments of the Dal Lake.[11] With high levels of siltation (due to deforestation in the surrounding mountains), added to the encroachments, the lake is fast contracting (Mahapatra 2003; Heeter 2005). Reclamation of the lake was being practiced earlier too, but the process accelerated during the 1990s. In the absence of tourists and income from that source, the lake dwellers started reclaiming more land for cultivation. This has substantially altered the physical landscape of the lake, and the dwellers are now caught in a bind as the floating islands that are so charming as impermanent formations lose their attraction for visitors when they are made permanent. Residents whom I interviewed informed me that tourism generates a higher income for them than the cultivation and sale of flowers and vegetables. Yet they are still unwilling to dismantle the new reclamations, as they do not have the confidence that the violence in the valley will recede and the tourists will continue to come (Figure 16.3).

Figure 16.3 Patrolling the houseboats on Dal Lake (Photo by Tim Winter)

For Kashmiris involved with handicrafts and souvenirs too, these are still troubled times. Over the past five centuries, Kashmiri traders have been among the most enterprising in the country. Itinerant traders have carried Kashmiri shawls, rugs, papier-mâché items and woodwork, along with saffron and dry fruits, to shops and directly to homes across India and beyond. The traders have been forced to move out even more over the past 16

Figure 16.4 Living under the gaze of the security forces (Photo by Tim Winter)

years. While a few of them have prospered outside, commercial activity in Kashmir has stagnated.

The difficulties of living with the conflict are also experienced in other ways. The Kashmiris cannot ignore the barbed wires and the sandbags, much less the intrusive presence of the security forces. Even as tourism is sought to be encouraged, and the tourist protected, life for the average Kashmiri is made no easier. Maneuvering the various security checks, answering the endless questions thrown at them, constitutes not just a physical impediment but also seems to mark a boundary between Kashmir and the rest of India (Figure 16.4).

Securing the land for the tourists

In recent years, there have been strong calls for 'demilitarization,' for the reduction in the numbers of security forces in the valley. Their overwhelming presence seems to restrict possibilities at every step. Somewhat ironically, however, in the past decade and a half, the security forces have contributed to the economy of Kashmir in different ways. The army has been buying rations and other essential goods in large quantities, and the service personnel themselves have constituted a regular market for handicraft products, dry fruits and souvenirs. Even now as the men in uniform constrain the hosts, they make the guests feel secure – and thus provide some solace to the Kashmiris dependent on tourism.

The army's most direct and large-scale involvement in tourism has been in the Amarnath *yatra*. Especially after 1994, the army has taken the lead in security arrangements and even contributed to arranging the logistics for the pilgrimage. In 1993, the most holy mosque in Kashmir, Hazratbal, was surrounded by security personnel in a bid to evict a group of militants who had taken shelter inside. The siege lasted for over a month and though it ended peacefully, a couple of militant groups vowed to take revenge by targeting the Amarnath pilgrims. Most of the local Kashmiri groups have consistently opposed any disturbance to the pilgrimage, but since 1994 militants have managed to periodically attack pilgrim camps causing many casualties. This has not deterred the pilgrims, and with support from the central and state governments and the army, the pilgrimage has grown rapidly in numbers through the past decade. The numbers are bound to have adverse ecological consequences on a fragile, mountain zone. The extreme importance accorded to the success of the *yatra* can also be seen as a sign of the government's appeasement of rightwing Hindu forces (Navlakha 2006). However, even though commentators may be critical of the government's policies, Kashmiris themselves are more equivocal. Employees of the Jammu and Kashmir Bank – which annually sells tickets for the *yatra* through its branches around the country – think the government's promotion is 'a good thing.' The staff, whom I met at a branch of the bank in Bangalore in August

2006, even gave credit to the Amarnath pilgrims for their role in restarting tourism. It was the pilgrims from Amarnath, who began re-visiting the valley in the mid-1990s and initially carried the message that 'things are not so bad.'

The overt involvement of the army in Amarnath – and even more in the periodic border skirmishes – has created its own brand of tourism. The army's exploits, particularly against the Pakistani forces in Kargil in May 1999 were hailed in the media and created many new heroes. The Indian army successfully managed to dislodge militants and Pakistani soldiers from some Indian posts they had occupied around Kargil, north of Srinagar. It was India's first televised war, and many of the soldiers involved became household names. Capitalizing on this sentiment, a number of movies and television serials were produced that further glorified the soldiers and projected the army in a very positive light. Among the prominent movies were *LOC: Kargil* (Line of Control), released in 2003 and *Lakshya* (Aim) in 2004. The extensive media coverage and the movies have together contributed to a relatively new phenomenon of tourists greeting soldiers, shaking their hands and posing for photographs with them.

However, the tourists, by applauding the security personnel, also seem to be expressing their approval of the measures adopted by the government to ensure their safety. The government has given them the extra protection, the security to travel again to their dreamland. It is a dreamland replete with images from early Hindi romances, and now of sites of fighting immortalized in later films and the media. The strong hold of Kashmir in the Indian imagination is exemplified in the revival of tourism today. It is the middle-class families, the young and the old included, who are visiting Kashmir in their hundreds of thousands, not adventurous youth. In fact, the young people who come here on their own are usually 'honeymoon couples' during winter – the high season for weddings in North India. It is difficult to think of any other conflict zone where so many people travel, seemingly unmindful of the attendant and very real dangers.

However, Kashmir is perceived as a place on the margins, and the aspirations of the Kashmiris are continually undermined. The movies valorizing the Indian army have never been shown in Kashmir, because cinema halls there have been closed since 1990 after threats and attacks by the militants.[12] The Kashmiris, however, are aware of the movies and the success they have achieved. These movies imply a repudiation of their movement for autonomy, yet most Kashmiris welcome the audience of these movies as tourists.

Their desire for tourists to return in large numbers was evident in the reactions to the violent attacks on tourists in July 2006. Since 1995–96, when there were incidents of kidnapping and killing of tourists, no leisure tourists had deliberately been harmed in the valley. All the militant groups seem to have arrived at an explicit or implicit understanding that tourists are critical for Kashmir's economy, and should not be harmed. Breaking from that stand, in a series of incidents in July 2006, domestic tourists were deliberately targeted – grenades were thrown and bombs exploded, resulting in many casualties. No one claimed responsibility for these incidents, and as unprecedented as the attacks was their condemnation from all quarters. There were conflicting allegations about the involvement of the army and the militants in these attacks, and rumors also circulated that travel agents and hotel owners from the neighboring state of Himachal Pradesh were responsible (Sethi 2006). No clear answers have still emerged, but all Kashmiris I spoke to are sure that no Kashmiri would have organized such attacks that undermined tourism.

Conclusion

The desire for tourists to return is clear, yet the revival seems to be coming with a price. The ideas of 'return to normalcy' and the 'safety of tourists,' which are essential prerequisites for tourism, create their own constraints. As the Kashmiris are being encouraged, they are also simultaneously being controlled. The gap thus created also forecloses possibilities of engagement between the hosts and the tourists. This paradox, like others I have highlighted, does not just represent the situation, it is constitutive of it. The binds around tourism in a conflict zone manifest themselves variously.

The interest of the Indian state in creating a situation of 'normalcy' and thus procuring a revival in tourism is clear. The conception of a nation, of the coexistence of many people in a demarcated space under a common law, necessitates that all should be seen to be consenting to that control. The Indian government, to maintain its territorial integrity, has to highlight the happiness and prosperity of the populace under Indian rule. Building up economic and social links, through trade and tourism, with the rest of the country would also lessen the desire of Kashmiris to secede. Also, as various commentators have recognized, Kashmir – as a Muslim majority province – is too critical in India's self-representation as a secular state to ever be allowed sovereignty. The discourse of 'normalcy' has to prevail.

Most Kashmiris too, at this juncture, do not want to foreground the conflict. The past two decades of violence and suffering have yielded nothing. Now most of them want to get on with their lives, and rebuild their homes and businesses. Tourism is important in this design. And tourism itself, as an activity where people go on a holiday to relax and enjoy themselves, is premised on a disengagement from politics. Yet the attempt to ignore the unresolved conflict, to sweep it all under a beautiful Kashmiri carpet, seems to constitute another familiar chapter in the history of Kashmir. As has been noted by other commentators, visions of the alluring landscape of Kashmir have always excluded the Kashmiri people (Zutshi 2003; Rai 2004). Most Indians have always sought to erase the presence of Kashmiris – with their dreams and their aspirations, their hopes and their sorrows – while enjoying the land

and its material products. The theme of 'paradise regained' too hinges on this exclusion.

The tumultuous, violent history of Kashmir has seemingly always been at odds with its tranquil beauty – and it is at this intersection that tourism in Kashmir is located today. For though the violence of the conflict has been contained, the issue is still unresolved and life – and tourism – in the valley remain enmeshed in the dispute. So though everyone involved wants tourism in Kashmir to flourish again, the journey from the margin to the center cannot be linear. The multitudinous entanglements of tourism in a conflict zone make this impossible.

Notes

1 Another set of studies has focused on issues of tourism management in areas of conflict, with discussions of strategies and measures to revive tourism (Richter 1999; Akama 2002; Ospina 2006).

2 Leisure tourism in the valley preceded Independence, and began with the consolidation of British rule in the nineteenth century, with hundreds of British families traveling to Kashmir every summer to escape the heat (Gole 1993: 156; Keenan 2006). After Independence, tourism to the region would continue to thrive, this time through domestic Indian visitors.

3 My brief narrative of the conflict is based on many readings (books, journal articles, and newspaper reports) and interviews with Kashmiris caught in the conflict. For general reading, Singh (1995), Behera (2000), Sikand (2001), and Schofield (2003), among others, provide reviews of the conflict – from somewhat varying perspectives.

4 It left India in control of most of the valley, as well as Jammu and Ladakh, while Pakistan gained control over a part of the valley and over the Northern territories of Gilgit and Baltistan.

5 The conflict, however, has spawned its own economy, with large benefits to some sections of the bureaucracy, the armed forces, and the militants (Waldman 2002).

6 This was legislated through the state's constitution, as a mode of defining 'permanent residents' of Kashmir (Dhavan 2004).

7 Interview with Salim Jahangir, Manager, Bangalore, Jammu and Kashmir Bank, 16 August, 2006.

8 Other studies too have emphasized how governments seek to gain political legitimacy by promoting tourism (Hall and Ringer 2000).

9 The accounts in this chapter are based on my two field trips to Kashmir in April and July 2006. The interviews with the various informants were also conducted during these trips.

10 According to popular reports, the British introduced houseboats in the 1880s to get around the law forbidding them from owning property in Kashmir. However, this tale is not strictly true. Though the British were critical for the development of the industry in the last quarter of the nineteenth century, the houseboats themselves were adaptations by Kashmiri boatmen of their own boats, the *doongas* (Khan 2007: 75–6).

11 This is done through a process akin to reclamation. Vegetables are grown on the lake on rafts of reeds. As the reeds decompose, more layers can be added, and in a few years, a floating island results. Over time, soil is added to the island,

and thus is land created out of water. The floating islands can be towed and adjoined to dry land in order to expand an existing plot.

12 In the valley where so many movies have been filmed over the decades, there is only one cinema hall functioning today and that too is struggling to survive (Ahmed 2005; Hamid 2007; Mushtaq 2007).

17 Staging the nation, exploring the margins

Domestic tourism and its political implications in northern Thailand

Olivier Evrard and Prasit Leepreecha

Introduction: non-Western tourists, nationalism and the state

While the number of books and articles on tourism in the social sciences has increased sharply in the past decade, there are at least two domains of research which have remained relatively understudied. First, and as the Introduction to this volume has indicated, the anthropology of tourism has for long overlooked the practices and representations of non-Western tourists. This 'Northern bias' (Ghimire 2001a) can be considered both a blindness and a denial; non-Western tourists are not as often studied because many cannot help but consider non-Westerners as being only benevolent and dependent hosts. This neo-colonial attitude is certainly reflected in the current state of the anthropology of tourism (Alneng 2002). Even when non-Western tourists are mentioned, they are usually considered as late avatars of their Western counterparts, and thus denied their own originality.

As Winter notes in the Conclusion here; since most historical studies on tourism have either focused on Northern Europe or considered this region as the birthplace of 'modern' travel, there is a tendency to equate modern tourism with culturally bounded forms of mobility. In so doing, tourism analysts have neglected the fact that each culture has its own way of defining boundaries between 'holiday' and 'everyday' (echoing the boundaries between culture and nature, ourselves and the other), and also of regulating appropriate and acceptable leisure (Franklin and Crang 2001: 7). While the development of tourism has drawn on similar patterns in different countries (for instance, the leading role of an urban middle class and the romanticization of travel), the cultural value of these patterns, their conditions of emergence and the outcomes of their combinations could be locally different. Far from being a defense of relativism, the study of non-Western tourism considers tourism to be a 'total social fact' with cultural, political and historical variations.

A second problem is that the social sciences have long focused on the recreational aspect of tourism while ignoring its political implications, especially the role of the state in the development of travel. In several recent and stimulating books and articles, Adrian Franklin rejected the idea that tourism was the 'natural' consequence or product of people's desire for escape from their everyday life. Borrowing from the emergent sociology of ordering, which combines aspects of Foucault's notion of governance with Latour's relational materialism, Franklin insisted on the desirability of travel as a concept that needed to be 'constructed' and for which important means of persuasion and innovative techniques have been deployed, sometimes by the private sector, but also primarily by the state. He argues that nationalism (and colonialism) have transformed places/landscapes into something attractive, worthy of being visited and preserved. He contends 'it was not difference and the extraordinary that created tourism but the opposite, the extension of belonging, the prospect of taking up a place in the new national cultures that beckoned them' (Franklin 2004: 298). In that respect, tourism deserves primarily a historical and political anthropology to understand how, in a given place or country, a tourist culture emerges and becomes an 'ordering process.'

While following Franklin's recommendation to take tourism 'more seriously,' we shall challenge, or at least try to complement, some aspects of his analysis. Like Bauman (2000) and Urry (1990) before him, Franklin divides the history of tourism into two periods: first, the development and the propagation of a dominant culture (internal colonialism, more or less until the 1950s) and, later on, the valorization of local cultures into objects of desire. Franklin considers this reversal as a consequence, among other causes, of the development among the tourists of a 'generalized receptivity and predisposition to objects of everyday,' a process which he terms 'aestheticization' (2003: 71). We would like to insist rather on a political aspect quite obvious in non-Western countries today: local cultures and their symbols (places, objects and people) become objects of desire and marketing for tourists as part of a process of control and pacification of social relations. In other words, they are subject to commoditization and fetishism (rather than aestheticization) either because they are no longer perceived as a threat to the nation–state, or because there is a need to soften and domesticate their difference.

Our discussion focuses on the mountain of Suthep (Doi Suthep, 1,600 m) which overlooks the city of Chiang Mai and which has become one of the main destination for tourists (both Thai[1] and foreign) visiting Northern Thailand (Figure 17.1). It is estimated that Doi Suthep receives 160,000 visitors each month, 120,000 of whom visit its most sacred and oldest attraction, the Wat Phra That temple,[2] built in the last decades of the fourteenth century. The tourists also simultaneously enjoy various attractions in the vicinity of the temple (waterfalls, statues, royal palace and garden, ethnic village, souvenir shops), two of which bear special political and social significance: the royal palace of Phuphing and the Hmong village of Doi Pui. We focus on these two attractions since they provide crucial insights on the history of domestic tourism in Thailand: its similarities and differences with previous forms of aristocratic travels, its relations with the new idealization of the rural and its role in the pacification of the relations between the Thai state and its geographic and social margins.

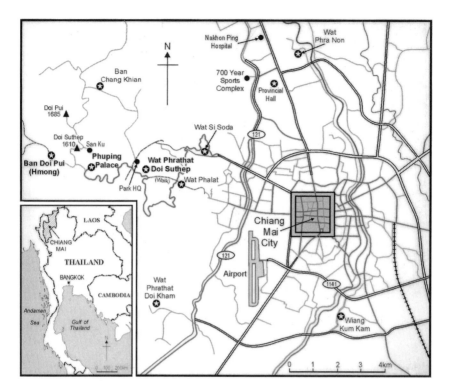

Figure 17.1 Map of Chiang Mai and Doi Suthep in northern Thailand

The monarchy, Thai travel culture, and the 'gaze toward the North'

Phuping Palace was built in 1961, three years after the first visit of King Bhumibol to Chiang Mai, and serves as a royal residence for the King, his family and his guests especially during the winter months (January to March) (Figure 17.2). Other royal palaces in Thailand have also become tourist destinations in the past decades (Royal Palace in Bangkok and summer residence of Chonburi, for instance), but Phuping Palace bears a special significance since its construction coincided more or less with the development of domestic mass tourism in Chiang Mai Province at the beginning of the 1960s. Its location near one of the most sacred temples of Northern Thailand and on one of its most scenic roads contributed directly to the transformation of Doi Suthep into a kind of 'total tourist complex' in which sightseeing, as part as leisure, involves also a loyalty toward Buddhism and respect to the monarchy and to the nation (Peleggi 2002: 69). Indeed, the construction of Phuping Palace can be seen as a symbol of the transformation of traditionally pilgrimage-oriented forms of travel in the mountain

Figure 17.2 Phuphing Palace, winter residence of the royal family (Photo by authors)

into a modern domestic and multi-purpose mass tourism. It is also the most recent manifestation of the special and ambiguous relationship that the Siamese aristocracy has developed with its northern margins.

The construction of Phuping Palace is part of an old historical trend which saw the Siamese power trying to subordinate the sanctity of any sacred place in the country to the royal rule. In the Tai-Yuan culture, sacred places (i.e., containing relics of the Buddha) are usually found outside the city (*müang*), often on mountains once honored by fertility cults, whereas in the Siamese cosmogony, these relics stand (or are brought) in the royal center. Richard O'Connors (cited in Baker 2004: 396) has perfectly summarized this tension between the two conceptions of place and power:

> Overall, we might call this a shift in the goal of traditional rites. Where all Tai seek prosperity, Yuan and many others focus on fertility. Their cults thus grant power to places if only to tap it. In contrast, the Siamese subsume this animistic fertility in a Buddhist quest for order or discipline. In the end, this 'order' arises from royal rule, not sacred places. So it neutralizes or at least subordinates every place but one – the royal centre.

With the Phuphing Palace, we have another example of this subordination process: the royal power cannot deny the sanctity of the place, but it is taking it over to increase its own legitimacy.

Among the Thai tourists, the popularity of the palace is related to its location, its rose gardens[3] and, of course, to the royal presence itself. The palace seems to constitute the fusion and embodiment of both a traditional imagery of the North and of certain aspects of the King's life, especially his education in Switzerland and his taste for long walks in the mountains. Among the Thai visitors that we interviewed, Switzerland was the place most often cited as an ideal tourist destination. This cannot be explained only by the contrasting landscapes or climates; it has to be linked with the identification to a living model. Such identification played also a role in the increasing popularity of trekking among the urbanized middle class. During his stays at Phuphing Palace, the King is said to have walked regularly in the mountains to contemplate nature and to pay the occasional visit to the neighboring Hmong village of Doi Pui (more on this below). Indeed, the path leading to Doi Pui village, which has been transformed into a concrete road today, is said to have been the first mountain walk opened to tourists in the Chiang Mai area. The Royal Projects, created in 1969 for agricultural development and opium eradication in highland villages, also recently included the promotion of (so far mainly domestic) tourism in their targeted villages with the slogan 'Follow the King's footsteps!'

However, this is not to say that modern Thai tourism should be conceived simply as an emulation of an élite behavior since this would surely be a misleading shortcut. Rather, contemporary Thai domestic tourism should be understood as the result of a double shift. First, travels by the aristocracy set up the conditions of the new state of mind necessary for domestic leisure travel. Several decades later, mass tourism (including mass domestic tourism) developed mainly through the intervention of the state and through a commoditization of local culture.

There is a long tradition of travel among the Thai aristocracy going back to the end of the nineteenth century. These travels were the prerequisite for the construction of a 'Siamese geo-body' (Thongchai 1994), that is, an *ordering* both of a physical, social and mental landscape which turned travel into something appealing and provided landmarks, rituals and objects for transformation into attractions. It was also during that time that a fundamental shift occurred at a discursive and cognitive level. A new conceptual frame or state of mind emerged which made travels both necessary (in controlling the territory) and appealing while they were at first considered a painful separation from one's place of origin. Analyzes of the early Thai 'travel' literature (see Thongchai 2000; Reynolds 2006), for instance, show how an old form of poetry called *nirat* was progressively transformed into a kind of travelogue, giving less emphasis to themes like 'longing for love' than to the description of the places actually visited. Melancholy did not completely disappear but came second to the exaltation of travel discoveries and the mapping of the Siamese interior.[4] Such a conceptual shift is also obvious in the emergence and development of a visual culture among the aristocracy (Morris 2000: 209–10). The 'uncivilized North' is thus progressively turned into a phantasmagorical 'northern pastness' which, in turn, becomes then an object of discourse and gaze for the Thai élite.

While travels by the aristocracy allow us to understand how a desire for travel came into being, a closer look reveals two kinds of sociological and technical discrepancies with modern forms of mass tourism. First, an obvious difference is that the first travelers – aristocrats, the King, administrators – were 'interrogators' and there was no pretense at close intimacy. In fact, most of these travelers displayed negative attitudes toward the locals, said to be uncivilized and dirty (Renard 1999). Second, mass tourism required both a well-developed infrastructure network and a transformation of the image of the North through new (visual) media and state-sponsored policies.

The development of new means of transport (first, the train in 1921, and then later the plane) was accompanied by the organization of special promotional tours such as the one organized by the Railway Company in 1931 for the *songkhan* festival (Renard 1999: 95). The Tourism Authority of Thailand (TAT, created in 1960) opened an office in Chiang Mai in 1968, and launched marketing campaigns to promote travels in the Northern provinces (highlighting temples, handicraft, landscapes and beautiful girls) while training their inhabitants to become hosts for the tourists.[5] In the 1980s, the airport was expanded, numerous hotels were built and bus trips from Bangkok to Chiang Mai were organized for Thai urban middle classes who paid 3,000–4,000 baht (approximately US$80–105) for a three-day tour (Richter 1989: 90). At the end of the 1980s, roughly two million Thai domestic tourists were visiting Chiang Mai each year and this number has remained constant up to now. The 'voluntary' creation of a domestic tourist market by the national authorities shows clearly that previous forms of aristocratic mobility did not mechanically generate modern domestic mass tourism. It was not until the development of a full-fledged industry and travel advertisements that this process could really flourish, and that Thai citizens could really begin 'dreaming' of being tourists.

This 'Thai tourist dream' was also nurtured by heritage policies and the idealization of the rural. Preservation of historical monuments started under the reign of Rama VI (1910–25) but became a truly important issue only at the end of the 1970s which, interestingly, was a period of profound divisions among Thai civil society. In addition to the communist guerrillas in various border areas, this period was also marked by the events of October 1973 when a civil government took control of the country, and by the massacres at Thammassat University in October 1976, after which the military regained control. From that time on, the politics of heritage became a national concern closely linked with the celebration of the monarchy. Historical Parks such as Sukhothai and Ayuthya (UNESCO World Heritage Sites in 1991) became symbols of the longevity and the fame of the Thai kingdom, as well as support for Thai popular nationalism.

During the same period, in the academic and intellectual spheres, a new paradigm emerged which idealized the rural world. In sociology, the 'School of Community Culture' (*watthanatham chumchon*) insisted on independence and egalitarianism of traditional rural societies, as well as their problematic encounters with capitalism and with the state. In history, the project of 'Local History' (*prawattisat thongthin*) rejected the official historiography based on royal chronicles, investigating instead the history of small principalities *müang* and insisting on the relative political independence they were able to sustain until the beginning of the twentieth century. While these works have certainly led to important achievements from an academic perspective,[6] it is also quite obvious that they relied on and perpetuated two ideological biases: first, the rural/local is seen to be a symbol of an idyllic past (*rural-ness* is equated with *past-ness*) endangered by modernity and, second, the solutions to present problems can be found in lessons from the past.

On the whole, the improvements in communications networks, the multiplication of 'local histories,' the idealization of the rural, the politics of heritage as well as the onslaught of numerous magazines, journals and travel guides devoted to these subjects directly contributed to the development of a leisure mobility among Thai citizens, and consequently of a domestic mass tourism industry. Under the influence of an idyllic, traditionalist and nostalgic vision of the countryside, rural spaces have been reinvented and transformed into appealing visual and conceptual archetypes which sustain discourses on national identity and history. Such 'landscaping' processes are qualitatively different from those which occurred at the end of the nineteenth century: while cultural difference was at that time encountered, it is now sought after; while it was equated with backwardness and danger, it is now considered as something picturesque and pleasurable.

In Chiang Mai, as in other places in the country, these conceptual reversals allowed the rise of domestic tourism since the end of the 1970s. The city became 'subjected to a discourse of culture premised on the fetishism of appearance' (Morris 2000: 237). The 'Lanna culture'[7] revivalism – once considered a potential disruption of national cohesion – became associated with the origin of the Thai nation, with large-scale production of 'traditional' artifacts and souvenirs and also with specific rituals such as the wearing of Lanna costume each Friday to the office. Here, tourism is involved in a pacification of the relations between the center and the periphery: from fears of separatism to promotion of regionalism, from a contemptuous attitude to a nostalgic gaze. It also perpetuated an internal colonialism, through self-identification (including self-censorship[8]) and displacements. The Northern Thai turned themselves into objects of desire for mobile urban dwellers and at the same time also enacted the same process toward their own margins, the so-called 'Hill Tribes' (*cao khao*).

Domestic tourism in the highlands: from 'the other within' to 'the fancy other'

At the very end of the Doi Suthep road, more than 20 km from the city walls, lies the Hmong village of Doi Pui. This destination is the 'ethnic' component of the package tour sold by the red taxis (*doysan*) at the bottom of the mountain. Today, most of the visitors who go to the temple, then to the palace and eventually to the Hmong village are Thai, not foreigners. This was not always the case since Doi Pui village became a true domestic tourist attraction only when the road between the palace and the village was improved, in the mid-1980s. Previously, there was only a dirt track and most of the visitors were Westerners.

Hmong of Doi Pui village originally migrated from Southwestern China to upper Northern Thailand, at the end of the nineteenth century. Around the 1920s, Hmong began to settle in the vicinity of Suthep-Pui Mountains. In 1951, Hmong communities in this area were disturbed by fights between government officers and Yunnanese opium traders. A few years later, five Hmong families settled in their fields at the contemporary location of Doi Pui. Later on, other Hmong villagers joined them and formed a new village. In addition to Hmong, Yunnanese Chinese from urban Chiang Mai and elsewhere also joined them in the village. Village economy in those days was largely based on self-sufficiency. The villagers practiced swidden agriculture to grow rice for household consumption, maize for family animals and humans. The only commercially oriented production was opium which was sold to increase family income and to tide over unexpected medical expenses. Though the area was declared a protected forest in 1949 and opium growing and smoking were officially banned in 1959, there was no clear policy implementation at that time. The real change came during the 1960s and once again, it was closely linked to political integration and more precisely, direct contact between the monarchy and the villagers.

After Phuping Palace was built in 1961, the royal family spent a few months annually in Northern Thailand (December to March), regularly visiting the highland community of Doi Pui as well as other communities in neighboring districts and provinces. While there was certainly, as we have noted before, a leisure aspect in the treks undertaken by the King and his relatives, one cannot completely ignore their political motivations. This was a time when Thailand was facing the 'threat of communism' both in neighboring countries (through its support to US military actions) and on its own territory (via the Communist Party of Thailand). As usual, the Hmong had a bad reputation: they were opium growers and in constant contact with the Haw traders, and they were feared for their military skills and for their border-crossing ability. The concern of the King for the Hmong of Doi Pui, among other Hmong villages in the area, pertained to the 'concept of a volatile alterity' (Race 1974: 105) which would prove dangerous if the villages fell under the influence of Communism. The kingdom could not just let them live as previously on the margins; it had to control them more directly, to lessen their strangeness in order to ensure their faithfulness to the country.

Doi Pui was one of the first villages in the country to have a Royal Project in 1969. The aim of the project was officially to promote commercial agriculture and crop substitution, as well as to eradicate the opium industry.

Figure 17.3 The opening of the first souvenir shop in Doi Pui in 1971 in the presence of the King of Thailand (Courtesy of the Royal Project)

Concretely, however, its main role was to enforce the regulations of National Park Agency. However, villagers felt that the project constrained commercial economy and had little direct effect on agricultural development since it did not distribute enough seeds. Lychee plantations, for instance, were developed primarily through contacts with Haw traders rather than with project officials. As for tourism, a somewhat different discourse prevailed. The King contributed to the opening of the first souvenir community store in the village in 1971 with his own fund (Figure 17.3). Although the store failed because the village headman took the benefits for himself, it led to the development of an increasing number of privately owned shops. During the first few years, some villagers expressed concern over the reliance of tourism as a tool for economic development. While some pointed to the multiplication of young beggars who were taught by their parents to ask for money from foreigners, others remarked that tourism favored the production, sale and consumption of opium in the village. These problems eventually disappeared at the end of the 1980s when the number of tourists increased sharply and the income generated was several times higher than that of agricultural activities.

Today, Doi Pui receives an average of 300 visitors per day but it can reach 1,000 in high season, especially during the *songkhan* festival (in April). These visits generate around 70 million baht of income for the villagers or around 50,000 baht per villager per year (more than US$1,300). There are a total of 135 tourist-oriented stores and 11 restaurants in the village which numbers only 134 households and 1,391 people. Souvenirs include Hmong costumes, resins, old coins, herbal medicines, pickled fruits, postcards, ornaments, seasonal agricultural products, etc. (Figure 17.4). Outside Doi Pui, Hmong villagers travel to sell souvenirs in different places throughout the country such as Phuping Palace, Doi Suthep temple, Chiang Mai, the weekend markets in Bangkok and even as far as Hua Hin and Phuket. Most of these souvenirs are standardized objects and only a few are actually produced in the village or relate directly to Hmong culture. One of the most significant consequences of the development of the souvenir economy was the installation in the village of non-Hmong people. Doi Pui village today, for example, includes seven Chinese, four Karen, 13 lowland Thai households and even two Nepalese individuals who sell typical Indian or Nepalese objects such as *mandala* paintings.

The Hmong of Doi Pui were so successful economically (apart from tourism revenues, they also produced fruits and vegetables for sale in Chiang Mai) that they could successfully oppose relocation projects that wanted to force them out of the National Park. More recently, they have also opposed the Forestry Bill which was intended to strengthen the control of the state over forested areas used by the highland farmers. In the meantime, the tourist economy encountered a radical change: Doi Pui attracted fewer Western

Figure 17.4 A Thai tourist dressed with rented Hmong clothes has her picture taken by a Hmong guide near the village museum (Photo by authors)

visitors but increasingly more Thai tourists. Road improvements and the homogenization of the souvenir trade in Chiang Mai played an important role. This shift is also a consequence of the emergence, at the end of the 1980s, of a new discourse on ethnic minorities among the media and especially the Thai newspapers (Krisadawan 2000). Following the creation of numerous NGOs representing the interests of the highlanders (called 'indigenous groups' today), the 'wild' and even frightening other of the 1970s became, in the eyes of Thai travelers, a pacified and appealing one.

The example of Doi Pui village leads to a few reflections on tourism and 'ethnic' identities. First, the other is engaged in a process of 'representation and commoditisation of itself as an object of desire' (Peleggi 2002: 72) which has important implications for ethnographic knowledge and methodology. In the case of the Hmong, for instance, some traditional rituals have been transformed and used to impart a better group image. This is the case of the *ntoo xeeb* ritual, which traditionally serves to call and appease the spirit of the place *thwvtim*, and is organized at the base of one of the oldest trees in the village vicinity. Today, this ritual has been transformed to appear as the Hmong equivalent of the Thai ritual *buat pha*, the ordination of trees practiced by the Thai Buddhists (Leeprecha 2004). The two rituals are completely different, both in their sequence and in their meaning but they have nonetheless become symbolically associated and the Hmong ritual is now conceived as the symbol of their attachment to the forest in the 'indigenous' public discourse.

This representation of self on the part of the ethnic minorities is not exempt from contradictions. For example, one of the two small museums constructed by the Hmong of Doi Pui to attract tourists and exhibit their culture presents some of the most controversial symbols attached to Hmong identity, and for which the Hmong often claim to be misunderstood (by Thai and Westerners alike). For instance, the tourists will notice the poppies and marijuana grown in front of the entrance, presented here as a symbol of the past. They will also observe within the museum a reconstitution of the traditional so-called wedding by abduction when a young man takes his future wife out of her village and lets his relatives arrange the compensation to his in-laws, a practice officially banned by the Thai state. These are but only outward inconsistencies. Linking cultural features to familiar practices among the majority group (such as the case of the *ntoo xeeb* as previously mentioned) or associating them with purely historical, non-threatening features (opium, wedding abduction) are two sides of the same 'domestication' process.[9]

An optimistic analysis would conclude that through the pacification of social relations, tourism plays a critical role in a pluralist, though official, narrative of the nation. This is certainly true in the case of the Hmong of Doi Pui where the Royal patronage, added to their ability to cope with the commercial economy, prevents them from being too heavily dependent upon tourism. Indeed, they have even developed some protection mechanisms to keep the tourist economy spatially confined to the main street of the village. In short, tourism favors economic development and allows the villagers to openly manifest both their cultural differences and their position of citizen-subjects. However, this is not the case everywhere in Thailand since the hidden (though obvious) undercurrent of tourism lies sometimes precisely in the impossibility of the 'ethnic other' accessing full citizenship. The (in)famous 'ethnic zoos' of the so-called 'long-necked' Kayan on the Burmese border or the less well-known Mlabri in Nan Province clearly show how the tourist gaze nurtures itself on a symbolic and physical violence. The mobility of some privileged people needs the immobility of others, thereby keeping them in their marginal position.

A second reflection concerns the contrasting and partially contradictory ways through which staged identities are consumed by international and domestic tourists. In the case of Doi Pui, the former began avoiding the village as soon as it became attractive to the latter. The same process occurs nearly everywhere, even in an extreme case such as the Kayan 'ethnic zoo;' indeed, some villages are particularly popular with domestic tourists while others are popular with international visitors, and the organization of their tourist space and services differs markedly from each other. A possible reason for this differing popularity is that different tourists seek different experiences. The search for authenticity – even reduced to some basic social interactions – predominates among foreign visitors, and this has led paradoxically to the development of a full-scale tourist economy in some villages, including queues of photographers waiting to take their shot of the same 'long-necked' person and the sale of standardized souvenirs obviously unrelated to the village.

On the other hand, domestic tourists favor *sanuk* (or fun) over authenticity: the 'difference' must be enjoyable, in order to be an object of desire but not too different. An interesting example lies in the practice of wearing 'ethnic dress' and having one's photograph taken in a picturesque village setting amidst gardens and waterfalls (a similar practice may be found in Vietnam and China too). Such dressing-up is sometimes described by the Thai people as 'fancy.' Old pictures taken at the beginning of the twentieth century suggest that this practice was already common among the members of the aristocracy (Turton 2000: 362–3) although we do not know precisely when it was introduced. Recent photographs also show members of the royal family wearing 'hill tribe' attire whenever they visit the Doi Pui village. The fact that such a practice caught on with Thai tourists, however, goes beyond a simple popularization of aristocratic pastime. Instead it reflects a process of making the other 'consumable' and 'imaginable': after all, if we were to refer to a dictionary, we realize that the term 'fancy' may be applied to a costume, as well as a whim, taste, fantasy, an illusion and even cookery! Hence, wearing ethnic clothing should not be conceived as a process of assimilation but as the desire for inclusion shared by the locals themselves:

> As peripheral communities and populations were incorporated into the state, it became necessary for them to appear in a manner that

represented their acquiescence to the state and it is in this moment that the demand for ethnic costume begins to be made. In effect, costumes come to work as the signs of a double status, evoking both anteriority vis-à-vis the nation and encompassment by the state. The one who wears ethnic costume is not so much a subject-citizen as a sign of difference abstracted.

(Morris 2000: 210)

The other is domesticated and at the same time, difference is made appealing through a standardized code. Western tourists are not attracted by such practices because these practices do not 'speak' to them as they do to Thai people: the 'code' used here does not match their representation of authentic travel and interactions with local people. Paradoxically, wearing 'fancy' dress became a way of asserting a modern Thai identity.

Conclusion

To conclude, we have come full circle. What do a famous Buddhist temple, a royal palace and a Hmong village have in common? They all became domestic tourist attractions scattered along the same road and they all contribute to the sense of 'feeling Thai.' An interesting detail is that one of the very first attractions on the road of Doi Suthep, namely, the Wat Srisoda, relates symbolically to the last one, the Hmong village of Doi Pui. Wat Srisoda was built in the 1920s to promote Buddhism among the ethnic minorities. In 1965, the Project Dhamma Jarika was implemented by this temple under the responsibility of the Department of Social Welfare; it was also at this time that the Buddhist *sangha* worked hand in hand with the royal administration to prevent the spread of Communism among the so-called 'Hill Tribes.' In 2006, with 360 monks and novices coming from highland villages, most of them Karen (260) but also Hmong (70), Akha and Lahu (30), the Wat Srisoda symbolizes the links between the monarchy, Buddhism and development in peripheral areas of the kingdom.

The two attractions studied in this chapter reveal an aspect of the social dynamics of domestic tourism in Thailand. The example of the royal palace offers an opportunity to understand how a tourist culture emerged in Thailand, and more precisely the role of the élites, the State and also the middle class in the construction of a 'gaze from Bangkok to the North' (Reynolds 2006: 278). Such a northward gaze may be regarded a manifestation of internal colonialism, which later became associated with fetishism and mass consumption. This transformation of the Northerners and of the Northern culture in objects of desire also had important implications for the so-called 'ethnic minorities' who lived on the margins of the Tai social space, as shown by the case of the Hmong village of Doi Pui. Here, tourism allows the creation of a 'fancy other' or in other words, of a domesticated difference which can mirror and support the sense of national belonging. It also stages the cultural diversity in a way which does not always cope, and sometimes even contradicts, the exoticism expected by Western tourists.

Notes

1 As is usual in most academic works, we distinguish Thai (citizens of Thailand) from Tai (culturally and linguistically related populations, including Yuan, Lue, Lao, Shan etc.).
2 Wat Phra That Doi Suthep temple (said to have been built in 1371) is strongly associated with a Northern variant of *theravada* Buddhism, called Yuan Buddhism, itself directly linked with Northern Thai people (*khon müang*) culture and language (*kam müang*). It was also the focus of a religious movement during the twentieth century and still highlights the problematic relation between the 'revitalized' Northern Thai identity and the Siamese kingship (see Keyes, 1975; Cohen, 2001).
3 Chiang Mai is known as the 'city of the rose' (*kularb vieng ping*). On floral tourism and the origin of rose in Chiang Mai, see Renard (1999: 94).
4 One can argue that melancholy of those left behind, such as that expressed in the old style of *nirat* resurfaces as nostalgia in the modern travel. There is a double reversal in this process. While melancholy expressed the homesickness of the traveler, nostalgia refers to something irremediably lost or supposedly so. More importantly, nostalgia in modern travel takes, as its objective, the destination of the travel (as symbol of what has been lost at home), while in classical *nirat* melancholy refers to one's place of origin (the loved ones or home atmosphere left behind). This shift (from melancholy to nostalgia) is crucial since it set up the conceptual frame, or state of mind, for travel to be seen as appealing.
5 By 1990, about 40 percent of all commercial enterprises in Chiang Mai were working directly or indirectly within the tourist industry (Anchalee 1999: 77).
6 On 'Community culture,' see the detailed bibliography in Rigg and Richie (2002), and Hirsch (1993). For 'Local history,' see Peleggi (2002).
7 The Lanna (million of rice fields) kingdom, in which Chiang Mai was the capital, extended its control to what is today North Thailand between the thirteenth and the sixteenth centuries. It was later integrated into the Thai kingdom.
8 The locals conform themselves and their culture to what travelers expect to see and how they want to see it, but this process also involves negotiation of their own image and self-censorship. For instance, there is reluctance to publicly stage pre-Tai and pre-Buddhist cultural backgrounds onto which Northern Tai identity unfolds. An example is the ritual held each year on *Doi Kham* for the Lawa spirits Phu Sae and Ya Sae, the two guardians of Chiang Mai. Once a popular tourist attraction (until the end of the 1980s), it involves a buffalo sacrifice and the performance by a medium possessed by spirits. This ritual is now held more discretely since the villagers had expressed their concern at being seen as backward and unfaithful to Buddhism if images of this were broadcast on national television.
9 The process of 'museumification' is always closely linked with the 'pacification' of social relations. For example, in Nan Province, the previous sanctuaries of the Communist Party have now been turned into historic tourism attractions (Anonymous 2005).

18 Cultural preservation, tourism and 'donkey travel' on China's frontier

Robert Shepherd

Introduction

As the editors to this volume highlight, in anthropology and sociology, much attention has been paid to the impact of tourism, mainly from the 'West,' on local cultural practices in non-Western societies (cf. Greenwood 1989; MacCannell 1992; Linnekin 1997). Implicit in these concerns has been an assumption that increased tourism flows to a site inevitably lead to a dilution of authentic cultural practices as local residents take on performative roles and become 'Westernized' (cf. Ritzer and Liska 1997: 97–101). The net result of this process becomes what Claude Lévi-Strauss in *Tristes Tropiques* (1957) lamented as a futile search for a 'vanished reality,' as authentic cultural practices forever remain beyond the grasp of (Western) visitors.

China in general and Tibet in particular appear to be awkward candidates for this model. The China National Tourist Office in 2005 reported approximately 100 million domestic tourist trips and 100 million visitors from Hong Kong, Taiwan, and Macau, far exceeding the 20.2 million international tourist arrivals (CNTO 2006b). In 2006, the Tibetan Autonomous Region received 2.35 million visitors, only 145,000 of whom were foreigners (*Xinhua* 2006).

Based on these statistics, Western tourists play only a minor role in the 'opening up' of Tibet to tourism. My point is not to argue for a place or places untouched by global forces, like a *Lonely Planet* guidebook that promises its readers a chance to encounter people who have never met a 'Westerner.' Instead, I wish to note that an unreflective belief in the inevitable destruction of other people's cultures by Western tourism practices is of limited use in examining the place of tourism in contemporary Tibet, where the overwhelming majority of tourists are Han Chinese.

This tourism boom in Tibetan regions has raised new concerns among critics, as concerns over Chinese attempts to forcibly assimilate Tibetans into a broader Chinese cultural landscape under Maoism have been replaced by a fear that tourism will achieve what Mao could not: a Tibet emptied of any authentic cultural differences. A recent travel article in the *New York Times* is an example of this worry. It begins by evoking a timeless Tibet of prostrating worshippers and chanting monks before disrupting this image with the specter not of communist modernization but of mass tourism:

> In front of one of the holiest sites in Tibetan Buddhism, the Jokhang Temple in Lhasa, hundreds of pilgrims fall on the ground, spread-eagled, prostrating themselves so forcefully their hands bleed from being smacked to earth . . . several seem so overcome to have arrived at the Jokhang that they sob controllably or stare into the temple as if entranced. Then the trance snaps. Behind one of the pilgrims, a tourist climbs onto one of the Jokhang's massive golden prayer wheels, pulls out a cell phone camera, and starts snapping away.
>
> (Kurlantzick 2006: n.p.)

What follows is a lament for an authentic Tibet rapidly disappearing as it is transformed by development and tourism, and a warning for foreigners to experience Tibet 'while they can still recognize its unique culture and fragile environment' (ibid.: n.p.). While Kurlantzick trots out the usual tropes one encounters in such travel writing, such as the writer as a privileged insider who is not a tourist and somehow gains access to 'real' culture, he adds something new to this set narrative: not only are the people who are destroying Tibet tourists instead of Maoists or Red Guards, these tourists are no longer the middle-class and working-class Europeans and North Americans usually blamed for such acts of destruction, but rather Han Chinese. In other words, race and ethnicity are layered on to the usual class-driven tourist–traveler divide: Tibet is being ruined not simply by tourism, but by *Chinese* tourism.

This ethno-racial narrative about the destruction of a 'real' Tibet is appealing to some Europeans and North Americans because it fits their conceptions of this land. In this narrative, Tibet was once a place of isolation, harmony and peace that, beginning in 1951, was assaulted by a (foreign) Maoist attempt to destroy its cultural and spiritual uniqueness. Now, having survived Mao, Tibet is confronted with the destructive power of tourism (Adams 1996: 515). As Adams notes, angst about Tibetans in Tibet becoming 'Sinicized' takes precedence in this narrative over concerns about Tibetans living abroad in exile becoming 'Westernized,' as if the former carries more coercive force than the latter (ibid.: 521). These concerns about the harm done to Tibetan culture by Chinese tourists have been heightened by the opening in July 2006 of a direct rail link between Xining, the capital of Qinghai province, and Lhasa. With onward rail connections from Xining to major cities such as Beijing, Shanghai, and Guangzhou, Tibet as a travel destination is now a practical reality for millions of urban Chinese residents.

Yet, while this despair over a (forever) disappearing Tibet is understandable in the context of a continued Euro-American fascination with Tibet as Shangri-La, it misses the broader implications of state tourism policies in Tibet. Although officially described as an economic development strategy and condemned by outside critics as a tactic aimed at cultural destruction, these policies seek to transform Tibet into a de-politicized space of 'culture' and 'tradition' securely within the People's Republic, much like New Order tourism policies under former President Suharto in Indonesia that were aimed at increasing the state presence in non-Javanese regions of the country (Adams 1997: 156–8). In both cases, these policies enable state actors to make a claim on an imagined unitary national past, thereby justifying contemporary state boundaries and strengthening national standing (Errington 1998: 37; Tuohy 1991: 201).

Equating increased Han Chinese tourism in Tibetan cultural areas with the destruction of Tibetan culture is therefore highly questionable. Indeed, from a practical policy perspective, a key goal of a policy premised on utilizing cultural 'resources,' suitably de-politicized, for development purposes is the *preservation* of performative differences, not their erasure. It is more useful to view these tourism policies as one aspect of a broader policy aimed at the pacification of Tibet through the aesthetization of Tibetan culture, led by government-directed efforts to protect this by working with the United Nations Education, Scientific, and Cultural Organization (UNESCO) to save and preserve Tibetan cultural sites from the dangers of, paradoxically, tourism.

This leads to three questions. First, why has the Chinese government promoted tourism in Tibetan areas after decades of limiting outside access to this region for both Han Chinese and foreigners? Second, why have state authorities actively cooperated with UNESCO in protecting Tibetan cultural sites as examples of 'world heritage?' Finally, why might Han Chinese citizens be attracted to Tibet despite widespread negative stereotypes about Tibetans in Chinese popular culture?

In this chapter, I argue that this state effort to both 'protect' Tibetan heritage and promote Tibet as a tourist destination is linked to broader attempts to undercut Tibetan claims of cultural and hence historical difference. In other words, issues of Tibetan cultural authenticity and the effects tourism has on this are less important than a state strategy that seeks to depoliticize questions of culture.

I begin with a brief review of the place of tourism in Chinese society, linking the rapid growth in domestic tourism in the past decade to the transformation of spatial policies in a post-Maoist era. I then turn to the role played by UNESCO in Chinese state policies that seek to harness Tibetan culture in service to a greater China. Finally, I turn to the issue of Han Chinese tourists in Tibet, arguing that different types of tourists are visiting Tibet for different reasons.

Space, mobility and consumption

Beginning in 1986, Chinese state tourism policies focused on the rapid development of foreign tourism as a means of generating foreign exchange earnings. Yet, while foreign tourism has steadily increased since the beginning of the reform process, the most dramatic increases have been in domestic tourism (Ghimire and Li 2001: 87–91). This rapid rise in domestic tourism can be connected to policy changes in the aftermath of the 1989 Tiananmen protests that have benefited urban residents. Increased personal autonomy and an emphasis on consumption have created an urban middle class with the means and desire to travel. However, the most important factor in this radical transformation has been a relaxation of spatial control and citizen mobility. Quite simply, without the ability to travel, tourism cannot exist. Yet for much of the post-1949 era in China the ability of citizens to move was extremely limited.

The suspicion of spatial movement in China long predates the establishment of the People's Republic in 1949. Indeed, this suspicion lies at the core of Confucianism. From a Confucian perspective, people living outside of their family group are presumed to be not just out of place but also to be unanchored from the productive constraints of family ties and responsibilities and hence liable to engage in selfish or anti-social pursuits. Beginning in the Ming Dynasty, household registers (*baojia*) were required for all subjects. These enabled authorities to track people's movements and served as a basis for tax levies. During the Republican era (1911–49), surveillance techniques based on identity cards were common in both government and communist-controlled areas (Cheng and Sheldon 1994: 645). The post-1949 régime mandated population registration in urban areas in 1951, and established a nation-wide family registration system (*hukou*) in 1960 (Kam and Li 1999: 819–21). Modeled on the Soviet internal passport system, this policy was aimed at the same problem Soviet planners faced in attempting rapid economic modernization: in a largely rural society, how to prevent peasants from leaving rural areas and moving to cities? A registration system that tied all citizens to their place of birth appeared to be the logical answer.

The result was not just economic growth but the codification of a new type of inequality. In seeking to erase economic class differences, authorities created a new and more rigid social marker of difference, based not on social class but on place of birth. As Gong Xikui has noted, 'the reproduction of the household register [was] the reproduction of difference . . . it was originally the outcome of people's activity, but it quickly changed to become a precondition for social activity' (Gong 1998: 83).

In urban areas, residents were assigned to a 'work unit' (*danwei*), where they lived, labored, shopped, ate, socialized, often married, and eventually died. Cities were in essence large collections of walled work unit compounds; public space in the normative Euro-American sense was thus highly limited. Travel, for either business or pleasure, was also highly restricted. While hotels existed, the ability to stay in a hotel depended on having a reason, which meant a letter from one's work unit boss explaining why a person was 'out of place.' Buying a train ticket required the same sort of authorization. In such an environment, what little tourism that existed functioned as an extension of the work unit.

Economic reforms beginning in 1978 have not just radically transformed economic production in China but have also fundamentally altered social relationships. As work units have privatized their housing stock and state employment has declined, control over the movement of urban residents has largely broken down. In regard to tourism, several trends are evident. Travel for both pleasure and for economic necessity is closely connected to this breakdown in state control of space and institutional limits to citizens' ability to move. This breakdown, necessitated by market pressures for a mobile and flexible labor force, has created both the affluence that enables some people to travel as tourists and the poverty that requires peasants to move to urban areas in search of work. Second, economic affluence for some has not displaced the normative view of people who are 'out of place.' In Chinese, the character *liu*, 'to float or move,' is culturally and historically rooted in a concern for being 'in place.' Those who are out of place include *liumang* 'criminals,' *liumin* 'refugees,' and *mangliu*, literally 'blindly floating' people, migrants who seek work in places they are not from. The hyper-modernization of urban areas has not erased traditional urban views of 'the countryside' or 'country bumpkins,' but has in fact further solidified these.

Yet, despite this, tourism among urban residents to rural areas is booming. Yet why would city people want to visit those places from where the migrants whom they blame for daily social problems come? It is to this issue I turn in the final section of this chapter when I discuss tourism in Tibet. Before this, however, I examine the relationship between UNESCO and state authorities in Tibet.

Cultural heritage and state-building

Like national museums and monuments, cultural heritage programs are inevitably political, given that they seek to shape accepted narratives about specific aspects of the past. In the context of Tibet, cultural heritage programs also assist state-directed development efforts that are explicitly linked to a national project of modernization. State authorities and the Communist Party position themselves as both guides to modernization and shields against the negative effects of modernization. This claim to being the protector of culture against an unrestrained market process mirrors UNESCO's emphasis on protecting cultural practices from tourism (UNESCO 1995: 184). From a critical perspective, this simultaneous state celebration of cultural difference *and* claimed role as protector of this difference turns both tangible and intangible culture into an aesthetic performance.

Despite this political reality, UNESCO's focus in Tibet, as in many other places, is on protecting cultural heritage sites from the presumed destructive intent of economic processes, including tourism. This approach transforms the political issue of control over the narratives told about cultural sites in places such as Tibet into technical questions of physical preservation. UNESCO thus is necessarily a complicit partner in the transformation of 'culture' into both a development resource and an object requiring state protection from the effects of these very same development policies.

The enthusiastic acceptance of the concept of world heritage in minority regions by Chinese state authorities neatly fits the state vision of what Tim Oakes has termed a government-imagined 'landscape of nostalgia' (1997: 42). For example, the official application for World Heritage status for the Potala Palace states that it deserves inclusion not because it is symbolic of Tibet nationhood or Tibetan culture but because it 'embodies the outstanding skills of the Tibetan, Han, Mongol, Man, and other nationalities and the high achievements of Tibetan architecture in terms of the overall layout of the Palace as well as its civil engineering, its metalwork, its sculptures, and its wall paintings' (UNESCO 1993: 5). In other words, the Potala is significant because from the state perspective it reflects the joint technical and aesthetic achievements of the *peoples* of China, not of the separate nation of Tibet.

The UNESCO response to this claim is mute, although for understandable reasons. Some staff members no doubt take the pragmatic view that preservation of tangible cultural sites on any terms is better than no preservation, particularly in the case of Tibet, given that Chinese authorities directed the destruction of numerous Tibetan cultural sites in the 1950s and 1960s during the initial occupation of Tibet and Cultural Revolution (1966–76). And in response to the Chinese government's application for World Heritage status for the Potala complex, members of the International Council on Monuments and Sites (ICOMOS), the primary organization responsible for evaluating all such applications, did note its dissatisfaction with government plans to redevelop areas around the Potala (UNESCO 1993: 9). Yet the Council limited its critique to urging 'responsible authorities to give careful consideration to a possible reappraisal of the overall plan' (ibid.) and, more recently, has suggested authorities 'develop an articulated strategic program for the conservation and rehabilitation of the historic fabric of Lhasa' so as to 'make the most appropriate use of the historic Shol area' (UNESCO 2004: 104).

These calls have not been heeded. Instead, the area directly below the Palace (known as inner Shol), until recently home to approximately 300 Tibetan families and numerous small Tibetan-run shops, is being redeveloped into, ironically, a museum, while across the main boulevard, Beijing Road, the area known as outer Shol was demolished and replaced in 1995 by a large square modeled on Tiananmen Square in Beijing (Potala Palace Management Office 2005). These changes highlight the underlying paradox in the relationship between UNESCO and the Chinese state: UNESCO marks sites as worthy of protection because of their cultural value, and Chinese authorities then transform these sites into elements in the state narrative of Chinese culture and civilization.

Yet this on-going government effort to harness the Tibetan past for contemporary political interests is not uncontested. On the one hand, Tibetan exile groups continue to criticize Chinese policies in Tibet (though most also support UNESCO programs in Tibet for their own reasons). More importantly, shaping narratives about the past are clearly easier than controlling how these narratives are consumed in the present. Thus, state tourism policies in Tibet, as in other minority areas such as Yunnan and Guizhou Provinces, only succeed to the extent that first, local subjects accede to these state efforts and accept their roles, and second, that tourists validate and authenticate state-sanctioned tourist/cultural sites through visiting these (Oakes 1998: 80; Ashworth 1994: 18).

In doing so, tourism certainly impacts local cultural practices, though this happens in ways that exceed worries about the purity of cultural practices versus the pollution of tourism desires and claims. For example, Oakes (1997) has shown how the state-encouraged transformation of Dong and Miao villages in Guizhou into tourist destinations has led not to a decline in the authenticity of cultural practices but to a situation in which being marked as a state-sanctioned space of cultural importance has become an intimate aspect of local identity and a source of capital, both cultural and social (ibid.: 55). This is similar to what has occurred in Bali, as its tourist status as both a site of unique (Bali-Hindu) culture and as an idealized tropical beach destination have shaped what it means to be Balinese within a Muslim-dominated nation–state (Picard 1997). Something similar appears to be happening in the case of Tibet and Tibetans.

Touring Tibet and other places on the frontier

Because of the size of Tibet, the region's few urban centers, and its still rudimentary road system, the rapid increase in tourist arrivals has been limited almost exclusively to the Lhasa region. Why do so many Han Chinese visit Lhasa, given the way Tibetans have been portrayed in popular media and in school textbooks for decades as backwards and primitive people, and within Chinese culture at large as recalcitrant and suspect?

One response would be to view this from a Euro-American perspective and explain such travel in terms of the relationship between self and nature. In other words, urban Han Chinese visit minority areas such as Tibet to cultivate the 'I' of their identity, engaging in the paradoxical process of 'finding themselves' (coming to more intimately know their own self) among strangers, by literally 'finding themselves among strangers' through travel. For example, Kolås tentatively suggests these tourists seek to experience a natural world they no longer recognize in their urban lives (2004: 273), while Swain argues that such tourists aim to confirm their own modernity and the distance both in space and time between them and ethnic minorities such as Tibetans (2001: 136–8).

However, as Nyíri (2006) persuasively argues, these trips are for many Han Chinese tourists aimed at consuming *mingsheng* (scenic spots), already-marked sites of historical or cultural importance, and doing so in the company of others. In other words, a good trip is not only faithful to the text (i.e., it meets expectations) but is also a social experience (it is good because it is experienced with others). This is a very different travel expectation than the idealized view of travel which circulates in the Euro-American canon. From this perspective, a good Chinese experience is a *bad* travel experience, since the point of travel is supposed to be to achieve a moment of insight spurred by an experience that does not replicate expectations but somehow exceeds these, and does so in a solitary setting, if not literally alone then among complete strangers. For the latter, estrangement is good ('I'm alone, even if surrounded by lots of people whose language I do not understand'); for the former, estrangement is simply strange ('I'm alone, and so either bored or lonely').

This certainly appears to be the case for the legions of middle-class group travelers in China, often on packaged tours from the same work units or companies. As Nyíri illustrates, these types of travelers are quite content to consume the social experience of already-marked travel destinations, surrounded by like-minded others. For such travelers, places such as Tibet, like Jiuzhaigou National Park in Sichuan, are not toured for their authenticity, be this of nature or material culture. Instead, cultural performance is both expected and valued – not the reality of everyday life (Nyíri 2006: 64–7).

Of course, a rejoinder to this would be to assert that what these people experience is not travel but tourism. Travel, or so it is sometimes asserted, has the depth, thickness, and emotional weight that tourism is supposed to lack. To what extent might this be true in the case of Tibet, and to what extent does this affect the broader state project of depoliticizing Tibetan culture?

In the Tibetan quarter of Lhasa a growing number of small hotels and cafés that once catered to foreign backpackers now increasingly host young Chinese urban residents. These travelers are called 'friends of donkeys' (*luzi pengyou*, shortened to *luyou*), a phonetic pun on the characters for tourism (also pronounced *luyou*). This label also quite effectively describes the sight of one of these backpackers, trudging down a street with his or her load. Among Chinese who frequent these hostels and cafés, Tibet and Tibetans are no longer primitive, dirty, superstitious, and dangerous, but exotic, spiritual, authentic and mystical. Or, more accurately, they are 'primitive' and therefore exotic, not yet modern and therefore mystical. Tibet appeals to these backpackers because of experiential differences from their normative experiences, both in terms of physical environment and social life. In other words, these backpackers appear to imagine Tibet as a place to visit not to confirm their own superiority, as Swain argues, or cultivate already existing social ties, as is the case with the package tourists Nyíri analyzes, but to grasp at something they do not have. Thus, Kolås may be partially right; for these donkey travelers, the goal is, broadly conceived, 'nature' – not, however, what he calls a 'nostalgic rejuvenation' (2004: 273) for what they have lost, but an idealized nostalgia for something they have never experienced.

Lu Xue is a typical example of these backpackers. The son of a former colleague, I met him in Beijing recently, shortly after his return from a six-week trip by train and bus through Qinghai and Tibet with two school friends.

Having just graduated from college, Lu had put off finding a job to take this trip. When I asked him what he had been looking for in Tibet, he promptly told me: a 'real spiritual place.' When I asked him to explain this, he said he had been looking for 'real people':

> Tibetans, you know, they are fierce people but also very spiritual. They know about mystical and magical things. I wanted to see these people in their own place. And I wanted to experience their nature, because it is a cleaner place then here. They are not yet modern (*xiandaide*). They still are traditional (*gudaide*), more like real people.
>
> (personal interview, June 2007)

His comments are strikingly similar to those of another group of young tourists I met at Labrang Monastary in Xiahe, a Tibetan town near Lanzhou in Gansu Province. Xiao Wang worked as an administrative assistant in a media company in Nanjing and had met her five travel companions through a website run by Chinese backpackers. The six of them were on a two-week vacation, and planned to continue by bus from Xiahe to Qinghai Lake at the edge of the Tibetan plateau. According to Xiao Wang, what kept her from traveling longer was a lack of money and time, not a lack of desire. She did not think it unusual for her to go traveling alone:

> People always say to me, 'You're a girl, what are you doing riding hard buses around the countryside with a backpack?' I tell them my mother went down to the countryside (*xiaxiang*) during her school days, so why shouldn't I? I think she likes what I am doing, because I learn about the real social situation. And what do I care about what other people say?
>
> (personal interview, August 2004)

Xiao Wang's reference to her mother's experience being sent to a rural area during the Cultural Revolution is thick with meaning. Between 1968 and 1975, approximately 12 million youth were 'sent down' to the countryside to learn from peasants. This massive spatial movement, known as 'going up to the mountains and down to the villages' (*shangshan xiaxiang*), was the defining event in the lives of many of these youth. It is the so-called 'little Emperors and Empresses,' many of them the children of these returned Red Guards, who make up urban China's first generation of single children to grow up with the wealth and ability to travel.

Xiao Wang and her companions were unanimous in their reasons for traveling in Tibetan regions. While not on a spiritual quest or a religious pilgrimage (they appeared to be baffled by the behavior of both monks and worshippers), they also were not the sort of Han Chinese visitors who serve as foils in so much of the contemporary travel writing about Tibet. Instead, they spoke about Tibet's 'mystery' and 'magic.' 'Tibetans are special people,' Xiao Wang told me. 'They have special practices and beliefs.' For 'special' she used both *te bie*, which translates as 'unique' and 'unusual', and *shen mi*, which connotes mystery and secrecy. Chen, one of her companions, added that he thought Tibetans were 'superstitious' people, which initially confused me. In Chinese, 'superstition' (*mi xin*) carries a sense of over-enthusiasm for a subject, to the point where a person becomes bewildered, confused, and ultimately lost. For most of the twentieth century, to describe a person as *mi xin* was to classify them as trapped in the past and not-yet modern: people to 'fix,' not observe, or, to observe in order to improve. Yet Chen was not out to 'develop' Tibetans and make them modern, he was content to simply see their 'superstitions' in practice.

A Chinese travel writer in Beijing explained why city people wanted to go to Tibet in this way:

> 'Superstitious' was a derogatory word to describe people 30 years ago, now it mostly likely means so-called diversity of culture, which attracts people from all over China. Why? Because they all think, dream, dress, eat, play in the same way, so seeing differences is cool . . . I guess most tourists to Tibet view religious stuff like temples, Lamas, and worshipping rites as something they put on their must-see list. They must see these just because they are special and mysterious. That doesn't mean they have any interest in religion. It's just like you don't have to be an art lover to see a show in Las Vegas. It's just a tourist attraction.
>
> (personal communication, May 2007)

Seeing Tibetan beliefs and practices certainly appeared to be enough for Xiao Wang. Neither she nor her companions expressed any desire to transcend their positions as observing subjects and enter a backstage into a more authentic zone of cultural reality, which so much of tourism theory assumes to be the point of such travel. Quite the contrary: when I posed this question of moving beyond surface encounters to a deeper level of meaning, Xiao Wang stared at me, perplexed. 'I'm not Tibetan,' she told me. 'How could I be like them?' Shen, one of the boys in the group, laughed. 'I don't understand anything they say! What would I do? And why would I want to?'

Conclusion

New forms of travel by Chinese citizens, ranging from rural laborers floating from city to city, to middle-class professionals on package tours to state-sanctioned scenic spots, to urban youth participating in their own form of 'going up to the mountains and down to the countryside,' influence how Chinese view themselves, their fellow citizens, and their country. In regard to Tibet, for Chinese citizens to imagine Tibet and Tibetans to be 'mysterious' and 'magical' is certainly another example of the late Edward Said's Orientalism at work. Yet this is very different from thinking of Tibetans as primitive and fierce peoples in need of saving from their own traditions – a belief that, once given ideological weight by Maoism, led to widespread destruction and death in the name of 'liberation.'

This shift in attitudes, however, has not occurred outside the broader state project of harnessing Tibetan 'culture,' reduced to a performative motif, as a resource in both the economic development of Tibet and a means of further incorporating Tibet into the national state. This shift in state policy towards Tibet, from an emphasis on forced assimilation under Mao to one of difference captured for the market, succeeds to the extent that cultural differences remain 'cultural' and not political. It is thus a policy that assiduously promotes the (Western) Shangri-la image of Tibet (Tibet as strange and 'colorful,' and in need of protection from modernity), but without the political implications of this (that strangeness implies fundamental differences).

Even among the emerging class of urban backpackers in China, the exoticization of Tibet and Tibetans, while rooted in these Shangri-la narratives of Western outsiders, remains firmly situated at the level of spectacle. In this sense, these backpackers, like other types of Han Chinese tourists, remain participants in the broader state tourism project in China that situates those who are toured as happy, 'colorful' minorities (Nyíri 2006: 84). Yet this is a different encounter than that of the idealized Euro-American reader of *The Lonely Planet*, who is promised both complete difference ('Go there, because there are no outsiders') and the means of identifying with this differentiated subject ('You, too, can become Tibetan-like'). If the prototypical Euro-American backpacker fantasizes about being like Tibetans (if only temporarily) these Chinese donkey travelers do not. As Shen said: 'Why would I want to (be like them)?'

Where these narratives meet is in their inability to conceive of Tibet and Tibetans as anything other than dreamlike; in doing so they collectively deny Tibet a place in history and Tibetans a role as active agents in the shaping of their own reality (Norbu 2001: 378).

19 Gastronomy and tourism

A case study of gourmet country-style cuisine in Hong Kong

Sidney C.H. Cheung

Food is also one of the important aspects of the 'environmental bubble' that surrounds most tourists on their travels. Many tourists eat the same food on holidays as they would do at home. Mass tourist resorts can often be divided spatially on the basis of cuisine – English tourists in English pubs, German tourists in the *Bierkeller*. Some tourists still engage in the habit of taking their own food with them on holidays.

(Richards 2002: 4–5)

Introduction

From what I have heard, some Japanese tourists take soya sauce with them during their trips in order to make foreign food taste familiar and acceptable, while some Hong Kong tourists take instant noodles, assuming that they might not have appropriate or sufficient food during their trip. In fact, the choice of food among tourists can really vary. There are also as many tourists who are willing to try local indigenous food in order to have an authentic cultural experience during their travels. As a cosmopolitan city, the people of Hong Kong are not only exposed to food from different parts of the world on their own home ground, but rising affluence has also given ample opportunity for many to travel for food. Hong Kong nationals can go to Japan for a sushi meal or to Cuba for a box of Havana cigars if they can afford the travel expenses. While economic success and political freedom in Hong Kong have opened the way to how food habits have developed, especially the internationalization of food, in this chapter, I analyze the connections between food, domestic (heritage) tourism and local identity with a view to underscoring the implications of Asians traveling within Asia.

Research on the anthropology of food has in the past centered largely on taboos, feasts, diets, communion and offerings, employing cultural symbolism for a better understanding of social relations among people and their interactions with others and/or the supernatural world (Messer 1984; Mintz and Du Bois 2002). More recent research is multidisciplinary, including issues of cultural identity, gender, ethnicity, social change, cultural nationalism, globalization/localization, memory, etc. with food, sharing the interests not only of anthropologists, but also historians, feminists and political scientists (Mintz and Du Bois 2002; Holtzman 2006; Phillips 2006). In recent research in various studies in Asia, it is not difficult to find that food and eating have been viewed as important markers of cultural identity, hence their changing meanings have been studied to discern various kinds of social and political issues within a local context (see Arnott 1975; Watson 1997; Wu and Tan 2001; Nestle 2002; Wu and Cheung 2002; Anderson 2005; Watson and Caldwell 2005; Wilk 2006). Consequently, as tourism has become a major activity for both visitors and local host societies in many Asian countries, it is important to pay attention to the significance of food in tourism for an understanding of relevant social values and cultural meanings beyond economic and polit-ical development in the fast globalizing world (Hjalager and Richards 2002; Cohen and Avieli 2004).

When talking about gastronomic tourism, people tend to think of destina-tions in which the original version of a particular kind of gourmet food or drink is produced, e.g., Italian pasta, Swiss chocolate, Australian seafood, French wine, Chinese tea, etc. With the support of tourism agents and local government in place-making through gastronomic attractions, some tourist attractions are eager to promote local food for tourists to enjoy, which can be Japanese sake, Korean imperial cuisine, Singaporean street food, Cantonese seafood, etc. Unheard of in the past, gastronomic tours are now popular. According to Hjalager (2002: 33), there are four levels of gastro-nomic tourism, with the emphasis upon four different orders of attitude toward gastronomy varying from how tourists enjoy the food, understand the food, experience the food, and exchange knowledge about the food. Even though Hjalager did not provide many cases for clarification of the above four-order model, it is beyond doubt that there exists, many different kinds of gastronomic tours in various countries exist. In this case study, I seek to investigate the meanings of gastronomy for Hong Kong society, with par-ticular reference to the relations between one's gastronomic experiences and domestic tourism. As *puhn choi* (meaning 'basin cuisine') becomes more and more popular, I investigate its meanings for Hong Kong visitors to the New Territories and unveil what this representative country-style cooking has implied for domestic heritage tourism since the early 1990s.

Food and eating in Hong Kong society

Hong Kong, part of the previous Hsin-an County in Guangdong Province, was taken by the British in the mid-nineteenth century. The southern part of the Kowloon Peninsula with all its surrounding islands, including Hong Kong Island, was ceded to Britain by the Treaty of Nanking in 1842. A large part of the peninsula, called the New Territories, which starts from Boundary Street in the southern part of Kowloon peninsula and reaches the border between Shenzhen and Hong Kong in the north, was leased to the British Government in 1898 for 99 years. In the colonial era, the Hong Kong Colonial

Government was the highest authority in policy-making for the entire society. Chinese residents, however, numbering more than 95 percent of the total population, were still given enough religious, academic, press and economic freedom to ensure that there was comparatively little hostility towards the British. The alternative to staying in Hong Kong was to migrate overseas, which many did, or to return to China with its own turbulent history.

In the past 50 years, Hong Kong has undergone dramatic changes in industrial and financial development stemming from both economic growth and changing political relations with mainland China. During two large-scale immigration waves from the mid-1940s to the early 1950s, Hong Kong's population grew from 600,000 in 1945 to 2,340,000 by the end of 1954. While these migrants included both Hong Kong residents who had previously fled the Japanese occupation and mainland Chinese who left China after the Communist Revolution in 1949, most came from the Pearl River Delta area in South China, while the rest came from different parts of the mainland. With the stability offered by new public housing for most working-class people, a large, low-cost labor force emerged and helped to develop Hong Kong's light industry. By the mid-1960s, Hong Kong had achieved great success in economic development; at the same time, the Cultural Revolution was unfolding in China, beginning a period of great suffering and turmoil on the mainland. In response, the Hong Kong Government began local campaigns to create a sense of belonging among the people living in Hong Kong. Campaigns such as 'Clean Hong Kong,' 'Against Corruption,' and the 'Hong Kong Festival' were aimed at helping the residents claim a sense of ownership over the territory. In addition, the use of the Cantonese language in the mass media, e.g., television and radio, which began in the late 1960s, cemented the Hong Kong identity as separate from China or even Guangdong. Cantonese serials on television became the popular culture and further solidified the Hong Kong identity. Generally, most scholars (Lau and Kuan 1988; Siu 1996) agree that it was in the late 1960s that a 'Hong Kong identity' emerged. Consumption became an important means of expressing status, prestige and power as the people's living standards improved. Besides spending money on imported brand-name products, travel and dining out were also associated with wealth and status. The popular destinations to visit were Singapore, Malaysia, Thailand, the Philippines and Taiwan rather than mainland China. Starting in the 1980s, however, mainland China was added to the list. With more vacation time and money for leisure, families and friends were looking for greater choice and food tours became one of the spin-offs of this new wealth wherein people started going on expensive gastronomic tours. Tours to Japan, led by famous food writers, complete with five-star hotel stays and business-class flights, are examples of the gastronomic expeditions available for Japanese gourmet food aficionados. Such packages cost more US$5,000 for a five-day guided tour.

Likewise, we can observe that as Hong Kong's changing material culture became more international, individuals sought to use food as a cultural marker of identity and status. International cuisine at restaurants serves to provide a means for people to compete as equals in the international arena. Food consumed at home is far more traditional and conservative, characterized by concerns for safety, health, traditional hot/cold (*yin–yang*) balance, and ritual taboos. A well-defined boundary is maintained between eating at home and outside and this negotiation between traditionalism and cosmopolitanism is clearly evident in Hong Kong. The ingredients used at home are similar for most families, with little variation in cooking style. For example, boiled soup, steamed fish, fried seasonal green vegetables with small pieces of meat and bean curd are all typical family dishes, with rice almost invariably served as the staple food in Hong Kong homes. The difference between eating habits inside and outside the home is a telling one, and reflects the dichotomy of Hong Kong itself. Hong Kong is a cosmopolitan city boasting international sophistication on the one hand, while on the other it is an extension of Chinese culture with long-standing Cantonese traditions. This is a notable point because it explains in part the popularity of *puhn choi* which is traditional home cooking extended to community members and captures the essence of an imagined past or heritage which is no longer available in cosmopolitan and urban Hong Kong.

Domestic tourism in Hong Kong

Hong Kong's prosperity has been paralleled by the active and rapid development of its tourism industry. In 2006, Hong Kong experienced 25.25 million tourist visits, generating HK$117.3 billion (approximately US$15.1 billion) in income and making the tourism industry the second largest generator of foreign currency (Tourism Commission 2007). However, with the rapid development of tourism in Macau and South China, Hong Kong's inbound tourism has faced considerable competition from neighboring destinations, with local residents tempted to leave the country on vacation. This means that Hong Kong is faced with a dual challenge: to entice international tourists to stay longer, to shop more and to do more sightseeing, as well as to provide local attractions for domestic tourists so that residents can enjoy weekend breaks and day-trips at home instead of traveling to Macau or Shenzhen.

Thus, cultural as well as heritage tourism activities have enjoyed considerable prominence in domestic tourism during the past two decades. Domestic tours are mostly one-day package tours typically featuring cultural heritage in the New Territories or experiences of pre-colonial and rural Chinese lifestyles or natural scenery away from the city. For example, a tour with heritage visits to the Ping Shan Heritage Trail draws attention to the traditional, rural side of Hong Kong. With the development of convenient transportation, domestic tours have begun allowing people to make voyages of discovery to experience rural traditions in the New Territories, a region that was considered remote until the 1980s. Also, popular domestic package tours generally include a meal of local food (usually *puhn choi*, seafood or vegetarian dishes) after visiting historic villages in order to reinforce the idea that there is a traditional Hong Kong that comprises the heritage of the local people. In other words, going into the inner, rural part of the New Territories is, for urban Hong Kong residents, a journey of discovery into their past. The search for what is traditional and old Hong Kong reflects an identity crisis felt among its residents which the handover of 1997 amplified (Cheung 1999, 2005a, 2005b).

The emphasis upon the local, rural and pre-colonial in domestic Hong Kong tourism is significant. According to information I have collected from various domestic heritage tours in the late 1990s while I was conducting research on the impacts brought by tourists after the establishment of Ping Shan Heritage Trail in the New Territories, popular package tours generally involve a schedule including local food, rural scenery and a visit to historic villages or temples (Cheung 1999, 2003). The tours include authentic Chinese culinary tradition such as a *puhn choi* meal which is banquet food found in many of Hong Kong's local villages, vegetarian food served at well-known temples, and goose and pigeon cooked in country style. Thus, food with local characteristics have been greatly preferred in domestic heritage tours, especially if the eating places in the New Territories, islands, and coastal areas are located in relatively untouched places.

In addition to cultural heritage, the Hong Kong Tourism Board also emphasizes the green side of Hong Kong. After the 1997 handover of Hong Kong from British jurisdiction to the People's Republic of China, Hong Kong's tourism industry started to decline. In an attempt to redress this decline, a new campaign entitled 'We are Hong Kong, City of Life' was launched in May 1998, emphasizing a diversity of tourist experiences including the region's diverse ecological and natural environment. Despite the dominant metropolitan image of Hong Kong, the HKSAR government has devised multiple strategies to encourage nature-based tourism, one of which is through the sustainable utilization of natural resources. The potential for tourism of hitherto neglected, rich natural resources finally received attention in the 1990s. With the success of the Hong Kong Wetland Park, opened in 2006, the time is ripe to review the growth of domestic nature-based tourism and the accompanying changes regarding wildlife conservation and education (also see Cheung 2007). Some of the park's more heavily promoted nature-based travel and leisure activities include dolphin-watching, bird-watching, butterfly-watching, recreational and educational centers, nature trails, coastal walks, and hiking. Food is still a basic component of the new tourism because the tourists are out of the city.

The emergence of gastronomic tourism

Gastronomy is an important cultural marker of identity in many globalizing Asian societies, and analysis of different aspects of food and cuisine can provide insights into the development of society. Apart from studying regular daily food as many scholars have done, I suggest that food promoted to and eaten by domestic tourists should not be overlooked in the contemporary Hong Kong society. Such food might previously be exclusive food specially prepared for local events, and is widely produced for mass tourists who are interested in trying authentic, inexpensive and local food. Here, I would like to make use of a local case regarding how the choice of tourist food depends on the social political atmosphere which changes people's social taste in many different ways. Let's look at the 'urbanization' of *puhn choi*. Historically speaking, this country-styled dish is a festive food commonly prepared during ancestor worship rites and wedding banquets among the indigenous inhabitants of Hong Kong's New Territories. Usually prepared in the kitchen of the ancestral hall, it is the main and usually only dish served in the meal. All ingredients are served together in one basin, or *puhn*, from which everyone at the table eats communally. This dish usually comprises layers of inexpensive, local ingredients such as dried pig skin, dried eel, dried squid, radish, tofu skin, mushroom and pork stewed in soy bean paste. The banquet may occasionally have several side dishes, but the main basin dish is always the focus. Among local villagers in the New Territories, the dish is usually called *sihk puhn* (meaning 'eat the basin'), and boasts an oral history longer than that of colonial Hong Kong. More importantly, *sihk puhn*'s contemporary manifestation as *puhn choi* is being promoted in the media (e.g., guidebooks, web sites and travel magazines) through different stories of its so-called origin. Yet, the tradition of eating *puhn choi* in Hong Kong appears to have attracted domestic tourists only after their visits to the region's traditional village settlements and particularly to heritage sites in the New Territories, visits to the latter being more common since the 1990s.

There are many different versions of how *puhn choi* supposedly originated. For example, it has been said that *puhn choi* began as leftovers from a village banquet and was highly appreciated by the Qing Emperor Qianlong when he was visiting Kwangtung (Watson 1987: 394). Another popular version says that *puhn choi* was originally given to the Emperor Song Bing and his entourage when they moved to the south during the invasion of the Mongolians in the late Song period; it was later named *puhn choi* because there were not enough containers to hold food for everyone, so washing basins used by villagers became the containers for the army's feast (Tang 2002: 4). These stories reflect a historical consciousness of the state from the local level up. *Puhn choi*, functioning as a local food among Chinese family lineages settled several centuries ago, speaks of the 'exotic' for most Hong Kong residents who are not familiar with cultural traditions in the New Territories. With *puhn choi*'s dual identity as both local and exotic, it has been promoted widely in domestic tourism for its 'taste of tradition.' However, the change from eating the traditional *sihk puhn* to the modern *puhn choi* needs further examination. Historically speaking, *sihk puhn* has been served as banquet food in many local, single-surname villages, marking corresponding ethnic boundaries, and is ceremonially used to signify an entire lineage joined by the way they eat together; furthermore, *sihk puhn* not only reinforces the *punti* (local) single-surname lineage system, but also seems to exclude Hakka migrant groups from *punti* local Chinese groups within the New Territories' political context. In other words, *sihk puhn* is metaphorically considered the real food of the New Territories, dating back to its very earliest inhabitants (Watson 1987). As Watson (ibid.: 391–2) stated, the practice of *sihk puhn* is an indicator of equality and commonness:

> Each guest collected his own chopsticks from a tray and picked up an individual bowl of steamed rice. The basin was carried to an unoccupied corner of the hall. Earlier arrivals were already eating at the few makeshift tables that had been assembled near the kitchen. I could not help but notice that one of the wealthiest men in rural Hong Kong (an emigrate millionaire) was sitting between a retired farmer and a factory worker . . . No ceremonies of any kind were performed; no complicated codes of etiquette were observed. No one acted as host for our small group and there was no ranking of diners, nor was there a head table reserved for important quests. People were fed on a first come, first served basis. No speeches were delivered and no toasts proposed. Everyone ate at their own place and left when they pleased.

Nowadays the majority of *puhn choi* eating does not recall rural scenery, yet, it is labeled as 'nostalgic food' to people who have not really experienced the past but intend to construct an exotic experience of the 'good old days' by eating 'food from the past;' this was described by Appadurai (1996: 30) as 'nostalgia without memory.' From the early 1990s, Hong Kong urbanites who participated in 'discovery voyages' of the New Territories' local and domestic traditions and their affiliated expectations of exoticism reasserted their Hong Kong-ness on the path to the 1997 handover. In other words, local traditions in the New Territories were constructed as a unique local Hong Kong culture distinct from mainland China. Besides nostalgia-inspired village tradition, infrastructure development in the New Territories is probably also a significant reason for the drastic increase in demand for *puhn choi* in contemporary Hong Kong society.

Besides being served the traditional way, 'take away' *puhn choi* in a large bowl for 10–12 people is also popular. Thus, one can enjoy this food with friends and relatives at home instead of at traditional venues – village halls or cemeteries for festive and ceremonial occasions. Most interestingly, during the Lunar New Year in 2003, it was widely reported in the media that *puhn choi* was one of the best sellers despite the economic depression; in particular, many take-away *puhn choi* meals were sold on the second day of the Lunar New Year, serving as the first family meal of the year at which all family members were in attendance. In the following two years, the demand for *puhn choi* remained consistent and some versions of this dish were served and sold (as take-away) in high-end seafood restaurants. Its rising popularity caused the Hong Kong Government to issue a press release (HKSARG 2005a, 2005b) outlining the hygiene involved in the preparation and subsequent consumption of *puhn choi*. Again in January 2005, the most popular local Chinese food magazine – *Eat and Travel Weekly* – contributed a special issue on the varieties of *puhn choi*, ranging from traditional meals prepared in an ancestral hall to expensive meals with fresh seafood or dried marine products. In still another variation, miniature *puhn choi* (using a small pumpkin as the basin that contains a few pieces of chicken, mushrooms and vegetables) was actively promoted by some local fast food chains and served in single portions as well as a single dinner set. Conveying an image of family meals and symbolizing Hongkong-ness, *puhn choi* has entered Hong Kong daily life in many ways (Chan 2007).

Considering the food items which used to be local but have now became nationwide commercial items, Noguchi (1994: 328) described the development of *ekiben* (train station lunch boxes) in Japan, and emphasized that its increased popularity was related to the fact that *ekiben* 'are powerful symbols in Japan because they mediate the new age of speed in travel and the venerated past.' This might also be one of the many reasons for explaining why *puhn choi* has become popular in Hong Kong in the past decade. On the one hand, convenient transportation promotes voyages of discovery of rural traditions. On the other hand, *puhn choi*, with an emphasis on local tradition, represents an exotic element in domestic tourism and developed as a nostalgic food with an emphasis on its rural cooking style to satisfy Hong Kong people's search for a sense of cultural belonging during the run-up to the handover. Carrying this political message, *puhn choi* moved from its original function as a focus for lineage gathering in the New Territories to a symbol of Hong Kong heritage that everyone can share. Besides actual participation in domestic tours, many Hong Kong people learned about *puhn choi* through mass media channels such as TV programs, popular food magazines and Chinese dailies.

Travel programs fast forward gastronomic tourism

Modern mass media can create new or influence consumption habits. Advertisements give guidelines for or teach people how to choose and purchase goods and services. The mass media bombards the public with all sorts of images via television advertisements, newspapers, magazines, mail, Internet, radio broadcasts and posters on the subways. In this exact manner, gastronomic tourism has also harnessed the mass media to its advantage.

The development of Hong Kong television cooking shows can be divided into three phases. In the first phase, cooking was demonstrated as evidence of competent domestic skills for women. Such presentations were usually performed by an elegant woman who gave tips on what to cook on particular days and shared her personal experiences about how to keep everyone in the family healthy by serving traditional Cantonese simmered soups and fresh seasonal dishes. This kind of cooking show can still be found in afternoon programming as part of various housekeeping series; books and videos are also available on this topic. The second phase emerged with the rapid increase in Hong Kong's living standard in which travel abroad, luxurious living and gourmet dining were enjoyed by a rising middle class eager to express social status; this is especially the case with the consumption of expensive food introduced by pop stars, celebrities and food writers on many of Hong Kong's televised travel programs. Celebrities introduced local foods and cuisines and famous eateries of particular tourist destinations. They also explained how local people prepared and cooked the dishes they ate and, in addition, some exotic ingredients and other aspects of the food were introduced. The third phase that combines travel and food with a focus on the Pearl River Delta area is perhaps the most interesting. Instead of expensive and luxurious foods, it emphasizes basic traditional cooking, hailing back to how things were 'originally' done.

Among all the food critics and chefs who are the most active in the Hong Kong media, Hua (pseudonym given by author) should be considered the most prominent promoter of country-style food as well as New Territories local village food. Hua's restaurant was successful in serving dishes developed from the traditional *puhn choi* and bringing different local home-style food into the commercial sphere. Besides being a renowned chef, Hua is famous for his television show and enjoys the reputation of knowing where good food can be found. In his television show, viewers follow Hua on his travels to locate high quality ingredients. Unlike other popular food critics in the media, Hua does not emphasize the use of luxury, high-end, expensive meals, but rather focuses on traditional country food prepared with care. He discusses the difference between good and bad ingredients and how, during cooking, one can make full use of local food's tastes, textures and characteristics.

Between December 2002 and July 2003, Hua published four books on traditional food: the first is a cookbook on village (or *wai tsuen*) food in the New Territories; the second is about eating in the Pearl River Delta area, while the third and fourth are cookbooks that include the history of traditional sauces, hints for choosing ingredients and culinary techniques compiled after a popular television series on looking for good food in the Pearl River Delta area. Between August 2003 and July 2004, Hua published three additional books with similar themes showcasing simple cooking methods with local ingredients, reinforcing how this aspect of everyday material culture had assumed center stage in a transformed cultural practice of the time. Apart from the recipes and illustrations of different kinds of dishes, Hua also described some of the personal experiences through which he learned of these dishes, always reminding his readers of the close relationship between local ingredients and their environment.

Conclusion

To summarize, regarding the domestic tourist's search for food through heritage tourism, the development of *puhn choi* demonstrates Hong Kong nationals' response to social change at a time when Hong Kong people were psychologically and politically preparing themselves for the 1997 handover to mainland China. Beginning in the early 1990s, there was an obvious identity crisis among Hong Kong urbanites who went on to participate in 'discovery voyages' in search of local tradition through domestic heritage tourism in the New Territories (Cheung 1999). *Puhn choi*, with its emphasis on country-style cooking is an important component of Hong Kong people's search for a sense of cultural belonging. *Puhn choi* became more and more popular as the boom in domestic (heritage) tourism got underway and itself became a metaphor for what is traditionally Hong Kong and rooted in history.

Media as one of the central cultural institutions in Asia has helped the development of gastronomic tourism both worldwide and locally. Television food shows and food and travel programs have done much to change people's attitude towards the idea of eating interesting local food while traveling and have brought into the public eye traditional foods and how they are cooked. For Hong Kong, TV food programs and advertisements have contributed to the interest of locals in domestic tourism. Hua's food and travel program is one of the most successful in Hong Kong and has sustained the phenomenal interest in *puhn choi*.

In this chapter, I have shown the link between food, travel and identity. Using the case of *puhn choi*, I have shown how crucial local food is for the development of domestic tourism. As Asia becomes more and more affluent, there are similar developments in Japan, South Korea, mainland China, Singapore and Taiwan. *Ekiben* in 'Discover Japan' is a case in point. Without a doubt, Asians are on tour and what needs further investigation is the implication of this for domestic tourism which this chapter has expanded upon for Hong Kong. Further work is needed to think through the implications of gastronomic tourism within Asia as the shared heritage of ethnic Chinese (not to mention Muslim food or Hindu vegetarian food) have yet to begin an odyssey of discovery.

Part V

Tourism and new social networks

20 'My mother's best friend's sister-in-law is coming with us'

Exploring domestic and international travel with a group of Lao tourists

Charles Carroll

Introduction

> We're in Vientiane, the Lao People's Democratic Republic and the video recording begins. It's 19 April 2006. With the morning sun streaming through an opened window behind her, *PhaaKung*, my wife's aunt, kneels on the floor of my wife's wooden house carefully folding banana leaves into small cones. The cones will hold offerings of money that we will present to the seven Buddhist monks who are due to arrive shortly. *PhaaKung* spent much of the morning making the elaborate *pa kwan* flower arrangement that will stand at the center of the day's spirit-calling ceremony. In a few moments we are joined by the in-law of *PhaaKung* and both women spend the remainder of the morning fulfilling the role of maternal aunts, guiding my wife and me through an elaborate ceremony to prepare our newly remodeled house for use.
>
> (Excerpt from field notes dated 20 April 2006)

In this chapter I provide an observation of how travel is conducted by citizens of the Lao People's Democratic Republic. Using an anthropological approach of participant observation, I document how a group of five tourists from Lao PDR journey to Chiang Mai, Thailand. The details provided in this analysis are useful and contribute insights into the social nature of tourism practices in a country where there is a lacuna of information on outbound travel by local people. I start this chapter by looking at an event six years after the 2000 trip. The presence of *PhaaKung* and her in-law at the ceremony cannot be fully understood without examining the journey we took together six years before, nor can the inclusion of *PhaaKung* and her in-law on the journey be fully understood without examining their presence at the spirit-calling ceremony in 2006.

Lao PDR is becoming increasingly popular as a tourist destination (Vongsam-ang 2006). Total tourist arrivals in Lao PDR first passed the million mark in 2005. By 2006, Asia and Pacific tourist arrivals alone were 1,008,663, with 891,807 of those coming from other ASEAN member countries (Figure 20.1). While the Lao National Tourism Administration gathers a great deal of data on tourists coming to Lao PDR, there is very little information available on the tourism practices of the Lao themselves. We do know that Lao citizens travel (Figure 20.2) but there is a dearth of information regarding how they travel; this is one of the first contributions to filling this gap.

My social proximity to members of this group enabled the research of this journey. I recorded it on video, and used the tapes to re-observe the group members' practices of tourism, to develop questions about their practices

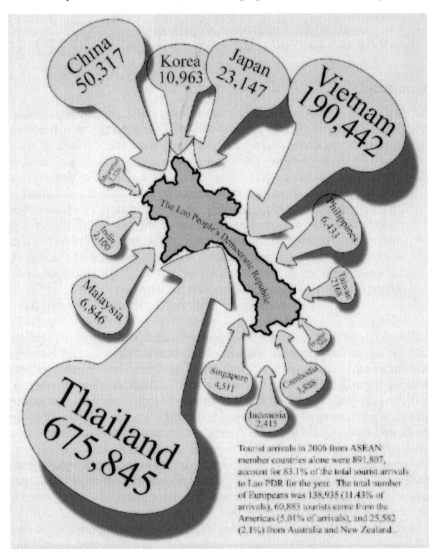

Figure 20.1 Asian tourist arrivals to Laos by nationality in 2006 (*Source*: Lao National Tourism Administration, arranged by the author)

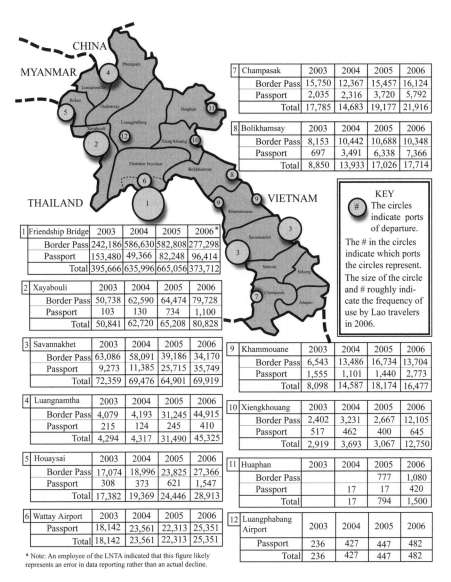

CHINA

MYANMAR

THAILAND

VIETNAM

7	Champasak	2003	2004	2005	2006
	Border Pass	15,750	12,367	15,457	16,124
	Passport	2,035	2,316	3,720	5,792
	Total	17,785	14,683	19,177	21,916

8	Bolikhamsay	2003	2004	2005	2006
	Border Pass	8,153	10,442	10,688	10,348
	Passport	697	3,491	6,338	7,366
	Total	8,850	13,933	17,026	17,714

KEY
The circles indicate ports of departure.
The # in the circles indicate which ports the circles represent. The size of the circle and # roughly indicate the frequency of use by Lao travelers in 2006.

1	Friendship Bridge	2003	2004	2005	2006*
	Border Pass	242,186	586,630	582,808	277,298
	Passport	153,480	49,366	82,248	96,414
	Total	395,666	635,996	665,056	373,712

2	Xayabouli	2003	2004	2005	2006
	Border Pass	50,738	62,590	64,474	79,728
	Passport	103	130	734	1,100
	Total	50,841	62,720	65,208	80,828

3	Savannakhet	2003	2004	2005	2006
	Border Pass	63,086	58,091	39,186	34,170
	Passport	9,273	11,385	25,715	35,749
	Total	72,359	69,476	64,901	69,919

4	Luangnamtha	2003	2004	2005	2006
	Border Pass	4,079	4,193	31,245	44,915
	Passport	215	124	245	410
	Total	4,294	4,317	31,490	45,325

5	Houaysai	2003	2004	2005	2006
	Border Pass	17,074	18,996	23,825	27,366
	Passport	308	373	621	1,547
	Total	17,382	19,369	24,446	28,913

6	Wattay Airport	2003	2004	2005	2006
	Passport	18,142	23,561	22,313	25,351
	Total	18,142	23,561	22,313	25,351

* Note: An employee of the LNTA indicated that this figure likely represents an error in data reporting rather than an actual decline.

9	Khammouane	2003	2004	2005	2006
	Border Pass	6,543	13,486	16,734	13,704
	Passport	1,555	1,101	1,440	2,773
	Total	8,098	14,587	18,174	16,477

10	Xiengkhouang	2003	2004	2005	2006
	Border Pass	2,402	3,231	2,667	12,105
	Passport	517	462	400	645
	Total	2,919	3,693	3,067	12,750

11	Huaphan	2003	2004	2005	2006
	Border Pass			777	1,080
	Passport		17	17	420
	Total		17	794	1,500

12	Luangphabang Airport	2003	2004	2005	2006
	Passport	236	427	447	482
	Total	236	427	447	482

Figure 20.2 Out-going Lao travelers by year and port of departure (*Source*: Lao National Tourism Administration, arranged by the author)

of travel, and used these questions in subsequent interviews. In the five years between our tour together and the interviews, all but one of the group members had participated in additional tourism domestically and abroad. The interview questions were designed to probe their practices of international tourism, and delve into how their international tourism compares and contrasts with their tourism inside the borders of the Lao PDR.

I concur with Graburn (1997: 200): 'there is no one homogeneous process of "tourism" but many tourisms;' my intention is not to paint with broad brushstrokes to provide a generalized picture of 'the tourism practices of the Lao.' Rather, I detail the experience of this group of lowland Lao tourists with the hope that these details will inform theories and practices concerning Asians on tour. This study opens up understandings of how people with very limited financial resources are able to leverage social relationships to make tourism affordable and feasible. As such, the findings could prove relevant for those studying the movements of similar populations throughout Asia and around the globe.

Obligations to kin: formation of destination and the social unit for travel

The tape begins to roll on the Thai bank of the Mekong River in the winter of 2000. My lens is focused on the distant shore, on the Lao People's Democratic Republic. With me is my wife, Aire, a citizen of Lao PDR and resident of Vientiane. This was her first visit back to Southeast Asia after two years in the United States. On this trip, Aire felt obliged to see two people – her biological mother in Lao PDR, and a woman in Chiang Mai, Thailand, whom Aire considers her second mother. Originally Aire and I planned to meet Aire's biological mother at the border in Nong Khai, Thailand, and together, travel by train to Chiang Mai. Before our small family travel group could depart we needed to congregate in Nong Khai.

The border checkpoint at the Friendship Bridge connecting Nong Khai, Thailand and Thadua, Lao PDR, is the most frequently used border checkpoint for incoming international tourists and out-going Lao travelers (Lao National Tourism Administration 2006: 16–17). A Lao national may use two documents to pass through the checkpoint – a short-term border pass, or a passport. Participants explained that they primarily use the border pass for shopping, medical visits, and one- to three-day trips to nearby destinations. They use passports for longer-term tourism in Thailand. Aire's mother was to meet us in Nong Khai with her passport in her hand.

The mobile phone boom had not fully arrived in Vientiane. Cross-border communication with Aire's family was accomplished in two ways – calling Aire's mother's neighbor who would take the message to Aire's family, and we would call again to hear a response; or, family members or friends would travel across the river on a short-term border pass and bring information in person.

On arriving in Nong Khai we heard through the neighbor that Aire's stepfather had been granted vacation time to join us; our travel group grew by one. While he waited for his passport, Aire's younger sisters came across the river to join us and stay at the guesthouse. Aire's sisters brought with them more information: Aire's mother's best friend would also join us on the trip. Explaining the best friend's inclusion in our travel group Aire told me: 'If she didn't come with us my mother wouldn't have fun.' Our travel group now stood at five.

Lao systems of social classification are essential for understanding the formation of this social unit of travelers, the determination of destinations, as well as the means through which these Lao travelers finance their tourism. In English Aire refers to *PhaaKung* as 'my mother's best friend,' but in the Lao language the name *PhaaKung* has the meaning 'my maternal aunt whose eldest child is named Kung.' In his study of lowland Lao migrants Barber (1979: 315) stressed: 'Simple kinship terms in Lao are . . . indicators of social category, which do not necessarily reflect the indicated blood relationships.' Aire's family views the mother's best friend as belonging to the social category of a maternal aunt. Although she is not biologically a blood relative, her social category is that of a biological relative. Her participation in family ceremonies, celebrations and on tour is as a maternal aunt.

Tambiah's (1970) research on Thai societies provides valuable insights into some Lao social practices which are similar in nature. It is particularly useful for explaining the composition of this travel group, the obligations related to financing the journey, and the obligations that determined the destination of the tour. Tambiah views the ordering of persons in the regional social categorization as having two axes, 'the vertical generational (which defines respect and authority relations) and the lateral "sibling" (which defines sexual accessibility and approved marriage). Both axes embody concepts of social privilege and obligation' (ibid.: 17). Using this social organization, we can see that the aunt simultaneously occupies multiple positions of social privilege and obligation. Simply being of Aire's mother's generation affords *PhaaKung* social obligations and privileges vertically. By adding the dimension of a maternal sibling, these social obligations and privileges are increased. As a maternal aunt, *PhaaKung* occupies a social position with privileges and obligations that are close to those Aire affords her biological mother.

There is only one family friend occupying a higher position of obligations and privileges than *PhaaKung*, and that is the woman living in Chiang Mai whose home constituted the initial destination of our journey. The woman in Chiang Mai cared for Aire with a great deal of love, helping to raise her when Aire was young and supporting her when Aire was a teenager. In many respects the woman in Chiang Mai took on the obligations of Aire's biological mother. Because of her social role in Aire's life, this woman is referred to as Aire's *mae hak*. The word *mae* means mother, and *hak* means love. Aire's *mae hak* occupies a social position that is as close as one can get to that of a biological mother. Aire felt obliged to visit her mother during this return trip to the region. In a similar manner she felt obliged to visit her *mae hak*. These two obligations initiated the tour. Our time and finances for visiting in the region were limited, so Aire decided it would be best to consolidate the two obligatory visits and maximize the amount of time she could spend with both, by bringing Aire's biological mother to the home of the *mae hak*.

Travel and the social production of kin: leveraging hospitality/establishing obligations

Upon hearing that her stepfather had received his visa, we sent word back to Vientiane telling the travel group to meet us at a guesthouse in Nong Khai. On the morning of the day of departure, the tour group stood at five: Aire, her stepfather, Aire's biological mother, *PhaaKung* and myself. This was Aire's stepfather's first travel experience outside of Lao PDR, and his first use of a Lao passport. All other members of the traveling group had participated in tourism in Thailand before.

When the group arrived we noticed an unfamiliar woman who turned out to be the mother of the man married to *Kung* who is the eldest daughter of *PhaaKung* (i.e., the in-law of *PhaaKung*). After conversing with *PhaaKung* a little more, Aire turned with a smile and informed me: 'My mother's best friend's sister-in-law is coming with us.' Aire's gentle smile and the direct statement made it clear that this was not a point of negotiation.

Six years after the trip I asked the in-law to reflect upon how she became a part of the travel group. The tone of her answer was that of one patiently informing the oblivious of the obvious: 'You are the *luuk-hack luuk-phaeng* of the mother of my son's wife, therefore you are my *luuk-hack luuk-phaeng* as well. There are feelings of *hak*, feelings of *phaeng*.' The in-law of *PhaaKung* refers to Aire and myself as *luuk-hack luuk-phaeng*. The term *luuk* translates to child/children and the terms *hack* and *phaeng* are both terms for love. The word *phaeng*, however, is most commonly reserved for describing or expressing the love between a parent and child, an uncle/aunt and nieces/nephews, the children of one's closest and dearest friend, etc. Combined the words form an idiom expressing the closest of parental-like relationships. The use of terms for close kinship in this situation is best understood by the circumstances under which their use was initiated (i.e. the desire to include the in-law in our family travel group).

In examining how kinship terms govern social relations, Tambiah (1970: 17) wrote: 'Close kin are naturally more important than more distant kin, but which of the close kin (outside ego's families of procreation and orientation) depends on situational circumstances and not on jural norms.' Jural norms did not govern who was included in our travel group, but clearly an argument for the inclusion of the in-law was difficult to counter once she was socially positioned in such a manner. It was the situation of travel that initiated the social positioning through the use of kinship terms. By using the phrase *luuk-hack luuk-phaeng* to describe my wife and myself, the in-law positioned herself as having a social relation to us that is akin to being a parental blood relative, and thus logically included as a sponsored participant in our family journey.

Understanding kinship and the obligations of mutual hospitality that kinship entail are essential for understanding the domestic tourism of this group of Lao tourists. Barber's (1979: 313) research reveals how Lao kinship and hospitality are related:

The expression used in Lao to refer to people with whom one has a kin relationship of some kind is *phi nong* (literally: 'elder sibling/younger sibling'). This term, undifferentiated in singular and plural, can cover all consanguine and affinal kin, both genuine and fictitious. In the most general sense its use expresses the feeling that the person or persons referred to will be, or should be, ready to offer the facilities which are expected from a blood relative, or conversely that they will expect to receive those facilities from the speaker. Thus a person planning a journey might say to his companions, 'Don't worry. I have *phi nong* in Vang Vieng' (and therefore we have no need to worry about food or accommodation). The first obligation prescribed among kin is therefore that of mutual hospitality.

Interviews with each participant in this travel group revealed a clear pattern of domestic and international travel. Within Lao PDR, tourism that includes overnight stays is made to the homes of persons considered to be relatives. Hospitality of relatives makes this travel affordable and feasible. Though not biologically related, *PhaaKung* and Aire's mother have an *euay nong* or 'elder sister, younger sister' relationship. Whenever Aire's mother travels domestically, *PhaaKung* is invited to join. The overnight destinations for all of Aire's mother's domestic journeys depend upon the hospitality of people whom she considers relatives. *PhaaKung* would consider these people to be relatives as well. When Aire's mother, *PhaaKung*, and the in-law travel and stay overnight domestically, they travel with family members to the homes of family members. The kin are the destinations, and the hospitality of kin is what makes the overnight stay affordable.

Family vs. *toowa*: domestic and international travel differences

For the participants in our journey, the social composition and size of domestic and international traveling units are usually different. This Chiang Mai journey was an exception to the norm. Aire's mother, *PhaaKung* and her in-law explained that unlike domestic travel where the traveling unit is composed of two or three members of one's kin, their international tourism experience had primarily been with a *toowa*. The international *toowa* group can be as large as 70 unrelated people. The word *toowa* is clearly derived from the word 'tour,' however, the use of the word *toowa* by these participants denotes the practices of group travel they have personally experienced, not necessarily forms of tourism that the term 'tour' may connote or imply in English.

The in-law explained that when she traveled on *toowa* to both Vietnam and Thailand, the travel companies were Vietnamese or Thai companies respectively. The guides were always Lao, and all members of the *toowa* were Lao citizens. She learnt about tour destinations and determined which she would join by reading printed brochures. The mode of transport was either a bus or mini-van, depending on the size of the group. The overnight accommodations were shared spaces. If they stayed in a hotel, the *toowa* participants decided with whom they would share a room.

The participants in our trip to Chiang Mai all preferred family travel over *toowa* travel, as the in-law explained:

> When you go on a *toowa* you go with a group. Going in a group is not enjoyable. When you go with family you can stop anywhere you want. When you go with family you can eat affordably together sharing just a small serving of food. Too many people is not fun.

Those who traveled with us to Chiang Mai use the Lao word *kob kua* (family) as the term for the travel unit, and the Lao word *moo* (group) for the travel unit of a *toowa*. For these travelers, tourism is always conducted in a social unit, never alone.

As my interview with his wife concluded, the in-law's husband reflected upon what we had discussed and what he had witnessed in his hometown, Vang Vieng, a popular tourist destination north of Vientiane:

> When people come from abroad, such as those who come from Europe to visit Vang Vieng, they will travel in groups of two, or even travel alone. One person, hiking alone, one person. But not a person from Lao. A Lao person wouldn't do that, would we? Lao people don't travel alone. We always go in groups, two people, or three people. What are Lao people afraid of?

I asked the participants why Lao people wouldn't travel alone. The common response was: 'I don't know, it is just something Lao people wouldn't do.' No matter how I rephrased it, this was the question for which I had the most difficulty eliciting an in-depth reply. The interviewees' reaction to this question makes me believe that the thought of a Lao traveling alone for pleasure is such an illogical thought that their consideration of the question would be illogical as well. Aire's stepfather was the only participant who would reflect upon this at length.

Aire's stepfather had worked as a baggage handler at the airport for almost three decades, affording the opportunity to observe countless international tourists. Clearly he had pondered the question long before I presented it. 'Foreigners when they travel internationally by themselves,' he began in an authoritative tone tinged with observational curiosity,

> ... foreigners have knowledge, an understanding that's deeper than the Lao knowledge. They have a higher understanding and knowledge of the law, a higher education than the Lao. They have knowledge. They go and they aren't scared, they aren't scared to go by themselves. Lao people might not understand. If a Lao person traveling by himself is stopped

by a police officer 'Stop! Don't go!' they would stop. The foreigner would question the officer as to why they are being stopped. They have this higher level of knowledge.

From his perspective, travel group size is correlated with levels of fear. Levels of fear are inversely related to knowledge/understanding of laws and an individual's rights under those laws. Foreigners who have had a relatively greater opportunity to learn about laws and rights granted to individuals under laws have less fear and as a result have less need for group travel.

Fear and the resulting desire for social security might be factors contributing to the lack of solo travel among the participants in this group, but another factor is found in Aire's explanation of *PhaaKung*'s presence on the journey: If she didn't come with us my mother wouldn't have fun.' The enjoyment of the journey is in making it in the company of others, i.e., in the socializing. Another factor is the financial cost of sharing food and of staying with 'relatives.' By traveling with others, the costs of travel are shared.

Financing travel: the roles of children, family and the group

Aire's stepfather's, her mother's, *PhaaKung*'s, and the in-law's domestic and international tourism began once their children were old enough to finance their travels. Children must be understood in the broad use of kinship terminology described above, although it is primarily biological children providing the funds for the travel of their parents and assistance with the costs of their parents' travel companions.

The parents' travel is limited by the funds available to the children. *PhaaKung* and her in-law have older employed children, this affords them more tourism to distant locations than Aire's mother who has younger children with fewer financial resources. The children of someone considered kin are frequently leveraged to provide financial assistance for a journey. For the journey to Chiang Mai, Aire and I provided most of the financial support for the entire traveling unit. For other trips, it was the children of *PhaaKung* who provided the financial support for both Aire's mother and *PhaaKung*.

Aire's stepfather stated: 'Americans coming on tour here are mainly students and grandparents. The Japanese as well, students and grandparents.' I asked if this was also the pattern for Lao international travelers. He laughed and replied that Lao tourists aren't going to be students; Lao tourists are 'only grandparents.' The 'grandparents' in this travel unit have expended much of their resources raising their children and supporting the immediate needs of their families. Finances were not available for these grandparents to support travel for their children; rather, travel financing has a unidirectional flow from the younger generation to the older.

Obligations to kin resulted in Aire and I financing the tour to Chiang Mai. Those traveling with us had an understanding that they would not bankrupt us in the process. The travelers arrived with plans to insure that the expenses for the journey would not rise despite the increase in number of participants. After informing us of the addition of the in-law, they shared their plan for making the trip affordable: we would all travel in the cheapest class of transportation, room together in one common room, and share meals. Aire's stepfather found creative ways to ensure I followed their cost-saving plan, for example, when I tried to purchase train tickets for an air-conditioned express coach, he quickly informed me that air-conditioning would make him ill. Their planning helped us spend less on six people than we originally planned to spend on a trip for three. Aire explains the travel patterns of *the family* as follows: 'You know when they go they aren't going to buy expensive things like Americans. They go and want to see things, to have fun, and stay in a cheap place.' Inexpensive accommodations and not purchasing expensive things are two factors controlling the cost of their travel; a third factor is the group itself.

The family/group enables the primary expenses (transportation, accommodation, and food) to be shared among multiple members. As with domestic tourism, the larger number of participants in a *toowa* means that the transportation and lodging costs can be divided making the international travel more affordable. The cost of a *toowa*, though minimal by US standards, represents a considerable expense for a family whose primary income earner may be a government employee earning the equivalent of US$50 each month.

Gendered movements: Buddhism and the navigation of tourist space

Practices of Theravada Buddhism in Thailand and Lao PDR share common historical roots, albeit with local and transnational influences producing regional variation (see Keyes 1995: 65–112; de Casparis and Mabbett 1999: 291–304). Transnational practices of Buddhism provide a socio-cultural foundation upon which the travelers who accompanied me to Chiang Mai practice international tourism. Gendered asymmetries inherent in the way Buddhism is practiced results in dissimilar patterns of male and female transborder travel and movement through the toured Buddhist space.

Toowa operators in Thailand capitalize on the commonality of Buddhist practices to attract Lao *toowa* participants and make travel economically feasible. Hotel costs, could easily push the expense of a *toowa* out of the price range of many Lao travelers. Some *toowa* operators use Buddhist temples for overnight lodging, eliminating the cost of accommodation. Aire's mother stated that Thai temples offering overnight stays for the public do so free of charge, typically providing accommodation in communal spaces such as the open-walled, roof-covered communal *sala* structures.

In 2006, Aire's mother and *PhaaKung* traveled on a *toowa* to northeastern Thailand and stayed overnight at a Buddhist temple. The temple had organized funeral services for a prominent monk, and musicians playing for this occasion were a feature that attracted visitors from Lao PDR. The *toowa* operators did not reap profits from the overnight stay, or the events, but rather through providing mini-bus transportation at a cost of 150 Baht per person (US$4). If an overnight stay at a hotel were added to the *toowa* price, the fee would put the journey outside the financial limitations of Aire's mother and *PhaaKung*. Temple accommodations are also used as affordable overnight stops on the route of *toowa* heading to subsequent destinations. While each of the older people interviewed had stayed overnight at a Buddhist temple in Thailand, none of them had stayed overnight at a temple in Lao PDR. Their overnight accommodations within Lao PDR are always with kin.

Keyes writes that a 'structural asymmetry' between men and women in rural Theravada Buddhist societies results in communities where males (i.e., those males not serving in the Buddhist order of monks) are 'conspicuously less diligent in their support of the religion – in 'making merit' – than are women' (Keyes 1984: 233). Each interviewee mentioned that a *toowa* to Thailand is composed primarily of female participants. The gendered asymmetry of merit-making practices appears to be one of the factors responsible for the asymmetrical inclusion of Lao women in international travel. Aire's mother explained that Lao men simply aren't interested in going to destinations where *toowa* go: 'On a *toowa* there aren't usually men, just women, if there are men it won't be more than two, two men and a large number of women. Men don't want to go.' She described the composition of a recent tour and temple stay in Thailand: 'There were 21 women and three men; 24 people in total, and only three men.'

Merit making is also responsible for many domestic movements by women. For example, Aire's mother makes a considerable number of day trips in and around Vientiane for the purposes of merit-making. The phrase used to describe such an activity is *bai leing Pha* which can be translated roughly as 'going to provide support for the monks.' It is a very different concept from the activities associated with the phrases *bai tio* (to go on a pleasure trip), *bai len* (to go out playfully), *bai toowa* (to go touring). For Aire's mother and the women in her village, *bai leing Pha* typically involves waking in the early morning to prepare food for the monks, renting a vehicle, loading it to capacity with people from the local temple, and traveling to various temples on the outskirts of the city (sometimes as many as five temples in a day) to deliver food and supplies to monks. Participants in these merit-making trips are almost entirely women. I speculate that these long-standing practices of travel have helped enforce the concept: 'Lao men don't like to go on trips.'

On our journey I noted asymmetrical movements of family members through the toured Buddhist spaces. One such setting was the mountainside temple of Doi Suthep. From the parking lot there are two ways of reaching the temple: visitors can climb a 300-step dragon-lined staircase, or take a tram. Believers view the stair climb as an act of merit. Every woman in our group climbed the stairs. Aire's stepfather took the tram. The expenditure of energy to climb the stairs was not worth the merit he would make from the climb.

While traveling, Aire's stepfather made considerable efforts to contact his elderly uncle who lives as a monk in Bangkok. Aire's stepfather hoped that he could complete his journey with a visit to this uncle, that is, leveraging the hospitality of kin to provide overnight accommodations at a Buddhist temple. Gender and Buddhism combined to transform the typical patterns of hospitality towards kin once they reached the temple: Aire's father was welcomed to stay overnight in the residence of his uncle, and the women (unable to enter the residence of a monk) spent the night in the temple's collective space. The leveraging of kin, combined with a historically situated social production of gendered space, resulted in the participants' divergent movements through the final destination.

Reciprocity: family tourism as the beginning of a journey

I respect Aire's stepfather as a keen observer of human behavior. Commenting on travel and differences between tourists from abroad and Lao he stated:

> When Lao people go abroad, they are interested in looking at things, many kinds of things, but they are not going to be taking pictures as souvenirs. They go to look, just look with their eyes and come back . . . It is different than people from abroad. People from abroad when they disembark from the aircraft they may take a picture of the plane that brought them. Lao people aren't interested in this – they go on a trip and come back.

A woman listening to the interview interjected an idiom at this point: 'Lao people wipe their butts and are done.' The point Aire's stepfather and this interjector were making is that Lao people are not going to devote time to reflecting on the tour with material objects brought back from the tour.

At the journey's end these Lao travelers don't return with the durable-good souvenirs and photographs foreign travelers collect, rather these Lao travelers bring back goods that are either too expensive to buy on a regular basis in Vientiane, or items that are seasonally unavailable. I questioned the in-law about what she brings back, and she explained: 'It depends on the season, if it is the season for mangosteen I buy mangosteen, if it is the season for durian I buy durian . . . if it is the season for lychee I buy lychee.' During our visit to Warowot Market in Chiang Mai, each of the women purchased a bag of durian-paste candies. These items are not durable-goods purchased with the intention of providing a lasting reminder of their journeys, but rather these are items brought back with the intention of immediate consumption in the company of family and friends.

Importantly, these travelers return to Vientiane with social relations produced through travel. An understanding of the social world of these Lao tourists necessitates a movement from focusing on the tourist as a 'consumer' (e.g., Wang 2002), towards understandings of dialectical forms of production/ consumption, in which the production and consumption of social obligations are 'directly coincident,' 'mutually dependent,' and in which the production of social obligations is only completed with the consumption of social obligations (here I draw on Hall's 1973 description of dialectics). Allow me to turn our attention to the in-law, the production of kin, and the concomitant mutual obligations. Leveraging kinship through employing the phrase *luuk-hack luuk-phaeng*, the in-law positions herself as the equivalent of a close blood relative of our parents' age, and logically the recipient of our hospitality and finances. The production of kinship was the basis of her inclusion/ participation in our *family* unit of travel. The obligations initiated through the use of kinship terminology are not unidirectional, but rather mutual. That is, by enacting this terminology the sister-in-law simultaneously positioned herself as reciprocally obligated to Aire and myself. Just as Aire and I were obligated to treat her with hospitality in regards to the journey, she, in turn, has social obligations towards us. Acts of reciprocity need not be identical or immediate. To understand the ways in which obligations are reciprocated we must examine social relations across a span of years.

I opened this chapter with the description of a spirit-calling ceremony in Vientiane six years after our journey to Chiang Mai. The mutual obligations generated through kin-based tourism can be understood through examining this ceremony. Aire and I held the ceremony on the advice of a number of elders in our village. Aire had recently renovated our home, using reclaimed wood from three older homes. The elders believed the renovation and use of reclaimed-wood disturbed the spirits residing in the original structures. During the ceremony, living kin call on the spirits of deceased kin to look over and protect those residing in the home.

Through participation in this and similar ceremonies *PhaaKung* and the in-law enact their obligations as maternal aunts, supporting and guiding their *luuk-hak luuk-phaeng* through ceremonial procedures. *PhaaKung* supplied the chairs, tables, pots, and utensils to host the monks and guests. The in-law and *PhaaKung* made substantial financial contributions. Both guided Aire and myself through the ritual. The roles of *PhaaKung* and the in-law in the ceremony cannot be fully understood without examining the journey six years earlier. Prior to the journey, *Phaa Kuung* and the in-law were peripheral participants in the social activities of our lives. *Family* tourism was the catalyst initiating the use of the phrase *luuk-hack luuk-phaeng*. Once initiated, mutual social obligations of kin continue post-travel. Aire's mother, her stepfather, *PhaaKung*, and the in-law did not come back to Vientiane with photographs and souvenirs, rather, they returned with obligations to 'kin' – obligations to the children who had sponsored their travel. The formation of this tour group was an act of producing social identities; an act of the social positioning of the self in relation to others. The tour was a catalyst for verbalizing and enacting what are now ongoing relations of obligations and privileges between my wife and myself, and those who consider us kin.

Conclusion

Lao forms of 'family' travel are replete with practices of leveraging kinship and concomitant obligations of kin; kinship obligations factor into the determination of destinations, the social unit of travelers, accommodation, and the financing of travel. The Lao tourism industry is primarily focused on incoming travelers from abroad. Should the industry choose to 'promote' Lao domestic and international overnight tourism, a challenge they will face is finding and using systems of accommodation that can incorporate kinship. Those organizing *toowa* to Thailand have successfully tapped into social obligations (the obligations of Buddhist merit-making) to form *toowa* of interest to female Lao travelers. In addition, *toowa* operators have found forms of accommodation that fall within the Lao travelers' finances. Finding ways to successfully stir feelings of obligations to kin (as the in-law did with Aire and I) would be an essential step in promoting Lao family travel domestically and abroad. The post-revolution resettlement of kin in international locations such as France, the USA, Australia, etc., combined with the Lao government's recent relaxation of travel permit requirements, could contribute to expanding the geographical reach of Lao family travel practices. Nonetheless, out-going Lao family travel will remain limited by finances and the visa restrictions of destination countries.

For the participants in this journey, family tourism is a practice in the production of kin and the long-term mutually beneficial relations that come with kinship. While this study may not disrupt theories of the 'tourist moment' (Hom Cary 2004), it does suggest that fundamental and related experiences of 'self-discovery and communal belonging' resulting from certain forms of Asian tourism culminate long after the end of the physical movements across geography. Longitudinal studies, with a focus on the social practices of travelers before, during, and after travel, may prove essential for expanding our understandings of Asians on tour.

21 'Donkey friends' in China

The Internet, civil society and the emergence of the Chinese backpacking community

Francis Khek Gee Lim

Introduction

A significant phenomenon has lately emerged in the tourism landscape of China: groups of young Chinese backpackers, often with expensive gear, have become a ubiquitous sight. The absence of the Chinese backpacking phenomenon from the tourism literature in the late 1990s shows how recent this phenomenon has been. Superficially, these Chinese backpackers – usually carrying haversacks and donning outdoor adventure attire – seem similar to their Western counterparts. However, the particular historical moment that led to the emergence of the Chinese backpackers, and the specificities of the political and social environment within which they conduct their various activities, make the study of the Chinese backpackers especially useful for the comparative study of backpacking in tourism studies. Such a study is also illuminative of the broader cultural transitions that China is currently undergoing. I argue in this chapter that while the Chinese backpackers manifest certain features common to backpackers portrayed in tourism studies, they do exhibit specific 'Chinese characteristics.' This study highlights the importance of examining the backpacking phenomenon in its diverse cultural and social contexts, as well as the necessity of examining the impact of the Internet on the formation of travel communities.

Data for this chapter were gathered mainly through two avenues: first, participant observation and interviews with backpackers and hostel owners in eastern Tibet and Yunnan and, second, content analysis of major Chinese independent-travel websites. Participant observation and interviews were conducted from April to July 2005, and from May to July 2006, when I joined six backpacking groups traveling in Yunnan and Tibet, with trips lasting between four to ten days. I conducted informal interviews with a total of 37 Chinese backpackers, comprising 23 men and 14 women, mostly between 23 and 35 years of age. Two female and three male backpackers were in their late 40s. Eight of the interviewees had a high school education, while the rest were university graduates. Most were employed in what might be called 'white-collar' jobs, such as managers, engineers, designers, accountants; three of the interviewees were self-employed. All the backpackers were based in urban areas such as Chengdu, Shenzhen, Shanghai, and Beijing. Apart from personal information relating to education, family background, and occupation, I was interested to hear their motivation for engaging in backpacking as a form of travel, where they obtained travel information, and their itineraries. I also interviewed seven owners of budget accommodations popular among independent travelers.

Backpacking in the tourism literature

The term 'backpacking' has come to refer to a particular mode of travel that emphasizes freedom and mobility (Ateljevic and Doorne 2004: 60). Erik Cohen's (1973) early characterization of the backpacker as a 'drifter' has been influential in our understanding of the backpacking phenomenon. Taken together with MacCannell's (1976) argument that the pursuit of touristic activities is a reflection of a rootless and alienated modern life, the backpacker tends to be considered an example of an alienated individual who seeks out 'experimental' and 'existential' experiences of more 'authentic' lifestyle (Cohen 1979). Aided by the ease of international travel, the proliferation of budget hotels, and motivated by the intense desire to take time out from stressful modern life, the backpacker is characterized as wandering through global backpackers' enclaves in search of experiences that would give him/her a sense of mastery of the self and the environment (Vogt 1976).

It is such features of travel that have prompted Richards and Wilson (2004) to use the term 'global nomad' as a metaphor for the backpacker. 'Global' here refers to the widespread geographical dispersion of backpackers, mainly of Western origins. There has been a recent increase in research on this global phenomenon (Loker-Murphy and Pearce 1995; Murphy 2001; Scheyvens 2002; Uriely *et al.* 2002; Sørensen 2003; Noy 2004). One shortcoming of the backpacking literature is its dominant focus on Western backpackers, although a small number of studies on Asian backpackers has emerged (e.g., Teo and Leong 2006). Cohen (2004) had called for the widening of the scope to emergent backpacking markets from non-Western countries, and to take into account the historical and social contexts within which backpacking takes place. Such detailed studies from other countries 'would enable us to formulate a comparative framework relating the crucial experiences of the youths in their different countries of origin' (Cohen 2004: 56). It is in this regard that the present study of the Chinese backpackers is significant.

Civil society, Chinese backpacking and the Internet

'Civil society' is usually conceptualized as a social space analytically separated from, but also mediating, the spheres of the state and family (Cohen and Arato 1992; Bobbio 1988). The theorizing of this concept can be traced to European political theories that seek to understand state–society relations resulting from the emergence of capitalism and the creation of 'bourgeois' society (Keane 1988; Kumar 1993; Seligman 1995). The concept has recently received much attention by scholars of Chinese affairs, as Deng Xiaoping's reform programs since the late 1970s put China on the path towards market economy and greater openness. The challenge for Chinese scholars lies in the applicability of the concept to the Chinese context, where the state still exerts enormous control and influence over both public and private life. Under such a condition, it would be erroneous to view civil society as a space largely separated from the state or the family (Ma 2006). Regardless whether civil society has a long history in China, or whether it is a recent phenomenon (Chamberlain 1993; Yu 1993; He 1994), there is general agreement that a Chinese civil society is emerging and slowly taking shape, albeit in a 'constructive interaction' (*liangxing hudong*) with a strong, intrusive Chinese state (Deng and Jing 1992).

The concept of 'civil society' has been rendered in Chinese in a number of ways, such as '*gongmin shehui*' (citizen society) and '*shimin shehui*' (townspeople society). A more apt expression for the present purpose is the term '*minjian shehui*,' referring to a social space of the ordinary people which is not directly under political control. As Liang (2001: 67–8) puts it: 'It is in this world that people live their familiar lifestyle and pursue their respective interests; also, it is associated with this or that kind of social organizations such as clans, trade associations, village organizations, religious groups and secret society.' While the Chinese gloss of the civil society concept as 'citizen society' or 'townspeople society' carries certain political connotations, civil society as '*minjian shehui*' places greater emphasis on the associative nature of a popular space, where citizens come together voluntarily to form organizations for explicitly non-political purposes. The numerous independent travel websites that have lately emerged should be considered part of the 'popular organizations' (*minjian tuanti*) that have arisen in the context of China's recent reform program and its embrace of the market economy.

The emergence of the Chinese backpackers (*beibaoke*) is intimately tied to the increasing popularity of 'independent travel' (*zizhu lüyou*) and the proliferation of budget hotels in China (Nyíri 2006: 87–90). In contrast to the dominant characterization in tourism literature of backpackers as mainly young 'non-institutionalized drifters,' the Chinese backpackers present a unique case by being a group of highly educated, largely urban-based, upwardly mobile professional adults who are among the chief beneficiaries of China's recent socio-economic development. Known colloquially as 'donkeys' (*lüzi*) or 'donkey friends' (*lüyou*), these backpackers mainly engage in cultural and adventure tourism within the country. As a nation-wide movement held together by decentralized, independent but interconnected websites, the Chinese backpacking community has the potential of undermining the organized, up-market tourism favored by the Chinese authorities, and also of becoming a significant cultural influence in China's rapidly evolving civil society.

As a mode of 'independent travel,' backpacking mostly attracts the younger Chinese. While some are now starting to venture abroad, most Chinese backpackers still travel primarily within the country. An understanding of Chinese backpacking thus requires an examination of recent developments in China's domestic tourism. China's domestic tourism did not develop until a couple of decades ago. Previously, the tourism industry was stifled due to social unrest and political restrictions. The Communist régime under Mao Zedong severely restricted people's freedom of travel (Zhang 1997), while its effort at eradicating 'traditional' cultures for socialist development meant that China's cultural heritage was considered a hindrance rather than a resource for modernization (Sofield and Li 1998: 363). In the rapid industrialization period of the 1950s and 1960s, tourism was regarded a propaganda tool rather than as a viable economic activity (Qiao 1995). Foreign dignitaries were invited to China mainly to witness the country's 'achievements' in industrialization and social engineering, and not so much to enjoy its natural beauty and cultural heritage. During the Cultural Revolution, it was also common for the Red Guards to travel to prominent sites associated with the Communist Revolution as part of their 'ideological work' (Nyíri 2006: 3).

In the late 1970s, the Chinese government began to realize tourism's potential in contributing to the country's economic development and fostering national pride (Xiao 2006). Laws were designed to strengthen the conservation of China's heritage in order to build up socialism and modernization (Sofield and Li 1998: 371). Many ethnic minority areas were opened to visitors, partly to stimulate economic development, and partly to showcase how well the ethnic minorities had been integrated into the 'motherland' (Matthews and Richter 1991; Oakes 1998). This initial phase of tourism development was directed towards international tourism, aiming to increase China's foreign exchange earnings. It was only towards the end of the 1980s, when China was experiencing rapid growth and the burgeoning of the middle class that the government began to develop domestic tourism. The number of domestic tourists rose from 744 million to 1,102 million between 2000 and 2004, while the annual average expenditure per domestic tourist increased by around 48 percent in the same period (National Bureau of Statistics 2005).

Meanwhile, the Chinese government gradually liberalized the hotel industry to attract more local private investment and to facilitate private ownership of hotels. According to one estimate, 'economy'-type hotels now constitute around 80 percent of the total number of tourist accommodation in China (Zou and Chen 2003: 160). According the proprietor of 'The Hump,' a popular hostel in Kunming (Yunnan province), most of her clients in the late 1990s were Western backpackers, followed by Asians from Japan, South Korea and Singapore. However, starting around five years ago, the Chinese backpackers constituted around 40 percent of her clientele. While Western-oriented backpacking started with the development of international tourism in the 1960s, Chinese backpacking emerged due to the development of domestic tourism. What then are the distinctive features of Chinese backpacking? The discussion below highlights three key characteristics.

A web-based phenomenon

While the rapid growth of China's domestic tourism has been recognized by tourism researchers, what is less noted is that this has occurred in conjunction with the rapid expansion of Internet use in China. The emergence of the Chinese backpacker community cannot be separated from the development of the Internet and the proliferation of travel websites. In 2000, there were an estimated 16.8 million Internet users in China; by 2006, the number was roughly 123 million (CNNIC 2007). A study has estimated that during this period, the earnings of web-based travel businesses rose from RMB$260 million in 2002 (US$35 million) to RMB$1.91 billion in 2006 (http://www.pday.com.cn/research/2006/6209_etravel.htm). As a form of independent travel, Chinese backpacking can be traced to the popular Internet travel forums of the late 1990s such as www.sina.com, where a group of young people discussed travel-related issues and exchanged information. It was in this particular forum that the various Chinese neologisms for 'backpacking' and 'independent' travel first emerged. A significant moment occurred when those unhappy with then-existing travel forums set up their own non-profit travel organizations online. In contrast to the state-led development of international tourism and domestic tourism, independent travel and backpacking have therefore arisen largely through the voluntary efforts of individuals who shared a common passion for a particular form of travel and lifestyle.

One of the earliest and most popular of these web-based organizations was the Green Wilderness (*Lüye*), founded in 1998 by a group of outdoor enthusiasts mostly based in Beijing and its surrounding regions. Positioning themselves as 'innocent' (*zhipu*) and 'romantic' (*langman*), the founders wanted to provide a 'free platform for the promotion of outdoor activities based on the AA [equal-sharing] system' (Green Wilderness 2007). The group's website emphasizes its non-profit and idealistic nature, and highlights freedom, equality and innocence as some of its values. All members are supposedly 'equal in terms of rights, obligations and dignity,' and as long as they obey the rules, 'everyone has the freedom to express their opinions.' This illustrates another feature of Chinese backpacking: In addition to the global backpacking enclaves discussed in the tourism literature, the Chinese case shows that backpacking enclaves also include online spaces in the form of travel websites (Sørensen 2003: 860–1). Recent research on Internet use in China has shown how participants in online forums have formed virtual communities revolving around particular interests. Such online communities are part of the rapidly evolving contours of the Chinese civil society where strong state control over the public media has spurred citizens to rely more on the Internet for information as well as to form social groupings (Hughes and Wacker 2003; Giese 2004; Lagerkvist 2006; cf. Dean 2001). Travel websites form part of the current proliferation of interest-based online communities in China, and are important spaces where Chinese backpackers create their online enclaves.

One reason behind the success of travel websites such as the Green Wilderness is that almost anyone can initiate an activity or a trip by posting a 'notice' (*tiezi*) on them. The content of the notice should include information such as the destination, date, specific route or activity, estimated cost, and group size. Here is a typical travel notice:

> October 1st Gongka hike seeking 2–3 companions 7 Troublesome
> 06-09-13 13:40

This notice includes date of travel, destination, and the number of companions sought. The author is identified by his/her username, in this case 'Troublesome,' and the date and time of the posting is also shown. '7' refers to the number of written responses to the notice. By clicking on the notice, one is led to another page containing more detailed information about the trip. Whether the call for participants is successful depends not only on factors such as the timing of the activity or attractiveness of the destination; another important element is the author's reputation. Some members and their usernames like 'Happy Monkey,' 'No Borders,' or 'Deep Breath,' are more widely known than others, due to their active participation in travel forums and other online activities. These more experienced and popular members would normally have better response rates compared to new members. On very popular websites, newer members would have greater difficulty attracting response to their notices; many receive no response at all. To become well known, the newer members often have to join outings organized by the more established members and to participate more actively in various forums.

These travel websites have certain features that facilitate the creation of an online community. First, they allow members to post notifications of activities, thus crucially locating agency within individual members to initiate events. In a sense, the various notifications for activities can be considered 'projects' over which their initiators could gain a certain degree of control in shaping both the content and final outcome of these projects. Someone posting a notice is also, at the same time, claiming ownership over the project. The travel websites must also host one or more online forums where members can post their views, questions, and comments on matters of common interest. Some, like the Green Wilderness, have forums dedicated to different types of activities such as general travel, trekking, mountain sports, and clothing and equipment. Most websites would also allow members to post their travelogues and photographs online, where fellow travelers on the same trips could read and comment on the postings. It is such online interactions, straddling pre-travel organization and post-travel activities, that are crucial to the formation of a community where groups of individuals get to know, and keep in constant touch with, one another. A good travel website will contain hyperlinks to other travel-related websites, such as those of youth hostels, budget accommodation, airlines, shops selling travel clothing and equipment, etc.

Someone who wishes to go backpacking can thus start by either posting a notice or signing up for activity online, followed by participating in the actual activity offline, and then moves online again after the event to post travelogues, pictures and comments about what had transpired, and to maintain contact with fellow travelers. One's reputation as a backpacker can be made or tarnished in the process. A person, or specifically his/her username, can become famous for being a good travel writer, photographer, or travel companion. Conversely, because members can post travelogues and comments, those who 'misbehave' during the course of the activities risk having their antics exposed by other fellow travelers on the forums (and thus face criticism and ostracism). The Chinese backpacking experience therefore usually comprises a continuous movement of participants between physical and virtual spaces, both of which are 'real' in the sense that they constitute a complete backpacking experience. Apart from the various services provided by the online independent travel websites, another indication of the important link between backpacking and the Internet in China is that a unique set of vocabulary among Chinese backpackers has evolved from online travel forums. These linguistic codes have since become popularized among other Chinese tourists.

Backpacking vocabulary and code of behavior

If language is one of the key cultural markers of a community, then the existence of a set of unique vocabulary extensively used by those engaging in backpacking marks them out as a distinct cultural group in the Chinese civil society. To trace the emergence of such vocabulary, we have to turn our attention to another travel website, 'The Mill' (*Mofang*). The Mill was set up in 2000 in Shenzhen by a group of travelers who were formerly active in the travel forum at www.sina.com. It was in this forum where participants first used the word 'donkeys' to refer to themselves as backpackers or independent travelers. As these travelers felt they had led a harder life in Shenzhen compared to their counterparts in other locales, they started to call the places they gather – whether in physical or virtual spaces – as 'the mill,' i.e., where donkeys engage in excruciating labor. Today, the word 'donkey' is widely used to refer to the backpacker. 'Donkey' in Mandarin Chinese is *lü*, which sounds similar to the word for 'travel.' Since independent travelers often carry huge haversacks, much like donkeys carrying loads, backpackers in China have come to be known as 'donkeys.' The phrase 'to go traveling' can also be rendered playfully as 'donkey travel.' Backpackers refer to each other affectionately as 'donkey friends' (*lüyou*), with the more experienced among them known as the 'old donkeys' or 'head donkeys' (*laolü, toulü*). Those who prefer adventure sports such as mountain climbing and caving are called 'mules' (*luozi*). Travel websites or forums are called 'donkey forums' (*lütan*).

Tourism scholars arguing for a 'postmodern' turn in tourism point out that tourists tend to seek not so much 'original' sites and 'authentic' experiences, but hedonistic activities, irony, and 'fun' (Ritzer and Liska 1997). Thus, theme parks such as the 'Windows of the World' in Shenzhen and Beijing which showcase replicas of famous sites from around the world become the emblems of post-modern tourism. Here, copies are enjoyed by visitors with as much, or even greater relish, than original sites and landscapes. For the post-tourists, the essential ingredient of tourism is the inherent thrill and sensual stimulation of the experience, rather than the search for authenticity in a manufactured world.

The distinction between 'modern'/'postmodern' forms of tourism does not seem to apply as much to the Chinese case, in which both the quest for authenticity and self-actualization co-exist with the pursuit of hedonism and play. In his (2006) book, *Scenic Spots*, Pal Nyíri discusses the Chinese cultural construction of tourist sites as 'scenic spots' (*jingdian*), and how the Chinese tourists (including the backpackers) tend to refer to their activities at scenic spots as 'playing' (*wan*). My research shows that the Chinese backpacking community has developed two broad categories of 'playing.' The first category is known as 'masochism' (*zinüe*), usually abbreviated in online discussions as 'ZN,' which refers to physically challenging activities such as hiking, mountain climbing, water-rafting, camping, caving, traveling to relatively remote areas inhabited by ethnic minorities (cf. Elsrud 2001). The second category is called 'debauchery' (*fubai*), or 'FB,' which encompasses more 'pleasurable' activities such as eating in restaurants, drinking in bars, dancing, etc. The terms 'masochism' and 'debauchery' should be seen as being used with playful irony by the backpackers. While backpackers usually have to go through the 'masochistic' phase before indulging in 'debauchery,' these days numerous travel websites would allow members to organize these two categories of activities independent of each other. However, one could participate in both even while hiking for an extended period of time: after a day's hike in the mountains, backpackers could enjoy a sumptuous dinner and get themselves drunk – in other words, partake in 'debauchery' – and continue their tiring journey the next day.

For the Chinese backpackers, 'playing' also involves the search for an allegedly more authentic, traditional way of life, or 'folkways' (*minfeng*), which is deemed to have been lost in places where the backpackers live and work. Such traditional way of life is believed to be found either in the rural areas, or in the areas where the ethnic minorities live. In the famous Tiger Leaping Gorge in northern Yunnan, some backpackers trekking in the area complained to me that the 'folkways' there had been 'corrupted' (*minfeng baihuai*) by mass tourism, seemingly unaware of the irony that the arrival of many backpackers like them contributed to the erosion of the local 'folkways.' After a three-day trek, the same group of backpackers then went back to the nearby 'ancient' town of Lijiang to engage in 'debauchery' – eating, drinking and singing in the restaurants and bars.

Core values and ethos

> I like backpacking because it gives me the sense of freedom. I can design
> my own itinerary, go online to look for fellow travelers, and if we get a
> small group, then off we go! If we don't like each other during the trip,
> we could always split and go our separate ways . . . Everyone is equal
> during the trip, we should all help each other.
>
> (Chen, graphic designer from Shenzhen, female, 27)

Compared to packaged tours, one of the main attractions of backpacking
is the relative freedom to choose one's itinerary and mode of travel. An interesting feature about Chinese backpacking is that while the notion of 'freedom' is also prominent, it is only one of the few values that constitute a set
of ethos. In order to understand what these 'core values' and ethos are, it is
necessary to analyze the reasons Chinese backpackers offer for engaging in
this form of travel, as well as the rhetoric used in independent travel websites.
The assumption here is that the values contained in these self-created websites resonate strongly with the values either held or sought by the people
who seek out these websites, and who participate in independent travel and
backpacking. Many websites offer descriptions of a particular travel ethos
which emphasizes freedom, equality, democracy, altruism, etc. For example,
the Green Wilderness website states that the founders 'are not motivated by
self-interest, but by an idealism that holds fast to freedom and innocence'
(Green Wilderness 2007). In the Green Wilderness community, 'members share
the resources while shouldering the obligation for its protection and development.' The website's rhetoric appeals to a sense of altruism when it says
that, 'from the beginning, all the tasks of Green Wilderness are voluntarily
undertaken by its members.'

'Equality' is also highly valued by the backpacker community, and this is
demonstrated in a number of ways. For example, all members of a travel
website can in theory participate in its forums and post notices to initiate
activities. The Mill website stresses 'equality as the basis' for interactions among
its members, and that all the activities are based upon the 'equal sharing,'
or 'AA,' system (The Mill 2007). This 'AA' system refers not only to the
sharing of costs and responsibilities, but also, as highlighted by the Green
Wilderness website, 'equality with regards to rights, obligations and dignity.'

While the AA system has become the *modus operandi* of most backpacking groups, the full range of practices encompassed within the notion of
'equality' is seldom realized. For one thing, most backpacking groups will
have a leader, sometimes called the 'head donkey.' This person is either selected
by fellow travelers, or has naturally emerged through the course of travel.
Often the 'head donkey' is the initiator of the trip, especially if he (the leader
is usually male) is already a well-known personality in the Internet community. From my participation observation with a number of backpacking groups in Yunnan, the leaders in backpacking groups often take on a

paternalistic role, such as ensuring the overall well-being of the group, bargaining with guesthouse owners over the price of food and accommodation, leading discussions, resolving disputes among members, and allocating tasks and responsibilities.

There is also often a marked gender division of labor in mixed groups, especially among those who engage in activities such as hiking and camping. In such cases, the men, generically referred to as 'elder brothers' (*gege*, abbreviated online as 'GG,' regardless of their age), are expected to carry the heavier equipment such as tents and cooking utensils, while the women, generically referred to as 'younger sisters' (*meimei*, abbreviated online as 'MM'), will carry lighter things such as food and medical supplies. Men are expected to do most of the manual chores, such as pitching the tents, while female group members would cook and wash. If someone misbehaves or acts contrary to the ethos of backpacking during the trip, other members could post comments on this person's behavior on the travel website forum, thus ensuring that this person will not be welcomed in future activities. In such instances, the person concerned would either have to defend him/herself in the forum, or to leave the site and move to another online travel community. For example, a controversy erupted in the Green Wilderness community recently concerning an 'old donkey' who had allegedly outraged the modesty of a few fellow female travelers. One of the women in the group subsequently complained about the man's behavior on the forum page, provoking a vigorous defense by the accused. Accusations and counter-accusations were traded back and forth on the online forum. The possibility of being criticized and ostracized by the community puts strong pressure on backpackers traveling in groups to conform to the backpacking ethos.

The preceding discussion suggests that Chinese backpacking is in some ways shot through with contradictions. While 'freedom' is emphasized, backpacking in China is often a very organized affair, from the initial notification posted on the travel website, to the planning of the trip and the division of responsibilities, to the post-mortem whereby comments, travelogues and pictures are posted online. Furthermore, the emphasis on 'equality,' as manifested in the AA system, is overlaid with a gender division of labor and gender hierarchy that define men as generically 'older' and 'stronger' than women, regardless of their actual age. Finally, altruism and self-sacrifice are expected of backpackers, who are themselves the chief beneficiaries of a market capitalism that is founded upon profit-making and self-interest.

Conclusion

This chapter has examined the emergence of the Chinese backpacking as one of the many 'popular' (*minjian*) movements that have evolved with the expansion of an associative social space brought about by increasing usage of the Internet in China. Given the strong control the state still exercises over both the public and private spheres of Chinese society, these travel websites or clubs often state explicitly that their activities are non-political. It is largely due to this fact that I refrain from characterizing these independent travel clubs as 'non-governmental organizations' (NGOs), given the term's political connotation in the social sciences literature. In line with the Chinese context, it would be more appropriate to classify these as 'popular organizations' (*minjian tuanti*). Early studies of civil society groups in China have tended to note their lack of autonomy due to strong governmental control. However, as Harwit and Clark (2001) point out, these studies were mostly conducted before the widespread use and popularity of the Internet. Recent developments in Internet technology have enabled the formation of a multiplicity of independent groups that make full use of the possibilities that the Internet offers. One such independent group is the backpacking community.

While the Chinese backpackers exhibit certain common features with their Western counterparts, such as the emphasis on 'freedom' and preferred attire (e.g., backpacks, casual outdoor wear), this chapter has examined backpacking with 'Chinese characteristics.' First, it is a predominantly web-based phenomenon, such that both online and offline activities are constitutive of the whole backpacking experience. The implication for general research is that, in this age of the Internet, tourism research on backpacking should complement the investigation of backpackers' physical enclaves with research on the online enclaves. Both these spaces are equally important sites where social interactions occur and where community is built. Second, Chinese backpacking has evolved particular linguistic and behavioral codes that make this community a distinct cultural entity. The circulation of terms such as 'donkey friend,' 'donkey travel,' 'masochism,' and 'debauchery' has moved beyond the specific sphere of backpacking community to become part of a unique set of vocabulary shared by Chinese independent travelers in general. Lastly, far from the carefree style portrayed of Western backpackers in the tourism literature, Chinese backpacking entails particular core values and ethos that govern social interactions among its practitioners. The enforcement of such values and ethos is enacted mainly through the continuous movement between the two interlinked contexts of face-to-face interactions and online activities. The possibility of one's misbehavior being publicized by fellow travelers for all to see on the Internet forum constitutes an effective sanction in enforcing desirable dispositions. While studies from different parts of the world reveal certain commonalities and differences in both the form and the content of backpacking (cf. Loker-Murphy and Pearce 1995; Uriely *et al.* 2002), equally important would be the cultural and national specificities that make backpacking a diverse experience.

22 Still vision and mobile youth

Tourist photos, travel narratives and Taiwanese modernity

Joyce Hsiu-yen Yeh

Introduction

This chapter examines the dynamic interplay among tourist photographic practices, youth mobility and modernity. I begin with an examination of parallel trends in photography and tourism studies and a call to study the meanings of photographic images and tourism in contemporary Asian society. I then go on to consider tourist products, like photos and stories, as products of modernity. This is a socio-cultural study of the visual culture of tourism in a larger context of modernity rather than a study of the imperialism of Western tourist narratives. In Ong's words, it seeks 'to consider how non-Western societies themselves make modernities after their own fashion, in the remaking of rationality, capitalism and the nation in ways that borrow from but also transform Western universalizing forms' (1996: 64). Through emphasizing and unpacking the relationships of materiality in tourist productions, I believe we can gain a richer understanding of tourism practices and provide new ways to contextualize the relationships between travel and modernity in Asian societies. By looking more closely at the narratives contained within the travel photos of Asian young people, I seek to dissect their complex visual practices and their experiences of the meanings of Taiwanese modernity within a contemporary tourism context. The chapter also aims to call into question the complexity of Asian travel experiences and to investigate the role of travel photography as an agent of modernity. I argue that a clear understanding of youth travel requires an appreciation of a wider frame of social and cultural factors, including global influences and the technological development of photography and its link with the growth of mass tourism.

Photography, tourism and modernity

Photography was invented in 1839/40 and was one of the typifying characteristics of the nineteenth century (for a history of photography, see Benjamin 1978; Tagg 1982, 1988). The development of photography (Jeffrey 1981) coincides with the growth of mass tourism (Crawshaw and Urry 1997: 180).

As both photography and tourism have changed over time, in conjunction with social and technological change, both have become accessible to more and more people. Crawshaw and Urry thus describe the role of photography as 'the most significant component of a new economy of value and exchange in which visual images are given extraordinary mobility and exchange-ability' (ibid.: 82). The impact of technology and the opening up of these visual forms had a profound influence on what we see and how we understand the world as well as on modes of traveling (Larsen 2001). The uses of photography in everyday life also interact with the global proliferation of visual images and the increasing democratization of personal travel around the globe (Slater 1991).

Photography reflects a powerful sense of what tourists see in the world around them. This way of seeing and knowing is thus part of what Roland Barthes calls 'a kind of intractable supplement of identity' (1982: 109) by which people incorporate their systems of thoughts and embodied movements into photographic images. Photographs are images of information and, as Berger suggests, 'every image embodies a way of seeing' (1972: 10). For tourists, to travel is to 'see,' or rather to catch on film, a way to perform their identities of being tourists somehow distinct from their daily routines and everyday practices.

Photography is a central touristic ritual, the recording and capturing of the moment of gazing (Taylor 1994; Edwards 1999, 2001; Osborne 2000; West 2000). The link between tourism and photography suggests a symbiosis. Susan Sontag, in her critique of photography, acknowledges the inseparable relationship between the two. In *On Photography*, she notes that 'travel becomes a strategy for accumulating photographs' (1979: 9). She goes on to suggest that 'most tourists feel compelled to put the camera between themselves and whatever is remarkable that they encounter: unsure of other responses, they take a picture' (ibid.: 10). Such a strategy can be incorporated into the travel patterns of tourists and become a recognizable tourist performance.

Several attempts have been made to find the theoretical and empirical interconnections between photography and tourist practices (Albers and James 1988; Taylor 1994; Crawshaw and Urry 1997; Edensor 1998; Osborne 2000; Larsen 2001). Crawshaw and Urry have argued that an empirical understanding of the dynamics of tourism and photographic practices provides insights into how photographic images are tied up with the 'construction of touristic memories' (1997: 179). They further argue that such 'memory-production' is central to the significance of sociability and 'photography is a socially organized set of rituals' (ibid.: 179, 183). Such reassessment requires an examination not only of how the photographic act takes place, but also of how productions of tourist narratives contribute to informing and shaping modernity within the tourism context.

It is clear that in certain respects the practices of the photographing act of a domestic tourist differ from those of an international tourist. Each practice seemingly fits a specific, though culturally embedded, way of enacting and engaging a site. Edensor argues that 'tourism has blended into a mélange of consuming activities, typified by a structure of feeling which is instantaneous, depthless, affective and fragmented, a condition which apparently thwarts an enduring sense of identity' (1998: 5). Awareness of tourist sight at the tourist site is essential to understanding why the photographic act has become one of the imperative forms of the touristic performance of being modern.

This literature offers us complex connections between photography practices and tourism. It does little, however, to help us explore how tourists use their photographic practices and self-made souvenirs to construct their sense of new culture self and to mediate their social interactions in touristic settings and at home. These accounts fail to offer sufficient evidence for explaining what the tourist gazes upon through photographic practices and what tourists do with their travel photos afterwards, introducing broader questions of modernity and representation. Photographs taken by Asian tourists remain largely unexplored and few empirical studies have addressed the issue from the perspectives of mobility, visuality and modernity.

Tourism, as the Chinese scholar Ning Wang suggests, is 'no longer simply regarded as a universal and homogenous phenomenon . . . it is essentially a contemporary phenomenon and thus needs to be analyzed in terms of the larger context of modernity' (2000: 11). This way of seeing tourism is related to the question of the perception of modernity and requires the identification of the subject of modernity. Tim Oakes (1998) had earlier applied the concept of modernity to examine tourism practices in China. Oakes's study embeds many of the conflicting imaginings and representations of modernity in his analysis of the tourist political economy of Guizhou villages in China. He argues that tourism is actively used to construct, negotiate and perform a sense of modernity. I draw upon this framework and suggest that the development and experience of tourism are integrally connected to this globalizing culture. The process of travel and interpretation of travel are elements of social interaction by which tourists define and reconfirm their identities.

Research sites and data collection

This chapter uses travel photographs as research 'sites' to explore the complexity of tourist photos, stories, and their sense of modernity. I focus on the context in which photographs are selected by the tourists themselves and how they are interpreted and transformed into accounts and illustrations of their sense of modernity. Additionally, I emphasize how young people use their photographs to present their views as a form with which to study the 'world' and convey such 'knowledge' to others through their photographic discourses as an objectification of modernity. In other words, it examines how a group of Taiwanese youth use their travel photos as ways to trace the connections and disconnections between here and there, then and now, as well as the local and the global. From a socio-cultural perspective I will discuss what these chosen photos can tell us about these Taiwanese youth's mobilities and their performance of modernity through their vacation travel photographs. In this study, I refer to youth in economic and socio-cultural terms, that is being young is not only seen as relating to a particular age group, but also an act through which people tell others their identity.

This qualitative research draws on data from 150 self-selected traveling photos and narratives from 30 university students who took Cultural Studies of Tourism, taught by the author at Dong Hwa University, Taiwan in 2005–6. Informant backgrounds and their traveling experiences are: age: 20–22; 25 female, 5 male; 10 indigenes (6 tribes, 20 Han Taiwanese; 26 have traveled abroad before: 22 joined packaged tours, 4 backpacking). All the interviews and written essays were done in Chinese. English translations in this chapter are done by the author and have been approved by the interviewees to avoid the misreading or misinterpretation of the original Chinese texts. The analysis of the narratives of young tourists presented here seeks to answer to the following research questions. How does photographic acting contribute to a sense of self and a means of encounters? How does photography shape youth mobilities and constitute their modernity? What can we tell from tourist images and narratives? And what are the functions of tourist photographs and their photo-centered narratives? Based on data collection and analysis, the following discussion addresses two key sets of findings: (1) a reflexive self in which photography as way of understanding 'self;' and (2) encountering 'otherness' in which photography as a way to comprehend the 'world' and all forms of 'other' within the context of tourism.

Reflexive self

Tourism, for John Jakle, 'is a significant means by which modern people assess their world, defining their own sense of identity in the process' (1985: xi). Given the intimate links between 'modern' conditions and tourism practices, there is little doubt the mobility of subjects has become an active ingredient in their identity constructions. For young people in particular, it has its own symbolic meanings and powerful effects that underpin such processes. For example, a female student who has traveled to 13 countries with her parents put it this way:

> I keep thinking what can I get from this journey? What can I see? There are many questions in my mind – about myself, about places that I am going to visit and even about my relationship with my parents. There are so many things that are waiting for me to learn, to discover and find the answers, but there are also many uncertainties!! To me, now travel is no longer just for fun!
>
> (February 2006)

The discourse of 'seriousness' of traveling-to-learn is not new at all. For instance, Judith Adler (1989) reminds us that the Grand Tour is associated with the aristocratic youth in the eighteenth century and has been generally understood as a means of gaining some kind of 'uplifting' life experience for young people. In undertaking these interviews it became apparent that the benefits of foreign travel to life experiences and that exposure to other cultures leads to more 'open-mindedness' and a sense of cosmopolitan identity: as the following examples illustrate:

> Traveling abroad is a way of connecting to the world. Who said that travel is just for fun? In my journeys I bring back full of memories and experiences. Every recalled memory is a departure of another journey. From there I am not only a Taiwanese person, but a world citizen.
>
> (December 2005)

One of the indigenous male students who traveled to New York to perform indigenous cultural dance wrote in his photo caption:

> Mountain is forever a mountain
> Mountain is also my home
> We are the children of the mountain.

In a later interview, the student went on to stress the sense of self-identification and cultural identity through the natural landscape he interprets:

> I have never had such a strong sense that nature means so much to me and to an indigene. When I was in busy New York I knew how I missed my family, my nation and my mountain . . . Now I look at beautiful mountains in Hualien [the east coast of Taiwan] I know that's the place where I come from and no other place can replace it in my mind. That is why I chose this picture [see Figure 22.1] to represent my traveling experiences. After the trip to New York, I have started getting involved with some environmental activities to conserve the sustainability of our natural environment.
>
> (December 2005)

Narratives such as this are not only about traveling experiences and reviewing tourist landscapes, but may also further illustrate the sophistication of self-identity and the reflexive modernity of a contemporary society in which environmental issues are deeply troubling. Being thought of as environmentally aware through tourist traveling experiences suggests that contemporary young touristic practices reflect the desire to be associated with the environmental movement, which is an important signifier of being 'modern' in Taiwanese society. Immediately we can see from this narration that sense of place and sense of environmental duty are intertwined. The implications for

Figure 22.1 Natural landscape as a cultural belonging (Photo by Shih-wei Lin)

selfhood involve acculturation of mobility and part of 'being-in-the-world.' The passage encompasses questions of a young tourist's identity construction and how modernity is experienced.

Several respondents also pointed out that being Taiwanese and letting other people know the differences between Taiwanese and other Asian peoples, especially Chinese, were important to their own identities. As one student claimed:

> I hate people to think that I am Japanese or Chinese. But sometimes it is so difficult to explain to them. Actually that is the reason after my trip to Australia I actually learn English better. I hope I can use English to explain to the world that I am from Taiwan which is a different country from China. I have never thought being a Taiwanese is a big deal but when I was in a foreign country then is very important.
>
> (January 2006)

Such an identity construction is complex and indeed a process of negotiation. For these mobile youth, traveling experiences between 'home' and 'away' constitutes a partial process of construction of who they are and their cultural belonging. Among the 30 young students faced with the question of which of the tourist elements they had taken they preferred most, 18 out of 30 informants chose scenery, including landscape, nature and famous sights, as their top choice. There is a tendency evident in my case studies that young tourist narratives are associated with sense of identity and on-going reconstruction of local meaning for a place, city, and landscape that is meaningful to them in the globalizing world.

The stereotypical image of Asian tourists is of people endlessly taking pictures of themselves on their holidays abroad (see Parr 1995). This characteristic also fits the Taiwanese young tourists. Of the 150 photographs tourists chose to represent their traveling experiences, 96 are of people. Most of the pictures of people are self-portraits in front of buildings, sites and sights in which those still images indicate that those youth are on the move. Images relating to tourists themselves are especially important, such as self-portraits, group shots with old friends, classmates and new friends in a variety of sites (see Figure 22.2). Undoubtedly, however, there are differences in their decisions to photograph themselves or not. Nonetheless their individual travel experiences, feelings, memories, or self-understandings are often integrated with their expressions of mobility. One female informant regarded travel pictures as a record of her 'rite of passage':

> It is hard for me to choose only five travel photos. I have a series of travel photos that are my records of growing up. From local tours to abroad, these photos keep my experiences and memories alive. They also show how time, my family and Taiwanese society have changed.

Figure 22.2 Frame of friendship and sociability (Photo by Shih-chieh Chuang)

I am not a little girl any more which is a mixed feeling. I had many pictures that were taken locally before because we could not travel abroad at that time. In recent years I have many pictures that were taken in the foreign countries. It is because most people can afford overseas holidays now.

(December 2005)

Such shifting connections between the individual and society are significant. These comments suggest that tourist photos are useful for investigating tourist experiences and reflecting their socio-cultural meanings from a non-Western perspective. The narrative shows not only the change of destinations of an Asian youth's mobility, it demonstrates the economic growth of an Asian society in which overseas holiday has become a common leisure practice.

As I have previously noted, photographs are souvenirs of travel and can be used as evidence of being there to prove what tourists have said, seen and done. The act of photographing, as Osborne remarks, 'has become an act necessary to the tourist's engagement with the moment when the fabulous object registers itself on the body and emotions of the visitor as a shock of recognition – and of transcendence' (2000: 118). Osborne explains the functions of the tourists' photographs:

> Tourists use the photographic images of tourism, including their own photographs, as both proofs, records and mementos of tourists actualities while accepting these same actualities as set-up performances, idealizations or romanticizations – fictions.

(ibid.: 77)

With such romantic souvenirs tourists are potentially able to create a more heroic romanticized self. These self-selected photos suggest that Taiwanese young people use their mobility as a performing platform to stage a 'better' self on the road around the globe. Through travel photos they move between and across time and space and their traveling experiences are 'recaptured' by these still 'visions' 'on the materiality of images' (Edwards and Hart 2004). The contradictory tensions between 'seen' and 'not seen' are very much a part of tourist encounters. Photography, especially holiday snapshot photography, has played an important role in driving leisure travel and continues to be an important factor for travel when combined with leisure purposes (Chalfen 1979, 1987). Photography visualizes the tourists' gaze, turning what they survey into visible images. In other words, it formulates and individualizes what tourists see and how they see the world.

Encountering otherness

Traveling provides many possible encounters. As Trinh T. Minh-ha has highlighted:

Every voyage is the unfolding of poetic. The departure, the cross-over, the fall, the wandering, the discovery, the return, the transformation . . . the complex experience of self and other (the all-other within me and without me) is bound to forms that belong but are subjects neither to 'home,' nor to 'abroad;' and it is through them and through the cultural configurations they gather that the universes over there and over here can be named, accounted for, and become narrative.

(1994: 21–2)

Like many young people elsewhere, Taiwanese young people want to travel and perform their own 'modernity' (Yeh 2003). Many young people use traveling as a means to situate themselves and connect themselves with the world (Desforges 1998, 2000). Luke Desforges in his study describes how 'collecting places' are Western young travelers' strategies to 'authenticate their knowledge and experiences' (1998: 181). Here we see the linkage between travel and knowledge recognized in contemporary travel practices, and young people are becoming selective about where to travel. Desforges observes that the use of certain destinations and modes of traveling are ways of distinguishing 'us' from 'them' among mobile youth and others as well. For these young Taiwanese this process of an emergent self ascribed modernity is especially important. Rather than stay inside the bubble of their familiar environment and cultural backgrounds, Taiwanese youth also follow the flow of modernity to explore other parts of the world first hand in order to participate within what Bauman called 'liquid modernity' (2000) and to cultivate their own 'aesthetic cosmopolitanism' (Urry 1995: 167). One interviewee stated:

Here I am at the beach and I can tell that I'm so fortunate to be here [Bali, Indonesia]. I'm a student but I have a part-time job which allows me to save money for my travel. I'm fortunate also because my parents understand the importance of holidays for modern people.

(December 2005)

For many young student tourists, their travels enable them to make comparisons and connections, and through their narrations they express their desired modernities. It is clear that money, time and holidays are all characteristics of 'being modern.' Taiwanese young people present an image of themselves as people who are interested in the process of mobility, visiting other countries and encountering the 'other.' One female student said:

When I was in Paris last year it was so hot too. The funny thing is that they do not have air-conditioners or even a fan in the hotel . . . Then when we arrived in England the desserts there were always too sweet . . . I thought I was too fat, but in England I became so 'thin' and 'little.'

English girls really look much older than me. When I told them I had my 20th birthday last month they were shocked.

(January 2006)

Using this example it is not my intention to underestimate or oversimplify the multiple layers of cultural differences; nor do I in any way mean to reinforce national stereotypes. One important point must be understood: this chapter is an attempt to provide a Taiwanese case study as an example of how Asian young people travel to consume the services provided by the people in the 'First World.' From this perspective, 'otherness' acquires other meanings and functions and is refracted through a dynamic hybrid of (re)visions of the self and the other. Nelson Graburn calls such a quest 'the sacred journey' in which tourists engage in a search for selfhood in the destination (1989: 21–36). Such journeys, therefore, are 'rites of passage' (Van Gennep 1960) as travel to otherness allows the traveling selves to position and distinguish themselves by commenting on the culture and behavior of others that they encounter on their journeys. As one informant explains:

When my sister and I were trekking in Nepal we learned how a simple life can bring so much happiness. I looked those kids who even do not have shoes I know I am lucky. After Nepal I became a vegetarian and I am also much happy about what I have now.

(December 2005)

From the perspective of tourists, othering helps inform self-definition and the figuring out of how different aspects of life are conceptualized and experienced. The development of cultural tourism is central to this process (see Figures 22.3 and 22.4). As one student pointed out:

I like to take pictures of others. I especially like Westerns as they look different from us [Taiwanese]. Their hair is just like the doll that I played when I was little. And people in Indonesia speak funny English, but I think it's very cute. I also like men wear flowers (*sic*) in their hair.

(February 2006)

The photos of people who are like, and not like ourselves – permit looking at 'the other;' explored through the juxtaposition of images and analysis of relationships. Through photographic practices and materiality, Taiwanese study tourists make their own constructed images of various cultures: self-referential systems of representation of self and other which they take home and display to multiple audiences. Recognizing how holiday photographs are used by individuals to form satisfying relationships and convey information about others, tourists take an active role in creating 'social' and 'cultural' capital, to use Bourdieu's (1984) expression, which are both a mark of personal distinction as well as a way of framing, interpreting and representing

Figure 22.3 Encounterings of Otherness (Photo by Hui-ling Tai)

Figure 22.4 More encounterings of otherness (Photo by Kuan-ling Chen)

their socio-cultural encounters and networks. Here is one example in which the student uses her travel photos to share her experiences and encounters:

> All my friends like to see me with foreigners together in the photos. By pointing this picture to them I can tell them my traveling experiences in Germany which they want to know more. Even though I still cannot speak German at all, these pictures make me feel like I know them much better than my friends and they can learn something from my travel stories as well.
>
> (January 2006)

The notion of othering in this chapter has been examined and presented through the perspective of Taiwanese students. I argue that the experiences of encountering the other involves not only physically 'being-there,' but also every aspect of emotional being, including anticipation, experiences, fantasy, anxiety, excitement and memories. Asian tourist experiences of the quest for the other tend to be under-represented in tourism and travel studies. My intention here has been to use photographic images to convey such encounters within a framework of performed modernity.

Conclusion

Travel photos are tourist mementos through which they reflect on their interactions with time, places and peoples. They refresh and reconstruct tourist memories and document the places they visited. They capture experiences and memorialize journeys and convey the essence of tourist experiences. I argue that holiday snapshots are never just souvenirs; they can be regarded as an objectification of modernity. We need to consider their productions, interpretations and representations of tourist experiences in a globalizing world. Holiday photographs act as indexical signs of self-expressions that frame the tourist gaze, and thus contribute to how others understand touristic experiences in various settings. The photo-stories of tourists that potentially extend non-traveler visions of the world might seem plausible, since travel tales can involve encounters with people, places and other cultures.

To tourists themselves, travel stories, whether bad or good, are representational forms of their performances and therefore are significant. As John Steinbeck observed: 'One goes, not so much to see but to tell afterward' (quoted in Jakle 1985: 9). It is not that they veridically recall tourist experiences, for they are selectively acquired, retained, and presented. Rather, they help to construct narratives of self that are flattering and self-affirming. They reveal not only the tourist landscape, but also the cultural expectations that shape their ideas of what tourists are meant to be. They make their journeys into stories, highlighting the sites and events that were most 'memorable' and locating themselves in the tourist landscape. These personal mementos reveal more than just the various routes followed or the 'sights' visited. They show the consciously constructed visual, verbal and physical narrative of the actual and imagined journeys. These self-selected tourist photos shed light on the dynamic cultural interplay that defines the tourist experience in the context of modern society. In this context, photographic images become hybrids and are important objectifications of empowerment which young people use to define themselves and express their own identities, crossing many boundaries. What is involved here is not just the functions of photographic images, but also the confirmation of the overlapping and complex relations between photography and tourists performing acts of being modern. Despite the fact that one tourist photograph may be identical to those of other tourists, the moment of the photographic act is very individual and subjective. Once the photograph has been taken, the tourists present a kind of individual 'creation' of the 'reality' that belongs to how they see and sense the world around them. Through tourist photographic objects and narrations this chapter displays a visual approach demonstrating how rich Asian tourism is and how its study immediately moves us beyond tourism itself.

The mobility of youth can help us understand certain values and meanings associated with tourism and modernity in the context of Asia today. Travel and tourism are also regarded as educational experiences. They have crucial roles to play in the processes of learning and the 'transformation of self' (Bruner 1991; Yeh 2003). The emphasis here is on demonstrating how the discourse of traveling-to-learn is still reiterated and performed by contemporary Taiwanese youth's narration of their own travel culture. The research findings suggest that travel photos are not only used as interpretations of sightseeing and site-seeing, but also as ways of articulating reflexivity and consciously producing a sense of modernity. They also convey various notions of Asian modernity through mobility that shapes their visions and views of the world, their interpretations of that travel, and their interconnected sense of places. Modernity means many things and the process of formation can be traced through various markers. I argue that an understanding of visual material objects as vehicles for articulating ideas concerning sets of modernity leads us to the analysis of broader social and narrative questions. Tourism involves a set of tastes and cultural generative practices that provide a means of rethinking the visual material and travel narratives that characterize modernity in general. I have demonstrated how Taiwanese young people use their mobility and photographic images as performing platforms to promote 'grand' narratives of reflexive self and encountered others. I believe that such an approach can be productively applied to the analysis of other Asian tourism practices, particularly when the social meanings are deeply embedded in the complex and dynamic relationships between mobility, visuality and modernity.

23 Conclusion

Recasting tourism theory towards an Asian future

Tim Winter

Introduction

As we move into the new millennium we are constantly told this will be the 'Asian century.' By 2050, India and China will be the powerhouses of the global economy. If this is the case, then it can be safely assumed that modernization, development and vast increases in wealth for hundreds of millions of people will lead to unprecedented levels of travel. Urry's (2007) suggestion that contemporary globalization demands us to re-conceive societies in terms of 'mobilities' holds extremely important consequences for understanding and making sense of the rapid changes now occurring in Asia. The near overnight growth of budget airlines across the region and the launch of a car costing US$2,500 by Tata that will bring the freedom of movement to hundreds of thousands of families are just two indicators of a mobile future. Is the world of academia, and in particular the field of tourism studies, institutionally and intellectually equipped to address the profound social changes Asian tourism will inevitably bring? I believe it isn't. In this final chapter I want to spell out why not and offer some initiatives that might help us better address the myriad challenges and possibilities Asian tourism poses. The chapter begins by highlighting some of the key problems that continue to lie at the heart of scholarship on tourism. This is followed by a discussion of how such issues might be tackled in ways that create a more pluralistic, less Western-centric discourse.

Anglo-Western centrism and beyond

From around 2000 onwards, there have been increasingly loud calls for a fundamental rethink about the paradigms and norms which shape scholarship on tourism. As more and more scholars have aired their feelings of discontent publicly, it appears we have entered a period of sustained reflexivity; one that calls for a 'new era,' and a new generation of researchers capable of stepping out of the analytical and disciplinary straitjackets that have formed over the past three to four decades. Aitchison (2001), for example, points to the need for greater gender equality. To understand the complexities of today's tourism, Coles *et al.* (2006: 293) suggest researchers 'would benefit greatly from a post-disciplinary outlook, i.e. a direction "beyond disciplines" which is more problem-focused, based on more flexible modes of knowledge production, plurality, synthesis and synergy.' Back in 2000, the journal *Tourist Studies* was established with the specific aim of offering a platform for more critical, social science-based approaches to tourism. More recently, Adrian Franklin (2007: 132), one of the co-founders of the journal, goes as far as saying the development of new theories is not the solution, but a whole new thinking about the ontology of the field is required: a new way of describing what tourism is/does. For Tribe (2006, 2007), however, first we have to understand a series of 'truths' by making explicit the ideological and hegemonic values which together constitute the belief systems of tourism research. He suggests researchers continue to work within a number of 'isms,' citing managerialism, Marxism and consumerism as examples (2007: 33). He also raises the specter of ethnocentrism. But by building on Teo's earlier analysis (Chapter 3), I argue here that the full implications of this term have yet to be discussed by Tribe or others, and that in its current usage it only offers partial clarity. To really appreciate the ethnocentric problems facing tourism studies today we have to dig down to its foundations and excavate another pervasive and persistent 'ism,' that of Anglo-Western centrism.

It is a critical perspective that has been offered by others. In what must be the most provocative and stimulating diatribe on the subject, Alneng refers to 'the ethnocentric cartography of tourism studies' (2002: 138). Reflecting on the preoccupation of many post-MacCannell researchers for ever more elaborate tourist typologies, he states:

> Rather than having ethnographic accounts speak of cultural complexity, these typologies have done little more than splitting the Tourist into halves and ascribing these different motifs that do not ultimately contest MacCannell's unitary Tourist – they all dwell in a culturally barren landscape of modernist construed universality. While questions of class and age, and recently also gender, have sometimes been noticed, cultural variations of ethnicity and nationality have been left trivialized.
>
> (ibid.: 123)

In a similar vein, Edensor (1998), Ghimire (2001a) Gladstone (2006) and others have all questioned why there is an underlying and persistent assumption that tourists reside in Western, industrialized societies of the global North. Correctly, Williams *et al.* (2004) complain that such assumptions sustain major geographical imbalances in research. And yet, despite the publication of these various critiques, I believe their message largely remains unheeded and that the field of tourism studies, understood in its broadest sense, has hardly begun to grasp the multitude of implications that arise from it. The Western-centric *modus operandi* of research and teaching which endures today means the geographic, cultural and racial biases in the field remain a common blind spot.

It is crucial that we recognize that nearly all the field's key concepts have been grounded in societal changes occurring in Western Europe or North America. As we noted in the Introduction, histories of 'the beach' as a sexualized space of leisure, have focused predominantly on Britain, Southern Europe and California. Urry's (1990) idea of the *tourist gaze* puts its roots down in the emergence of clock time, trains, timetables, and work/leisure dichotomies in an industrializing Europe. The *grand tour* is the story of the élite of Northern Europe traveling south to learn about the high art, architecture and history of the region's classical civilizations (Towner 1996). The *flâneur* has its origins in Paris (Tester 1994). The *package tour* is the contribution of Thomas Cook and Thomson holidays (Withey 1997; Cobb 2002). *Mass tourism* began with working-class seaside holidays in Victorian Britain, morphed into Butlin's resorts and eventually moved to the Mediterranean with the invention of the jet engine and charter flights (Inglis 2000; Lofgren 2002). And, of course, MacCannell's (1976) *tourist* was based on an American character. As tourism became increasingly global, these concepts formed the backbone of analyses for countries as diverse as Thailand, Mexico and Egypt. The development of tourist industries around the world has thus largely been interpreted through a tool-bag of theories conceived and re-conceived in the socio-cultural particularities of Euro-American societies. In essence, the normative use of expressions like package tour, mass tourism and the seaside now hides their cultural and historical roots.

Of course, there is little denying that the emergence of large-scale tourism has been driven by citizens living in the increasingly wealthy, technologically advanced, 'modern' societies of Western Europe and North America. It is therefore understandable that analytical frameworks emerged which attempted to make sense of these historical patterns. And it is surely not surprising that as academics reflected on their holidays, their interest in *the* subject grew from being *its* subject. Perhaps the scale, scope and complexity of tourism and its practice have indeed been less 'developed' in regions outside Europe and North America, but I would also argue that there has been a widespread failure to look more closely and incorporate non-Western forms of leisure travel into mainstream discussions and theories about tourism. In the case of Asia, for example, it would be difficult to defend a position that denies a long history of tourist mobility both within and beyond the region. Just because 'package tours' were not the industry standard in India in the years after World War II, can we assume traveling for leisure was not widespread during this time? Or that the absence of railway travel in nineteenth-century Laos meant the aesthetic appreciation of landscape failed to emerge in the country? Or that seventeenth-century Japanese Buddhists traveling to Angkor didn't rely upon local guides and forms of hospitality? Indeed, in raising such questions I would suggest the history of 'modern tourism' has been written from a Eurocentric perspective. It is an account that centers Europe as the birthplace of modern tourism, an industry that became increasingly global as citizens of Western, industrialized countries traveled further and further afield. It is also an account that has used these citizens to construct 'the tourist' as a globally recognizable, supposedly universal subject.

At this point, it is worth pausing for clarification. I am suggesting this centrism takes on two forms. First, while it would be misleading to say that non-Western tourism has been totally overlooked and that a number of valuable studies have not been made, there is little doubting that the vast majority of research to date has cast its gaze on 'Western' tourists and their cultural, social and economic impacts. Crucially, this imbalance has both contributed to, and reflected a second form of Anglo-Western centrism: the accepted norm of uncritically applying certain analytical and theoretical approaches conceived in particular historical circumstances to all forms of tourism everywhere. English language scholarship on tourism has all too rarely torn up its 'Western' roots to interpret 'non-Western' tourist practices and industries.

In essence, then, the critical voices of Alneng, Edensor, Williams *et al.* and the various studies conducted on domestic and regional tourism in regions outside Europe and North America have yet to disturb the ethnocentric foundations of the field, which emerge from the widely held assumption that tourists come from the West and that 'the modern tourism industry' is essentially Western in its origins. The essays collected in the 2007 volume *The Critical Turn in Tourism Studies* are symptomatic of this ongoing problem. In what is a highly stimulating and thought-provoking volume, a number of well-known and up-and-coming authors explore an array of issues concerning current tourism theory, with many suggesting various intellectual and institutional reforms. In Chapter 1, Pritchard and Morgan (2007: 11), two of the book's editors, offer a persuasive account of why there needs to be an 'intellectual de-centering in the universe' of tourism scholarship. They begin by calling for changes in the academy, through a deconstruction of the 'hierarchies which exert power in and control over the tourism field' (ibid.: 14, see also Williams *et al.* 2004). Citing previous studies that have looked at the locations of leading scholars, journals and PhD programs, they demonstrate why the USA, the UK, Australia, Canada and New Zealand are 'the key power bases of the academy' (ibid.: 16). To analyze the centers of power within these countries they rightfully pay particular attention to the patriarchal values embedded in the field and the gender imbalances which characterize appointments to university faculties and journal editorial boards. They suggest 'not only are our academy's gatekeepers typically male, first generation scholars, it also emerges that they are more likely than not to be grounded in Western Anglo-centric epistemic research traditions' (ibid.: 16). Accordingly, they revisit the critique expressed by a number of earlier observers concerning the predominance of positivist and post-positivist approaches, particularly in the context of management and business studies departments. Indeed, as we know, the epistemic paradigms pursued in such environments invariably rest upon the foundations of scientistic rationalism which prioritizes objectivity, empiricism, quantitative data and predictability.

In considering which voices and approaches are marginalized, they once again highlight the neglect of gender issues and the trivialization of women's studies.

In order to de-center this universe, Pritchard and Morgan argue 'as researchers, we must begin to articulate and confront the ethnocentricity, which has shaped much of tourism research' (ibid.: 21). This is deemed necessary because 'the conceptualization and scholarship related to extant tourism literature has been created largely by white, Anglo-centric masculine voices. Other voices (particularly those of women, ethnic minorities and aboriginal peoples) have struggled to be heard' (ibid.: 22). They continue: 'we must act to decenter the tourism academy and respond to the challenges and critiques being articulated by indigenous scholars so that we may begin to create knowledge centred on indigenous epistemologies and ontologies' (ibid.: 22). These are clearly good and well-meant intentions.

There remains, however, a fundamental problem in this account. Reference to ethnic minorities and aboriginal peoples reflects a strong geographical bias. Their claim that we need to bring to the fore the epistemologies and ontologies of indigenous peoples and ethnic minorities rests on the idea that these are marginalized in societies of white majorities. To clarify this, they indicate 'future tourism research needs to comprehend, resist and transform the crises related to the effects of colonization on indigenous peoples and the ongoing erosion of indigenous languages, knowledge and culture as a result of colonization' (ibid.: 22). Clearly then in framing the concept of indigenity in such terms, we are in the realm of *native peoples*, *first nations*, or *aborigines* who have suffered white Anglo-Saxon forms of colonization. And so while we have seen their critique of tourism studies highlights the hegemony enjoyed by institutions and scholars in the USA, the UK, Australia, Canada and New Zealand, their concern for ethnic minorities and indigenous peoples essentially only speaks to, and about, these five countries.[1] Indeed, in an account focusing primarily on the epistemic and institutional reforms required in these five countries, their proposed 'new approach' remains silent about the challenges and opportunities facing tourism studies in the rest of the world.

To be more inclusive and overcome these 'Eurocentric tourism imaginaries' we need to move far beyond a language of ethnic minorities and colonized indigenous peoples. It is a definition of inclusion that continues to ignore the majority of the world's population. It gives no place for perspectives on tourism from scholars living in Thailand, Japan, Russia, Kenya or Dubai, to cite just a few examples. It is a discussion of margins and the marginalized that fails to question, and thus disrupt, the position of these five Western countries, and the English language, as the global center of scholarship on tourism. In Pritchard and Morgan's desire to include the indigenous voice, we also hear a concern to addressing exploitation and injustice. They argue:

> to decentre the tourism academy . . . academic decolonization is a necessity and a responsibility. It must be based on dialogues characterized by respect,

reciprocity, equality, collectivity, and empathy between indigenous minorities, indigenous researchers, and their non-indigenous counterparts.

(ibid.: 22)

Evidently, in sentiments where aboriginals and minorities remain victims we see the discomfort of the *white man's burden*. Although driven by noble ideals, such expressions of anguish, even guilt, are nevertheless highly problematic. The merits and drawbacks of discourses flavored by ideas of victimization and exploitation have long been debated by feminist and post-colonial scholars. But as their fields evolved it became apparent that such conversations were of limited value. In this context, given the historical and thematic links between colonialism and tourism, it is a discourse that implies the agents of exploitation remain the same, and that we merely need alternative voices and perspectives capable of countering the hegemonic narrative. Through this lens of social justice and 'ongoing erosion' the villains and victims of the touristic encounter remain in their same positions. It appears in their account that the 'native' has yet to be liberated as the agent of tourism, and take on the role of the tourist.

Many of the themes outlined in this introductory chapter are pursued in greater detail in the book's subsequent chapters. Read together, the authors deliver a richly detailed and, at times, provocative analysis of the field. Once again, however, the principal topics of concern are theoretical and disciplinary boundaries, the importance of critical paradigms, gender or the need for new methodological approaches. Beyond the broad recognition that the field is dominated by research emanating from the English-speaking, neo-liberal institutions in North America, Australasia and the UK, there is little discussion concerning how this situation creates a range of geographic, intellectual and thematic biases. Even some of the book's most insightful writing on the state of tourism theory today retains this assumption. Franklin's (2007: 140) chapter of the 'ordering of tourism,' for example, while innovative in its analysis, firmly situates tourism in a history of nation-building in Europe, as we can see from the following passage:

I have tried to locate the specific origins and contingencies of modern tourism in nation formation processes, which at least provide the possibility of exploring the detailed nature of agency in a socio-political problem and movement. I have also tried to identify using the early British travel writings of John Byng to show the startling absence of (or indeed indifference to) a popular traveling culture or tourism during the eighteenth century, prior to the main period of nation formation movements in the nineteenth century. John Byng and Thomas Cook after him were extremely influential and *unusual* at the same time. While the conditions for the emergence of modern tourism were contingent and generally given in the currents of nation formation, it still required people of imagination to dream the dream, to envisage something entirely new

... For what they both did was create the *idea* of tourism where none had existed before.

We see similar patterns elsewhere. The recent volume *Histories of Tourism* (Walton 2005: back cover), for example, also offers Europe as the sole empirical base for developing a 'closer relationship between history and tourism studies.' To build this analytical relationship the book focuses on stories like travel and empire and travel journalism in nineteenth-century Britain, the development of resorts in Spain, Nazi tourism, the English Lake District and Austrian travel literature. Although it undoubtedly fills an important void in our knowledge, the volume tells us nothing about non-European developments in recreational travel.

It can thus be seen that this privileging of Europe and the USA in the annals of tourism means we still overlook parallel developments in other parts of the world. In response, then, I believe we need to move on from treatise that retain hierarchies of the oppressed or minority and embrace an approach that sees pluralism as its starting point. By this I mean an approach that is at once geographically, politically and epistemologically plural. Only by doing so can we understand the inherent complexities of tourism, and the major shifts now occurring in this ever more globalizing industry. The collection of essays presented in *Asia on Tour* vividly illustrates why the Western-centric orthodoxies of tourism and tourism research need to be addressed urgently. The rapid, long-term growth of Asian tourism at both the regional and global level forces us to rethink our approaches, our ways of looking, our points of entry, and our existing theoretical dialogues. As we have already highlighted in this volume, this does not mean advocating a position of cultural determinism, nor am I suggesting the cultural and social complexities of the region be reduced to constructs of a homogenous Asia. Attempts to delineate the 'Asian tourist' as a conceptual category, for example, will be counterproductive. And I am certainly not suggesting research requires 'an Asian eye' or should head in the directions of an analytical 'nativism': a perspective which entails a widespread rejection of Western knowledge. But until we begin to seriously question the universalisms at the core of tourism studies we will not know when we need to embark on radical overhauls, and where we need to merely adjust and fine-tune, swerve and nudge.

Future directions

Frameworks of cultural and political pluralism have become important ways of constructing a critique that exposes the privileging of certain positions. To think about addressing the dynamics between majority/minority voices, however, we need to move far beyond the idea that the *a priori* majority is Anglo-Saxon white. A pluralist standpoint asks us to reflect upon broader interplays characterized by urban/rural, ethnic, religious, gendered and other distinctions. Of course, such ontological positions often remain ideals and aspirations, with their advocates frustrated by power and resistant social, institutional structures. As Ateljevic *et al.* (2007) correctly point out, to overcome the *status quo* we need to pursue more critical approaches. Accordingly, in the final part of this chapter I offer some directions for developing a more critical dialogue, one that will hopefully help address the Anglo-Western imbalances in the field. A shift towards a more pluralist perspective is not merely an intellectual or political concern; the ongoing growth of non-Western forms of travel is the empirical impetus for cultivating new approaches and perspectives. The following six points certainly do not pretend to be a panacea. Naturally, the problems of gender, knowledge force-fields and disciplinary outlooks raised by Aitchison, Tribe, Teo and Coles, Hall and Duval respectively are highly pertinent here. However, rather than rehearse their remarks, I wish to extend the analysis offered by Teo earlier by concentrating on some issues and challenges that are deemed most relevant to the arguments outlined above. Indeed, I limit my discussion to the development of critical scholarship on Asia. And to move the conversation away from the bureaucratic and disciplinary issues facing European and North American researchers, the six points that follow pay particular attention to the development of critical tourism scholarship within the Asian region itself.

One, writing histories of Asian tourism. To better interpret current developments and future trends in Asian tourism we need to understand where they have come from. It is also imperative we situate the historical growth of travel within and across sub-regions within their appropriate societal changes. This is no easy task. The archives of knowledge vary immensely both within and between countries, and framing the rise of leisure travel in the wider social contexts of industrialization, urbanization and modernity is fraught with analytical problems. The historiography of Asian travel is also faced with the problem of making visible existing ideas of culture, peoples and places constructed from Orientalist and Eurocentric colonial/post-colonial perspectives. Nonetheless, the lack of historical accounts is a major problem that warrants the attention of numerous conferences, PhDs, books and detailed empirical studies.

Two, develop grounded theory and alternative discourses. This is perhaps the trickiest issue of all, and the one that requires the most careful attention. Clearly, a discussion of issues such as intellectual imperialism, the geo-politics of scholarship, and post-colonial theory are far beyond the scope of this closing chapter. However, I just want to briefly note that the uncritical transplantation of ideas like modernity and post-modernity, risk and performance into accounts of Asian tourism is of very limited value. The arguments offered by Alatas in his recent book *Alternative Discourses in Asian Social Science: Responses to Eurocentrism* provide some instructive guidance here. As Alatas highlights this problem of 'mimesis' – that of uncritically adopting or imitating Western social science models – is a long one (2006: 32). In response he lays out a series of 'alternative discourses,' ones that are:

informed by local/regional historical experiences and cultural practices in Asia in the same way that the Western social sciences are. Being alternative means a turn to philosophies, epistemologies, histories, and the arts other than those of the Western tradition. These are all to be considered as potential sources of social science theories and concepts, which would decrease academic dependence on the world social science powers.

(ibid.: 82)

Alatas carefully spell outs why such alternative discourses make a positive contribution to the field of knowledge. The production of non-Western epistemologies is not driven by a desire to reject Western approaches *in toto* (ibid.: 85). He highlights collaborative approaches, for example, albeit with heavy words of caution, as a strategy for delivering richly detailed interpretations. Equally, he recognizes the benefits of cultivating multiple centers of theory. Of course Alatas's arguments sit within far-reaching, complex debates. Without extending this present discussion further into those debates, it is worth noting one further point that is particularly pertinent to the concerns expressed earlier regarding the enduring prevalence of positivism in tourism research. He suggests:

the formation of a social-science tradition which involves the raising and treatment of original problems and new research questions as well as the generation of new concepts. It involves the critique of positivist social-science to the extent that models of society epistemologically founded in the physical sciences obstruct the interpretative understanding of local situations.

(ibid.: 89)

What we see here is a call for new ways of looking, and a willingness to risk alternative, untried avenues of analysis. In foregrounding interpretative approaches, it is also a perspective that points towards the need for humanist, qualitative, value driven research. Clearly, as both Alatas and a number of chapters in this volume illustrate, it is a philosophical perspective towards research and knowledge production that needs to be at the heart of tourism scholarship across the region.

Three, create the institutional homes in Asia that support and promote critical perspectives. The rapid growth in leisure travel in Asia means the study of tourism is too important to leave to tourism departments alone. To date, much of the teaching and research in India, Hong Kong, China and Southeast Asia has been on hospitality and tourism management. As Teo has pointed out, while courses in these areas undoubtedly address important skills voids, it is crucial the field is not merely examined in vocational or technological institutions. The debates concerning the positioning of tourism research and its intellectual foundations noted above should be central concerns for planning teaching and research programs in Asia's universities. To understand and interpret the wider societal impacts of tourism, and how domestic and intra-regional travel is reshaping the cultural, social and physical landscapes of Asia, we need to embed tourism-related scholarship in sociological, anthropological, development studies, heritage studies, environmental studies, and cultural geography environments. Only by working towards more rigorous intellectual foundations can we realistically address the merits of inter- versus post-disciplinary outlooks. Finally, here, by critical perspectives I mean approaches that engage with issues like power, structure, inequality and human rights. If these are to emerge, institutions need to retain a healthy degree of political autonomy from state and other transnational groupings. With funding clearly being the key challenge here, lobbying government departments and other stakeholders, both domestic and foreign, about the merits of critical thinking will undoubtedly be an arduous, but necessary task.

Four, centering scholarship from Asia. The chapters presented here and the authors cited throughout this book show that social science scholarship on tourism is continuing to gain greater traction in Asia's most respected universities. Driven in large part by the ever growing pool of students in countries like China, there is also a strong pattern of growth in the number of collaborations and partnerships between institutes in Asia and with universities in the USA, the UK, Australia, Spain, Netherlands, Denmark, etc. More and more early career academics living and working in Asia are undertaking exciting research. Seen together, these developments give strong reasons to be optimistic. A number of challenges, however, remain: the extant imbalances in journal editorial boards; academia's inbuilt biases concerning the location of publications; the pressures imposed on early career researchers to publish in a select number of rated journals; the widespread use of English at conferences; poor visibility and distribution of Asian publications outside the region; and the dominance of English language publishing.[2] There is also the danger that Asia will be seen as a form of 'area studies,' with its own regionalized debates and theoretical concerns. In essence, to ensure pluralism is the starting point of theory generation, and in particular critical theory generation, the core–periphery hierarchies which characterize the field today need to be overcome.

Five, address country imbalances. Like governments, companies and entrepreneurs around the world, academia is rushing to China. It is crucial that efforts are made to understand the region's less dynamic and 'spectacular' countries. Over the longer term, domestic and in-bound regional tourism will undoubtedly have a major impact on the societies of Burma, Sri Lanka, Aceh, Nepal, and Laos. There is a risk these countries will continue to be overlooked, given the current growth of studies on Japanese, Hong Kong, mainland Chinese and Singaporean tourism. At the conceptual level, it is also vital that the immense cultural, political and historical differences across the region are not dissolved by an analytical conflation, whereby

China comes to speak for the whole of Asia. Particular efforts are therefore required to raise the visibility of institutions and scholarship in smaller countries. Initiatives here might include more collaborative partnerships and the cross-translation of research and publications.

Six, get critical thinking on tourism into policy. The ongoing growth of tourism will be intimately tied to the transformation of cities, rising economic inequalities, prostitution, migration, nationalisms, environmental damage, heritage management, the consumption of non-renewable energies, and so forth. Tourism as a force for cultural, economic and political change needs to be a recognized component of policy formulation. At present, the contradictions and complexities of tourism are rarely integrated into the planning strategies of governmental and non-governmental agencies. As more and more national economies turn to domestic and regional tourism for economic growth, it is crucial that tourism is not treated merely as a 'sector' of industry or commerce.

To sum up then, it is worth reiterating that the subject matter and issues at stake are far too complex for these six points to be anything like prescriptive or comprehensive. Instead, they are offered in the hope that they stimulate, provoke and unsettle discussions about the future directions of tourism research. I believe the long-term growth in Asian tourism necessitates a re-thinking about how tourism is both researched and taught. The pursuit of critical, empirically grounded approaches is the only way to achieve that, and at the same time make sense of the wider societal consequences emanating from this ongoing growth in Asia. The sustained analysis of this phenomenon is undoubtedly a journey we need to embark upon urgently. And just like tourists, researchers need road maps and guidebooks to make sense of the unfamiliar territories now being entered. It is our hope that *Asia on Tour* will help make the foreign seem less alien, the native less exotic, the modern less threatening, and the familiar a little less habitual.

Acknowledgements

I would like to thank Ien Ang, TC Chang, Ong Chin Ee, Laavanya Kathiravelu and Peggy Teo for comments on earlier drafts of this chapter.

Notes

1 Of course, the concept of indigeneity is relevant to other parts of the world, beyond the 'colonized' populations of these five countries. But as the thrust of this chapter suggests, the merits of non-indigenous versus indigenous perspectives need to form part of a wider concern for real cultural, geographic and political pluralism.
2 Indeed, the dilemma of how to better integrate non-English scholarship, whether it emanates from Europe, Asia or Africa, into the English language academy is a problem faced by many fields of scholarship today.

Bibliography

Acciaioli, G. (1985) 'Culture as art: from practice to spectacle in Indonesia,' *Canberra Anthropology*, 8(1 & 2): 148–72.

Adams, K. (1997) 'Touristic "primadonnas": tourism, ethnicity, and national integration in Sulawesi, Indonesia,' in R. Wood and M. Picard (eds), *Tourism, Ethnicity and the State in Asian and Pacific Societies*, Honolulu: University of Hawaii.

Adams, K. (1998) 'Domestic tourism and nation building in south Sulawesi,' *Indonesia and the Malay World*, 2(75): 77–96.

Adams, K. (2006) 'Terror and tourism: charting the ambivalent allure of the urban jungle,' in C. Minca and T. Oakes (eds), *Travels in Paradox: Remapping Tourism*, Lanham, MD: Rowman & Littlefield.

Adams, V. (1996) 'Karaoke as modern Lhasa, Tibet: Western encounters with cultural politics,' *Cultural Anthropology*, 11(4): 510–46.

Adler, J. (1989) 'Origins of sightseeing,' *Annals of Tourism Research*, 16(2): 7–29.

Ahmed, F. (2004) 'Sayeed wants security forces out of hotels,' *South Asia Monitor*. Online. Available HTTP: <http://www.southasiamonitor.org/focus/2004/dec/10kash2.shtml> (accessed 4 September 2007).

Ahmed, M. (2005) 'J & K cinemas fail to gain, turn into hospitals,' *Rediff India Abroad*, 3 October. Online. Available HTTP: <http://us.rediff.com/news/2005/oct/03cinema.htm> (accessed 8 September 2007).

Aitchison, C. (1996) 'Partriachal paradigms and the politics of pedagogy: a framework for feminist analysis of leisure and tourism studies,' *World Leisure and Recreation*, 38(4): 38–40.

Aitchison, C. (2001) 'Gender and leisure research: the codification of knowledge,' *Leisure Sciences*, 23(1): 1–19.

Akama, J.S. (2002) 'The role of government in the development of tourism in Kenya,' *International Journal of Tourism Research*, 4(1): 1–13.

Alatas, S.F. (2006) *Alternative Discourses in Asian Social Science: Responses to Eurocentrism*, London: Sage.

Albers, P. and James, W. (1988) 'Travel photography: a methodological approach,' *Annals of Tourism Research*, 15(1): 134–58.

Alneng, V. (2002) 'The modern does not cater for natives: travel ethnography and the conventions of form,' *Tourist Studies*, 2(2): 119–42.

Alsayyad, N. (2001) 'Hybrid culture/hybrid urbanism: Pandora's box of the "third place",' in N. Alsayyad (ed.), *Hybrid Urbanism: On the Identity Discourse and the Built Environment*, Westport, CT: Praeger.

Alter, J. (2000) *Gandhi's Body: Sex, Diet and the Politics of Nationalism*, Philadelphia, PA: University of Pennsylvania Press.

Anagnost, A. (1997) *National Past-Times: Narrative, Representation, and Power in Modern China*, Durham, NC: Duke University Press.

Anchalee Singhanetra-Renard (1999) 'Population mobility and the transformation of village community in Northern Thailand,' *Asia Pacific Viewpoint*, 40(1): 69–87.

Anderson, B. (1983) *Imagined Communities*, London: Verso.

Anderson, E. (2005) *Everyone Eats: Understanding Food and Culture*, New York: New York University Press.

Anonymous (2004) *Mekong Blue*, Stung Treng Women's Development Center promotional brochure, Phnom Penh: Stung Treng Women's Development Center.

Anonymous (2005) 'Revisiting history in the hills of Nan,' *Bangkok Post*, 15 December: 111.

Ap, J. (2003) 'An assessment of theme park development in China,' in A.A. Lew, L. Yu, J. Ap and G. Zhang (eds), *Tourism in China*, New York: The Haworth Hospitality Press.

Appadurai, A. (1996) *Modernity at Large: Cultural Dimensions of Globalization*, Minneapolis: University of Minnesota Press.

Appelgren, S. (2007) 'Huis ten Bosch: mimesis and simulation in a Japanese Dutch town,' unpublished PhD thesis, University of Göteborg, Sweden.

Arlt, W.G. (2006) *China's Outbound Tourism*, New York: Routledge.

Arlt, W.G. (2007) 'Chinese tourists' behavior in "Elsewhereland",' in J. Cochrane (ed.), *Asian Tourism: Growth and Change*, Burlington, MA: Elsevier Publishing Ltd.

Arnold, W. (2005) 'Chinese tourists getting a bad image,' *International Herald Tribune*, 23 October. Online. Available HTTP: <http://www.iht.com/articles/2005/10/21/business/tourists.php> (accessed 10 September 2007).

Arnott, M.L. (ed.) (1975) *Gastronomy: The Anthropology of Food and Food Habits*, The Hague: Mouton.

Artisans d'Angkor (2006) *Artisans d'Angkor: vocation*. Online. Available HTTP: <http://www.artisansdangkor.com/html/artisans_angkor/notre_vocation.php> (accessed 10 August 2006).

Ashcroft, B., Griffiths, G. and Tiffin, H. (1998) *Key Concepts in Post-colonial Studies*, London: Routledge.

Ashworth, G.J. (1994) 'From history to heritage: from heritage to identity,' in G.J. Ashworth and P.J. Larkham (eds), *Building a New Heritage*, London: Routledge.

Ashworth, G.J. and Tunbridge, J.E. (2000) *The Tourist-Historic City: Retrospect and Prospect of Managing the Heritage City*, Oxford: Pergamon.

Askew, M. and Logan, W.S. (eds) (1994) *Cultural Identity and Urban Change in Southeast Asia: Interpretative Essays*, Geelong, Victoria: Deekin University Press.

Ateljevic, I. and Doorne, S. (2004) 'Theoretical encounters: a review of backpacker literature,' in G. Richards and J. Wilson (eds), *The Global Nomad: Backpacker Travel in Theory and Practice*, Clevedon: Channel View Publications.

Ateljevic, I., Pritchard, A. and Morgan, N. (eds) (2007) *The Critical Turn in Tourism Studies: Innovative Research Methods*, Oxford: Elsevier.

Bae, Y.J. (2005) 'Pae Yong-jun ssika ponaeon kŭlimnita' (A statement by Bae Yong-jun). Online. Available HTTP: <http://www.byj.co.kr/pop_index.asp?tag=2&langs=kr> (accessed 11 October 2007).

Baer, H. (2003) 'The work of Andrew Weil and Deepak Chopra – two holistic health/new age gurus: a critique of the holistic health/new age movements,' *Medical Anthropology Quarterly*, 17(2): 233–50.

Baker, C. (ed.) (2004) *The Society of Siam, Selected Articles for the Siam Society's Centenary*, Bangkok: The Siam Society.

Bandyopadhyay, R. and Morais, D. (2005) 'Representative dissonance: India's self and western image,' *Annals of Tourism Research*, 32(4): 1006–21.

Bannerjee, M. (2002) 'Power, culture and medicine: Ayurvedic pharmaceuticals in the modern market,' *Contributions to Indian Sociology*, 36(5): 435–67.

Baranay, I. (1994) 'Arriving in the 1980s,' in A. Vickers (ed.), *Travelling to Bali: Four Hundred Years of Journeys*, Kuala Lumpur: Oxford University Press.

Barber, M.J.P. (1979) 'Migrants and modernisation: a study of change in Lao society,' unpublished PhD thesis, University of Hull.

Barnes, T. (2006) 'Between deduction and dialectics: David Harvey on knowledge,' in N. Castree and D. Gregory (eds), *David Harvey: A Critical Reader*, Oxford: Blackwell.

Barr, M.D. (2000) 'Lee Kuan Yew and the "Asian Values" debate,' *Asian Studies Review*, 24(3): 309–34.

Barthes, R. (1982) *Camera Lucida: Relations on Photography*, London: Jonathan Cape.

Bartling, H. (2006) 'Tourism as everyday life: an inquiry into the villages, Florida,' *Tourism Geographies*, 8(4): 380–402.

Basham, A.L. (1959) *The Wonder That Was India: A Survey of the Culture of the Indian Subcontinent Before the Coming of the Muslims*, New York: Grove.

Bauman, Z. (2000) *Liquid Modernity*, Cambridge: Polity Press.

Beech, H. (2005) 'Deals and diplomacy, China's influence in Southeast Asia is growing as its trade and investments boom,' *Time Asia*, 30(May): 14–20.

Beeson, M. and Yoshimatsu, H. (2007) 'Asia's odd men out: Australia, Japan and the politics of regionalism,' *International Relations of the Asia-Pacific*, 7(2): 227–50.

Behera, N.C. (2000) *State, Identity and Violence: Jammu, Kashmir and Ladakh*, New Delhi: Manohar.

Belfrage, C. (1937) *Away From it All: An Escapologist's Notebook*, New York: Simon & Schuster.

Belo, J. (1970) *Traditional Balinese Culture: Essays*, New York: Columbia University Press.

Benjamin, W. (1978) 'A short history of photography,' in D. Mellor (ed.), *The New Photography: Germany, 1927–33*, London: Arts Council of Great Britain.

Berger, J. (1972) *Ways of Seeing*, London: Penguin.

Berking, H. (2003) ' "Ethnicity is everywhere": on globalization and the transformation of cultural identity,' *Current Sociology*, 51(3 & 4): 248–64.

Bhabha, H. (1994) *The Location of Culture*, London: Routledge.

Bhattacharyya, D.P. (1997) 'Mediating India: an analysis of a guidebook,' *Annals of Tourism Research*, 24(2): 371–89.

Black, H. and Wall, G. (2001) 'Global-local inter-relationships in UNESCO world heritage sites,' in P. Teo, T.C. Chang and K.C. Ho (eds), *Interconnected Worlds: Tourism in Southeast Asia*, Oxford: Pergamon.

Blunt, A. and Wills, J. (2000) *Dissident Geographies: An Introduction to Radical Ideas and Practice*, Harlow: Prentice Hall.

Bobbio, N. (1988) 'Gramsci and the concept of civil society,' in J. Keane (ed.), *Civil Society and the State: New European Perspectives*, London: Verso.

Bochaton, A. and Lefebvre, B. (2006) 'Interviewing elites: perspectives from medical tourism sector in India and in Thailand,' paper presented at Asia Research

Institute workshop on Questions of Methodology: researching tourism in Asia, Singapore, 5–6 September.

Bochner, S. (2003) 'Culture shock due to contact with unfamiliar cultures,' in W.J. Lonner *et al.* (eds), *Online Readings in Psychology and Culture*. Online. Available HTTP: <http://www.wwu.edu/~culture> (accessed 13 June 2005).

Boniface, P. (1995) *Managing Quality Cultural Tourism*, New York: Routledge.

Boothroyd, P. and Pham, X.N. (eds) (2000) *Socioeconomic Renovation in Viet Nam: The Origin, Evolution, and Impact of Doi Moi*, Ottawa: International Development Research Center.

Bourdieu, P. (1984) *Distinction: A Social Critique of the Judgement of Taste*, London: Routledge.

Broinowski, A. (2003) *About Face: Asian Accounts of Australia*, Melbourne: Scribe Publications.

Brown, C.K. (2000) *Encyclopedia of Travel Literature*, Santa Barbara, CA: ABC-CLIO.

Brown, P., Sutikna, T., Morword, M.J., Soejono, R.P., Jakniko, E., Saptomo, E.W. and Due, R.W. (2004) 'A new small-bodied hominin from the late Pleistocene of Flores, Indonesia,' *Nature*, 431(28 October): 1055–61.

Bruner, E.M. (1991) 'Transformation of self in tourism,' *Annals of Tourism Research*, 18(2): 238–50.

Bruner, E.M. (1995) 'The ethnographer/tourist in Indonesia,' in J. Allcock *et al.* (eds), *International Tourism: Identity and Change Anthropological and Sociological Approaches*, London: Sage.

Bruner, E.M. (2001) 'The Masaai and the lion king: authenticity, nationalism and globalization in African tourism,' *American Ethnologist*, 28(4): 881–908.

Bruner, E.M. (2005) *Culture on Tour: Ethnographies of Travel*, Chicago: The University of Chicago Press.

Bruno, G. (2002) *Atlas of Emotion: Journeys in Art, Architecture, and Film*, New York: Verso.

Bunnell, T. (2004) *Malaysia, Modernity and the Multimedia Corridor: A Critical Geography of Intelligent Landscapes*, London: RoutledgeCurzon.

Burns, P. (2001) 'Interconnections, planning and the local-global nexus: a case from Vietnam,' in P. Teo, T.C. Chang and K.C. Ho (eds), *Interconnected Worlds: Tourism in Southeast Asia*, Oxford: Pergamon.

Carroll, C. (2006) ' "My mother's best friend's sister-in-law is coming with us": exploring domestic and international travels with a group of Lao tourists,' paper presented at the conference Of Asian Origin: rethinking tourism in contemporary Asia, Singapore, 7–9 September.

Cartier, C. (1998) 'Megadevelopment in Malaysia: from heritage landscapes to "leisurescapes" in Melaka's tourism sector,' *Singapore Journal of Tropical Geography*, 19(2): 151–76.

Cartier, C. (2001) *Globalizing South China*, Oxford: Blackwell.

Castree, N. and Gregory, D. (eds) (2006) *David Harvey: A Critical Reader*, London: Blackwell.

Causey, A. (2003) *Hard Bargaining in Sumatra: Western Travelers and Toba Bataks in the Marketplace of Souvenirs*, Honolulu: University of Hawaii Press.

Chalfen, R. (1979) 'Photography's role in tourism: some unexplored relationships,' *Annals of Tourism Research*, 6(4): 435–47.

Chalfen, R. (1987) *Snapshot Versions of Life*, Bowling Green, OH: Bowling Green State University Popular Press.

Chamberlain, H.B. (1993) 'On the search for civil society in China,' *Modern China*, 19(2): 199–215.

Chan, A., Kerkvliet, B.J.T. and Unger, J. (eds) (1999) *Transforming Asian Socialism: China and Vietnam compared*, Lanham, MD: Rowman & Littlefield.

Chan, K.S. (2007) '*Poonchoi*: the production and popularity of a rural festive cuisine in urban modern Hong Kong,' in S.C.H. Cheung and C.B. Tan (eds), *Food and Foodways in Asia: Resource, Tradition, and Cooking*, London and New York: Routledge.

Chan, Y.W. (2006) 'Coming of age of the Chinese tourists: the emergence of non-Western tourism and host-guest interactions in Vietnam's border tourism,' *Tourist Studies*, 6(3): 187–213.

Chang, P.M. (1985) *The Sino-Vietnamese Territorial Dispute*, New York: Praeger.

Chang, T.C. (1997) 'From "Instant Asia" to "Multifaceted Jewel": urban imaging strategy and tourism development in Singapore,' *Urban Geography*, 18(6): 542–62.

Chang, T.C. (1998) 'Regionalism and tourism: exploring integral links in Singapore,' *Asia Pacific Viewpoint*, 39(1): 73–94.

Chang, T.C. (2001) 'Configuring new tourism space: exploring Singapore's regional tourism forays,' *Environment and Planning A*, 33(9): 1597–619.

Chang, T.C. and Huang, S. (2004) 'Urban tourism: between the global and local,' in A. Lew, C.M. Hall and A.M. Williams (eds), *A Companion to Tourism*, Oxford: Blackwell Publishing.

Charras, M. (2005) 'The reshaping of the Indonesian archipelago after 50 years of regional imbalance,' in M. Erb, P. Sulistiyanto and C. Faucher (eds), *Regionalism in Post-Suharto Indonesia*, London: RoutledgeCurzon.

Cheng, T.J. and Sheldon, M. (1994) 'The origins and social consequences of China's hukou system,' *The China Quarterly*, 139 (September): 644–68.

Cheung, S.C.H. (1999) 'The meanings of a heritage trail in Hong Kong,' *Annals of Tourism Research*, 26(3): 570–88.

Cheung, S.C.H. (2003) 'Remembering through space: the politics of heritage in Hong Kong,' *International Journal of Heritage Studies*, 9(1): 7–26.

Cheung, S.C.H. (2005a) 'Consuming "low" cuisine after Hong Kong's handover: village banquets and private kitchens,' *Asian Studies Review*, 29(3): 259–73.

Cheung, S.C.H. (2005b) 'Food for tourists: second menus, special menus and specific menus,' *Cultura y Desarrollo* (Special Issue on Cultural Diversity and Tourism), 4: 60–68.

Cheung, S.C.H. (2007) 'Wetland tourism in Hong Kong: from birdwatcher to mass ecotourist,' in J. Cochrane (ed.), *Asian Tourism: Growth and Change*, London: Elsevier Science.

China Internet Network Information Center (CNNIC) (2007) *20th Statistical Survey on the Internet Development in China*. Online. Available HTTP: <http://www.cnnic.net.cn/download/2007/20thCNNICreport-en.pdf>. (accessed 3 November 2007).

China National Tourist Office (CNTO) (2006a) *China Tourism Statistics*. Online. Available HTTP: <http://www.cnto.org/chinastats.asp> (accessed on 26 October 2006).

China National Tourist Office (CNTO) (2006b) *Official China Tourism Statistics*. Online. Available HTTP: <http://old.cnta.gov.cn/lyen/index.asp> (accessed 7 January 2007).

Choe, Y.M. (2006) 'Affective tourism: domestic screen tourism in Korea and the Asian experience,' paper presented at the conference 'Of Asian origin: rethinking tourism in contemporary Asia,' Singapore, 7–9 September.

Chua, B.H. (ed.) (2000) *Consumption in Asia: Lifestyles and Identities*, London and New York: Routledge.

Chua, K.H. (2005) 'The rise of the ugly China tourist,' *The Straits Times*, 31 July: 1.

Clifford, J. (1997) *Routes: Travel and Translation in the Late Twentieth Century*, Cambridge, MA: Harvard University Press.

CLSA (2005) *Chinese tourists: Coming, Ready or Not!* Hong Kong: CLSA Asia-Pacific Markets.

Cobb, V. (2002) *The Package Tour Industry*, London: Blackie & Co.

Cohen, E. (1973) 'Nomads from affluence: notes on the phenomenon of drifter-tourism,' *International Journal of Comparative Sociology*, 14(1–2): 89–103.

Cohen, E. (1979) 'A phenomenology of touristic experience,' *Sociology*, 13(2): 179–201.

Cohen, E. (1993) 'Introduction: investigating tourist arts,' *Annals of Tourism Research*, 20(1): 1–8.

Cohen, E. (1996) *Thai Tourism: Hill Tribes, Islands and Open-Ended Prostitution – Collected Papers*, Bangkok: White Lotus Books.

Cohen, E. (2004) 'Backpacking: diversity and change,' in G. Richards and J. Wilson (eds), *The Global Nomad: Backpacker Travel in Theory and Practice*, Clevedon: Channel View Publications.

Cohen, E. and Avieli, N. (2004) 'Food in tourism: attraction and impediment,' *Annals of Tourism Research*, 31(4): 755–78.

Cohen, J.L. and Arato, A. (1992) *Civil Society and Political Theory*, Cambridge, MA: MIT Press.

Cohen, P.T. (2001) 'Buddhism unshackled: the yuan "holy man" tradition and the nation-state in the Tai world,' *Journal of Southeast Asian Studies*, 32(2): 227–47.

Coles, T. (2008) 'Citizenship and the state: hidden features in the internationalization of tourism,' in T. Coles and C.M. Hall (eds), *Tourism and International Business*, London: Routledge.

Coles, T., Hall, C.M. and Duval, D.T. (2006) 'Tourism and post-disciplinary enquiry,' *Current Issues in Tourism*, 9(4 & 5): 293–319.

Connell, J. (2006) 'Medical tourism: sea, sun, sand and . . . surgery,' *Tourism Management*, 27(6): 1093–100.

Covarrubias, M. (1937) *Island of Bali*, New York: Alfred A. Knopf.

Crawshaw, C. and Urry, J. (1997) 'Tourism and the photographic eye,' in C. Rojek and J. Urry (eds), *Touring Cultures: Transformations of Travel and Theory*, London: Routledge.

Crouch, D. (1999) *Leisure/Tourism Geographies: Practices and Geographical Knowledge*, London: Routledge.

Crush, J. (1994) 'Post-colonialism, de-colonization, and geography,' in A. Godlewska and N. Smith (eds), *Geography and Empire*, Oxford: Blackwell.

Dahles, H. (2001) *Tourism, Heritage and National Culture in Java: Dilemmas of a Local Community*, Richmond, Surrey: Curzon.

Dahles, H. and Bras, K. (1999) *Tourism and Small Entrepreneurs – Development, National Policy, and Entrepreneurial Culture: Indonesian Cases*, New York: Cognizant Communication Corporation.

Dash, B. (1999) *Fundamentals of Ayurvedic Medicine*, Delhi: Sri Satguru Publications.

Dean, J. (2001) 'Cybersalons and civil society: rethinking the public sphere in transnational technoculture,' *Public Culture*, 13(2): 243–65.

de Casparis, J.G. and Mabbett, I.W. (1999) 'Religion and popular beliefs of Southeast Asia before c. 1500,' in N. Tarling (ed.), *The Cambridge History of Southeast Asia: Volume One, Part One, from Early Times to c. 1500*, Cambridge: Cambridge University Press.

de Kadt, E. (1979) *Tourism: Passport to Development?*, Oxford: Oxford University Press.

Deleuze, G. and Guattari, F. (1983) *Anti-Oedipus: Capitalism and Schizophrenia*, trans. R. Hurley *et al.*, Minneapolis: University of Minnesota Press.

Deleuze, G. and Guattari, F. (1987) *A Thousand Plateaus*, trans. B. Massumi, Minneapolis: University of Minnesota Press.

Deng, Z.L. and Jing, Y.J. (1992) 'Jiangou zhongguo de shimin shehui' (Building a Chinese civil society), *Chinese Social Science Quarterly*, 1: 1–22.

Departemen Kebudayaan dan Pariwisata Indonesia (Indonesian Department of Culture and Tourism) (2006a) *Statistik Perkembangan Kunjungan Wisman ke Indonesia 2000–2005 (Foreign Tourist Arrival Statistics 2000–2005)*. Online. Available HTTP: <http://www.budpar.go.id/page.php?ic=521andid=160> (accessed 2 August 2006).

Departemen Kebudayaan dan Pariwisata Indonesia (Indonesian Department of Culture and Tourism) (2006b) *Statistik perkembangan wisatawan nusantara (wisnus) 2006 (Domestic Tourism Statistics 2006)*. Online. Available HTTP: <http://www.budpar.go.id/page.php?ic=521andid=1427> (accessed 12 August 2006).

Department of Export Promotion, Ministry of Commerce (2002) *Questionnaire Survey of Foreign Patients*, Nonthaburi, Thailand: Ministry of Commerce.

Desforges, L. (1998) 'Checking out the planet: global representations/local identities and youth travel,' in T. Skelton and G. Valentine (eds), *Cool Places: Geographies of Youth Culture*, London: Routledge.

Desforges, L. (2000) 'Travel the world: identity and travel biography,' *Annals of Tourism Research*, 27(4): 926–45.

Deshingkar, G. (1999) 'The construction of Asia in India,' *Asian Studies Review*, 23(2): 173–80.

Dewan, R. and Manzar, B. (2000) *Demystifying Kashmir: Developmental Potential of Horticulture and Tourism*, Srinagar: Kashmir Foundation for Peace and Developmental Studies.

Dhavan, R. (2004) 'The J & K Bill 2004,' *The Hindu*, 19 March: 8.

Dinas Pariwisata Provinsi Bali (Tourism Authority of the Province of Bali) (2004) *Statistik Bali (Bali Statistics)*, Bali: Dinas Pariwisata Provinsi Bali.

Dixon, D.P. and Jones III, J.P. (2004) 'What next?,' *Environment and Planning A*, 36(3): 381–90.

Doheny, K. (2006) 'A little sightseeing, a little face-lift,' *Los Angeles Times*, 29 January. Online. Available Http: <http://www.latimes.com/travel/la-tr-healthy29jan29, 1,4400053.column?coll=la-travel-headlines&ctrack=1&cset=true> (accessed 4 May 2006).

Doorne, S., Ateljevic, I. and Bai, Z. (2003) 'Representing identities through tourism: encounters of ethnic minorities in Dali, Yunnan Province, People's Republic of China,' *International Journal of Tourism Research*, 5(1): 1–11.

Dougoud, R. (2000) 'Souvenirs from Kambot (Papua New Guinea): the sacred search for authenticity,' in M. Hitchcock and K. Teague (eds), *Souvenirs: The Material Culture of Tourism*, Aldershot: Ashgate.

Duan Ying and Yang Hui (2001) 'Quanli bianyuan de Manchunman – Lüyou zuowei xiandaixing yu minzu yishi de gean yanjiu' (Manchunman at the periphery of power: tourism as a case study in modernity and ethnic consciousness), in Yang Hui, Tan Chee-Beng and Sydney C.H. Cheung (eds), *Tourism, Anthropology and China*, Kunming: Yunnan Daxue Chubanshe.

Dubey, N.K., Kumar, R. and Tripathi, P. (2004) 'Global promotion of herbal medicine: India's opportunity,' *Current Science*, 86(1): 37–41.

du Cros, H. (2004) 'Postcolonial conflict inherent in the involvement of cultural tourism in creating new national myths in Hong Kong,' in C.M. Hall and H. Tucker (eds), *Tourism and Postcolonialism: Contested Discourses, Identities and Representations*, London and New York: Routledge.

du Cros, H. and Lee, Y.F. (2007) *Cultural Heritage Management in China: Preserving the Cities of the Pearl River Delta*, London and New York: Routledge.

Echtner, C.M. and Prasad, P. (2003) 'The context of third world tourism marketing,' *Annals of Tourism Research*, 30(3): 660–82.

Eck, D. (1998) 'The imagined landscape: patterns in the construction of Hindu sacred geography,' *Contributions to Indian Sociology*, 32(2): 165–88.

Edensor, T. (1998) *Tourists at the Taj: Performance and Meaning at a Symbolic Site*, London and New York: Routledge.

Edensor, T. (2001) 'Performing tourism, staging tourism,' *Tourist Studies*, 1(1): 59–81.

Edensor, T. and Kothari, U. (2004) 'Sweetening colonialism: a Mauritian themed resort,' in D. Medina Lasansky and B. McLaren (eds), *Architecture and Tourism: Perception, Performance and Place*, Oxford: Berg.

Edwards, E. (1999) 'Photographs as objects of memory,' in M. Kwint, C. Breward and J. Aynesley (eds), *Material Memories*, Oxford: Berg.

Edwards, E. (2001) 'Material beings: objecthood and ethnographic photographs,' *Visual Studies*, 12(1): 67–75.

Edwards, E. and Hart, J. (eds) (2004) *Photographs Objects Histories: On the Materiality of Images*, London and New York: Routledge.

Edwards, P. (2006) *Cambodia: The Cultivation of a Nation 1860–1945*, Honolulu: University of Hawaii Press.

Elias, N. (1994) *The Civilizing Process*, Oxford: Basil Blackwell.

Elsrud, T. (2001) 'Risk creation in traveling: backpacker adventure narration,' *Annals of Tourism Research*, 28(3): 597–617.

Equipe MIT (2002) *Tourismes 1. Lieux communs (Tourisms 1. Common Places)*, Paris: Belin.

Erb, M. (2000a) 'Understanding tourists: interpretations from Indonesia,' *Annals of Tourism Research*, 27(3): 709–36.

Erb, M. (2000b) 'Work, consumption and the Indonesian crises in western Flores,' *Southeast Asian Journal of Social Science*, 28(2): 131–52.

Erb, M. (2000c) 'Understanding tourists: interpretations from Indonesia,' *Annals of Tourism Research*, 27(3): 709–36.

Erb, M. (2001) 'Le tourisme et la quête de la culture à Manggarai,' *Anthropologie et Sociétés*, 25(2): 93–108.

Erb, M. (2005) 'Limiting tourism and the limits of tourism: the production and consumption of tourist attractions in western Flores,' in C. Ryan and M. Aicken (eds),

Indigenous Tourism: The Commodification and Management of Culture, London: Elsevier.

Errington, S. (1998) *The Death of Primitive Art and Other Tales of Progress*, Berkeley, CA: University of California Press.

Evans, G. (1994a) 'Fair trade: cultural tourism and craft production in the third world,' in A. Seaton (ed.), *Tourism: The State of the Art*, Chichester: John Wiley and Sons.

Evans, G. (1994b) 'Whose culture is it anyway? Tourism in greater Mexico and indigena,' in A. Seaton (ed.), *Tourism: The State of the Art*, Chichester: John Wiley & Sons.

Evans, G. (2000) 'Contemporary crafts as souvenirs, artifacts and functional goods and their role in local economic diversification and cultural development,' in M. Hitchcock and K. Teague, K. (eds), *Souvenirs: The Material Culture of Tourism*, Aldershot: Ashgate.

Fawcett, C. (1998) 'The influence of L.M. Montgomery on Japan's view of Canada,' unpublished manuscript.

Feest, C. (1992) *Native Arts of North America*, London: Thames and Hudson.

Fforde, A. and De Vylder, S. (1996) *From Plan to Market: The Economic Transition in Vietnam*, Boulder, CO: Westview Press.

Florida, R.L. (2005) *The Flight of the Creative Class: Why America Is Losing the Competition for Talent*, New York: HarperBusiness.

Forbes, D., Hull, T.H., Marr, D.G. and Bogans, B. (eds) (1999) *Doi Moi: Vietnam's Renovation Policy and Performance*, Canberra: Department of Political and Social Change, Research School of Pacific Studies, Australian National University.

Foucault, M. (1967) 'Of other spaces,' *Architecture, Mouvement, Continuité (Architecture, Movement, Continuity)*, October 1984(5): 46–9. Online. Available HTTP: <http://foucault.info/documents/heteroTopia/foucault.heteroTopia.en.html> (accessed 7 January 1007).

Foucault, M. (1979) 'Truth and power: an interview with Alessandro Fontano and Pasquale Pasquino,' in M. Morris and P. Patton (eds), *Michel Foucault: Power/Truth/Strategy*, Sydney: Feral Publications.

Foucault, M. (1994) *The Order of Things: An Archaeology of the Human Sciences*, New York: Random House.

Franklin, A. (2003) *Tourism: An Introduction*, London: Sage Publications.

Franklin, A. (2004) 'Tourism as an ordering: towards a new ontology of tourism,' *Tourist Studies*, 4(3): 277–301.

Franklin, A. (2007) 'The problem with tourism theory,' in I. Ateljevic, A. Pritchard and N. Morgan (eds), *The Critical Turn in Tourism Studies: Innovative Research Methods*, Oxford: Elsevier.

Franklin, A. and Crang, M. (2001) 'The trouble with tourism and travel theory?,' *Tourist Studies*, 1(1): 5–22.

Ganai, N.A. (2007) 'Paradise on earth!,' *Greater Kashmir*, 5 January: 6.

Ganguly, S. (1996) 'Explaining the Kashmir insurgency: political mobilization and institutional decay,' *International Security*, 21(2): 76–107.

Gaur, B.L. (2002) *Understanding Ayurveda*, Jaipur: Publication Scheme.

Gebyar Wisata Program (2006) author's files.

Gell, A. (1998) *Art and Agency: An Anthropological Theory*, Oxford: Clarendon.

Ghimire, K.B. (ed.) (2001a) *The Native Tourist: Mass Tourism within Developing Countries*, London and Sterling, VA: Earthscan Publications Limited.

Ghimere, K.B. (2001b) 'The growth of national and regional tourism,' in K.B. Ghimire (ed.), *The Native Tourist: Mass Tourism within Developing Countries*, London and Sterling, VA: Earthscan Publications Limited.

Ghimire, K.B. and Li, Z. (2001) 'The economic role of national tourism in China,' in K.B. Ghimire (ed.), *The Native Tourist: Mass Tourism within Developing Countries*, London and Sterling, VA: Earthscan Publications Limited.

Ghosh, R.N., Siddique, M.A.B. and Gabbay, R. (eds) (2003) *Tourism and Economic Development: Case Studies from the Indian Ocean Region*, Aldershot: Ashgate.

Giese, K. (2004) 'Speaker's corner or virtual panopticon: discursive construction of Chinese identities online,' in F. Mengin (ed.), *Cyber China: Reshaping National Identities in the Age of Information*, New York: Palgrave Macmillan.

Gillespie, R. (2002) 'Architecture and power: a family planning clinic as a case study,' *Health and Place*, 8(3): 211–20.

Gladstone, D. (2006) *From Pilgrimage to Package Tour*, London: Routledge.

Globe Health Tours (2006) 'Hospital is the new destination,' *Globe Health Tours*, 22 April. Online. Available HTTP: <http://www.globehealthtours.com/medical_news/2006_04_16_archive.htm> (accessed 4 May 2006).

Go, F.M. and Jenkins, C.L. (eds) (1997) *Tourism and Economic Development in Asia and Australasia*, London: Cassell.

Goldstein-Goldini, O. (1997) *Packaged Japaneseness: Weddings, Business and Brides*, Honolulu: University of Hawaii Press.

Gole, S. (1993) 'The town of Srinagar in Indian maps,' *Environmental Design: Journal of the Islamic Environmental Design Research Centre*, 1–2: 156–63.

Gong, X. (1998) 'Household registration and the caste-like quality of peasant life,' in M. Dutton (ed.), *Street Life China*, Cambridge: Cambridge University Press.

Gorer, G. (1936) *Bali and Angkor, or, Looking at Life and Death*, London: Joseph.

Government of India, Ministry of Tourism and Culture (2002) *It's Time to Go for Domestic Tourism*. Online. Available HTTP: <http://www.tourismofindia.com/misc/time.htm> (accessed 26 October 2006).

Graburn, N. (ed.) (1976) *Ethnic and Tourist Arts*, Berkeley, CA: University of California Press.

Graburn, N. (1982) 'The dynamics of change in tourist arts,' *Cultural Survival Quarterly*, 6(4): 7–11.

Graburn, N. (1983) *To Pray, Pay and Play: The Cultural Structure of Japanese Domestic Tourism*, Aix-en-Provence: Centre des Hautes Etudes Touristiques (Les Cahiers du Tourisme).

Graburn, N. (1987) 'The evolution of tourist arts,' *Annals of Tourism Research*, 11(3): 393–420.

Graburn, N. (1989) 'Tourism: the sacred journey,' in V.L. Smith (ed.), *Hosts and Guests*, 2nd edn, Oxford: Blackwell.

Graburn, N. (1995a) 'The past in the present in Japan,' in R. Butler and D. Pearce (eds), *Change in Tourism, People, Places, Processes*, London: Routledge.

Graburn, N. (1995b) 'Tourism, modernity and nostalgia,' in A. Akbar and C. Shore (eds), *The Future of Anthropology: Its Relevance to the Contemporary World*, London: Athlone.

Graburn, N. (1997) 'Tourism and cultural development in East Asia and Oceania,' in S. Yamashita, H.D. Kadir and J.S. Eades (eds), *Tourism and Cultural Development in Asia and Oceania*, Bangi: Penerbit Universiti Kebangsaan Malaysia.

Gray, F. (2006) *Designing the Seaside: Architecture, Society and Nature*, London: Reaktion Books.

Greater Kashmir (2007) 'Listen to Ansari,' 27 November: 5.

Green Wilderness (2007) *Green Wilderness*. Online. Available HTTP: <http://www.lvye.org> (accessed 3 November 2007).

Greenblatt, S. (2004) *Cultural Mobility*. Online. Available HTTP: <www.fas.harvard.edu/curriculum-review/essays_pdf/Stephen_J_Greenblatt.pdf> (accessed 1 December 2005).

Greenlees, D. (2005) 'The subtle power of Chinese tourists,' *International Herald Tribune*, 6 October: 1, 8.

Greenwood, D. (1989) 'Culture by the pound: an anthropological perspective on tourism as cultural commoditization,' in V. Smith (ed.), *Hosts and Guests*, 2nd edn, Philadelphia, PA: University of Pennsylvania Press.

Grundy-Warr, C. and Perry, M. (2001) 'Tourism in an inter-state borderland: the case of the Indonesian-Singapore cooperation,' in P. Teo, T.C. Chang and K.C. Ho (eds), *Interconnected Worlds: Tourism in Southeast Asia*, Oxford: Pergamon.

Guizhou Tourism Bureau (2006) *Rural Tourism Plan 2006–2020 Compendium*, Guiyang: Guizhou Provincial Tourism Administration.

Guo Yingjie (2004) *Cultural Nationalism in Contemporary China*, London and New York: RoutledgeCurzon.

Gupta, A. and Ferguson, J. (1997) 'Beyond "culture": space, identity, and the politics of difference,' in A. Gupta and J. Ferguson (eds), *Culture, Power, Place: Explorations in Cultural Anthropology*, Durham, NC: Duke University Press.

Hall, C.M. (2001) 'Territorial economic integration and globalization,' in S. Wahab and C. Cooper (eds), *Tourism in the Age of Globalisation*, New York and London: Routledge.

Hall, C.M. and Page, S. (eds) (2000) *Tourism in South and South-east Asia*, Oxford: Butterworth-Heinemann.

Hall, C.M. and Ringer, G. (2000) 'Tourism in Cambodia, Laos and Myanmar: from terrorism to tourism?' in C.M. Hall and S.J. Page (eds), *Tourism in South and South-east Asia: Issues and Cases*, New York: Butterworth-Heinemann.

Hall, C.M. and Tucker, H. (eds) (2004) *Tourism and Postcolonialism: Contested Discourses, Identities and Representations*, London and New York: Routledge.

Hall, S. (1973) *A 'Reading' of Marx's 1857 Introduction to the Grundrisse*, Birmingham: Center for Cultural Studies.

Hamid, P.A. (2007) 'Dark entertainment in the Kashmir valley,' *Himal South Asian*, 20(7): 20–22.

Hamilton-Oerhl, A. (1998) 'Leisure parks in Japan,' in S. Linhart and S. Fruhstuck (eds), *The Culture of Japan as Seen through its Leisure*, New York: SUNY Press.

Han, S.-J. (1999) 'Asian values: an asset or a liability,' in Han S.-J. (ed.), *Changing Values in Asia: Their Impact on Governance and Development*, Japan Center for International Exchange, Tokyo.

Harrison, D. (1992) *Tourism and the Less Developed Countries*, London: Belhaven.

Harrison, J. (2003) *Being a Tourist: Finding Meaning in Pleasure Travel*, Vancouver: University of British Columbia Press.

Harrison, M. (1999) *Climates and Constitutions: Health, Race, Environment and British Imperialism in India 1600–1850*, London: Oxford University Press.

Harwit, E. and Clark, D. (2001) 'Shaping the internet in China: evolution of political control over network infrastructure and content,' *Asia Survey*, 41(3): 377–408.

He Guangwei (1992) 'Bianjing lüyou gongzuo xianzhuang yu fazhan' (speech at the First Border Tourism Work Conference, 16 August 1992); reprinted in *Zhongguo Lüyou Nianjian* (China Tourism Yearbook) (1993), Beijing: Zhongguo Lüyou Chubanshe.

He, Z.K. (1994) 'Shimin shehui gainian de lishi yanbian' (Historical evolution of the concept of civil society), *Chinese Social Science*, 5: 67–80.

Heeter, C. (2005) 'The messy clean-up of Dal Lake,' *AlterNet*. Online. Available HTTP: <http://www.alternet.org/envirohealth/23401/> (accessed 24 August 2006).

Hendry, J. (2000) *The Orient Strikes Back: A Global View of Cultural Display*, Oxford: Berg.

Hendry, J. (2005) 'Japan's global village: a view from the world of leisure,' in J. Robertson (ed.), *A Companion to the Anthropology of Japan*, Oxford: Blackwell.

Hepburn, S. (2002) 'Touristic forms of life in Nepal,' *Annals of Tourism Research*, 29(3): 611–30.

Hester, J.Y. (1999) 'Place making and the cultural politics of belonging in a mixed Korean Japanese local in Osaka, Japan,' unpublished PhD thesis, University of California at Berkeley, California.

Hillman, B. (2003) 'Paradise under construction: minorities, myths and modernity in northwest Yunnan,' *Asian Ethnicity*, 4(2): 176–88.

Hirsch, P. (ed.) (1993) *The Village in Perspective: Community and Locality in Rural Thailand*, Chiang Mai: Social Research Institute, Chiang Mai University.

Hitchcock, M. (1998) 'Tourism, Taman Mini and national identity,' *Indonesia and the Malay World*, 26(75): 124–35.

Hitchcock, M. (2000) 'Introduction,' in M. Hitchcock and K. Teague (eds), *Souvenirs: The Material Culture of Tourism*, Aldershot: Ashgate.

Hitchcock, M., King, V.T. and Parnwell, M.J.G. (eds) (1993) *Tourism in South-East Asia*, London: Routledge.

Hjalager, A. (2002) 'A typology of gastronomy tourism,' in A. Hjalager and G. Richards (eds), *Tourism and Gastronomy*, London: Routledge.

Hjalager, A. and Richards, G. (eds) (2002) *Tourism and Gastronomy*, London: Routledge.

Hollinshead, K. (1998) 'Tourism, hybridity, and ambiguity: the relevance of Bhabha's "third space" cultures,' *Journal of Leisure Research*, 30(1): 121–56.

Hollinshead, K. (2004) 'Tourism and new sense: worldmaking and the enunciative value of tourism,' in C.M. Hall and H. Tucker (eds), *Tourism and Postcolonialism: Contested Discourses, Identities and Representations*, London: Routledge.

Holt, C. (1967) *Art in Indonesia: Continuities and Change*, Ithaca, NY: Cornell University Press.

Holtzman, J.D. (2006) 'Food and memory,' *Annual Review of Anthropology*, 35: 361–78.

Hom Cary, S. (2004) 'The tourist moment,' *Annals of Tourism Research*, 31(1): 61–77.

Hong Kong Special Administrative Region Government (HKSARG) (2005a) 'Safety tips for enjoying "*poon choi*",' *Government Press Release*, 15 January.

Hong Kong Special Administrative Region Government (HKSARG) (2005b) 'Eat safely during Lunar New Year,' *Government Press Release*, 5 February.

Hook, D. and Vrdoljak, M. (2002) 'Gated communities, heterotopia and a "rights" of privilege: a heteropology of the South African security-park,' *Geoforum*, 33(2): 195–219.

Howe, L. (2005) *The Changing World of Bali: Religion, Society and Tourism*, London: Routledge.

Huang, P. and Zhao, S. (2005) 'Internal migration in China: linking it to development,' paper presented at the Regional Conference on Migration and Development in Asia, Lanzhou, China, 14–16 March.

Huber, T. (2006) 'The *skor lam* and the long march: notes on the transformation of Tibetan ritual territory in southern Amdo in the context of Chinese developments,' *Journal of the International Association of Tibetan Studies*, 2(August): 1–42.

Hughes, C. and Wacker, G. (ed.) (2003) *China and the Internet: Politics of the Digital Leap Forward*, London: RoutledgeCurzon.

Huis Ten Bosch (2000) *New Amsterdam in Nagasaki, Japan: Huis Ten Bosch Resort and Theme Park*. Online. Available HTTP: <www.HuistenBosch.co.jp> (access date unknown).

India Today (2006) Advertisement issued by the Jammu and Kashmir Tourism Department, 25 September: 9.

Inglis, F. (2000) *The Delicious History of the Holiday*, London: Routledge.

Ioannides, D. and Debbage, K. (1997) 'Post-Fordism and flexibility: the travel industry polyglot,' *Tourism Management*, 18(4): 229–41.

Ishimori, S. (1995) 'Tourism and religion: from the perspective of comparative civilization,' in T. Umesao *et al.* (eds), *Japanese Civilization in the Modern World*, IX Tourism Senri Ethnological Series, no. 38: 11–24, Suita: National Museum of Ethnology.

Isin, E.F. and Wood, P.K. (1999) *Citizenship and Identity*, London: Sage.

Ivy, M. (1995) *Discourses of the Vanishing, Modernity, Phantasm, Japan*, Chicago: University of Chicago Press.

Jackson, R. (2005) 'Converging cultures, converging gazes: contextualizing perspectives,' in D. Crouch, R. Jackson and F. Thompson (eds), *The Media and the Tourist Imagination: Converging Cultures*, New York: Routledge.

Jacobs, J. (1996) *Edge of Empire: Postcolonialism and the City*, London: Routledge.

Jacobs, J. (2002) 'From edge of empire: postcolonialism and the city,' in G. Bridge and S. Watson (eds), *The Blackwell City Reader*, Malden, MA: Blackwell.

Jafari, J. (2003) 'Research and scholarship: the basis of tourism education,' *Annals of Tourism Research*, 14(1): 6–16.

Jain, P. (2004) *Asia, Asian Values and Australia*, Asia Pacific Papers No. 3, Asia Pacific Research Centre, Kobe Gakuin University, Japan.

Jakarta Post (2003) 'Local leaders to boost tourism,' 25 October. Online. Available HTTP: http://www.thejakartapost.com/yesterdaydetail.asp?fileid=20031025.P12>. (accessed 12 August 2006).

Jakle, J. (1985) *The Tourist: Travel in Twentieth Century America*, Lincoln, NB: University of Nebraska Press.

Japan Travel Bureau (1999) *Hitori Yuki no Kyushyu* (*One Person's Going to Kyushu*), Tokyo: Japan Travel Bureau.

Jeffrey, I. (1981) *Photography: A Concise History*, London: Thames & Hudson.

Jeffrey, R. (2003) *Politics, Women and Well-being: How Kerala Became a 'Model,'* New Delhi: Oxford University Press.

Jeong, S. and Santos, C.A. (2004) 'Cultural politics and contested place identity,' *Annals of Tourism Research*, 31(3): 640–56.

Jin Hua (1994) 'Cong wulingyuan kan ziran fengjing kaifaqu de quyu shehui xiaoying' (Looking at the regional social impact of natural scenery development areas from Wulingyuan), *Jingji Dili/Economic Geography*, 14(4): 89–92.

Johnson, K. (2002) 'Catching a cure in Sri Lanka: healing holidays in old Ceylon,' *Time International*, 159(13): 9.

Jordan, M. (1999) 'Indian urbanites revive Ayurvedic Medicine,' *Wall Street Journal*, 27 December: 1.

Kahn, J.S. (1997) 'Culturalizing Malaysia: globalism, tourism, heritage, and the city in Georgetown,' in M. Picard and R.E. Wood (eds), *Tourism, Ethnicity, and the State in Asian and Pacific Societies*, Honolulu: University of Hawaii Press.

Kam Wing Chan and Li Zhang (1999) 'The Hukou system and rural-urban migration in China: processes and change,' *China Quarterly* 160(December): 818–56.

Kangwon Provincial Government Tourism Policy Department (2006a) 'Kangwŏndo, 2005 nyŏn uri torŭl ch'anŭn kwan'gwanggaek 10.2 per cent chŭngga' (Kangwon Province, number of tourists visiting our province sees 10.2 per cent hike in 2005), 7 March 2006, Kangwon Province: Tourism Policy Department, Republic of Korea.

Kangwon Provincial Government Tourism Policy Department (2006b) '2005 nyŏn kwan'gwangtonghyang' (Tourism trends in 2005), 7 March 2006, Kangwon Province: Tourism Policy Department, Republic of Korea.

Karla, V.S., Kaur, R. and Hutnyk, J. (2005) *Disapora and Hybridity*, London: Sage.

Keane, J. (1988) *Civil Society: Old Images, New Visions*, Cambridge: Polity Press.

Keating, P. (2000) *Engagement: Australia Faces the Asia-Pacific*, Sydney: Macmillan.

Keenan, B. (2006) *Travels in Kashmir: A Popular History of Its People, Places, and Crafts*, Delhi: Permanent Black.

Kelly, W.W. (1986) 'Rationalization and nostalgia: cultural dynamics of new middle class Japan,' *American Ethnologist*, 13(4): 603–18.

Kelner, S. (2001) 'Narrative construction of authenticity in pilgrimage touring,' paper presented at the 96th Annual Meeting of the Association of the American Sociological Association, Anaheim, California, 19 August.

Keyes, C.F. (1975) 'Buddhist pilgrimage centers and the twelve-year cycle: Northern Thai moral order in space and time,' *History of Religions*, 15(1): 71–89.

Keyes, C.F. (1984) 'Mother or mistress but never a monk: Buddhist notions of female gender in rural Thailand,' *American Ethnologist*, 11(2): 223–41.

Keyes, C.F. (1995) *The Golden Peninsula: Culture and Adaptation in Mainland Southeast Asia*, Honolulu: University of Hawaii Press.

Khan, M.I. (2007) *History of Srinagar, 1846–1947: A Study in Socio-Cultural Change*, Srinagar: Gulshan Books.

Kim, H.G. and Richardson, S.L. (2003) 'Motion picture impacts on destination images,' *Annals of Tourism Research*, 30(1): 216–37.

Kim, H.R. (2005) 'Hur Jin-ho kamtokŭi <Oechul> (2)' (Director Hur Jin-ho's <April Snow (Part 2)>), *cine21*. Online. Available HTTP: <http://www.cine21.com/Index/magazine.php?mag_id=28425> (accessed 1 February 2005).

Kim, S.K. (2002) *Yŏnghwa sok kamdongŭl ch'acha ttŏnanŭn sŭk'ŭrin t'uŏ (Screen Tours: In Search of the Emotions in Film)*, Seoul: Yŏksanet.

Kim, S.Y. (2005) 'Kŭdŭli oech'ŭlhaeya haettŏn iyu' (Why they had to go on an outing), *cine21*. Online. Available HTTP: <http://www.cine21.com/Index/magazine.php?mag_id=33722> (accessed 28 September 2005).

King, A.D. (1990) *Urbanism, Colonialism and the World Economy*, London and New York: Routledge.

King, A.D. (2003) 'Cultures and spaces of postcolonial knowledges,' in K. Anderson, M. Domosh, S. Pile and N. Thrift (eds), *Handbook of Cultural Geography*, London: Sage.

Kipp, R. (1993) *Dissociated Identities: Ethnicity, Religion, and Class in an Indonesian Society*, Ann Arbor, MI: University of Michigan Press.

Kitamura, K. (2006) 'For curious Japanese: nibbles of foreign cultures,' *New York Times*, 30 July: 3 (Travel Section).

Kleinen, J. (ed.) (2001) *Vietnamese Society in Transition: The Daily Politics of Reform and Change*, Amsterdam: Het Spinhuis.

Knight, J. (1993) 'Rural Kokusaika: foreign motifs and village revival in Japan,' *Japan Forum*, 5(2): 203–16.

Kolanad, G. (2005) *Cultureshock! A Survival Guide to Customs and Etiquette in India*, Singapore: Marshall Cavendish.

Kolås, Å. (2004) 'Tourism and the making of place in Shangri-La,' *Tourism Geographies*, 6(3): 262–78.

Kolås, Å. (2006) 'Ethnic tourism in Shangri-La: representations of place and Tibetan identity,' unpublished Dr. Polit. thesis, University of Oslo, Sweden.

Krisadawan Honladarom (2000) 'Competing discourses on hill tribes: media representation of ethnic minorities in Thailand,' *Journal of Humanities*, 3(1): 1–19.

Kumar, K. (1993) 'Civil society: an inquiry into the usefulness of a historical term,' *British Journal of Sociology*, 44(3): 375–95.

Kumar, S. (1999) 'Traditional Indian knowledge for sale,' *Lancet*, 353(9159): 1164.

Ku Ming-chun (2006) 'The construction of the self in the diversified references of pastness: domestic tourists in China's heritage tourism,' paper presented at the conference 'Of Asian Origin: rethinking tourism in contemporary Asia,' Singapore, 7–9 September.

Kurlantzick, J. (2006) 'Tibet now,' *New York Times*, 10 December. Online. Available HTTP: http://travel.nytimes.com/2006/12/10/travel/10Tibet.html (accessed 23 January 2007).

Kurup, P.N.V. (2004) 'Ayurveda: a potential global medical system,' in L.C. Mishra (ed.), *Scientific Basis for Ayurvedic Therapies*, Boca Rotan, FL: CRC Press.

Lagerkvist, J. (2006) 'In the crossfire of demands: Chinese news portals between propaganda and the public,' in J. Damm and S. Thomas (eds), *Chinese Cyberspaces: Technological Changes and Political Effects*, London: Routledge.

Lai, P.H. and Nepal, S.K. (2006) 'Local perspectives of ecotourism development in Tawushan Nature Reserve, Taiwan,' *Tourism Management*, 27(6): 1117–129.

Lanfant, M.F. (1995) 'Introduction,' in M.F. Lanfant, J.B. Allcock and E.M. Bruner (eds), *International Tourism: Identity and Change*, London: Sage.

Lanfant, M.F., Allcock, J.B. and Bruner, E.M. (eds) (1995) *International Tourism: Identity and Change*, London: Sage.

Langford, J. (2002) *Fluent Bodies: Ayurvedic Remedies for Postcolonial Imbalance*, Durham, NC: Duke University Press.

Lao National Tourism Administration (2006) *2005 Statistical Report on Tourism in Laos*, Vientiane: Lao National Tourism Administration.

Lao National Tourism Administration (2007) *2006 Statistical Report on Tourism in Laos*, Vientiane: Lao National Tourism Administration.

Larsen, J. (2001) 'Touristic snapshot photography,' paper presented to the Department of Geography, Roskilde University, Denmark, date unavailable.

Lash, S. and Urry, J. (1987) *The End of Organized Capitalism*, Madison, WI: University of Wisconsin Press.

Lau, S.K. and Kuan, H.C. (1988) *The Ethos of the Hong Kong Chinese*, Hong Kong: Chinese University Press.

Law, K.Y. and Lee, K.M. (2004) 'Citizenship, economy and social exclusion of mainland Chinese immigrants in Hong Kong,' *Journal of Contemporary Asia*, 36(2): 217–42.

Law, L. (2000) *Sex Work in Southeast Asia: The Place of Desire in a Time of AIDS*, London and New York: Routledge.

Laxson, J. (1991) 'How "we" see "them": tourism and Native Americans,' *Annals of Tourism Research*, 18(3): 365–91.

Lea, J. (1988) *Tourism and Development in the Third World*, London and New York: Routledge.

Lebra, T. (1993) *Above the Clouds: Status Culture of the Modern Japanese Nobility*, Berkeley, CA: University of California Press.

Leheny, D. (1995) 'A political economy of Asian sex tourism,' *Annals of Tourism Research*, 22(2): 367–84.

Leipziger, D.M. (1992) *Awakening the Market: Vietnam's Economic Transition*, Washington, DC: World Bank.

Lencek, L. and Bosker, G. (1998) *The Beach: The History of Paradise on Earth*, London: Secker and Warburg.

Lennon, J. and Foley, M. (2000) *Dark Tourism: The Attraction of Death and Disaster*, London: Continuum.

Leong, W.T. (1989) 'Culture and the state: manufacturing traditions for tourism,' *Critical Studies in Mass Communication*, 6(4): 355–75.

Leslie, D. (2005) 'Creative cities?,' *Geoforum*, 36(4): 403–5.

Leur, J.C. (1967) *Indonesian Trade and Society: Essays in Asian Social and Economic History*, The Hague: W. Van Hoeve Publishers.

Lévi-Strauss, C. ([1957] trans. 1972) *Tristes Tropiques*, trans. J. Russell, New York: Atheneum.

Lew, A. (2000) 'China: a growth engine for Asian tourism,' in M. Hall and S. Page (eds), *Tourism in South and Southeast Asia: Issues and Cases*, Oxford: Butterworth-Heinemann.

Lew, A. and Wong, A. (2005) 'Existential tourism and the homeland: the overseas Chinese experience,' in C. Cartier and A. Lew (eds), *Seductions of Place: Geographical Perspectives on Globalization and Touristed Landscapes*, London and New York: Routledge.

Lew, A. and Yu, L. (eds) (1995) *Tourism in China: Geographic, Political, and Economic Perspectives*, Boulder, CO: Westview Press.

Lew, A., Yu, L., Ap, J. and Zhang, G. (eds) (2003) *Tourism in China*, New York: The Haworth Hospitality Press.

Li, Z. (2003) 'Lun qian fada diqu lüyouqu de shehui xinli xiandaihua' (On the modernization of the social psyche in tourist areas of late developing regions), *Jihua yu shichang tansuo: A Journal on Planning and Market*, 11: 48–50.

Li, Z. (2005) 'Introduction to the work of the rural tourism demonstration project area of the Bala River valley in Guizhou,' in S. Yang (ed.), *Rural Tourism: A Strategy for Poverty Alleviation*, Guiyang: Guizhou Renmin Publishing Press.

Liang, Z.P. (2001) ' "Social space", "non-governmental society", and civil society: a re-examination of the civil society concept (*'minjian,' 'minjian shehui'* and civil society: civil society *gainian zai tantao*),' *Contemporary China Studies*, 72(1): 63–89.

Lim, F. (2006) ' "Donkey friends" in China: the internet, civil society, and the emergence of the Chinese backpacker community,' paper presented at the conference 'Of Asian Origin: rethinking tourism in contemporary Asia,' Singapore, 7–9 September.

Linnekin, J. (1997) 'Consuming cultures: tourism and the commoditization of cultural identity in the island Pacific,' in R. Wood and M. Picard (eds), *Tourism, Ethnicity, and the State in Asian and Pacific Societies*, Honolulu: University of Hawaii Press.

Liu Fei (1998) 'Wo guo guonei lüyouye fazhan chutan' (Our domestic tourism business: a preliminary discussion), *Beijing Shangxueyuan Xuebao*, 2: 61–4.

Liu, X. (2000) *In One's Own Shadow*, Berkeley, CA: University of California Press.

Lloyd, K. (2003) 'Contesting control in transitional Vietnam: the development and regulation of traveler cafes in Hanoi and Ho Chi Minh city,' *Tourism Geographies*, 5(3): 350–66.

Lofgren, O. (2002) *On Holiday: A History of Vacationing*, Berkeley, CA: University of California Press.

Loker-Murphy, L. and Pearce, P. (1995) 'Youth budget travelers: backpackers in Australia,' *Annals of Tourism Research*, 22(4): 819–43.

Luong, H.V. (2003) 'Wealth, power, and inequality: global market, the state, and local sociocultural dynamics,' in H.V. Luong (ed.), *Postwar Vietnam: Dynamics of a Transforming Society*, Singapore: Institute of Southeast Asian Studies and Rowman & Littlefield Publishers.

Ma, B. and Kou, M. (2006) 'Zhongguo chujing luyou fazhan ji qi yingxiang de chubu yanjiu' (A preliminary study of the development and impact of outbound Chinese tourism), *Tourism Tribune*, 21(7): 24–8.

Ma Huidi (2004a) *Zouxiang renwen guanhuai de xiuxian jingji (Toward a Leisure Economy with Humanistic Concerns)*, Beijing: Zhongguo Jingji Chubanshe.

Ma Huidi (2004b) *Xiuxian: renlei meili de jingshen jiayuan (Leisure: The Making of a Beautiful Home for the Human Spirit)*, Beijing: Zhongguo Jingji Chubanshe.

Ma Ping (2001) 'Xibu da kaifa dui dangdi minzu guanxi de yingxiang ji duice' (The impact of the Great Western Development project on local ethnic relations and ways of dealing with it), *Minzu Wenti Yanjiu*, 5: 37–42.

Ma, Q.S. (2006) *Non-Governmental Organizations in Contemporary China: Paving the Way to Civil Society?*, London and New York: Routledge.

MacCannell, D. (1973) 'Staged authenticity: arrangement of social space in tourist settings,' *American Journal of Sociology*, 79(3): 589–603.

MacCannell, D. (1976) *The Tourist: A New Theory of the Leisure Class*, New York: Schocken Books.

MacCannell, D. (1992) *Empty Meeting Grounds: The Tourist Papers*, New York: Routledge.

MacCannell, D. (1999) *The Tourist: A New Theory of the Leisure Class*, 2nd edn, Berkeley, CA: University of California Press.

MacCormick, N. (1996) 'Liberalism, nationalism and the postsovereign state,' *Political Studies*, 44(3): 553–67.

MacDonald, S. (2006) 'Undesirable heritage: fascist material culture and historical consciousness in Nuremberg,' *International Journal of Heritage Studies*, 12(1): 9–28.

Mahapatra, R. (2003) 'Peace isn't elusive,' *Down to Earth*, 31 May: 27–36.

Malam, L. (2004) 'Performing masculinity on the Thai beach scene,' *Tourism Geographies*, 6(4): 455–71.

Mars, G. and Mars, V. (2000) ' "Souvenir-gifts" as tokens of filial esteem: the meanings of Blackpool,' in M. Hitchcock and K. Teague (eds), *Souvenirs: The Material Culture of Tourism*, Aldershot: Ashgate.

Martinez, E. and Garcia, A. (1996) *What is Neoliberalism? A Brief Definition for Activists.* Online. Available HTTP: <http://www.corpwatch.org/article.php?id=376> (accessed 27 October 2006).

Massumi, B. (1996) 'The autonomy of affect,' in P. Patton (ed.), *Deleuze: A Critical Reader*, Oxford: Blackwell Publishers.

Massumi, B. (2002) *Parables for the Virtual: Movement, Affect, Sensation*, Durham, NC: Duke University Press.

Mathew, J. (2004) 'In search of a healthy holiday,' *Sanghamam Magazine on Ayurveda The Science of Life*, 1(36–40): 47–8.

Matthews, H.G. and Richter, L.K. (1991) 'Political science and tourism,' *Annals of Tourism Research*, 18(1): 120–35.

McGee, T. (1994) 'Foreword,' in M. Askew and W.S. Logan (eds), *Cultural Identity and Urban Change in Southeast Asia: Interpretative Essays*, Geelong, Victoria: Deekin University Press.

McIntosh, A.J. and Siggs, A. (2005) 'An exploration of the experiential nature of boutique accommodation,' *Journal of Travel Research*, 44(1): 74–81.

McNaughton, D. (2006) 'The "host" as uninvited "guest": hospitality, violence and tourism,' *Annals of Tourism Research*, 33(3): 645–65.

McPhee, C. (1946) *A House in Bali*, New York: J. Day Co.

Meethan, K. (2001) *Tourism in Global Society*, Basingstoke: Palgrave.

Menon, S. (2004) *No Place to Go: Stories of Hope and Despair from India's Ailing Health Sector*, New Delhi: Penguin Books.

Messer, E. (1984) 'Anthropological perspectives on diet,' *Annual Review of Anthropology*, 13: 205–49.

Messerli, H. and Oyama, Y. (2004) *Health and Wellness Tourism, Travel and Tourism Analyst*, London: Mintel International Group.

Michaud, J. and Turner, S. (2006) 'Contending visions of a hill-station in Vietnam,' *Annals of Tourism Research*, 33(3): 785–808.

Milne, S. and Ateljevic, I. (2001) 'Tourism, economic development and the global-local nexus: theory embracing complexity,' *Tourism Geographies*, 3(4): 369–93.

Milner, A. (1999) 'What's happened to Asian values?,' in D. Goodman and G. Segal (eds), *Beyond the Asia Crisis*, London: Routledge.

Ministry of Culture and Tourism (2006) *2005 nyŏn munhwa chŏngch'aek baeksŏ (2005 Cultural Policy White Papers)*, Seoul: Ministry of Culture and Tourism, Republic of Korea.

Ministry of Information, Communication and the Arts (2002) *Investing in Singapore's Cultural Capital.* Online. Available HTTP: <http://app.mti.gov.sg/data/pages/507/doc/ERC_SVS_CRE_Annex1.1(a).pdf> (accessed 13 July 2006).

Ministry of Tourism (2000) *Cambodia Tourism Statistical Report 2000*, Phnom Penh: Ministry of Tourism, Royal Government of Cambodia.

Ministry of Tourism (2003) *Tourism Statistical Report Year Book 2003*, Phnom Penh: Ministry of Tourism, Royal Government of Cambodia.

Mintz, S.W. and Du Bois, C.M. (2002) 'The anthropology of food and eating,' *Annual Review of Anthropology*, 30: 99–119.

Mitchell, D. (2002) 'Cultural landscapes: the dialectical landscape – recent landscape research in human geography,' *Progress in Human Geography*, 26(3): 381–9.

Mohamad, M. (1999) *A New Deal for Asia*, Selang Darul Ehsan: Pelanduk Publications.

Morales-Moreno, I. (2004) 'Postsovereign governance in a globalizing and fragmenting world: the case of Mexico,' *Review of Policy Research*, 21(1): 107–17.

Morand, P. (1932) 'Bali, or paradise regained,' *Vanity Fair*, 38(3): 40–1, 68.

Morris, R. (2000) *In the Place of Origins: Modernity and Its Mediums in Northern Thailand*, Durham, NC: Duke University Press.

Mowforth, M. and Munt, I. (1998) *Tourism and Sustainability: New Tourism in the Third World*, London: Routledge.

Muan, I. (2001) 'Citing Angkor: the "Cambodian Arts" in the age of restoration 1918–2000,' unpublished PhD thesis, Columbia University, New York.

Mudur, G. (2004) 'Hospitals in India woo foreign patients,' *British Medical Journal*, 328(5 June): 1338.

Mueggler, E. (2001) *The Age of Wild Ghosts: Memory, Violence, and Place in Southwest China*, Berkeley, CA: University of California Press.

Murphy, L. (2001) 'Exploring social interactions of backpackers,' *Annals of Tourism Research*, 28(1): 50–67.

Murphy, R. (2002) *How Migrant Labour is Changing Rural China*, Cambridge: Cambridge University Press.

Mushtaq, S. (2007) 'Braving violence, Kashmir's lone cinema plays on,' *AlertNet*. Online. Available HTTP: <http://www.alertnet.org/thenews/newsdesk/SP207033.htm> (accessed 8 September 2007).

Muzaini, H. (2006) 'Backpacking Southeast Asia: strategies of "looking local",' *Annals of Tourism Research*, 33(1): 144–61.

Muzaini, H. and Yeoh, B.S.A. (2005) 'War landscapes as "battlefields" of collective memories: "reading" reflections at Bukit Chandu, Singapore,' *Cultural Geographies*, 12(3): 345–65.

Nabae, K. (2003) 'The health care system in Kerala: its past accomplishments and new challenges,' *Journal of National Institutes of Public Health*, 52(2): 140–5.

Nagai, A. (2001) 'Getting away: secret religious history reduced to a memory,' *Yomiuri Shimbun*, 16 June: 10.

Nair, S. (2001) 'Social history of Western medical practice in Travancore: an inquiry into administrative process,' in D. Kumar (ed.), *Disease and Medicine in India: A Historical Overview*, New Delhi: Tulika Books.

Nankervis, A. (2000) 'Dreams and realities: vulnerability and the tourism industry in Southeast Asia,' in K.S. Chon (ed.), *Tourism in Southeast Asia: A New Direction*, New York: Haworth Press.

Nash, C. (2002) 'Cultural geography: postcolonial cultural geographies,' *Progress in Human Geography*, 26(2): 219–30.

National Bureau of Statistics (2005) *Statistics of Domestic Tourism*. Online. Available HTTP: <http://www.stats.gov.cn/tjsj/ndsj/2005/html/S1907E.HTM> (accessed 3 July 2007).

National Tourism Administration (NTA) (2004) *Yearbook of China Tourism Statistics 2004*, Beijing: NTA.

National Tourism Administration (NTA) (2005) *Zhongguo Lüyou Nianjian (China Tourism Yearbook)*, Beijing: NTA.

Navlakha, G. (2006) 'Pilgrim's progress causes regression,' *Economic and Political Weekly*, 41(27 & 28): 2975–7.

Navlakha, G. (2007) 'State of Jammu and Kashmir's economy,' *Economic and Political Weekly*, 42(40): 4034–8.

Neogi, S. (2004) 'Ayurvedic spas of Kerala,' *Sanghamam Magazine on Ayurveda, The Science of Life*, 1(2): 11–14.

Nestle, M. (2002) *Food Politics: How the Food Industry Influences Nutrition and Health*, Berkeley, CA: University of California Press.

Nguyen, M.H. (2001) *Buon Ban Qua Ben Gioi Viet-Trung (Vietnam-China Border Trade: History, Present Situation, and Future Prospects)*, Hanoi: Social Science Publishers.

Nichter, M. (1996a) 'Popular perceptions of medicine: a South Indian case study,' in M. Nichter and M. Nichter (eds), *Anthropology and International Health: Asian Case Studies*, Cornwall: Gordon and Breach.

Nichter, M. (1996b) 'Paying for what ails you: sociocultural issues influencing the ways and means of therapy payment in South India,' in M. Nichter and M. Nichter (eds), *Anthropology and International Health: Asian Case Studies*, Cornwall: Gordon and Breach.

Noguchi, P. (1994) 'Savor slowly: Ekiben – the fast food of the high-speed Japan,' *Ethnology*, 33(4): 317–40.

Norbu Jamyang (2001) 'Behind the lost horizon,' in T. Dodin and H. Rather (eds), *Imagining Tibet*, Boston: Wisdom Publications.

Nordstrom, C. (1989) 'Ayurveda: a multilectic interpretation,' *Social Science and Medicine*, 28(9): 963–70.

Notar, B. (2007) *Displacing Desire: Travel and Popular Culture in China*, Honolulu: University of Hawaii Press.

Noy, C. (2004) 'This trip really changed me: backpackers' narratives of self-change,' *Annals of Tourism Research*, 31(1): 78–102.

Nugaido (1997) *Watashi no Nihon* (My Japan), Okinawa: Nugaido.

Nyíri, P. (2005a) 'The "new migrant": state and market constructions of modernity and patriotism,' in P. Nyíri and J. Breidenbach (eds), *China Inside Out*, Budapest: CEU Press.

Nyíri, P. (2005b) 'Scenic spot Europe: Chinese travelers on the Western periphery,' *EspaceTemps.net*. Online. Available HTTP: <www.espacestemps.net/document1224.html> (accessed 25 March 2005).

Nyíri, P. (2006) *Scenic Spots: Chinese Tourism, Cultural Authority and the State*, Seattle: University of Washington Press.

Oakes, T. (1997) 'Ethnic tourism in rural Guizhou: sense of place and the commerce of authenticity,' in R. Wood and M. Picard (eds), *Tourism, Ethnicity, and the State in Asian and Pacific Societies*, Honolulu: University of Hawaii Press.

Oakes, T. (1998) *Tourism and Modernity in China*, London: Routledge.

Oakes, T. (1999) 'Selling Guizhou: cultural development in an era of marketization,' in H. Hendrischke and C.Y. Feng (eds), *The Political Economy of China's Provinces: Comparative and Competitive Advantage*, New York: Routledge.

Ohnuki-Tierney, E. (1993) *Rice as Self*, Princeton, NJ: Princeton University Press.

Ong, A. (1996) 'Anthropology, China and modernities,' in H.L. Moore (ed.), *The Future of Anthropological Knowledge*, London: Routledge.

Ong, A. (1999) *Flexible Citizenship: The Cultural Logics of Transnationality*, Durham, NC: Duke University Press.

Ooi, C.S. (2002) *Cultural Tourism and Tourism Cultures: The Business of Mediating Experiences in Copenhagen and Singapore*, Copenhagen: Copenhagen Business School.

Oppermann, M. (1997) 'The future of tourism in the Pacific Rim,' in M. Oppermann (ed.), *Pacific Rim Tourism*, Oxon: CAB International.

Osborne, P. (2000) *Travelling Light: Photography, Travel and Visual Culture*, Manchester: Manchester University Press.

Osella, F. and Osella, C. (2000) *Social Mobility in Kerala: Modernity and Identity in Conflict*, London: Pluto Press.

Ospina, G.A. (2006) 'War and ecotourism in the national parks of Colombia: some reflections on the public risk and adventure,' *International Journal of Tourism Research*, 8(3): 241–46.

Outlook Traveller (2003) Advertisement issued by the Jammu and Kashmir Tourism Department, September: 49.

Pachanee, C. and Wibulpolprasert, S. (2006) 'Incoherent policies on universal coverage of health insurance and promotion of international trade in health services in Thailand,' *Health Policy and Planning*, 21(4): 310–18.

Pacific Asia Tourism Association (PATA) (2003) *Annual Statistical Report 2002*, Bangkok: PATA.

Pacific Asia Tourism Association (PATA) (2007a) *Join PATA. Serious About the Travel and Tourism Industry in Asia Pacific?* Online. Available HTTP: <http://www.pata.org/patasite/index.php?id=13> (accessed 13 November 2007).

Pacific Asia Tourism Association (PATA) (2007b) *About Asia Pacific*. Online. Available HTTP: <http://www.pata.org/patasite/index.php?id=36> (accessed 13 November 2007).

Papoulias, C. (2004) 'Homi K. Bhabha,' in P. Hubbard, R. Kitchin and G. Valentine (eds), *Key Thinkers on Space and Place*, London: Sage Publications.

Park, S.O. (2003) 'Economic spaces in the Pacific Rim: a paradigm shift and new dynamics,' *Papers in Regional Science*, 82(2): 223–47.

Parr, M. (1995) *The Small World*, London: Magnum.

Patwardhan, B., Warude, D., Pushpangdan, P. and Bhatt, N. (2005) 'Ayurveda and traditional Chinese medicine: a comparative overview,' *eCAM*, 2(4): 465–73.

Peleggi, M. (2002) *The Politics of Ruins and the Business of Nostalgia*, Bangkok: White Lotus.

Peleggi, M. (2005) 'Consuming colonial nostalgia: the monumentalisation of historic hotels in urban southeast Asia,' *Asia Pacific Viewpoint*, 46(3): 255–65.

Pelley, P. (2002) *Postcolonial Vietnam: New Histories of the National Past*, Durham, NC: Duke University Press.

People's Daily Online (2003) 'Chinese tourists' unsocial behavior sparks concern at home,' 22 September. Online. Available HTTP: <http://English.peopledaily.com.cn> (accessed 6 September 2006).

Petersen, Y.Y. (1995) 'The Chinese landscape as a tourist attraction: image and reality,' in A. Lew and L. Yu (eds), *Tourism in China: Geographic, Political, and Economic Perspectives*, Boulder, CO: Westview Press.

Petruccioli, A. (1991) 'Gardens and religious topography in Kashmir,' *Environmental Design: Journal of the Islamic Environmental Design Research Centre*, 1–2: 64–73.

Phillips, L. (2006) 'Food and globalization,' *Annual Review of Anthropology*, 35: 37–57.

Picard, M. (1990) '"Cultural tourism" in Bali: cultural performance as tourist attraction,' *Indonesia*, 49: 37–74.

Picard, M. (1996a) *Bali: Cultural Tourism and Touristic Culture*, Singapore: Archipelago Press.

Picard, M. (1996b) 'Dance and drama in Bali: the making of an Indonesian art form,' in A. Vickers (ed.), *Being Modern in Bali: Image and Change*, New Haven, CT: Yale University Southeast Asian Studies.

Picard, M. (1997) 'Cultural tourism, nation-building and regional culture: the making of a Balinese identity,' in M. Picard and R.E. Wood (eds), *Tourism, Ethnicity and the State in Asian and Pacific Societies*, Honolulu: University of Hawaii Press.

Picard, M. (1999) 'The discourse of kebalian: transcultural constructions of Balinese identity,' in R. Rubinstein and L. Connor, (eds), *Staying Local in the Global Village: Bali in the Twentieth Century*, Honolulu: University of Hawaii Press.

Picard, M. and Wood, R. (eds) (1997) *Tourism, Ethnicity and the State in Asian and Pacific Societies*, Honolulu: University of Hawaii Press.

Poon, A. (1990) 'Competitive strategies for a "new tourism",' in C.P. Cooper (ed.), *Progress in Tourism, Recreation and Hospitality Management*, vol. 1, London: Belhaven Press.

Poon, A. (1993) *Tourism, Technology and Competitive Strategies*, Wallingford: CABI.

Potala Palace Management Office (2005) *Periodic Report on the Application of the World Heritage Convention, Lhasa, 5 September 2002*. Online. Available HTTP: <http://whc.unesco.org/archive/periodicreporting/cycle01/section2/707.pdf> (accessed 7 September 2005).

Powell, A.E. (1921) *Where the Strange Trails Go Down: Sulu, Borneo, Celebes, Bali, Java, Sumatra, Straits Settlements, Malay States, Siam, Cambodia, Annam, Cochin-China*, New York: C. Scribner's Sons.

Prasit Leepreecha (2004) 'Ntoo xeeb: cultural redefinition for forest conservation among the Hmong in Thailand,' in N. Tapp, J. Michaud, C. Culas and G.Y. Lee (eds), *Hmong/Miao in Asia*, Chiang Mai: Silkworm Books.

Pritchard, A. and Morgan, N. (2006) 'Hotel Babylon? Exploring hotels as liminal sites of transition and transgression,' *Tourism Management*, 27(5): 762–72.

Pritchard, A. and Morgan, N. (2007) 'De-centring tourism's intellectual universe, or traversing the dialogue between change and tradition,' in I. Ateljevic, A. Pritchard and N. Morgan (eds), *The Critical Turn in Tourism Studies: Innovative Research Methods*, Oxford: Elsevier.

Prunieres, H. (1931) 'Native Balinese music in Paris,' *The New York Times*, 27 September: 8x.

Purvis, A. (2001) 'Is it a hotel? Is it a trendy bar? No, it's a hospital,' *Guardian*, 5 August: 14–15.

Qiao, Y. (1995) 'Domestic tourism in China: policies and development,' in A. Lew and L. Yu (eds), *Tourism in China: Geographical, Political and Economic Perspectives*, Boulder, CO: Westview Press.

Race, J. (1974) 'The war in northern Thailand,' *Modern Asian Studies*, 8(1): 85–112.

Radcliffe, S. (2005) 'Development and geography: towards a postcolonial development geography,' *Progress in Human Geography*, 29(3): 291–8.

Rai, M. (2004) *Hindu Rulers, Muslim Subjects: Islam, Rights and the History of Kashmir*, New Delhi: Permanent Black.

Ramstedt, M. (2004a) 'Introduction: negotiating identities – Indonesian "Hindus" between local, national and global interests,' in M. Ramstedt (ed.), *Hinduism in*

Modern Indonesia: A Minority Religion between Local, National and Global Interests, London: RoutledgeCurzon.

Ramstedt, M. (2004b) 'The Hinduization of local traditions in South Sulawesi,' in M. Ramstedt (ed.), *Hinduism in Modern Indonesia: A Minority Religion between Local, National and Global Interests*, London: RoutledgeCurzon.

Raz, A.E. (1999) *Riding the Black Ship: Japan and Tokyo Disneyland*, Cambridge, MA: Harvard University Asia Center.

Rea, M.H. (2000) 'A *furusato* away from home,' *Annals of Tourism Research*, 27(3): 638–60.

Reid, D. (2003) *Tourism, Globalization and Development: Responsible Tourism Planning*, London: Pluto Press.

Renard, R.D. (1999) 'The image of Chiang Mai: the making of a beautiful city,' *Journal of the Siam Society*, 87(1): 87–98.

Renmin Ribao (1981) 'Guowuyuan zuochu jiaqiang lüyou gongzuo de jueding' (State Council issues decision on strengthening tourism work), 19 October: 1.

Reynolds, C.J. (2006) *Seditious Histories: Contesting Thai and Southeast Asian Pasts*, Seattle and Singapore: University of Washington Press.

Richards, G. (2002) 'Gastronomy: an essential ingredient in tourism production and consumption,' in A. Hjalager and G. Richards (eds), *Tourism and Gastronomy*, London and New York: Routledge.

Richards, G. and Wilson, J. (2004) 'Drifting towards the global nomad,' in G. Richards and J. Wilson (eds), *The Global Nomad: Backpacker Travel in Theory and Practice*, Clevedon: Channel View Publications.

Richter, L.K. (1989) *The Politics of Tourism in Asia*, Honolulu: University of Hawaii Press.

Richter, L.K. (1999) 'After political turmoil: the lessons of rebuilding tourism in three Asian countries,' *Journal of Travel Research*, 38(1): 41–5.

Rickover, R.M. (1975) *Pepper, Rice and Elephants: A Southeast Asian Journey from Celebes to Siam*, Annapolis, MD: Naval Institute Press.

Rigg, J. and Ritchie, M. (2002) 'Production, consumption and imagination in rural Thailand,' *Journal of Rural Studies*, 18(4): 359–71.

Riley, R., Baker, D. and Van Doren, C.S. (1998) 'Movie induced tourism,' *Annals of Tourism Research*, 25(4): 919–35.

Ritzer, G. and Liska, A. (1997) ' "McDisneyization" and "post-tourist": complementary perspectives on contemporary tourism,' in C. Rojek and J. Urry (eds), *Tourism Cultures*, London: Routledge.

Robison, R. and Goodman, D. (1996) *The New Rich in Asia: Mobile Phones, McDonald's and Middle-Class Revolution*, London: Routledge.

Rojek, C. (1997) 'Indexing, dragging and the social construction of tourist sights,' in C. Rojek and J. Urry (eds), *Tourism Cultures: Transformations of Travel and Theory*, London and New York: Routledge.

Rojek, C. (1998) 'Cybertourism and the phantasmagoria of place,' in G. Ringer (ed.), *Destinations: Cultural Landscapes of Tourism*, New York: Routledge.

Ronnas, P. and Sjoberg, O. (1990) *Doi moi: Economic Reforms and Development Policies in Vietnam*, Stockholm: SIDA.

Rutes, W.A., Penner, R.H. and Adams, L. (2001) *Hotel Design: Planning and Development*, Oxford: Butterworth-Heinemann.

Rutherford, A. (2003) 'Cinema and embodied affect,' *Senses of Cinema*, no. 25, March–April. Online. Available HTTP: <http://www.sensesofcinema.com/contents/03/25/embodied_affect.html> (accessed 15 July 2006).

Ryang, S. (ed.) (2000) *Koreans in Japan: Critical Voices from the Margin*, New York: Routledge.

Sahoo, A.K. (2006) 'Issues of identity in the Indian diaspora: a transnational perspective,' *Perspectives on Global Development and Technology*, 5(1–2): 81–98.

Said, E. (1978) *Orientalism*, New York: Vintage.

Sankar, D. (2001) *The Role of Traditional and Alternative Health Systems in Providing Health Care Options: Evidence from Kerala*, Delhi: Health Policy Research Unit, Institute of Economic Growth.

Scheyvens, R. (2002) 'Backpacker tourism and third world development,' *Annals of Tourism Research*, 29(1): 144–64.

Schofield, V. (2003) *Kashmir in Conflict: India, Pakistan and the Unending War*, London: I.B. Tauris.

Schwandner, G. and Gu Huimin (2005) 'Beer, romance and Chinese airlines: mindsets and travel expectations of Chinese tourism students,' in Suh Seung-Jin and Hwang Yeong-Hyeon (eds), *New Tourism for Asia-Pacific Conference Proceedings*, Seoul: Asia Pacific Tourism Association.

Scollay, S. (2000) 'The Kashmir shawl and the story of paisley,' *The World of Antiques and Art*, issue 58. Online. Available HTTP: <http://www.worldaa.com/article.cfm?article=35> (accessed 20 August 2006).

Sébastia, B. (2002) *Mariyamman-Mariyamman, the Virgin Mary of Velankanni in Tamil Country*, Pondy Papers in Social Sciences, No. 27, Pondicherry: Institut Français de Pondichéry.

Seligman, A. (1995) *The Idea of Civil Society*, Princeton, NJ: Princeton University Press.

Sethi, A. (2006) 'Lost horizon,' *Times of India*, 25 August: 10.

Sha, Y., Wu, Z. and Wang, L. (2007) 'Research and analysis on Longji terraces scenic area: Ping'an village residents' perceptions of tourism,' *Coastal Enterprises and Science and Technology*, 2(81): 151–4.

Shackley, M. (2002) 'Space, sanctity and service: the English cathedral as heterotopia,' *International Journal of Tourism Research*, 4(5): 345–52.

Shandong Youyi Shushi (1988) *Lüyou xiaobaike (Pocket Tourism Encyclopedia)*, Jinan: Shandong Youyi Shushi.

Sharma, D. (2001) 'India to promote integration of traditional and modern medicine,' *Lancet*, 358(9292): 1524.

Shavit, D. (2003) *Bali and the Tourist Industry: A History, 1906–1942*, Jefferson, VA: McFarland & Co.

Sheller, M. (2003) *Consuming the Caribbean*, London: Routledge.

Shiva, V. (1996) *Biopiracy: The Plunder of Nature and Knowledge*, Boston: South End Press.

Shoji, H. (ed.) (2004) *Taminzoku Nihon-Zainichi Gaikokujin no Kurashi (Multiethnic Japan: Life and History of Immigrants)*, Suita: National Museum of Ethnology.

Shouse, E. (2005) 'Feeling, emotion, affect,' *M/C Journal*, 8(6). Online. Available HTTP: <http://journal.media-culture.org.au/0512/03-shouse.php> (accessed 2 August 2006).

Shroff, F. (2000) 'Ayurveda: mother of indigenous health knowledge,' in G. Sefa Dei, B. Hall and D. Goldin Rosenberg (eds), *Indigenous Knowledge in Global Contexts: Multiple Readings of Our World*, Toronto: University of Toronto Press.

Shyam, V.I. (2004) 'Bridging the gulf: Arab world welcomes Ayurveda,' *Sanghamam Magazine on Ayurveda The Science of Life*, 1(2): 36–40.

Sidaway, J. (2002) 'Postcolonial geographies: survey-explore-review,' in A. Blunt and C. McEwan (eds), *Postcolonial Geographies*, New York: Continuum.

Siegenthaler, P. (2002) 'Hiroshima and Nagasaki in Japanese guidebooks,' *Annals of Tourism Research*, 29(4): 1111–37.

Sikand, Y. (2001) 'Changing course of Kashmiri struggle: from national liberation to Islamist jihad?,' *Economic and Political Weekly*, 36(3): 218–27.

Simon, D. (1998) 'Rethinking (post)modernism, post-colonialism, and post-traditionalism: South-North perspectives,' *Environment and Planning D: Society and Space*, 16(2): 219–45.

Sinclair, M. and Tsegaye, A. (1990) 'International tourism and export instability,' *Journal of Development Studies*, 26(3): 487–505.

Singapore Tourism Board (2005) *Tourism Focus 2005 December*. Online. Available HTTP: <http://app.stb.com.sg/Data/pages/12/b53b3a3d6ab90ce0268229151c9bde11/tourism_focus_-_december_2005.pdf> (accessed 3 May 2007).

Singh, T. (1995) *Kashmir: A Tragedy of Errors*, New Delhi: Viking.

Siu, H. (1996) 'Remade in Hong Kong: weaving into the Chinese cultural tapestry,' in T.T. Liu and D. Faure (eds), *Unity and Diversity: Local Cultures and Identities in China*, Hong Kong: Hong Kong University Press.

Slater, D. (1991) 'Consuming Kodak,' in J. Spence and P. Holland (eds), *Family Snaps: The Meanings of Domestic Photography*, London: Virago.

Smith, R. (1991) 'Beach resorts: a model of development evolution,' *Landscape and Urban Planning*, 21(3): 189–210.

Sofield, T. and Li, F. (1998) 'Tourism development and cultural policies in China,' *Annals of Tourism Research*, 25(2): 362–92.

Sontag, S. (1979) *On Photography*, Harmondsworth: Penguin.

Sørensen, A. (2003) 'Backpacker ethnography,' *Annals of Tourism Research*, 30(4): 847–67.

Spakowski, N. (1997) *Helden, Monumente, Traditionen: Nationale Identität und historisches Bewusstsein in der VR China* (Heroes, Monuments, Traditions: National Identity and Historical Consciousness in the PRC), Münster: LIT.

Sreekumar, T.T. and Parayil, G. (2002) 'Contentions and contradictions of tourism as development option: Kerala, India,' *Third World Quarterly*, 23(3): 529–48.

Stanley, N. (2000) 'Souvenirs, ethics and aesthetics: some contemporary dilemmas in the South Pacific,' in M. Hitchcock and K. Teague (eds), *Souvenirs: The Material Culture of Tourism*, Aldershot: Ashgate.

State Statistics Bureau International Statistics and Information Centre (Guojia Tongjiju Guoji Tongji Xinxi Zhongxin) (2002) *Chuguo renyuan guoji xinxi gailan (Brief Introduction of International Information for the Personnel Going Abroad)*, 4th edn, Beijing: China Statistics Press.

Stone, P.R. (2005) 'Dark tourism consumption: a call for research,' *E-review of Tourism Research*, 3(5). Online. Available HTTP: <http://ertr.tamu.edu> (accessed 17 September 2007).

Strange, C. and Kempa, M. (2003) 'Shades of dark tourism: Alcatraz and Robben Island,' *Annals of Tourism Research*, 30(2): 386–405.

Su, X.B. (2007) 'Place, capital and representation: the politics of heritage tourism in Lijiang, PR China,' unpublished PhD dissertation, National University of Singapore, Singapore.

Su, X.B. and Teo, P. (2005) 'The production of heritage landscapes for tourism in Lijiang Ancient Town, PRC,' paper presented at the International Conference on Border Tourism and Community Tourism Development, Xishuangbanna, China, 6–9 July.

Suehiro, A. (1999) 'A Japanese perspective on the perception of "Ajia" from Eastern to Asian Studies,' *Asian Studies Review*, 23(2): 153–72.

Sundar, K.M.S. (1998) 'Ayurveda in a nutshell,' *UNESCO Courier*, 51(2): 15–18.

Sun Wanning (2002) *Leaving China: Media, Migration, and the Transnational Imagination*, Lanham, MD: Rowman & Littlefield.

Swain, M. (2001) 'Cosmopolitan tourism and minority politics in the Stone Forest,' in Tan Chee-Bing, Sydney Cheung and Yang Hui (eds), *Tourism, Anthropology, and China*, Bangkok: White Lotus Press, pp. 125–45.

Swarbrooke, J., Beard, C., Leckie, S. and Pomfret, G. (2003) *Adventure Tourism: The New Frontier*, Oxford: Butterworth-Heinemann.

Tagg, J. (1982) 'The currency of the photography,' in V. Burgin (ed.), *Thinking Photography*, London: Macmillan.

Tagg, J. (1988) *The Burden of Representation: Essays of Photographies and Histories*, Basingstoke: Macmillan.

Talmadge, E. (1996) 'Theme parks let Japanese travel without leaving home,' *Daily News* (Los Angeles), 29 December. Online. Available HTTP: <ref="http://www.thefreelibrary.com/THEME+PARKS+LET+JAPANESE+TRAVEL+WITHOUT+LEAVING+HOME-a084037521"> (accessed 16 January 2008).

Tambiah, S.J. (1970) *Buddhism and the Spirit Cults in North-east Thailand*, Cambridge: Cambridge University Press.

Tan, C., Cheung, S. and Yang, H. (eds) (2001) *Tourism, Anthropology and China*, Bangkok: White Lotus Press.

Tang, K.C. (2002) 'A big bowl feast,' in Hong Kong Tourism Board (ed.), *Tell Your Hong Kong Story*, Hong Kong: Hong Kong Tourism Board.

Taniwaka, M. (2001) 'Japanese theme parks facing rough times,' *Associated Press*, 2 March: 1.

Taylor, J. (1994) *A Dream of England: Landscape Photography and Tourist Imagination*, Manchester: Manchester University Press.

Teague, K. (2000) 'Tourist markets and Himalayan craftsmen,' in M. Hitchcock and K. Teague, K. (eds), *Souvenirs: The Material Culture of Tourism*, Aldershot: Ashgate.

Teo, P. (2003) 'The limits of imagineering: a case study of Penang,' *International Journal of Urban and Regional Research*, 27(3): 545–63.

Teo, P. and Chang, T.C. (2007) 'Singapore's postcolonial landscape: boutique hotels as agents,' paper presented at the Annual Conference of the Association of American Geographers, San Francisco, 17–22 April.

Teo, P., Chang, T.C. and Ho, K.C. (eds) (2001) *Interconnected Worlds: Tourism in Southeast Asia*, Oxford: Pergamon.

Teo, P. and Leong, S. (2006) 'A postcolonial analysis of backpacking,' *Annals of Tourism Research*, 33(1): 109–31.

Teo, P. and Yeoh, B.S.A. (2001) 'Negotiating global tourism: localism and difference in Southeast Asian theme parks,' in P. Teo, T.C. Chang and K.C. Ho (eds), *Interconnected Worlds: Tourism in Southeast Asia*, Oxford: Pergamon.

Tester, K. (1994) *The Flâneur*, London: Routledge.

The Mill (2007) *The Mill*. Online. Available HTTP: <http://www.doyouhike.net> (accessed 3 November 2007).

The New Paper (2006) 'Peek-a-boutique hotel,' 26 March: 24–5.

The Straits Times (2004) 'More Indians go on overseas tours,' 12 April: A5.

The Straits Times (2005) 'No experience, you're hired,' 17 December: 30.

The Straits Times (2006a) 'The inn thing,' 25 February: 4–5.

The Straits Times (2006b) 'Singapore's most romantic places,' 11 February: S4–S5.

The Times of India (2004) 'Holiday now, pay later,' 3 September. Online. Available HTTP: <http://timesofindia.indiatimes.com/articleshow/830995.cmc> (accessed 9 September 2004).

Thongchai Winichakul (1994) *Siam Mapped: A History of the Geo-Body of a Nation*, Chiang Mai: Silkworm Books.

Thongchai Winichakul (2000) 'The others within: travel and ethno-spatial differentiation of Siamese subjects 1885–1910,' in A. Turton (ed.), *Civility and Savagery: Social Identity in the Tai States*, Richmond: Curzon.

Tiek, K.B. (1999) 'The value(s) of a miracle: Malaysian and Singaporean elite constructions of Asia,' *Asian Studies Review*, 23(2): 181–92.

Timbul, M. (2006) 'Press release on the controversy over Liang Bua,' July, author's files.

Tobin, J. (1992) *Re-Made in Japan: Everyday Life and Consumer Taste in a Changing Society*, New Haven, CT: Yale University Press.

Torchin, L. (2002) 'Location, location, location: the destination of the Manhattan TV tour,' *Tourist Studies*, 2(3): 247–66.

Tourism Authority of Thailand (TAT) (2005) *The Number of Foreign Patients in Thailand (2002–2004)*, Bangkok: TAT.

Tourism Commission (2007) 'Hong Kong: Asia's world city,' online. Available HTTP: <http://www.tourism.gov.hk> (accessed 8 October 2007).

Towner, J. (1996) *An Historical Geography of Recreation and Tourism in the Western World, 1540–1940*, Chichester: John Wiley & Sons, Ltd.

Traditional Knowledge Digital Library (TKDL) (2006) *Traditional Knowledge Digital Library Home*. Online. Available HTTP: <http://203.200.90.6/tkdl/langdefault/Common/home.asp?GL> (accessed 4 September 2007).

Trawick, M. (1995) 'Writing the body and ruling the land: Western reflections on Chinese and Indian medicine,' in D. Bates (ed.), *Knowledge and the Scholarly Medical Traditions*, Cambridge: Cambridge University Press.

Tribe, J. (2006) 'The truth about tourism,' *Annals of Tourism Research*, 33(2): 360–81.

Tribe, J. (2007) 'Critical tourism: rules and resistance,' in I. Ateljevic, A. Pritchard and N. Morgan (eds), *The Critical Turn in Tourism Studies: Innovative Research Methods*, Oxford: Elsevier.

Trinh, M.-H.T. (1994) 'Other than myself/my other self,' in G. Robertson *et al.* (eds), *Travellers' Tales, Narratives of Home and Displacement*, London: Routledge.

Tsu, T.Y. (1999) 'From ethnic ghetto to "gourmet republic": the changing image of Kobe's Chinatown in modern Japan,' *Japanese Studies*, 19(1): 17–32.

Tuohy, S. (1991) 'Cultural metaphors and reasoning,' *Asian Folklore Studies*, 50(1): 189–220.

Turley, W.S. and Seldon, M. (eds) (1993) *Reinventing Vietnamese Socialism: Doi Moi in Comparative Perspective*, Boulder, CO: Westview Press.

Turnbull, S. (1998) *The Kakure Kirishtan of Japan: A Study of Their Development, Beliefs and Rituals to the Present Day*, London: Curzon.

Turner, L. and Ash, J. (1976) *The Golden Hordes: International Tourism and the Pleasure Periphery*, New York: St. Martins Press.

Turton, A. (ed.) (2000) *Civility and Savagery: Social Identity in Tai States*, Richmond: Curzon Press.

United Nations Educational, Scientific and Cultural Organization (UNESCO) (1972) *Convention Concerning the Protection of the World Cultural and Natural Heritage,*

1972. Online. Available HTTP: <http://www.unesco.org>. (accessed 9 September 2005).

UNESCO (1993) *World Heritage List: Lhasa, Case No. 707, 26 October 1993*. Online. Available HTTP: <http://whc.unesco.org/en/decisions/&id_decision=227>. (accessed 9 September 2005).

UNESCO (1994) *World Heritage Committee, 18th Session, Phuket, Thailand, December 12–17*, Bangkok: UNESCO.

UNESCO (1995) *Our Creative Diversity: Report of the World Commission on Culture and Development*, Paris: UNESCO Publishing House.

UNESCO (2004) *World Heritage Committee, 28th Session, Suzhou, China, 18 June–7 July*, Bangkok: UNESCO.

United Nations World Tourism Organization (UNWTO) (2005) *Tourism Highlights*. Online. Available HTTP: <http://www.world-tourism.org/facts/menu.html> (accessed 12 September 2005).

Urashima, H. (1991) 'What is the theme of Hokkaido theme parks?' Online. Available HTTP: <http://www.zmag.org/content/showarticle.cfm?SectionID=69&ItemID=7325> (access date unknown).

Urbain, J. (2003) *At the Beach*, Minneapolis: University of Minnesota Press.

Uriely, N., Yonay, Y. and Simchai, D. (2002) 'Backpacking experiences: a type and form analysis,' *Annals of Tourism Research*, 29(2): 520–38.

Urry, J. (1990) *The Tourist Gaze: Leisure and Travel in Contemporary Societies*, London: Sage.

Urry, J. (1995) *Consuming Places*, London: Routledge.

Urry, J. (2002) *The Tourist Gaze: Leisure and Travel in Contemporary Societies*, 2nd edn, London: Sage Publications.

Urry, J. (2003) *Global Complexity*, Cambridge: Polity Press.

Urry, J. (2007) *Mobilities*, Cambridge: Polity Press.

van Gennep, A. (1960) *The Rites of Passage*, London: Routledge and Kegan Paul.

van Steenbergen, B. (1994) 'The condition of citizenship: an introduction,' in B. van Steenbergen (ed.), *The Condition of Citizenship*, London: Sage.

Vickers, A. (1989) *Bali: A Paradise Created*, Ringwood: Penguin.

Vickers, A. (1996) *Bali: A Paradise Created*, 2nd edn, Singapore: Periplus.

Vogt, J. (1976) 'Wandering: youth and travel behaviour,' *Annals of Tourism Research*, 4(1): 25–41.

Vongsam-ang, M. (2006) 'Tourism set for record highs,' *Vientiane Times*, 10 January: 3.

Waldman, A. (2002) 'Border tension a growth industry for Kashmir,' *New York Times*, 18 October. Online. Available HTTP: <http://query.nytimes.com/gst/fullpage.html?res=9A07E6DE133DF93BA25753C1A9649C8B63> (accessed 7 August 2006).

Wall, G. (1997) 'Indonesia: the impact of regionalization,' in F.M. Go and C.L. Jenkins (eds), *Tourism and Economic Development in Asia and Australasia*, London and Washington: Cassell.

Wall, G. (2001) 'Problemas en el paraiso. Turismo y medioambiente en Bali, Indonesia' (Problems in paradise: tourism and environment in Bali, Indonesia), *Estudios y Perspectivas en Turismo*, 10(3–4): 305–16.

Walton, J. (1983) *The English Seaside Resort: A Social History, 1750–1914*, Leicester: Leicester University Press.

Walton, J. (2005) *Histories of Tourism: Representation, Identity and Conflict*, Clevedon: Channel View.

Wang, F. (2005) *Organizing Through Division and Exclusion: China's Hukou System*, Stanford, CA: Stanford University Press.

Wang, N. (1999) 'Rethinking authenticity in tourism experience,' *Annals of Tourism Research*, 26(2): 349–70.

Wang, N. (2000) *Tourism and Modernity: A Sociological Analysis*, New York: Pergamon.

Wang, N. (2002) 'The tourist as peak consumer,' in G. Dann (ed.), *The Tourist as a Metaphor of the Social World*, New York: CABI.

Wang, N. (2005) 'Urbanscape as attraction: the case of Guangzhou,' in C. Cartier and A. Lew (eds), *Seductions of Place: Geographical Perspectives on Globalization and Touristed Landscapes*, London and New York: Routledge.

Wanshui Yifang (2006) *Yuenan ji xing (Notes on My Trip to Vietnam), 11 November*. Online. Available HTTP: <www.tianya.cn/New/PublicForum/Content.asp?flag=1&idWriter=0&idArticle=99550&strItem=travel> (accessed 22 March 2007).

Warner, J. (1999) 'North Cyprus: tourism and the challenge of non-recognition,' *Journal of Sustainable Tourism*, 7(2): 128–45.

Watson, J.L. (1987) 'From the common pot: feasting with equals in Chinese society,' *Anthropos*, 82: 389–401.

Watson, J.L. (ed.) (1997) *Golden Arches East: McDonald's in East Asia*, Stanford, CA: Stanford University Press.

Watson, J.L. and Caldwell, M.L. (eds) (2005) *The Cultural Politics of Food and Eating: A Reader*, Malden, MA: Blackwell.

Wei Xiaoan (2003) *Lüyou qiangguo zhi lu: Zhongguo lüyou chanye zhengce tixi yanjiu (Path to Great Tourism Country: Research on China Tourism Industry Policy System)*, Beiing: Zhongguo Lüyou Chubanshe.

Wen, J. and Tisdell, C. (2001) *Tourism and China's Development: Policies, Regional Economic Growth and Ecotourism*, Singapore: World Scientific.

Wen, T. (2002) 'On developing family inn industry: a case study of Dragon Ridge terrace scenic spot,' *Tourism Tribune*, 17: 26–30.

Werner, J. and Belanger, D. (eds) (2002) *Gender, Household, State: Doi Moi in Vietnam*, Ithaca, NY: Southeast Asia Program Publications.

West, N.M. (2000) *Kodak and the Lens of Nostalgia*, Charlottesville, VA: University Press of Virginia.

Whyte, M. (1998) 'Japan's obsession with Ann of Green Gables takes architectural form in a line of Emeryville Victorian "farmhouses",' *About Metropolis Online*, July. Weblink no longer available (access date unavailable).

Widana, I.G.K. (2001) *Hindu Berkiblat Ke India? Dan Pertanyaan Lain Tentang Hindu (Hinduism as Referred to in India? And Other Questions about Hinduism)*, Denpasar: Pustaka Bali Post.

Wilk, R. (ed.) (2006) *Fast Food/Slow Food: The Cultural Economy of the Global Food System*, Lanham, MD: Altamira Press.

Wilkinson, J. (2000) 'Tourism and Ainu identity, Hokkaido, Northern Japan,' in M. Hitchcock and K. Teague (eds), *Souvenirs: The Material Culture of Tourism*, Aldershot: Ashgate.

Williams, A.M., Hall, C.M. and Lew, A. (2004) 'Conclusions: contemporary themes and challenges in tourism,' in A. Lew, C.M. Hall and A.M. Williams (eds), *Companion to Tourism*, Oxford: Blackwell.

Williams, L. (1991) 'Film bodies: gender, genre, and excess,' *Film Quarterly*, 44(4): 2–13.

Williams, R. (1961) *The Long Revolution*, London: Chatto & Windus.

Winter, T. (2004) 'Landscape, Memory and Heritage: New year celebrations at Angkor, Cambodia' In: *Current Issues in Tourism*, No. 7 Vols. 4&5: 330–45.

Winter, T. (2007a) 'Rethinking tourism in Asia,' *Annals of Tourism Research*, 34(1): 27–44.

Winter, T. (2007b) *Post-Conflict Heritage, Postcolonial Tourism: Culture, Politics and Development at Angkor*, London: Routledge.

Withey, L. (1997) *Grand Tours and Cook's Tours*, London: Aurum Press.

Wong, P.P. (1988) 'Report: Singapore – Tourism development plans,' *Tourism Management*, 9(1): 73–6.

Wood, R. (1993) 'Tourism, culture and the sociology of development,' in M. Hitchcock, V. King and M. Parnwell (eds), *Tourism in Southeast Asia*, London: Routledge.

Wood, R. (1997) 'Tourism and the state: ethnic options and the constructions of otherness,' in M. Picard and R. Wood (eds), *Tourism, Ethnicity and the State in Asian and Pacific Societies*, Honolulu: University of Hawaii Press.

World Tourism Organization (WTO) (2005) *Compendium of Tourism Statistics 1999–2003*, Madrid: WTO.

World Tourism Organization (WTO) (2006) *Asian Tourism Ministers Debate Growth Strategies*. Online. Available HTTP: <http://www.world-tourism.org/newsroom/Releases/2006/june/asiantourism.html.> (accessed 26 October 2006).

World Travel and Tourism Council (WTTC) (2006) *World Travel and Tourism: Climbing New Heights*. Online. Available HTTP: <http://www.wttc.org/2006TSA/pdf/World.pdf> (accessed 26 October 2006).

Woronov, T.E. (2004) 'In the eye of the chicken: hierarchy and marginality among Beijing's migrant schoolchildren,' *Ethnography*, 5(3): 289–313.

Wu, D.Y.H. and Cheung, S.C.H. (eds) (2002) *The Globalization of Chinese Food*, Surrey: RoutledgeCurzon Press.

Wu, D.Y.H. and Tan, C.B. (eds) (2001) *Changing Chinese Foodways in Asia*, Hong Kong: The Chinese University Press.

Xiao, H. (2003) 'Leisure in China,' in A. Lew, L. Yu, J. Ap and G. Zhang (eds), *Tourism in China*, New York: The Haworth Hospitality Press.

Xiao, H.G. (2006) 'The discourse of power: Deng Xiaoping and tourism development in China,' *Tourism Management*, 27(5): 803–14.

Xiao, Q. (2005) 'Evaluation, unique features, divisions of labor and management and operational models for the development of rural tourism in Guizhou Province,' in S. Yang (ed.), *Rural Tourism: A Strategy for Poverty Alleviation*, Guiyang: Guizhou Renmin Publishing Press.

Xing, L., Fan, S., Lou, X. and Zhang, X. (2006) *Village Inequality in Western China: Implications for Development Strategy in Lagging Regions*, DSGD Discussion Paper No. 31, Washington, DC: International Food Policy Research Institute.

Xinhua (China News Agency) (2006) 'Tibet receives two million visitors in first six months,' 11 November. Online. Available HTTP: http://www.xinhuanet.com/english/. (accessed 5 January 2007).

Xu, G. (1998) *Tourism and Local Economic Development in China: Case Studies of Guilin, Suzhou and Beidaihe*, Surrey: Curzon.

Xu, G. (2005) 'The exploration and evaluation of the folklore tourism in Longji, Guangxi province,' *Guangxi Minzu Yanjiu*, 2: 195–201.

Yadav, S. (2004) 'Cultural and religious interaction between modern India and Indonesia,' in M. Ramstedt (ed.), *Hinduism in Modern Indonesia: A Minority Religion between Local, National and Global Interests*, London: RoutledgeCurzon.

Yadav, S. (2005) 'Ramayana to Bollywood, Indonesia still loves India,' *Hindustan Times*, 22 November. Online. Available HTTP: <http://www.hindustantimes.com/onlineCDA/PFVersion.jsp?article=http://10.81.141.122/2005/Nov/24/5967_1553773,001600060001.htm> (accessed 1 December 2005).

Yalouri, E. (2001) *The Acropolis*, Oxford: Berg.

Yamashita, S., Din, K.H. and Eades, J.S. (eds) (1997) *Tourism and Cultural Development in Asia and Oceania*, Bangi: Penerbit Universiti Kebangsaan Malaysia.

Yamashita, S. *et al.* (2004) 'Asian anthropologies: foreign, native and indigenous,' in S. Yamashita *et al.* (eds), *The Making of Anthropology in East and Southeast Asia*, New York: Berghan Books.

Yang, J. (2006) 'Zhongguo chujing luyou shuanggao geju yu zhengce quxiang bianxi' (An analysis of the double-high pattern of outbound Chinese tourism and the influences of policy orientations), *Tourism Tribune*, 21(6): 65–8.

Yapp, M.E. (1992) 'Europe in the Turkish mirror,' *Past and Present* (special issue: The Cultural and Political Construction of Europe), 137 (November): 134–55.

Yeh, J.H.-Y. (2003) 'Journeys to the west: traveling, learning and consuming Englishness,' unpublished PhD thesis, University of Lancaster, Lancaster.

Yeoh, B.S.A. (2001) 'Postcolonial cities,' *Progress in Human Geography*, 25(3): 479–91.

Young, R. (1990) *White Mythologies: Writing History and the West*, London: Routledge.

Yu, K.P. (1993) 'Makesi de shimin shehui lun ji qi lishi diwei' (Marx's theory of civil society and its historical importance), *Chinese Social Science*, 4: 59–74.

Yuginuma, T. (2000) 'Multicultural explorers go on Tokyo adventure,' *The Daily Yomiuri*, 15 September: 3.

Zhang, Ensheng and Guo Jie (2002) *Zui xin chuguo renyuan bi du (The Latest Must-read for Personnel Going Abroad)*, Beiing: Jincheng Chubanshe.

Zhang, G.R. (1997) *Zhongguo Bianjing Luyou Fazhan de Zhanlue Xuanze (The Strategic Choices of the Development of Border Tourism in China)*, Beijing: Jingji Guanli Chubanshe (Economic Management Publishers).

Zhang Gu (2000) 'Gengxin wu da guannian, jiakuai fazhan Sichuan lüyou chanye' (Refresh five big concepts, accelerate the development of Sichuan's tourism industry), *Lilun yu Gaige*, 5: 120–2.

Zhang, Q.H., Jenkins, C. and Qu, H. (2003) 'Mainland Chinese outbound travel to Hong Kong and its implications,' in A. Lew, L. Yu, J. Ap and G. Zhang (eds), *Tourism in China*, New York: The Haworth Hospitality Press.

Zhang, W. (1997) 'China's domestic tourism: impetus, development and trends,' *Tourism Management*, 18(8): 565–71.

Zhao, H.M. (2002) 'Zhongyue luyou hezuo de xianzhuang ji qianjing' (The present situation and future development of China-Vietnam cooperation in tourism), *Southeast Asia*, 73: 26–9.

Zhao, Q. (2007) 'Develop rural tourism, encourage the construction of the new countryside,' *Qiu Shi, 1.* Online. Available HTTP: <http://www.cnta.com/news_detail/newsshow.asp?id=A2007121324384827838> (accessed 26 March 2007).

Zhou, X. (2000) ' "Village museums": the breakthrough and problems of folk culture displays,' *Museum Studies Association Journal* (Taiwan), 14(1): 95–108.

Zimmerman, F. (1988) 'The jungle and the aroma of meats: an ecological theme in Hindu medicine,' *Social Science and Medicine*, 27(3): 197–215.

Zoete, B.D. and Spies, W. (1970) 'Dance and drama in Bali,' in J. Belo (ed.), *Traditional Balinese Culture*, New York: Columbia University Press.

Zou, Y.M. and Chen, Y.W. (2003) 'Preliminary inquiry into the business model of budget hotel in China' (woguo jingjixing fandian yingye moshi chutan), *Commercial Research*, 282(22): 158–60.

Zutshi, C. (2003) *Languages of Belonging: Islam, Regional Identity, and the Making of Kashmir*, New Delhi: Permanent Black.

Index